Fodor's 05

LAS VEGAS

Where to Stay and Eat
for All Budgets

Must-See Sights
and Local Secrets

Ratings You Can Trust

Fodor's Travel Publications   New York, Toronto, London, Sydney, Auckland
www.fodors.com

FODOR'S LAS VEGAS 2005
Editor: Sarah Sper

Editorial Production: Jacinta O'Halloran
Editorial Contributors: Mark Anderson, Bill Burton, Lenore Greiner, Satu Hummasti, Meredith McGhan, Heidi Knapp Rinella, Heidi Jo Walters, Mike Weatherford
Maps: David Lindroth, Inc.; Mark Stroud, Moon Street Cartography, *cartographers;* Rebecca Baer and Robert Blake, *map editors*
Design: Fabrizio La Rocca, *creative director;* Guido Caroti, *art director;* Moon Sun Kim, *cover designer;* Melanie Marin, *senior picture editor*
Production/Manufacturing: Robert B. Shields
Cover Photo: (Photo Montage): Ron Chapple/Taxi/Getty Images

SPECIAL SALES
This book is available for special discounts for bulk purchases for sales promotions or premiums. Special editions, including personalized covers, excerpts of existing books, and corporate imprints, can be created in large quantities for special needs. For more information, write to Special Markets/Premium Sales, 1745 Broadway, MD 6-2, New York, New York 10019, or e-mail specialmarkets@randomhouse.com.

AN IMPORTANT TIP & AN INVITATION
Although all prices, opening times, and other details in this book are based on information supplied to us at press time, changes occur all the time in the travel world, and Fodor's cannot accept responsibility for facts that become outdated or for inadvertent errors or omissions. So **always confirm information when it matters,** especially if you're making a detour to visit a specific place. Your experiences—positive and negative—matter to us. If we have missed or misstated something, **please write to us.** We follow up on all suggestions. Contact the Las Vegas editor at editors@fodors.com or c/o Fodor's at 1745 Broadway, New York, NY 10019.

PRINTED IN THE UNITED STATES OF AMERICA

10 9 8 7 6 5 4 3 2 1

DESTINATION LAS VEGAS

Illusion is everywhere in Las Vegas. A 50-story Eiffel Tower looms over the Strip, gondoliers "o sole mio" their way down an ersatz Grand Canal, and acres of neon turn night into multicolored day. Gamblers defy reason (and the considerable odds against winning) in their attempts to seduce the goddess of chance, while onstage extravaganzas manipulate reality with mind-bending special effects. Even a meal can be an adventure, whether at an over-the-top, all-you-can-eat buffet or in a celebrity chef showcase that you wouldn't expect to find in the Nevada desert. Head out of town and you'll come across otherworldly landscapes that nature has etched over the aeons. Yes, a trip to Las Vegas offers a chance to surrender to fantasy—and you'll have the time of your life doing it.

Tim Jarrell, Publisher

CONTENTS

Maps & Charts

CloseUp

ABOUT THIS BOOK

The best source for travel advice is a like-minded friend who's just been where you're headed. But with or without that friend, you'll be in great shape to find your way around your destination once you learn to find your way around your Fodor's guide.

SELECTION

Our goal is to cover the best properties, sights, and activities in their category, as well as the most interesting communities to visit. We make a point of including local food-lovers' hot spots as well as neighborhood options, and we avoid all that's touristy unless it's really worth your time. You can go on the assumption that everything in this book is recommended wholeheartedly by our writers and editors. Flip to On the Road with Fodor's to learn more about who they are. It goes without saying that no property pays to be included.

RATINGS

Orange stars ★ denote sights and properties that our editors and writers consider the very best in the area covered by the entire book. These, the best of the best, are listed in the Fodor's Choice section in the front of the book. Black stars ★ highlight the sights and properties we deem Highly Recommended, the don't-miss sights within any region. In cities, sights pinpointed with numbered map bullets ❶ in the margins tend to be more important than those without bullets.

SPECIAL SPOTS

Pleasures & Pastimes focuses on experiences that reveal the spirit of the destination. Also watch for Off the Beaten Path sights. Some are out of the way, some are quirky, and all are worth while. When the munchies hit, look for Need a Break? suggestions.

TIME IT RIGHT

Check On the Calendar up front and the Timing sections in the Exploring chapter for weather and crowd overviews and best days and times to visit.

SEE IT ALL

For a good overview of Las Vegas and its surroundings, use Fodor's exclusive Great Itineraries that begin the book as a model for your trip. In the Exploring chapter, Good Walks guide you to important sights on the Strip and in downtown; ▶ indicates the starting points of walks in the text and on the map.

BUDGET WELL

Hotel and restaurant price categories from ¢ to $$$$ are defined in the opening pages of each chapter—expect to find a balanced selection for every budget. For attractions, we always give standard adult admission fees; reductions are usually available for children, students, and senior citizens. Look in Discounts & Deals in Smart Travel Tips for information on destination-wide ticket schemes.

BASIC INFO

Smart Travel Tips lists travel essentials for the entire area covered by the book; city- and region-specific basics end each chapter. To find the best way to get around, see the transportation section; see individual modes of travel ("By Car," "By Train") for details.

ON THE MAPS	Maps throughout the book show you what's where and help you find your way around. Black and orange numbered bullets **1** **1** in the text correlate to bullets on maps.
BACKGROUND	We give background information within the chapters in the course of explaining sights as well as in CloseUp boxes and in Understanding Las Vegas at the end of the book. To get in the mood, review Books & Movies.
DON'T FORGET	Restaurants are open for lunch and dinner daily unless we state otherwise; we mention dress only when there's a specific requirement and reservations only when they're essential or not accepted—it's always best to book ahead. Hotels have private baths, phones, TVs, and air-conditioning and operate on the European Plan (aka EP, meaning without meals). We always list facilities but not whether you'll be charged extra to use them, so when pricing accommodations, find out what's included.

SYMBOLS

Many Listings
- ★ Fodor's Choice
- ★ Highly recommended
- ⊠ Physical address
- ✦ Directions
- ⌖ Mailing address
- ☎ Telephone
- 🖷 Fax
- ⊕ On the Web
- ✎ E-mail
- 🎫 Admission fee
- ☉ Open/closed times
- ► Start of walk/itinerary
- ▱ Credit cards

Outdoors
- ⛳ Golf
- ⛺ Camping

Hotels & Restaurants
- 🏨 Hotel
- ⇆ Number of rooms
- ♨ Facilities
- ⦿ Meal plans
- ✗ Restaurant
- ⟲ Reservations
- 🏛 Dress code
- ↘ Smoking
- 🍸 BYOB
- ✗🏨 Hotel with restaurant that warrants a visit

Other
- ⓒ Family-friendly
- 🛈 Contact information
- ⇨ See also
- ⊠ Branch address
- ☞ Take note

ON THE ROAD WITH FODOR'S

A trip takes you out of yourself. Concerns of life at home completely disappear, driven away by more immediate thoughts—about, say, what marvels will beguile the next day, or where you'll have dinner. That's where Fodor's comes in. We make sure that you know all your options, so that you don't miss something that's around the next bend just because you didn't know it was there. Because the best memories of your trip might well have nothing to do with what you came to Las Vegas to see, we guide you to sights large and small all over the region. You might set out to gamble away your bankroll on the Strip, but back at home you find yourself unable to forget hiking in Red Rock Canyon at sunrise or attending a performance by Cirque du Soleil. With Fodor's at your side, serendipitous discoveries are never far away.

Our success in showing you every corner of Las Vegas is a credit to our extraordinary writers. Although there's no substitute for travel advice from a good friend who knows your style, our contributors are the next best thing—the kind of people you would poll for travel advice if you knew them.

Mark Anderson covers University of Nevada–Las Vegas football and the Las Vegas Gladiators for the *Las Vegas Review-Journal*. He lives in Henderson, but before moving to the Las Vegas area, he wrote for the *Reno Gazette-Journal* and the *Tallahassee Democrat*.

Bill Burton is the casino gambling guide for About.com and is our gambling tutor. He writes for several national gaming publications, including *Chance & Circumstance* magazine and two newsletters, *The Crapshooter* and *Viva Las Vegas*. His book *Getting the Edge at Low Limit Texas Hold'em* was published in January 2002.

Lenore Greiner crosses the Mojave from her San Diego home for Vegas's shops, spas, and art museums. Sometimes she'll gamble but considers it a waste of valuable shopping time. A contributor to three Fodor's guides, she also has written for *Newsday, Delta Airlines' Sky,* and *Healing Retreats and Spas,* among others.

Meredith McGhan came to Las Vegas in 1999 for a UNLV graduate program and fell under the city's spell. In five short years she's watched the city grow in enthusiasm for culture and the arts as well as in population. Her post as the entertainment editor for the monthly *What's On: the Summerlin/Henderson Guide* keeps her entrenched in the ever-changing city; she's also written for the alternative weekly *Las Vegas CityLife* and published poetry and fiction in various venues.

Heidi Knapp Rinella has been reviewing restaurants for more than 20 years and currently is the restaurant critic for the *Las Vegas Review-Journal.* She has also spent plenty of time at the kids' table, while writing *The Lobster Kids' Guide to Exploring Las Vegas.* On top of that, she's published four other books, including *Personal Favorites: The Chefs of Las Vegas.*

Heidi Walters, our Where to Stay and Side Trips updater and a Nevada native, has written for newspapers in California and Nevada for the past 17 years, including two Las Vegas alternative newsweeklies. She's fond of side trips, and after a night sitting in a funky hot pool on the edge of Death Valley, looking up at the stars, she wondered if they might be the whole trip. That is, until she had to drag herself away from fine, sparkly Strip-side rooms, where she sank dream-deep in soft linens.

Mike Weatherford came to us well prepared for the task of revising the Nightlife & the Arts chapter of this book. He is an entertainment reporter for the *Las Vegas Review-Journal,* so he sees all the shows and visits all the clubs. He has lived in Las Vegas since 1987.

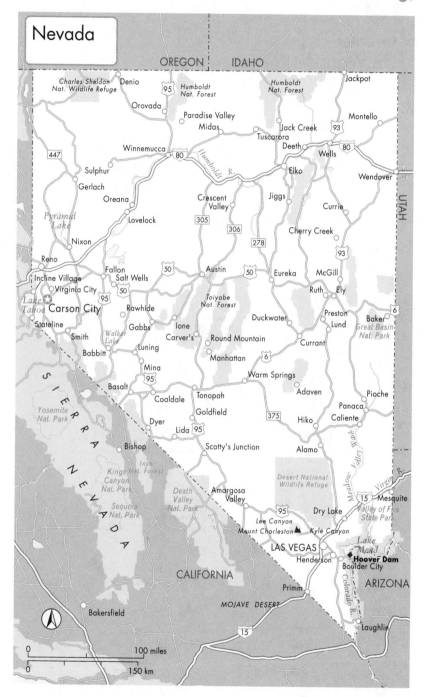

Nevada

OREGON | IDAHO

Charles Sheldon Nat. Wildlife Refuge
Denio
95
Humboldt Nat. Forest
Humboldt Nat. Forest
Jackpot

Orovada

Paradise Valley
Midas
Jack Creek
Montello
93
Tuscarora
Deeth

Winnemucca
80
Wells
80

447

Sulphur
Elko
Wendover

Gerlach

Oreana
Crescent Valley
Jiggs
Currie

Pyramid Lake
Lovelock
305
306
Cherry Creek

Nixon
278
93

Reno
50
Austin
50
Eureka
McGill

Incline Village
Fallon
Salt Wells
Ruth
Ely

Virginia City
50
Toiyabe Nat. Forest
Preston
Baker
6

Lake Tahoe
Carson City
Rawhide
Duckwater
Lund
Great Basin Nat. Park

Stateline
Gabbs
Ione
Round Mountain
Currant

Smith
Walker Lake
Carver's

Babbitt
Luning
Manhattan
6

Mina
Warm Springs

Basalt
95
Adaven
Pioche

S I E R R A
Coaldale
Tonopah
Panaca

Yosemite Nat. Park
Dyer
Goldfield
375
Hiko
Caliente

N E V A D A
Lida
95

Inyo Nat. Forest
Bishop
Scotty's Junction
Alamo

Kings Canyon Nat. Park
Death Valley Nat. Park
Desert National Wildlife Refuge

Sequoia Nat. Park
Amargosa Valley
15
Mesquite

Valley of Fire State Park

95
Dry Lake

Lee Canyon
Mount Charleston
Kyle Canyon

LAS VEGAS
Lake Mead
Hoover Dam

CALIFORNIA
Henderson
Boulder City

Primm
ARIZONA

Bakersfield
MOJAVE DESERT

0   100 miles
0   150 km

15
Laughlin

OREGON
IDAHO
UTAH
Humboldt R.
Meadow Valley Wash
Virgin R.
Colorado R.

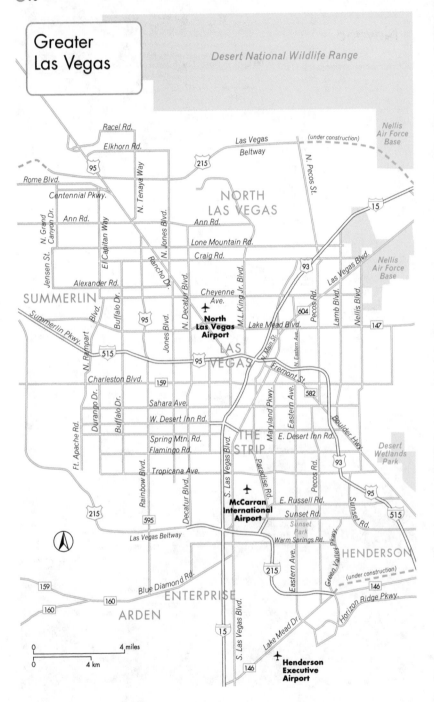

Greater
Las Vegas

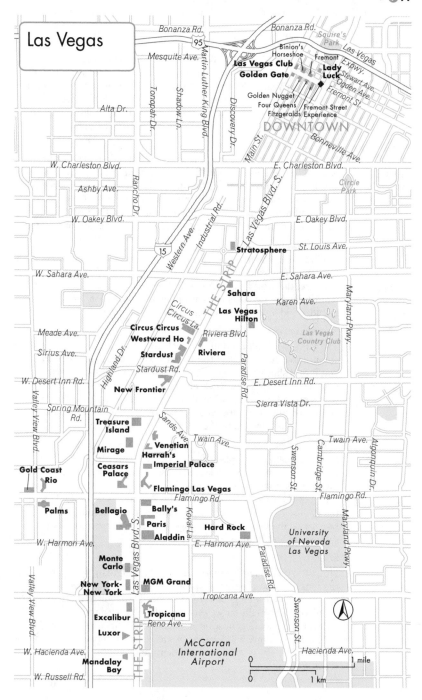

The Strip

Officially titled Las Vegas Boulevard South, the Strip runs north–south through the city. Without leaving this street you could sample all that's best in Las Vegas: the food, the shows, and the gambling. Almost all the major casinos are either on or just off the Strip. In fact, there's so much to see and do on the Strip that we've broken it down into South, Center, and North to help you navigate through the options.

Four Corners

If there's one part of the Strip that is worthy of special mention, it would have to be the Four Corners. The intersection of Las Vegas Boulevard and Flamingo Road has set the standards for excess ever since Bugsy Siegel first set up shop here with his Flamingo in 1946. Caesars, the Mirage, and now Bellagio have upped the stakes in their turn, and, as of yet, there appears to be no betting maximum at the hub of the Strip.

Downtown

You'll find the heart of downtown Vegas where Fremont Street meets Las Vegas Boulevard. It's also the epicenter of the Fremont Street Experience, the world's greatest collection of neon signs, covered by the world's largest electric sign. The hotels and casinos on Fremont tend to be older and less expensive than those on the Strip.

Paradise Road

The Paradise Road corridor parallels the Strip and increasingly is becoming an echo of its big brother to the west. Near and along Paradise you'll find shops and lots of good-quality restaurants, as well as such landmarks as the Hard Rock Hotel, Las Vegas Hilton, and Las Vegas Convention Center. Paradise also is generally less congested than the Strip—making it a good alternative route—but construction on the monorail has impeded traffic there to some extent.

West of the Strip

If you're looking for a place that's away from the often-crazy Strip traffic but retains much of the legendary street's glittery glamour, consider the area just to the west across I–15. The Rio and Palms are known for their hipster appeal—in Bikinis at the Rio, and Rain and Ghostbar at the Palms. The Gold Coast is primarily a locals casino, but its corporate sister, the Orleans, draws big-name entertainment to its intimate showroom and brand-new arena.

Summerlin

Howard Hughes left his mark on Las Vegas in many ways, and one of the biggest—and the one with the best chance for posterity—is Summerlin, named for Hughes's grandmother. He acquired the 22,500-acre chunk of desert in the far western part of the valley during the early '50s; today it's a sprawling, upscale planned community and the site of many shops, restaurants, and casinos, such as the Rampart Casino at JW Marriott Las Vegas, that draw residents and savvy visitors.

Henderson

It's said that Henderson was "born in America's defense." It was the site of the Basic Magnesium Plant, which supplied the U.S. War Department during World War II. Henderson almost died at the end of the war; the whole town was offered for sale in 1947. It managed to survive, and for a couple of decades wore its blue collar proudly. In the '80s, however, upscale developments began to spring up, and Henderson today is home to a mix of income groups and vies with Reno as the second largest city in the state. Two of the valley's best locals' casino-hotels are here, Sunset Station and Green Valley Ranch Station Casino.

Red Rock Canyon

You have probably seen Red Rock in the movies: it's a very popular location for Hollywood. A 13-mi scenic road loops through the red rock formations and unusual high-desert scenery of southern Nevada, only 20 minutes from the heart of the city.

Mt. Charleston

The eighth-highest peak in Nevada, Mt. Charleston is the perfect retreat for a day or two away from the madness of Las Vegas. It's also an ideal escape from the heat of summer, because temperatures on the mountain tend to be 15 to 20 degrees cooler than those in the valley. In wintertime, it's a local ski haven, and in summer hikers, mountain bikers, and campers hit the slopes.

Hoover Dam & Lake Mead

About 35 mi southeast of Las Vegas lies one of the seven industrial wonders of the world, the monster Hoover Dam. This 4.4-million-cubic-yard concrete beast dams the Colorado River, creating the 229 square mi of Lake Mead, the largest reservoir in the country. This is your destination for water sports if your ambitions extend beyond swim-up blackjack. Nearby Boulder City, built in the early 1930s to house workers who were constructing Hoover Dam, is the only community in Nevada where gambling is illegal.

Valley of Fire State Park

Nevada's first state park is about 55 mi northeast of Las Vegas. The name comes from the distinctive coloration of its rock formations, which range from lavender to tangerine to bright red. The lights of Las Vegas pale in comparison to the rays of sunset on this fantastic natural backdrop.

Las Vegas in 5 Days

You could easily spend a lifetime taking advantage of all Las Vegas has to offer, but if you're here for a short period, you'll need to wade through the seemingly limitless ways to spend your time (and money). The following suggested itinerary will help you structure your visit efficiently.

Day 1 The Strip is huge and offers lots of attractions, so it's best to divide it into two chunks. On Day 1, explore the southern end of the Strip, as far north as Flamingo Road. Take the monorail that runs the length of the Strip (set to open late summer 2004 at this writing) or hop on a Strip shuttle or CAT bus. Start with a look around Mandalay Bay, the Luxor, and the medieval kitsch of the Excalibur, then cross the Strip on an elevated pedestrian walk and take a peek at Old Vegas at the Tropicana.

Another elevated pedestrian walk and a few shorts steps and you'll find yourself inside the MGM Grand; be sure to check out the lion habitat. Then it's back across the Strip to New York–New York and the Monte Carlo.

Hop the tram at the Monte Carlo and cruise on up to the Bellagio. Just outside the tram stop you'll find the Bellagio conservatory with its amazing botanical gardens. Be sure to view the dancing waters from the sidewalk on the Strip. Then it's back up onto the pedestrian bridge to cross the Strip and explore Bally's, Paris, and the Aladdin. And don't miss the Aladdin's Desert Passage shopping area.

☉ *Works any day, though a weekday will be less crowded.*

Day 2 Pick up where you left off, and devote Day 2 to exploring the Strip north of the Flamingo Road intersection. Caesars Palace, the showpiece of this part of the Strip, is a good place to start. Then cross the Strip and take in, in succession, the Flamingo, the Imperial Palace, and the Venetian, maybe taking a quick break for a gondola ride. Cross the Strip at Spring Mountain Road to do a little shopping at Fashion Show Mall and, heading south now, tour the Treasure Island and the Mirage. If you time it right and it's after dark, you might see the volcano strut its stuff.

Then a good plan would be to hop some motorized transportation and head up to the Stratosphere to see the city from a whole different perspective—and maybe get a few thrills on the Big Shot.

Later that night, head downtown for the Fremont Street Experience sound-and-light show and a drink in Main Street Station's brewpub.

☉ *Works any day, though a weekday will be less crowded.*

Day 3 Take a quick morning break from casino madness in the awesome scenery of Red Rock Canyon, then fling yourself back into the fray in the afternoon by experiencing an "only in Vegas" attraction. Rise early and take Charleston Boulevard west to Red Rock Canyon and hike the desert or scramble up the sandstone. On the way back, stop off at the Rio to check out the "Masquerade Show in the Sky" and have lunch at its popular buffets. In the afternoon, take your pick of Las Vegas attractions—ride the Manhattan Express roller coaster at New York–New York, visit Adventuredome at Circus Circus, or get face to fin with ocean creatures at Mandalay Bay's Shark Reef. If museums are more to your taste, take in the Liberace Museum, Elvis-A-Rama Museum, Guggenheim-Hermitage Museum, or the Imperial Palace Auto Collection. Then settle back for an extravaganza such as *Blue Man Group,* Cirque du Soleil's *O,* or Celine Dion's *A New Day.*

☺ *Plan this day around the availability of the show you plan to see. The rest of the items on the agenda work any day of the week.*

Day 4 Today you can marvel at the civil engineering masterpiece that makes Las Vegas possible, and then gamble like a local. Begin by heading out to Boulder City and Hoover Dam. Tour the visitor center and dam, and maybe drive over to Lake Mead Marina. Then head to either of the "other" casino strips to mingle with the locals. You can see the parklike atrium as well as the laser and dancing water show at Sam's Town on the Boulder Strip or sample the sumptuous buffet at either Texas Station or Fiesta (or both!) on the Rancho Strip. Wind up the evening with a showroom seat at *Mystère, Lance Burton: Master Magician,* or *Danny Gans,* or a seat at a blackjack table or video-poker machine.

☺ *If your plans include a visit to a showroom, plan this day around your tickets. The other stops work any day of the week.*

Day 5 On your fifth day, you can head up to Mt. Charleston for a mountain (skiing or hiking) experience, hop a flight-seeing tour to the Grand Canyon, or drive down to Laughlin for a taste of gambling that's qualitatively different from Las Vegas.

☺ *Works any day.*

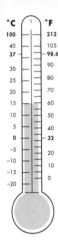

°C		°F
100		212
40		105
37		98.6
30		90
25		80
20		70
15		60
10		50
5		40
0		32
-5		20
-10		
-15		10
-20		0

Las Vegas is a year-round destination. Except for the first three weeks in December and weekdays during July, you can assume that Las Vegas will be running at full speed. Weekends, always crowded, are especially jam-packed for the Super Bowl, Valentine's Day, President's Day, the NCAA Final Four, Easter, Cinco de Mayo, Memorial Day, July 4, and Labor Day. The week between Christmas and New Year's is the most crowded week of the year. In addition, nearly 50 conventions of more than 10,000 participants are held here every year; prices skyrocket and availability plummets. Sporting events, such as boxing matches, golf tournaments, the National Finals Rodeo and the NASCAR Winston Cup Las Vegas 400, also have a major impact on the crowd situation. It's a good idea to contact the **Las Vegas Convention and Visitors Authority** (☎ 702/892–0711 ⊕ www.lvcva.com) to find out who or what will be in town at the time you're planning to visit.

During a "normal" week—that fairly rare time of no conventions, holidays, title fights, or local events—you can count on Sunday through Thursday being less crowded, less expensive, and less stressful than the weekend. During even a routine weekend, however, traffic jams can be ferocious—along with competition for room, restaurant, and show reservations, and spots at the slots or tables.

Climate

The most comfortable times to be in Las Vegas are the spring and fall. In March, April, and May, daytime temperatures range between 70 and 90°F. In September and October, the summer heat has abated.

Winter is a distinctly different season, with snowcapped mountains in the distance, windy and chilly days, and surprisingly cold nights. The three weeks before Christmas find Las Vegas nearly deserted, with rooms going for bargain rates and hardly a traffic jam on the Strip.

Summer is a time of dry, uncomfortably hot weather (sometimes 110°F in the shade), when lounging at an outdoor pool requires protection from the relentless desert sun. You'll probably find yourself continuously thirsty. At the height of the heat, however, hotels offer their lowest rates.

🎦 Forecasts **Weather Channel Connection** ☎ 900/932–8437 95¢ per minute from a Touch-Tone phone ⊕ www.weather.com.

LAS VEGAS

Jan.	60F	16C	May	89F	32C	Sept.	95F	35C
	28	-2		51	11		57	14
Feb.	66F	19C	June	98F	37C	Oct.	84F	29C
	33	1		60	16		46	8
Mar.	71F	22C	July	102F	39C	Nov.	71F	22C
	39	4		68	20		35	2
Apr.	80F	27C	Aug.	102F	39C	Dec.	60F	16C
	44	7		66	19		30	-1

Las Vegas is not known for specific celebrations—the Strip is the venue for a never-ending parade. Still, a number of annual events do attract wide attention. They are listed below, along with the major conventions that take place annually in Las Vegas, which affect everything from room rates and rental-car availability to lines at buffets and crowds at the crap tables.

ONGOING

Nov.–Mar.	It's basketball season at the University of Nevada–Las Vegas. ☎ 702/895–3900.
Feb.–June	It's football season indoor-style. The Arena Football League's Las Vegas Gladiators play at the Thomas and Mack Center on the Nevada–Las Vegas campus. ☎ 702/731–4977.
Apr.–Sept.	The Las Vegas 51s minor-league baseball team, a triple-A affiliate of the Los Angeles Dodgers, plays at Cashman Field near downtown Las Vegas. ☎ 702/386–7200.

WINTER

Early Dec.	National Finals Rodeo, the Super Bowl of rodeos, brings together 15 finalists to compete in each of seven events; there are 10 performances in nine days at the Thomas and Mack Center. When the rodeo comes to town, the showrooms all feature country music, and it seems as though everyone on the street is wearing jeans, boots, and a cowboy hat. ☎ 702/731–2115.
Mid-Dec.	In the Parade of Lights, boats large and small, all decked out in holiday lights, come together in a flotilla of illumination on Lake Mead. It's most fun to be on a boat, but it's also exciting to watch from the shoreline along Lakeshore Drive. ☎ 702/293–8947 or 702/293–8907.
Dec. 31	New Year's Eve is celebrated with fireworks over various casino-hotels all along the Strip and in downtown Las Vegas. ☎ 702/892–0711.
Early Jan.	The Consumer Electronics Show is a convention that attracts upward of 125,000 participants.
Late Jan.	The Las Vegas International Marathon draws more than 5,000 runners. The starting line changes from year to year, but the finish line of the 5K race is Vacation Village, 2 mi south of Mandalay Bay. ☎ 702/294–1588.
Mid-Feb.	The early spring Men's Apparel Guild Convention, aka MAGIC, attracts some 100,000 participants.

SPRING	
Early Mar.	The NASCAR Winston Cup Race is the largest sporting event of the year in Nevada. Some 135,000 racing fans converge on Las Vegas to watch the grueling 400-mi race on the 1½-mi track, with top national drivers competing for $3 million in prize money. ☎ 702/644–4444.
Mid-Mar.	The triennial Conexpo trade show is the largest show of its kind in the Western hemisphere, focusing on construction products (e.g., cement) and drawing more than 150,000 attendees over four days. The next show is scheduled for 2005.
Mar. 17	St. Patrick's Day in Las Vegas is a festive occasion, with many of the casinos decorated in green and serving bargain corned-beef-and-cabbage dinners.
Early Apr.	NHRA Drag Racing is one of the newer racing events in Las Vegas. The National Hot Rod Association races take place at the Las Vegas Motor Speedway, which has a ¼-mi drag strip and 80,000-seat grandstand. ☎ 702/644–4444.
Apr.	The LPGA Invitational golf tournament draws top women golfers. ☎ 702/894–9746.
	The Clark County Fair takes place 60 mi north of Las Vegas in Logandale. ☎ 702/398–3247.
Mid-Apr.	The National Association of Broadcasters convention fills the town with 125,000 attendees, including a bevy of major TV and movie celebrities.
Apr.–May	The World Series of Poker draws crowds to the Binion's Horseshoe casino to watch the poker faces of players from around the world. This month-long tournament culminates in a four-day final round in which nearly 300 players each invest $10,000 in the hope of winning first prize: $1 million. ☎ 702/382–1600.
May	The Gay Pride Parade is a five-day event, including a lighted night parade in downtown Las Vegas, plus parties and concerts. ☎ 702/395–4938.
SUMMER	
June	CineVegas Film Festival is a nine-day event featuring works by local filmmakers (including film students at UNLV) as well as movies about Las Vegas. ☎ 702/368–2890 or 800/675–8482.
Early July	Damboree Days is a weekend-long festival in Boulder City that coincides with the July Fourth holiday. It culminates in the largest fireworks event in the area. ☎ 702/293–2034.
Late Aug.	The early-fall Men's Apparel Guild Convention, aka MAGIC, attracts 100,000 participants.

AUTUMN	
Sept.	The International Las Vegas Triathlon draws top competitors to Lake Mead National Recreation Area.
Sept.	Masses of hot-air balloons take to the sky for the Las Vegas Balloon Classic. ☎ *702/247–6905.*
Mid-Sept.	Football season begins at the University of Nevada–Las Vegas. ☎ *702/895–3900.*
Mid-Sept.	The World Gaming Congress and Expo only attracts 25,000 to 30,000 attendees, so it barely makes a dent in hotel occupancy rates. But all the new-generation slot and video-poker machines, table games, and casino paraphernalia are on display at the Las Vegas Convention and Visitors Authority. ☎ *702/892–0711.*
Early Oct.	Art in the Park, one of the largest events of the year in Boulder City, is an early Christmas crafts fair, with artists and craftsmen displaying their wares in Bicentennial Park in downtown Boulder City. ☎ *702/293–2034.*
Mid-Oct.	The Las Vegas Invitational golf tournament, a five-day event, is played on three courses, with television coverage. ☎ *702/242–3018.*
Early Nov.	The AAPEX/Automotive After-market Products is a huge trade show bringing in more than 90,000 participants.
Mid-Nov.	The Comdex computer hardware, software, and electronics convention, held the week before Thanksgiving, is one of the largest conventions of the year in Las Vegas. It attracts 225,000 participants and fills the town to the gills.
Nov.	The Pro Bull Riders Finals is the two-day Super Bowl of the bull-riders circuit. The top 50 bull-riders compete for a $1-million purse. ☎ *800/739–0339.*

PLEASURES & PASTIMES

Downtown Neon It's a simple (and free) pleasure in downtown Las Vegas to bear witness to the extraordinary powers of electricity. The area has a collection of neon signs that only downtown Tokyo can claim to match. The 50-foot-tall neon cowboy Vegas Vic is perhaps the most famous sign. Once an hour, after dark, the modern-day wizards of odds fire up the Fremont Street Experience, all 2 million lightbulbs and 500,000 watts and four blocks of it, for a light-and-sound show unequaled anywhere on (and possibly off) the planet.

The High Rollers If you get a chance—that is, if it happens in one of the casinos' public rooms—just stand (in Las Vegas, chairs are for gamblers only) and watch one of the bigger players (aka, high rollers or whales) take on the tables. You have nothing to lose, but if the player hits a big streak and those chips start piling up, you can ride his or her adrenaline rush for free. This experience has become more rare in recent years, as the newest casinos shelter their biggest spenders in high-limit rooms, away from the eyes of the hoi polloi.

The Las Vegas Buzz Besides the renowned enticements of Las Vegas, there are other, more subtle ones. There's the twisting of time, noticeable, for example, in coffee shops, when at any hour some people are having breakfast, others lunch or dinner, and still others snacks or coffee. There's the unmistakable air—sounds, smells, sights—of a casino. And there's the phenomenon of a city that never closes or seems to sleep, that galvanizes and emblazons the familiar activities of daily life.

Magic & Song Nobody ever came to Las Vegas to see Shakespeare. The city has made famous a certain brand of entertainment based on big name entertainers, spectacular production values, sex, and illusion. Old reliable Wayne Newton packs them in and you can still catch a scantily dressed chorus line if you want. At some of the major hotels, however, a newer breed of show, the high-tech spectacular, has become a big draw and each show competes with the others for even more amazing special effects. They include Celine Dion's *A New Day* at Caesars Palace, the Cirque du Soleil productions *O* at Bellagio and *Mystère* at Treasure Island, *Blue Man Group* at the Luxor, and Bally's *Jubilee*, which with its topless showgirls and high-tech effects, bridges the gap between old and new.

Poolside Lounging As Las Vegas hotel-casino properties lavish ever more attention on their amenities, pool expansions have been part of the wave. And some of them are spectacular, such as the interconnected pools surrounded by lush tropical gardens at the Flamingo; the beach, wave pool, and lazy river at Mandalay Bay; the Roman-theme pool complex at Caesars Palace; the 8-acre rooftop pool area at the Las Vegas Hilton; and the five separate pools, including the 1,000-foot-long Backlot River pool, at the MGM Grand.

Shopping

Time was when Las Vegas was a great source for shocking-pink wigs, dice clocks, life-size Wayne Newton dolls—and not much else. Today, upscale shopping is the norm at the Forum Shops at Caesars, the Grand Canal Shoppes at the Venetian, and Via Bellagio, which bring Chanel, Tiffany, and Versace to Las Vegas. The Fashion Show mall on the Strip has four upscale department stores, and more proletarian offerings are available at the valley's three regional malls. You can find bargains at three huge outlet malls—two in town and one in Primm, Nevada.

Wining & Dining

Dining out in Las Vegas is an adventure in variety. The fun lies in choosing from the vast array of styles and price ranges, from cheap prime-rib joints to hip-and-happening eateries to big-name-chef restaurants. Every major hotel has at least four or five eating places, and independent restaurants are scattered about town. The fabulous buffets are a traditional treat, where you find yourself, plate in hand, standing before a mountain of all-you-can-eat food—some for as little as $4.99. But the big news in Las Vegas is the arrival of excellent—albeit expensive—new restaurants offering everything from the latest California fusion to the best aged steaks.

Winning & Losing

Times may change, but gambling is still the thing to do in Las Vegas. The first-timer is faced with a terrifying choice of possible bets—what seems like 1,001 different ways to part with your hard-earned dollars. But once you know your way around the casino, you'll quickly settle on your wagering thrill of choice. Blackjack, baccarat, and video poker offer the best odds for winning in a Las Vegas casino. The average bankroll of a Las Vegas gambler is $500, but you can experience either the excitement of winning or the frustration of losing for a lot less. The smaller casinos off the Strip are often the best bet for the amateur gambler; the pressure is less intense, the minimums are reasonable, and the staffs are friendlier.

FODOR'S CHOICE

Fodor'sChoice ★	The sights, restaurants, hotels, and other travel experiences on these pages are our editors' top picks—our Fodor's Choices. They're the best of their type in the area covered by the book—not to be missed and always worth your time. In the destination chapters that follow, you will find all the details.

LODGING

$$$$	**Four Seasons,** on the Strip. For those who want a stress-free Vegas visit, the Four Seasons offers its famed attention to detail and comfort, plus insulation from the madness on the casino floor.
$$$$	**Mandalay Bay,** on the Strip. Beautiful rooms, hot nightspots, an unbeatable pool, and the House of Blues add up to one of the most lively resorts in town.
$$$$	**Ritz-Carlton, Lake Las Vegas,** in Henderson. Escape the hectic pace of Vegas and indulge in a whimsical stay at the posh Mediterranean-style resort, complete with a replica of Florence's Pontevecchio Bridge.
$$$–$$$$	**Bellagio,** on the Strip. Quite simply, it's the most sophisticated and elegant joint on the whole of the Strip.
$$$–$$$$	**The Venetian,** on the Strip. Luxurious suites, a wealth of top restaurants, and over-the-top decor make this replica of Venice a winner.
$$–$$$$	**Caesars Palace,** on the Strip. The original theme-resort on the Strip, it's a classic still bustling with excess and opulence, and a wealth of entertainment and shopping.
$$–$$$$	**Monte Carlo,** on the Strip. Good deals on rooms, an inexpensive buffet, and a water park coexist with a palatial Mediterranean theme.
$$–$$$$	**The Palms,** on the West Side. The newest and most popular resort in town, with looser slots, hip nightclubs and restaurants, and a contemporary California decor and style.

BUDGET LODGING

$–$$	**Stardust,** on the Strip. The best neon sign in Las Vegas marks the spot for cheap rooms near the action.

RESTAURANTS

$$$$	**Le Cirque,** on the Strip. Mahogany woodwork and pastel silks hung across the ceiling reflect the rich French cuisine at the Bellagio's intimate and sophisticated branch of the famed New York City restaurant.
$$$$	**Picasso,** on the Strip. The Bellagio's top restaurant offers prix-fixe menus featuring innovative takes on the regional cuisines of France and Spain in a room adorned with Picasso originals.

$$$$ **Renoir,** on the Strip. Chef Alessandro Stratta presents his Franco-Italian culinary treasures in this elaborate restaurant in the Mirage, complete with paintings from the Impressionist master.

$$-$$$$ **Andre's French Restaurant,** Downtown. Although the original location is not on the nothing-is-what-it-seems Strip, Andre's will make you feel like you're somewhere else, too—in the French countryside, enjoying the best of Gallic foods.

$$-$$$$ **Commander's Palace,** on the Strip. This outpost at the Aladdin may not have quite the atmosphere of the New Orleans original, but the food and service are absolutely on par.

$$-$$$ **Rosemary's Restaurant,** on the West Side. Michael and Wendy Jordan have created an outstanding restaurant off the crowded Strip with a varied, contemporary menu but without the stratospheric prices.

BUDGET RESTAURANTS

$-$$ **Bonjour Casual French,** in South Las Vegas. Bonjour is just what the name implies—casual and comfortable, as well as being the source for some wonderfully updated French classics.

AFTER HOURS

Blue Man Group: Live at Luxor, on the Strip. Science-fair intellect collides with food-fight antics in a rocking, offbeat hit that plays against a larger canvas than in any other Blue Man city.

Ghostbar, on the West Side. You don't have to be young and single (though it helps) to enjoy a cocktail and penthouse view from the top of the Palms.

Mac King, on the Strip. A true bargain on a Strip no longer known for them. At Harrah's, King offers focused comedy-magic with a point of view, not just a cheap way to kill a hot afternoon.

O, on the Strip. A one-of-a-kind production at the Bellagio doesn't come cheaply, but those who can afford to splurge will be rewarded with a show that you really *can't* see anywhere else.

Ra, on the Strip. At Luxor, casino dollars prove that dance clubs can have a long shelf life with the help of a lavish "futuristic-ancient Egyptian" design that echoes the movie *Stargate* and, more important, an impressive rotation of visiting deejays.

CASINOS

Golden Nugget, Downtown. Those seeking the classic Las Vegas can still get a taste of it amid the gold-plated elevators, pay phones, and slot machines at this downtown institution.

Green Valley Ranch, in Henderson. Consider this a low priority if the pervasive spread of tribal gaming has put a casino in your backyard. If not, see how Las Vegas residents prefer to gamble—away from the Strip and where games have a minimum house edge.

Hard Rock Hotel, on Paradise Road. In direct contrast to the "supersizing" of most recent casino ventures, the Hard Rock is a modern version of the small casinos of the '50s. The action all stems from a circular center bar, where the weekend gatherings of singles make the whole casino feel like a party by extension.

Mandalay Bay, on the Strip. Gamblers of all but the lowest budgets will feel like high rollers in a sprawling casino that's comfortably spread out, yet surrounded by three live music lounges, an outsize sports book, and the Strip's most interesting array of nightclubs and specialty restaurants.

EXCURSIONS

Hermit's Rest, in the Grand Canyon. Head for this westernmost viewpoint on the South Rim at sunset for an awe-inspiring view.

Hoover Dam, near Boulder City. The civil engineering masterpiece brings life-giving water to the big city in the middle of the desert.

Pioche, in Lincoln County. From the Million-Dollar Courthouse to Boot Hill cemetery, this mining town is a living remnant of old Nevada.

Scotty's Castle, in Death Valley. Legends, tall tales, and an unforgiving desert surround this lonely manor house.

SHOPPING

Desert Passage at the Aladdin, on the Strip. Trek a North African mile around 140 stores, markets, bazaars, and a Lost City.

Fashion Outlets, in Primm. Reasons to travel to nearby Primm, Nevada: Versace, Burberry's, Neiman Marcus, Polo Ralph Lauren—we rest our case.

The Forum Shops at Caesars, on the Strip. Despite a Disney-esque atmosphere (animatronic shows, a changing sky), there's enough Fendi, Gucci, and Bulgari here to make the most jaded fashionista swoon.

Gambler's General Store, Downtown. Everything here for your own private casino: professional poker chips, casino-size roulette wheels, blackjack tables, or vintage slots, and the books to help you play the games.

Grand Canal Shoppes at the Venetian, on the Strip. Amid the most luxe jewelry and fashion boutiques, discover Ripa di Monti and Il

Prato, shops imported directly from beside those real Venetian canals, for fine mementos.

SIGHTS

Bellagio, on the Strip. Casino mogul Steve Wynn designed Bellagio to be the class act of the Strip, and it retains its title to that honor—at least until Wynn builds Wynn Las Vegas. Bellagio's dancing waters are among the best free shows in town.

Caesars Palace, on the Strip. One of the few remnants of Old Vegas, Caesars hasn't lost its edge, continually improving and adding new shows and attractions such as the Colosseum and Celine Dion's *A New Day.* And don't miss the over-the-top shopping in the Forum Shops at Caesars.

Mandalay Bay, on the Strip. Mandalay Bay is one of the three hippest casinos in town, after the Hard Rock Hotel and the Palms. Just how hip is it? The House of Blues, the A-list rumjungle, and an only-in-Las-Vegas beach should answer that question quite nicely.

The Palms, on West Flamingo Road. Catch a star or two at the too-cool hotel-casino that has plenty of those wild Vegas attractions: swim-up blackjack; a pool (painted lavender!) surrounded by cabanas; a tattoo parlor; a lavish spa; and a mega-nightclub, Rain, which has indoor "thunderstorms."

Paris, on the Strip. The half-scale replica of the Eiffel Tower is just the beginning; Paris is one of the most thoroughly themed of the theme casinos. You may not actually feel like you're in the City of Light, but it'll no doubt make you pine for the real thing.

SPORTS & THE OUTDOORS

Boating on Lake Mead. A lake in the middle of the desert? Yes, indeed—and the manmade Lake Mead is a fine choice for boating, fishing, and swimming.

Cheering for the Las Vegas 51s. This minor-league team, an AAA affiliate of the Los Angeles Dodgers, provides a taste of big-league action just minutes from downtown's Fremont Street.

Golfing at Bear's Best. Tee off at this best-of course, which replicates the top 18 holes from Jack Nicklaus–designed courses in the Southwest and Mexico.

Hiking Mt. Charleston. Not many desert communities can boast of a mountain recreational area just 45 minutes from the city center. Mt. Charleston offers hiking and skiing—or just an escape from the heat.

National Finals of Rodeo. Las Vegans can always tell when the rodeo's in town—all those 10-gallon hats, straight-leg jeans, and custom-made boots. NFR offers plenty of rompin', stompin' rodeo fun.

Rock Climbing in Red Rock Canyon. Contrasting bands of red sandstone and white limestone make Red Rock breathtaking, but the recreational opportunities—rock-climbing, rappelling, biking—might make you breathless in other ways.

SMART TRAVEL TIPS

Finding out about your destination before you leave home means you won't squander time organizing everyday minutiae once you've arrived. You'll be more streetwise when you hit the ground as well, better prepared to explore the aspects of Las Vegas that drew you here in the first place. The organizations in this section can provide information to supplement this guide; contact them for up-to-the-minute details. Happy landings!

ADDRESSES

The Greater Las Vegas area is in Clark County, Nevada and encompasses four cities: Las Vegas, North Las Vegas, Henderson, and Boulder City. There are also the planned communities of Summerlin, in the northwest part of the valley, and Green Valley, in Henderson. Sometimes the borders blur; areas cited as being in Summerlin or Green Valley often are well outside the communities' borders.

Streets are named at the whim of the developer, sometimes with unusual results (one neighborhood's streets were clearly named by a *Star Trek* fan). Some streets have more than one name, and others break for long sections and resume miles later, such as Maryland Parkway and Paradise Road.

AIR TRAVEL TO & FROM LAS VEGAS

McCarran International Airport (LAS) is well served by many nonstop and direct flights.

BOOKING

When you book, look for nonstop flights and remember that "direct" flights stop at least once. Try to avoid connecting flights, which require a change of plane. Two airlines may operate a connecting flight jointly, so ask whether your airline operates every segment of the trip; you may find that the carrier you prefer flies you only part of the way. To find more booking tips and to check prices and make online flight reservations, log on to www.fodors.com.

CARRIERS

All of the major airlines operate frequent service from their hub cities and between them offer one-stop connecting flights from virtually every city in the country. In addition to nonstop service to the "usual" hub cities (i.e., Atlanta, Chicago, Dallas, Denver, Houston, Minneapolis, St. Louis, Salt Lake City), nonstop service is offered to other destinations by some smaller airlines. Southwest remains the dominant airline (with nearly double the number of passengers carried as its closest competitor, America West), and it offers frequent flights to many cities in the south and west, including San Diego, Los Angeles, Oakland, Seattle, and Phoenix. Be sure to check rates for the newer discount airlines that serve Las Vegas, such as JetBlue, Song, and Ted. Many international carriers serve Las Vegas as well; their schedules include direct flights from Canada and the United Kingdom. Virgin Atlantic is the only airline providing nonstop service between Las Vegas and the United Kingdom, with four flights per week.

Major Airlines Air Canada ☎ 800/776-3000 ⊕ www.aircanada.ca. **AeroMexico** ☎ 800/237-6639 ⊕ www.aeromexico.com. **American** ☎ 800/433-7300 ⊕ www.aa.com. **America West** ☎ 800/235-9292 ⊕ www.americawest.com. **Continental** ☎ 800/525-0280 ⊕ www.continental.com. **Delta** ☎ 800/221-1212 ⊕ www.delta.com. **Japan Airlines** ☎ 800/525-3663 ⊕ www.jal.co.jp/en. **Northwest** ☎ 800/225-2525 ⊕ www.nwa.com. **Southwest** ☎ 800/435-9792 ⊕ www.southwest.com. **United** ☎ 800/241-6522 ⊕ www.united.com. **US Airways** ☎ 800/428-4322 ⊕ www.usairways.com. **Virgin Atlantic** ☎ 800/862-8621 ⊕ www.virginatlantic.com.

Smaller Airlines AirTran Airways ☎ 800/247-8726 ⊕ www.airtran.com. **Alaska Airlines** ☎ 800/426-0333 ⊕ www.alaskaair.com. **Allegiant Air** ☎ 877/202-6444 ⊕ www.allegiant-air.com. **Aloha** ☎ 800/367-5250 ⊕ www.alohaairlines.com. **American Trans Air/ATA** ☎ 800/435-9282 ⊕ www.ata.com. **Frontier Airlines** ☎ 800/432-1359 ⊕ www.frontierairlines.com. **Hawaiian Airlines** ☎ 800/367-5320 ⊕ www.hawaiianair.com. **Midwest Express** ☎ 800/452-2022 ⊕ www.midwestexpress.com. **Song** ☎ 800/359-6664 ⊕ www.flysong.com. **Spirit Airlines** ☎ 800/772-7117 ⊕ www.spiritair.com. **Sun Country Air** ☎ 800/359-6786 ⊕ www.suncountryairlines.com. **Ted** ☎ 800/225-5833 ⊕ www.flyted.com.

CHECK-IN & BOARDING

Always **find out your carrier's check-in policy.** Plan to arrive at the airport about two hours before your scheduled departure time for domestic flights and 2½ to 3 hours before international flights. You may need to arrive earlier if you're flying from one of the busier airports or during peak air-traffic times.

Las Vegas used to be the premiere destination for remote check-in facilities, a service that allowed passengers to check-in for flights at various hotels on the Strip and head straight for the departure gate with seat assignment and boarding pass. At this writing, however, all nonairport check-in was suspended until further notice due to heightened airport security measures.

To avoid delays at airport-security checkpoints, try not to wear any metal. Jewelry, belt and other buckles, steel-toe shoes, barrettes, and underwire bras are among the items that can set off detectors.

Assuming that not everyone with a ticket will show up, airlines routinely overbook planes. When everyone does, airlines ask for volunteers to give up their seats. In return, these volunteers usually get a several-hundred-dollar flight voucher, which can be used toward the purchase of another ticket, and are rebooked on the next flight out. If there are not enough volunteers, the airline must choose who will be denied boarding. The first to get bumped are passengers who checked in late and those flying on discounted tickets, so get to the gate and check in as early as possible, especially during peak periods.

Always **bring a government-issued photo ID** to the airport; even when it's not required, a passport is best.

CUTTING COSTS

The least expensive airfares to Las Vegas are priced for round-trip travel and must usually be purchased in advance. Airlines generally allow you to change your return date for a fee; most low-fare tickets, however, are nonrefundable. It's smart to call a number of airlines and check the Internet;

when you are quoted a good price, book it on the spot—the same fare may not be available the next day, or even the next hour. Always check different routings and look into using alternate airports. Also, price off-peak flights, which may be significantly less expensive than others. Travel agents, especially low-fare specialists (➪ Discounts & Deals), are helpful.

Always ask for package rates as these tend to be the best bargains to Las Vegas—airfare that includes hotel room and sometimes car rental.

Consolidators are another good source. They buy tickets for scheduled flights at reduced rates from the airlines, then sell them at prices that beat the best fare available directly from the airlines. (Many also offer reduced car-rental and hotel rates.) Sometimes you can even get your money back if you need to return the ticket. Carefully read the fine print detailing penalties for changes and cancellations, purchase the ticket with a credit card, and confirm your consolidator reservation with the airline.

🛄 Consolidators **AirlineConsolidator.com** ☎ 888/468-5385 ⊕ www.airlineconsolidator.com, for international tickets. **Best Fares** ☎ 800/880-1234 or 800/576-8255 ⊕ www.bestfares.com; $59.90 annual membership. **Cheap Tickets** ☎ 800/377-1000 or 800/652-4327 ⊕ www.cheaptickets.com. **Expedia** ☎ 800/397-3342 or 404/728-8787 ⊕ www.expedia.com. **Hotwire** ☎ 866/468-9473 or 920/330-9418 ⊕ www.hotwire.com. **Now Voyager Travel** ✉ 45 W. 21st St., Suite 5A, New York, NY 10010 ☎ 212/459-1616 🖷 212/243-2711 ⊕ www.nowvoyagertravel.com. **Onetravel.com** ⊕ www.onetravel.com. **Orbitz** ☎ 888/656-4546 ⊕ www.orbitz.com. **Priceline.com** ⊕ www.priceline.com. **Travelocity** ☎ 888/709-5983, 877/282-2925 in Canada, 0870/876-3876 in U.K. ⊕ www.travelocity.com.

ENJOYING THE FLIGHT

State your seat preference when purchasing your ticket, and then repeat it when you confirm and when you check in. For more legroom, you can request one of the few emergency-aisle seats at check-in, if you're capable of moving obstacles comparable in weight to an airplane exit door (usually between 35 pounds and 60 pounds)—a Federal Aviation Administration requirement of passengers in these

seats. Seats behind a bulkhead also offer more legroom, but they don't have under-seat storage. Don't sit in the row in front of the emergency aisle or in front of a bulkhead, where seats may not recline.

Ask the airline whether a snack or meal is served on the flight. If you have dietary concerns, request special meals when booking. These can be vegetarian, low-cholesterol, or kosher, for example. It's a good idea to pack some healthful snacks and a small (plastic) bottle of water in your carry-on bag. On long flights, try to maintain a normal routine, to help fight jet lag. At night, get some sleep. By day, eat light meals, drink water (not alcohol), and **move around the cabin** to stretch your legs. For additional jet-lag tips consult *Fodor's FYI: Travel Fit & Healthy* (available at bookstores everywhere).

All airlines flying into Las Vegas prohibit smoking.

FLYING TIMES

To Las Vegas: From New York, 5 hours; from Dallas, 2 hours; from Chicago, 4 hours; from Los Angeles, 1 hour; from San Francisco, 1½ hours; from London, 11 hours; from Sydney, 18 hours.

HOW TO COMPLAIN

If your baggage goes astray or your flight goes awry, complain right away. Most carriers require that you **file a claim immediately.** The Aviation Consumer Protection Division of the Department of Transportation publishes *Fly-Rights,* which discusses airlines and consumer issues and is available online. You can also find articles and information on mytravelrights.com, the Web site of the nonprofit Consumer Travel Rights Center.

🛄 **Aviation Consumer Protection Division** ✉ U.S. Department of Transportation, Office of Aviation Enforcement and Proceedings, C-75, Room 4107, 400 7th St. SW, Washington, DC 20590 ☎ 202/366-2220 ⊕ airconsumer.ost.dot.gov. **Federal Aviation Administration Consumer Hotline** ✉ For inquiries: FAA, 800 Independence Ave. SW, Washington, DC 20591 ☎ 800/322-7873 ⊕ www.faa.gov.

RECONFIRMING

Check the status of your flight before you leave for the airport. You can do this on your carrier's Web site, by linking to a flight-status checker (many Web booking services offer these), or by calling your carrier or travel agent.

AIRPORTS & TRANSFERS

The gateway to Las Vegas is McCarran International Airport (LAS), 5 mi south of the business district and immediately east of the southern end of the Strip. Some people choose to fly into Los Angeles International (LAX), rent a car, and drive the four hours to Las Vegas. Fares are usually lower into LAX but after adding the car rental it averages to about the same.

🚩 Airport Information **McCarran International Airport (LAS)** ☎ 702/261-5211 ⊕ www.mccarran. com. **Los Angeles International Airport (LAX)** ☎ 310/646-5252 ⊕ www.lawa.org

AIRPORT TRANSFERS

By shuttle van: this is the cheapest way from McCarran to your hotel. The service is shared with other riders, and costs $4 to $5 per person to the Strip, $5 to $7 to downtown, and $5.25 to $21 to outlying "locals" casinos. The vans wait for passengers outside the terminal in a marked area, near the cabs. Since the vans stop at many of the major hotels, it's not the best means of transportation if you're in a hurry.

By taxi: the metered cabs awaiting your arrival at McCarran are the quickest way of getting to your destination. The fare is $3.00 on the meter when you get in and $1.80 for every mile, plus an airport surcharge of $1.20. The trip to most hotels on the Strip should cost $11 to $18; the trip downtown should be about $20 to $25. Beware of drivers who suggest taking the quickest route. They may take you through the airport tunnel and up I–15, which may be a few minutes faster but will cost considerably more since taxis charge by the mile. Drivers who take passengers through the airport tunnel without asking are committing an illegal practice known as "long-hauling." Ask a hotel employee how to contact the taxi authority if you need to report a driver.

🚩 Taxis & Shuttles **Bell Trans** ☎ 702/739-7990 ⊕ www.bell-trans.com. **Checker/Yellow/Star Cab** ☎ 702/873-2000. **Gray Line** ☎ 702/739-5700 ⊕ www.grayline.com.

BUSINESS HOURS

Las Vegas is a 24-hour city, 365 days a year. Casinos, bars, supermarkets, almost all gas stations, even some health clubs and video stores cater to customers at all hours of the day and night (many people work odd hours here).

MUSEUMS & SIGHTS

Most museums and attractions are open seven days a week.

PHARMACIES

Most pharmacies are open seven days a week from 9–7.

🚩 24-Hour Pharmacies **Walgreens** ✉ 3765 Las Vegas Blvd. S ☎ 702/739-9645.

SHOPS

Most stores are open weekdays 10–9, Saturday 9–6, and Sunday 11–6. The souvenir shops on the Strip and downtown remain open until midnight and some are open 24 hours. Grocery stores are open around the clock.

BUS TRAVEL TO & FROM LAS VEGAS

Greyhound runs bus service in and out of Las Vegas; the bus terminal is downtown.

FARES & SCHEDULES

Call Greyhound or visit their Web site for fare and schedule information.

PAYING

Cash, travelers checks, and credit cards are accepted.

RESERVATIONS

Reservations are not accepted on Greyhound. Seating is on a first-come, first-served basis. The most frequently plowed route out of Las Vegas is the one to Los Angeles, with departures approximately every two hours around the clock. Arriving at the bus station 30 to 45 minutes before your bus departs to purchase tickets nearly always ensures you a seat. On Sunday evening and Monday morning, arriving an hour or more before departure is recommended as buses fill up quickly on those days.

🚩 Bus Information **Greyhound** ✉ 200 S. Main St., Las Vegas ☎ 702/384-9561 or 800/231-2222 ⊕ www.greyhound.com.

BUS TRAVEL WITHIN LAS VEGAS

The municipally operated Citizens Area Transit (CAT) runs local buses throughout the city and to most corners of the sprawling Las Vegas Valley. The overall quality of bus service along the main thoroughfares is decent. Most visitors only ride CAT buses up and down the Strip, between Mandalay Bay and the Stratosphere. Some continue on to the Downtown Transportation Center. If you're heading to outlying areas, you may need to change buses downtown. Mornings and afternoons the buses are frequently crowded, with standing-room only.

The Las Vegas Strip Trolleys are a bit more charming with their old-fashioned appearance, and they deliver you right to the door of most of the major casinos on the Strip. Bear in mind, however, that this door-to-door delivery makes them a little slower, as they have to fight the knots of cabs, limos, airport shuttles, and private vehicles that collect at every casino at any hour of the day.

FARES & SCHEDULES

The fare for CAT buses on the Strip is $2 (exact change required; one-dollar bills are accepted). The buses stop on the street in front of all the major hotels every 10 minutes (in a perfect world) between 5:30 AM and 12:30 AM and every 15 minutes between 12:30 AM and 5:30 AM. Since traffic is quite haphazard along the Strip, however, delays are frequent. Buses supposedly running every 15 minutes can take 25 minutes to show up. Other routes serve the Meadows and Boulevard shopping malls and Sam's Town Hotel and Casino on Boulder Highway. The schedule for all buses other than those along the Strip is 5:00 AM–1:00 AM daily; the fare is $1.25.

From 9:30 AM to 1:30 AM, the Las Vegas Strip Trolley travels every 15 to 20 minutes among Strip hotels, with stops at Fashion Show Mall and Wet 'n Wild. The exact fare of $1.75 is required.

F Bus Information **Citizens Area Transit** ☎ 702/228-7433. **Las Vegas Strip Trolley** ☎ 702/382-1404.

PAYING

Pay your bus fare when you board, with exact change or with tokens available at the Downtown Transportation Center. Pay your trolley fare when you board, with exact change.

F **Downtown Transportation Center** ✉ 300 North Casino Ctr. ☎ 702/229-6019

CAMERAS & PHOTOGRAPHY

Only a few casinos allow people to photograph or videotape the games or machines. This is a holdover from the bad old days, when gambling was considered a vice and people were ashamed to be caught doing it. Some players are still sensitive about having their picture taken while gambling, so most of the casinos generally prohibit it. If you want to take a photo, ask a nearby security guard for the casino's policy.

The *Kodak Guide to Shooting Great Travel Pictures* (available at bookstores everywhere) is loaded with tips.

F **Kodak Information Center** ☎ 800/242-2424 ⊕ www.kodak.com.

EQUIPMENT PRECAUTIONS

Windy and dusty conditions are not infrequent in Las Vegas, and your photo lenses can be quickly covered with a layer of sand. Always carry your equipment tightly sealed in protective covering and bring extra lens cleaner solution to wipe off lenses.

Don't pack film or equipment in checked luggage, where it is much more susceptible to damage. X-ray machines used to view checked luggage are extremely powerful and therefore are likely to ruin your film. Try to ask for hand inspection of film, which becomes clouded after repeated exposure to airport X-ray machines, and keep videotapes and computer disks away from metal detectors. Always keep film, tape, and computer disks out of the sun. Carry an extra supply of batteries, and be prepared to turn on your camera, camcorder, or laptop to prove to airport security personnel that the device is real.

CAR RENTAL

Rates in Las Vegas average about $23 a day and $115 a week for an economy car with unlimited mileage. This does not include the 7.5% (in Clark County) sales tax, a 6% "license tag" fee and a 4% "recovery fee." If you rent your car at the airport an additional 10% tax applies.

⑦ Alamo ☎ 800/327-9633 ⊕ www.alamo.com. **Avis** ☎ 800/331-1212, 800/879-2847 or 800/272-5871 in Canada, 0870/606-0100 in U.K., 02/9353-9000 in Australia, 09/526-2847 in New Zealand ⊕ www.avis.com. **Budget** ☎ 800/527-0700, 0870/156-5656 in U.K. ⊕ www.budget.com. **Dollar** ☎ 800/800-4000, 0800/085-4578 in U.K. ⊕ www.dollar.com. **Enterprise Rent-a-Car** ☎ 800/736-8222 ⊕ www.enterprise.com. **Hertz** ☎ 800/654-3131, 800/263-0600 in Canada, 0870/844-8844 in U.K., 02/9669-2444 in Australia, 09/256-8690 in New Zealand ⊕ www.hertz.com. **National Car Rental** ☎ 800/227-7368, 0870/600-6666 in U.K. ⊕ www.nationalcar.com. **Thrifty Car Rental** ☎ 800/847-4389 ⊕ www.thrifty.com.

CUTTING COSTS

Owing to the large number of visitors who rent cars, there are many deals to be had at the airport for car rentals. During special events and conventions rates frequently go up as supply dwindles, but during other times you can find bargains. For the best deals, check with the various online services, or contact a representative of the hotel where you'll be staying, as many hotels have business relationships with car-rental companies.

Although there are several local car rental companies along the Strip itself, they tend to be more expensive than those at the airport or elsewhere in the city.

For a good deal, book through a travel agent who will shop around. Also, price local car-rental companies—whose prices may be lower still, although their service and maintenance may not be as good as those of major rental agencies—and research rates on the Internet. Consolidators that specialize in air travel can offer good rates on cars as well (⇨ Air Travel). Remember to ask about required deposits, cancellation penalties, and drop-off charges if you're planning to pick up the car in one city and leave it in another. If you're traveling during a holiday period,

also make sure that a confirmed reservation guarantees you a car.

⑦ Local Agencies **Allstate/Payless** ☎ 702/736-6147. **Brooks Rent-A-Car** ☎ 702/735-3344. **Dream Car Rentals** ☎ 702/731-6452, 702/895-6661, or 877/373-2601. **Rent-a-Vette** ☎ 702/736-2592 or 800/372-1981.

INSURANCE

When driving a rented car you are generally responsible for any damage to or loss of the vehicle. You also may be liable for any property damage or personal injury that you may cause while driving. Before you rent, see what coverage you already have under the terms of your personal auto-insurance policy and credit cards.

For about $9 to $25 a day, rental companies sell protection, known as a collision- or loss-damage waiver (CDW or LDW), that eliminates your liability for damage to the car; it's always optional and should never be automatically added to your bill. In most states you don't need a CDW if you have personal auto insurance or other liability insurance. Some states, including Nevada, have capped the price of the CDW and LDW. However, **make sure you have enough coverage to pay for the car.** If you do not have auto insurance or an umbrella policy that covers damage to third parties, purchasing liability insurance and a CDW or LDW is highly recommended.

REQUIREMENTS & RESTRICTIONS

In Nevada you must be 21 to rent a car, and several of the major car rental agencies (such as Hertz) have a minimum age of 25. Those agencies that do rent to those under 25 may charge you higher rates. There is no upper age limit for car rental. Non-U.S. residents will need a reservation voucher, a passport, a driver's license, and a travel policy that covers each driver when picking up a car.

SURCHARGES

Before you pick up a car in one city and leave it in another, ask about drop-off charges or one-way service fees, which can be substantial. Also inquire about early-return policies; some rental agencies charge extra if you return the car before the time specified in your contract while others give you a refund for the days not used. To avoid a hefty refueling fee, fill the tank just before you turn in the car, but be aware that gas stations near the rental outlet may overcharge. It's almost never a deal to buy the tank of gas that's in the car when you rent it; the understanding is that you'll return it empty, but some fuel usually remains. Surcharges may apply if you're under 25 or if you take the car outside the area approved by the rental agency. You pay extra for child seats (about $8 a day), which are compulsory for children under five, and usually for additional drivers (up to $25 a day, depending on location).

CAR TRAVEL

Las Vegas is an easy city to navigate. The principal north–south artery is Las Vegas Boulevard (I–15 runs roughly parallel to it, less than a mile to the west). A 3½-mi stretch of Las Vegas Boulevard South is the Strip, where a majority of the city's hotels and casinos are clustered. Many of the major streets running east–west (Tropicana Avenue, Flamingo Road, Desert Inn Road, Sahara Avenue) are named for the casinos built at their intersections with the Strip.

Because the capacity of the streets of Las Vegas has not kept pace with the city's incredible growth, traffic can be slow in the late afternoon, in the evening, and on the weekend. At those times, **drive the streets that parallel Las Vegas Boulevard**: Paradise Road to the east, and Industrial Road to the west. The Industrial Road shortcut (from Tropicana Avenue almost all the way to downtown) will save you an enormous amount of time. You can enter the parking lots at Caesars Palace, the Mirage, Treasure Island, the Stardust, the New Frontier, and Circus Circus from Industrial Road.

Visitors from Southern California should at all costs try to avoid traveling to Las Vegas on a Friday afternoon and returning home on a Sunday afternoon. During these traditional weekend-visit hours, driving times can be twice as long as during other, nonpeak periods.

EMERGENCY SERVICES

You can call 911 from most locations in Nevada to reach police, fire, or ambulance assistance. Otherwise, dial the operator. If you have a cellular or digital phone, dial *647 to reach the Nevada Highway Patrol.

PARKING

You can't park anywhere on the Strip itself, and Fremont Street in the casino district downtown is a pedestrian mall closed to traffic. Street parking regulations are strictly enforced in Las Vegas, and meters are continuously monitored, so whenever possible it's a good idea to **leave your car in a parking lot.** Free parking is available at virtually every hotel, although you may have to hunt for a space and you can wind up in the far reaches of immense parking lots. To avoid this, simply make use of valet parking. Parking in the high-rise structures downtown is generally free, as long as you validate your parking ticket at the casino cashier.

ROAD CONDITIONS

It might seem as if every road in Las Vegas is in a continuous state of expansion or repair. Orange highway cones, road-building equipment, and detours are ubiquitous. But once the roads are widened and repaved, they're efficient and comfortable. The city's traffic-light system is state-of-the-art, and you can often drive for miles on major thoroughfares, hitting green lights all the way. Signage is excellent, both on surface arteries and freeways. The local driving style is fast.

For information on weather conditions, highway construction, and road closures call the Department of Transportation for the state you're traveling in.
🚗 Arizona Department of Transportation ☎ 888/411-7623. California Department of Transportation ☎ 916/445-7623. Nevada Department of Transportation ☎ 877/687-6237.

RULES OF THE ROAD

The speed limit on residential streets is 25 mph. On major thoroughfares it's 45 mph, though drivers often get impatient with people who obey the speed limit and pass on either side—in part because radar detectors are legal and widely used. On the interstate and other divided highways within the city the speed limit is a fast 65 mph; outside the city, the speed limit is 70 or 75 mph.

Police officers are vigilant about speeding laws within Las Vegas, especially in school zones, but enforcement in rural areas is rare. California's speed limit is 70 mph. Right turns are permitted on red lights after coming to a full stop in Arizona, California, and Nevada. Nevada requires seat-belt use in the front and back seats of vehicles. Chains are required on Mt. Charleston and in other mountainous regions when snow is fresh and heavy; signs indicate the conditions. Nevada has no restrictions on hand-held cellular phones.

Always **strap children under age five or under 40 pounds into approved child-safety seats.** In Nevada, children must wear seat belts regardless of where they're seated.

CHILDREN IN LAS VEGAS

Despite its determination to put the "sin" back in Sin City, Las Vegas, with all of its oddities and entertainment, actually can be a good family destination. Other than in the casinos, children are welcome everywhere. Branches of the Las Vegas–Clark County Library District host weekly storytimes for children in several age categories. For a schedule, call the main library number. The Lied Discovery Children's Museum and the Las Vegas Natural History Museum, which has exhibits of dinosaurs, whales, and Nevada fauna, are also good bets for kids. The Rainbow Company Youth Theatre group, which is part of the City of Las Vegas Cultural Affairs Division, frequently presents productions particularly suited to families. The *Las Vegas Review-Journal* and *Las Vegas Sun* (⇨ Media) also list activities of interest to families on their community-news pages, which run throughout the week. If you are renting a car, don't forget to arrange for a car seat when you reserve. For general advice about traveling with children, consult *Fodor's FYI: Travel with Your Baby* (available in bookstores everywhere).

🔢 Local Information **Las Vegas–Clark County Library District** ☎ 702/734-7323 ⊕ www.lvccld.org **Las Vegas Natural History Museum** ✉ 900 Las Vegas Blvd. N ☎ 702/384-3466 **Lied Discovery Children's Museum** ✉ 833 Las Vegas Blvd. N ☎ 702/382-3445 **Rainbow Company Youth Theatre** ☎ 702/229-6553.

BABYSITTING

One reliable independent local agency is Nanny's and Granny's, which charges a variable rate depending on the number of children (fees for one child begin with a minimum $60 for the first four hours). Babysitters are licensed and cleared through the local sheriff's department.

Several casinos also provide child care services, but they tend to be those that appeal to locals. The facilities at Sam's Town and the Gold Coast are free for casino patrons, three-hour maximum; you must stay in the building. At the Gold Coast and Sam's Town, children must be potty-trained. There's an hourly rate and a five-hour limit at Kids' Quest, the mega–play areas at Texas Station, Boulder Station, Palace Station, and Sunset Station. Kids' Quest offers sprawling, elaborate play structures; video games; and some structured activities. It's available to kids up to 12 years old.

🔢 Agencies **Nanny's and Granny's** ✉ 6440 W. Coley Ave., Las Vegas, 89117 ☎ 702/364-4700 ⊕ www.nanny4u.com.
🔢 Casinos **Boulder Station** ✉ 4111 Boulder Hwy., Boulder Strip ☎ 702/432-7569. **Gold Coast** ✉ 4000 W. Flamingo Rd., West Side ☎ 702/367-7111. **Orleans** ✉ 4500 W. Tropicana Ave., West Side ☎ 702/365-7111. **Palace Station** ✉ 2411 W. Sahara Ave., West Side ☎ 702/367-2411. **Sam's Town** ✉ 5111 Boulder Hwy., Boulder Strip ☎ 702/456-7777. **Sunset Station** ✉ 1301 W. Sunset Rd., Henderson ☎ 702/547-7773. **Texas Station** ✉ 2101 Texas Star La., Rancho Strip ☎ 702/631-8355.

FLYING

If your children are two or older, ask about children's airfares. As a general rule, infants under two not occupying a seat fly at greatly reduced fares or even for free. But if you want to guarantee a seat for an infant, you have to pay full fare. Consider flying during off-peak days and times; most airlines will grant an infant a seat without a ticket if there are available seats.

Experts agree that it's a good idea to use safety seats aloft for children weighing less than 40 pounds. Airlines set their own policies: if you use a safety seat, U.S. carriers usually require that the child be ticketed, even if he or she is young enough to ride free, because the seats must be strapped into regular seats. And even if you pay the full adult fare for the seat, it may be worth it, especially on longer trips. Do **check your airline's policy about using safety seats during takeoff and landing.** Safety seats are not allowed everywhere in the plane, so get your seat assignments as early as possible.

When reserving, request children's meals or a freestanding bassinet (not available at all airlines) if you need them. But note that bulkhead seats, where you must sit to use the bassinet, may lack an overhead bin or storage space on the floor.

LODGING
Most hotels in Las Vegas allow children under a certain age to stay in their parents' room at no extra charge, but others charge for them as extra adults; be sure to find out the cutoff age for children's discounts.

Hotels will usually provide cribs for babies and "rollaways" (cots) for children. Children are actively discouraged at the Bellagio, and they are allowed on the property only if they are accompanied by their parents and staying at the hotel.

Most major Las Vegas hotels provide extensive video-game arcades for their underage guests (though leaving children under the age of 14 or 15 alone in arcades and game rooms is not recommended). The Orleans is the casino closest to the Strip with a commercial child-care facility, Kids Tyme.

🎏 Best Choices **Orleans Hotel and Casino** ✉ 4500 W. Tropicana Ave. ☎ 800/675-3267.

SIGHTS & ATTRACTIONS
The free spectacles, the thrill rides (both big and small, actual and virtual), the many movie theaters, bowling alleys, video-game arcades, amusement and water parks, children's museums, and other activities make Las Vegas a fun place for youngsters. Places that are especially appealing to children are indicated by a rubber-duckie icon (🐤) in the margin.

CONCIERGES
Concierges, found in many hotels, can help you with theater tickets and dinner

reservations: a good one with connections may be able to get you seats for a hot show or prime-time dinner reservations at the restaurant of the moment. You can also turn to your hotel's concierge for help with travel arrangements, sightseeing plans, services ranging from aromatherapy to zipper repair, and emergencies. **Always tip** a concierge who has been of assistance (⇨ Tipping).

CONSUMER PROTECTION
Whether you're shopping for gifts or purchasing travel services, **pay with a major credit card** whenever possible, so you can cancel payment or get reimbursed if there's a problem (and you can provide documentation). If you're doing business with a particular company for the first time, contact your local Better Business Bureau and the attorney general's offices in your state and (for U.S. businesses) the company's home state as well. Have any complaints been filed? Finally, if you're buying a package or tour, always consider travel insurance that includes default coverage (⇨ Insurance).

🎏 **Council of Better Business Bureaus** ✉ 4200 Wilson Blvd., Suite 800, Arlington, VA 22203 ☎ 703/276-0100 🖷 703/525-8277 ⊕ www.bbb. org. **Better Business Bureau of Southern Nevada** ✉ 2301 Palomino La., Las Vegas, NV 89107 ☎ 702/ 320-4500 🖷 702/320-4560 ⊕ www.vegasbbb.org.

CUSTOMS & DUTIES
IN AUSTRALIA
Australian residents who are 18 or older may bring home A$400 worth of souvenirs and gifts (including jewelry), 250 cigarettes or 250 grams of cigars or other tobacco products, and 1,125 ml of alcohol (including wine, beer, and spirits). Residents under 18 may bring back A$200 worth of goods. Members of the same family traveling together may pool their allowances. Prohibited items include meat products. Seeds, plants, and fruits need to be declared upon arrival.

🎏 **Australian Customs Service** 🖉 Regional Director, Box 8, Sydney, NSW 2001 ☎ 02/9213-2000 or 1300/363263, 02/9364-7222 or 1800/020-504 quarantine-inquiry line 🖷 02/9213-4043 ⊕ www. customs.gov.au.

IN CANADA

Canadian residents who have been out of Canada for at least seven days may bring in C$750 worth of goods duty-free. If you've been away fewer than seven days but more than 48 hours, the duty-free allowance drops to C$200. If your trip lasts 24 to 48 hours, the allowance is C$50. You may not pool allowances with family members. Goods claimed under the C$750 exemption may follow you by mail; those claimed under the lesser exemptions must accompany you. Alcohol and tobacco products may be included in the seven-day and 48-hour exemptions but not in the 24-hour exemption. If you meet the age requirements of the province or territory through which you reenter Canada, you may bring in, duty-free, 1.5 liters of wine *or* 1.14 liters (40 imperial ounces) of liquor *or* 24 12-ounce cans or bottles of beer or ale. Also, if you meet the local age requirement for tobacco products, you may bring in, duty-free, 200 cigarettes and 50 cigars. Check ahead of time with the Canada Customs and Revenue Agency or the Department of Agriculture for policies regarding meat products, seeds, plants, and fruits.

You may send an unlimited number of gifts (only one gift per recipient, however) worth up to C$60 each duty-free to Canada. Label the package UNSOLICITED GIFT—VALUE UNDER $60. Alcohol and tobacco are excluded.

⑦ Canada Customs and Revenue Agency ⊠ 2265 St. Laurent Blvd., Ottawa, Ontario K1G 4K3 ☎ 800/461-9999 in Canada, 204/983-3500, 506/636-5064 ⊕ www.ccra.gc.ca.

IN NEW ZEALAND

All homeward-bound residents may bring back NZ$700 worth of souvenirs and gifts; passengers may not pool their allowances, and children can claim only the concession on goods intended for their own use. For those 17 or older, the duty-free allowance also includes 4.5 liters of wine or beer; one 1,125-ml bottle of spirits; and either 200 cigarettes, 250 grams of tobacco, 50 cigars, *or* a combination of the three up to 250 grams. Meat products, seeds, plants, and fruits must be declared upon arrival to the Agricultural Services Department.

⑦ New Zealand Customs ⊠ Head office: The Customhouse, 17-21 Whitmore St., Box 2218, Wellington ☎ 09/300-5399 or 0800/428-786 ⊕ www.customs.govt.nz.

IN THE U.K.

From countries outside the European Union, including the United States, you may bring home, duty-free, 200 cigarettes, 50 cigars, 100 cigarillos, or 250 grams of tobacco; 1 liter of spirits or 2 liters of fortified or sparkling wine or liqueurs; 2 liters of still table wine; 60 ml of perfume; 250 ml of toilet water; plus £145 worth of other goods, including gifts and souvenirs. Prohibited items include meat and dairy products, seeds, plants, and fruits.

⑦ HM Customs and Excise ⊠ Portcullis House, 21 Cowbridge Rd. E, Cardiff CF11 9SS ☎ 0845/010-9000, 0208/929-0152 advice service, 0208/929-6731, 0208/910-3602 complaints ⊕ www.hmce.gov.uk.

DISABILITIES & ACCESSIBILITY

Las Vegas gets a B-plus when it comes to accommodating travelers with disabilities. It's not perfect, but because so much major construction—from sidewalks to megaresorts—is recent, accessibility is very good for most places. Also, Las Vegas is well laid out for people who use wheelchairs: flat, wide sidewalks (especially in the tourist areas) and curb cuts, ramps, and wheelchair elevators and lifts are almost everywhere. Only the crowds make it at all difficult for people in wheelchairs to get around efficiently.

HELP of Southern Nevada refers callers to the proper social agency. Assistance is also available from the Las Vegas Convention and Visitors Authority ADA coordinator.

⑦ Local Resources HELP of Southern Nevada ⊠ 953 E. Sahara Ave., 35B-208, Las Vegas 89104 ☎ 702/369-4357. **Las Vegas Convention and Visitors Authority ADA Coordinator** ⊠ 3150 Paradise Rd., Las Vegas 89109 ☎ 702/892-7525.

LODGING

Despite the Americans with Disabilities Act, the definition of accessibility seems to differ from hotel to hotel. Some properties may be accessible by ADA standards for people with mobility problems but not for people with hearing or vision impairments, for example.

If you have mobility problems, ask for the lowest floor on which accessible services are offered. If you have a hearing impairment, check whether the hotel has devices to alert you visually to the ring of the telephone, a knock at the door, and a fire/emergency alarm. Some hotels provide these devices without charge. Discuss your needs with hotel personnel if this equipment isn't available, so that a staff member can personally alert you in the event of an emergency.

If you're bringing a guide dog, get authorization ahead of time and write down the name of the person with whom you spoke.

Generally, the layouts of most Las Vegas hotels and casinos are such that you have to cross long distances to get from one place to another. These resort-casinos are so big—3,000 rooms, a dozen restaurants, extensive retail areas, and huge gambling halls—that they're no less than minicities under one roof. Whether you're walking or moving around in a wheelchair, you have to cover a lot of ground.

The Imperial Palace has the most facilities accommodating people with disabilities, including more than 100 accessible rooms, many of which feature roll-in showers, transfer chairs, and features for people with hearing impairments. Most hotels have some rooms that are accessible to travelers in wheelchairs.

🔢 Wheelchair-Accessible Accommodations Aladdin Resort and Casino ✉ 3667 Las Vegas Blvd. S ☎ 702/785-5555 or 877/333-9474. Caesars Palace ✉ 3570 Las Vegas Blvd. S ☎ 702/731-7110 or 800/634-6661. Excalibur Hotel and Casino ✉ 3850 Las Vegas Blvd. S ☎ 702/597-7777 or 800/937-7777. Lady Luck Casino and Hotel ✉ 206 N. 3rd St. ☎ 702/477-3000 or 800/523-9582. Luxor Resort & Casino ✉ 3900 Las Vegas Blvd. S ☎ 702/262-4000 or 888/777-0188. Mandalay Bay Resort & Casino ✉ 3950 Las Vegas Blvd. S ☎ 702/632-7777 or 877/632-7800. MGM Grand Hotel and Casino ✉ 3799 Las Vegas Blvd. S ☎ 702/891-1111 or 877/880-0880. Mirage Hotel and Casino ✉ 3400 Las Vegas Blvd. S ☎ 702/791-7111 or 800/374-9000. Riviera Hotel and Casino ✉ 2901 Las Vegas Blvd. S ☎ 702/734-5110 or 800/634-6753.

RESERVATIONS
When discussing accessibility with an operator or reservations agent, ask hard questions. Are there any stairs, inside or out? Are there grab bars next to the toilet and in the shower/tub? How wide is the doorway to the room? To the bathroom? For the most extensive facilities meeting the latest legal specifications, opt for newer accommodations. If you reserve through a toll-free number, consider also calling the hotel's local number to confirm the information from the central reservations office. Get confirmation in writing when you can.

SIGHTS & ATTRACTIONS
All major attractions in Las Vegas are accessible for persons with physical disabilities, in accordance with the Americans with Disabilities Act. Call ahead for specific information.

TRANSPORTATION
Citizens Area Transit (☎ 702/228-7433) operates buses in Las Vegas that accommodate persons with disabilities.

🔢 Complaints Aviation Consumer Protection Division (⇨ Air Travel) for airline-related problems. Departmental Office of Civil Rights ✉ For general inquiries, U.S. Department of Transportation, S-30, 400 7th St. SW, Room 10215, Washington, DC 20590 ☎ 202/366-4648 🖷 202/366-9371 ⊕ www.dot.gov/ost/docr/index.htm. Disability Rights Section ✉ NYAV, U.S. Department of Justice, Civil Rights Division, 950 Pennsylvania Ave. NW, Washington, DC 20530 ☎ ADA information line 202/514-0301, 800/514-0301, 202/514-0383 TTY, 800/514-0383 TTY ⊕ www.ada.gov. U.S. Department of Transportation Hotline ☎ For disability-related air-travel problems, 800/778-4838 or 800/455-9880 TTY.

TRAVEL AGENCIES
In the United States, the Americans with Disabilities Act requires that travel firms serve the needs of all travelers. Some agencies specialize in working with people with disabilities.

🔢 Travelers with Mobility Problems Accessible Vans of America ✉ 9 Spielman Rd., Fairfield, NJ 07004 ☎ 877/282-8267 or 888/282-8267, 973/808-9709 reservations 🖷 973/808-9713 ⊕ www.accessiblevans.com. CareVacations ✉ No. 5, 5110-50 Ave., Leduc, Alberta, Canada, T9E 6V4

☎ 780/986-6404 or 877/478-7827 🖷 780/986-8332 ⊕ www.carevacations.com, for group tours and cruise vacations. **Flying Wheels Travel** ✉ 143 W. Bridge St., Box 382, Owatonna, MN 55060 ☎ 507/451-5005 🖷 507/451-1685 ⊕ www.flyingwheelstravel.com.

🚹 Travelers with Developmental Disabilities **New Directions** ✉ 5276 Hollister Ave., Suite 207, Santa Barbara, CA 93111 ☎ 805/967-2841 or 888/967-2841 🖷 805/964-7344 ⊕ www.newdirectionstravel.com. **Sprout** ✉ 893 Amsterdam Ave., New York, NY 10025 ☎ 212/222-9575 or 888/222-9575 🖷 212/222-9768 ⊕ www.gosprout.org.

DISCOUNTS & DEALS

Some hotels offer "funbooks" with gambling coupons (bet $5 and win $7 on an even-money wager, for example) and discounts for food and attractions. Inquire at the front desk when you check in. The Las Vegas Convention and Visitors Authority has coupon books for discounts and deals at hotels, restaurants, and casinos.

Be a smart shopper and compare all your options before making decisions. A plane ticket bought with a promotional coupon from travel clubs, coupon books, and direct-mail offers or purchased on the Internet may not be cheaper than the least expensive fare from a discount ticket agency. And always keep in mind that what you get is just as important as what you save.

DISCOUNT RESERVATIONS

To save money, look into discount reservations services with Web sites and toll-free numbers, which use their buying power to get a better price on hotels, airline tickets (⇨ Air Travel), even car rentals. When booking a room, always **call the hotel's local toll-free number** (if one is available) rather than the central reservations number—you'll often get a better price. Always ask about special packages or corporate rates.

🚹 Hotel Rooms **Accommodations Express** ☎ 800/444-7666 or 800/277-1064 ⊕ www.acex.net. **Hotels.com** ☎ 800/246-8357 ⊕ www.hotels.com. **Quikbook** ☎ 800/789-9887 ⊕ www.quikbook.com. **Turbotrip.com** ☎ 800/473-7829 ⊕ www.turbotrip.com.

PACKAGE DEALS

Don't confuse packages and guided tours. When you buy a package, you travel on your own, just as though you had planned the trip yourself. Fly/drive packages, which combine airfare and car rental, are often a good deal. In cities, ask the local visitor's bureau about hotel and local transportation packages that include tickets to major museum exhibits or other special events.

GAY & LESBIAN TRAVEL

Las Vegas has a growing gay community; contact the Gay and Lesbian Community Center of Southern Nevada for information on local services and events. For details about the gay and lesbian scene, consult *Fodor's Gay Guide to the USA* (available in bookstores everywhere).

The *Las Vegas Bugle* is a local gay publication.

🚹 Gay- & Lesbian-Friendly Travel Agencies **Different Roads Travel** ✉ 8383 Wilshire Blvd., Suite 520, Beverly Hills, CA 90211 ☎ 323/651-5557 or 800/429-8747 (Ext. 14 for both) 🖷 323/651-5454 ✉ lgernert@tzell.com. **Kennedy Travel** ✉ 130 W. 42nd St., Suite 401, New York, NY 10036 ☎ 212/840-8659, 800/237-7433 🖷 212/730-2269 ⊕ www.kennedytravel.com. **Now, Voyager** ✉ 4406 18th St., San Francisco, CA 94114 ☎ 415/626-1169 or 800/255-6951 🖷 415/626-8626 ⊕ www.nowvoyager.com. **Skylink Travel and Tour/Flying Dutchmen Travel** ✉ 1455 N. Dutton Ave., Suite A, Santa Rosa, CA 95401 ☎ 707/546-9888 or 800/225-5759 🖷 707/636-0951; serving lesbian travelers.
🚹 **Gay and Lesbian Community Center of Southern Nevada** ✉ 953 E. Sahara Ave. ☎ 702/733-9800. *Las Vegas Bugle* ☎ 702/369-6260.

HEALTH

The dry desert air in Las Vegas means that your body will need extra fluids, especially during the punishing summer months. Always drink lots of water even if you're not outside very much. When you're outdoors wear sunscreen in summer and always carry water with you if you plan a long walk.

HOLIDAYS

Major national holidays are New Year's Day (Jan. 1); Martin Luther King Day (3rd Mon. in Jan.); Presidents' Day (3rd Mon. in Feb.); Memorial Day (last Mon. in May); Independence Day (July 4); Labor

Day (1st Mon. in Sept.); Columbus Day (2nd Mon. in Oct.); Thanksgiving Day (4th Thurs. in Nov.); Christmas Eve and Christmas Day (Dec. 24 and 25); and New Year's Eve (Dec. 31).

INSURANCE

The most useful travel-insurance plan is a comprehensive policy that includes coverage for trip cancellation and interruption, default, trip delay, and medical expenses (with a waiver for preexisting conditions).

Without insurance you'll lose all or most of your money if you cancel your trip, regardless of the reason. Default insurance covers you if your tour operator, airline, or cruise line goes out of business—the chances of which have been increasing. Trip-delay covers expenses that arise because of bad weather or mechanical delays. Study the fine print when comparing policies.

U.K. residents can buy a travel-insurance policy valid for most vacations taken during the year in which it's purchased (but check preexisting-condition coverage).

Always **buy travel policies directly from the insurance company**; if you buy them from a cruise line, airline, or tour operator that goes out of business you probably won't be covered for the agency or operator's default, a major risk. Before making any purchase, review your existing health and home-owner's policies to find what they cover away from home.

🗂 Travel Insurers In the U.S.: **Access America** ✉ 2805 N. Parham Rd., Richmond, VA 23294 ☎ 800/284-8300 🖷 804/673-1491 or 800/346-9265 ⊕ www.accessamerica.com. **Travel Guard International** ✉ 1145 Clark St., Stevens Point, WI 54481 ☎ 715/345-0505 or 800/826-1300 🖷 800/955-8785 ⊕ www.travelguard.com.

FOR INTERNATIONAL TRAVELERS

For information on customs restrictions, *see* Customs & Duties.

CAR RENTAL

When picking up a rental car, non-U.S. residents need a reservation voucher for any prepaid reservations that were made in the traveler's home country, a passport, a driver's license, and a travel policy that covers each driver.

CAR TRAVEL

In Las Vegas gasoline cost $1.69 a gallon at this writing. Stations are plentiful. Most stay open late (24 hours along large highways and in big cities), except in rural areas, where Sunday hours are limited and where you may drive long stretches without a refueling opportunity. Highways are well paved. Interstate highways—limited-access, multilane highways whose numbers are prefixed by "I–"—are the fastest routes. Interstates with three-digit numbers encircle urban areas, which may have other limited-access expressways, freeways, and parkways as well. Tolls may be levied on limited-access highways. So-called U.S. highways and state highways are not necessarily limited-access but may have several lanes.

Along larger highways, roadside stops with restrooms, fast-food restaurants, and sundries stores are well spaced. State police and tow trucks patrol major highways and lend assistance. If your car breaks down on an interstate, pull onto the shoulder and wait for help, or have your passengers wait while you walk to an emergency phone (available in most states). If you carry a cell phone, dial *55, noting your location on the small green roadside mileage markers.

Driving in the United States is on the right. Do obey speed limits posted along roads and highways. Watch for lower limits in small towns and on back roads. Nevada does require front-seat passengers to wear seat belts. On weekdays between 6 and 10 AM and again between 4 and 7 PM expect heavy traffic. To encourage carpooling, some freeways have special lanes for so-called high-occupancy vehicles (HOV)—cars carrying more than one passenger.

Bookstores, gas stations, convenience stores, and rest stops sell maps (about $3) and multiregion road atlases (about $10).

CONSULATES & EMBASSIES

The following all have consulates in Los Angeles.

🗂 Australia **Australian Consulate-General** ✉ Century Plaza Towers, 19th fl., 2049 Century Park

E, Los Angeles, CA 90067 ☎ 310/229-4800 🖷 310/277-2258.

🚩 Canada **Canadian Consulate General** ✉ 550 South Hope St., 9th fl., Los Angeles, CA 90071 ☎ 213/346-2700 🖷 213/346-2767.

🚩 New Zealand **New Zealand Consulate-General** ✉ 12400 Wilshire Blvd., Suite 1150, Los Angeles, CA 90025 ☎ 310/207-1605 🖷 310/207-3605.

🚩 United Kingdom **British Consulate-General** ✉ 11766 Wilshire Blvd., Suite 1200, Los Angeles, CA 90025 ☎ 310/481-0031 🖷 310/481-2960.

CURRENCY

The dollar is the basic unit of U.S. currency. It has 100 cents. Coins are the copper penny (1¢); the silvery nickel (5¢), dime (10¢), quarter (25¢), and half-dollar (50¢); and the golden $1 coin, replacing a now-rare silver dollar. Bills are denominated $1, $5, $10, $20, $50, and $100, all mostly green and identical in size; designs and background tints vary. In addition, you may come across a $2 bill, but the chances are slim. The exchange rate at this writing is US$1.82 per British pound, 76¢ per Canadian dollar, 77¢ per Australian dollar, and 67¢ per New Zealand dollar.

ELECTRICITY

The U.S. standard is AC, 110 volts/60 cycles. Plugs have two flat pins set parallel to each other.

EMERGENCIES

For police, fire, or ambulance, **dial 911** (0 in rural areas).

INSURANCE

Britons and Australians need extra medical coverage when traveling overseas.

🚩 Insurance Information In the U.K.: **Association of British Insurers** ✉ 51 Gresham St., London EC2V 7HQ ☎ 020/7600-3333 🖷 020/7696-8999 ⊕ www.abi.org.uk. In Australia: **Insurance Council of Australia** ✉ Insurance Enquiries and Complaints, Level 12, Box 561, Collins St. W, Melbourne, VIC 8007 ☎ 1300/780808 or 03/9629-4109 🖷 03/9621-2060 ⊕ www.iecltd.com.au. In Canada: **RBC Insurance** ✉ 6880 Financial Dr., Mississauga, Ontario L5N 7Y5 ☎ 800/668-4342 or 905/816-2400 🖷 905/813-4704 ⊕ www.rbcinsurance.com. In New Zealand: **Insurance Council of New Zealand** ✉ Level 7, 111-115 Customhouse Quay, Box 474, Wellington ☎ 04/472-5230 🖷 04/473-3011 ⊕ www.icnz.org.nz.

MAIL & SHIPPING

You can buy stamps and aerograms and send letters and parcels in post offices. Stamp-dispensing machines can occasionally be found in airports, bus and train stations, office buildings, drugstores, and the like. You can also deposit mail in the stout, dark blue, steel bins at strategic locations everywhere and in the mail chutes of large buildings; pickup schedules are posted. You can deposit packages at public collection boxes as long as the parcels are affixed with proper postage and weigh less than one pound. Packages weighing one or more pounds must be taken to a post office or handed to a postal carrier.

For mail sent within the United States, you need a 37¢ stamp for first-class letters weighing up to 1 ounce (23¢ for each additional ounce) and 23¢ for postcards. You pay 80¢ for 1-ounce airmail letters and 70¢ for airmail postcards to most other countries; to Canada and Mexico, you need a 60¢ stamp for a 1-ounce letter and 50¢ for a postcard. An aerogram—a single sheet of lightweight blue paper that folds into its own envelope, stamped for overseas airmail—costs 70¢.

To receive mail on the road, have it sent c/o General Delivery at your destination's main post office (use the correct five-digit ZIP code). You must pick up mail in person within 30 days and show a driver's license or passport.

PASSPORTS & VISAS

When traveling internationally, carry your passport even if you don't need one (it's always the best form of ID) and **make two photocopies of the data page** (one for someone at home and another for you, carried separately from your passport). If you lose your passport, promptly call the nearest embassy or consulate and the local police.

Visitor visas aren't necessary for Canadian or European Union citizens, or for citizens of Australia who are staying fewer than 90 days.

🚩 Australian Citizens **Passports Australia** ☎ 131-232 ⊕ www.passports.gov.au. **United States Consulate General** ✉ MLC Centre, Level 59, 19-29 Martin Pl., Sydney, NSW 2000 ☎ 02/9373-9200,

1902/941-641 fee-based visa-inquiry line ⊕ usembassy-australia.state.gov/sydney.

Canadian Citizens **Passport Office** ⊠ To mail in applications: 200 Promenade du Portage, Hull, Québec J8X 4B7 ☎ 819/994-3500, 800/567-6868, 866/255-7655 TTY ⊕ www.ppt.gc.ca.

New Zealand Citizens **New Zealand Passports Office** ⊠ For applications and information, Level 3, Boulcott House, 47 Boulcott St., Wellington ☎ 0800/22-5050 or 04/474-8100 ⊕ www.passports.govt.nz. **Embassy of the United States** ⊠ 29 Fitzherbert Terr., Thorndon, Wellington ☎ 04/462-6000 ⊕ usembassy.org.nz. **U.S. Consulate General** ⊠ Citibank Bldg., 3rd fl., 23 Customs St. E, Auckland ☎ 09/303-2724 ⊕ usembassy.org.nz.

U.K. Citizens **U.K. Passport Service** ☎ 0870/521-0410 ⊕ www.passport.gov.uk. **American Consulate General** ⊠ Danesfort House, 223 Stranmillis Rd., Belfast, Northern Ireland BT9 5GR ☎ 028/9032-8239 🖷 028/9024-8482 ⊕ usembassy.org.uk. **American Embassy** ⊠ For visa and immigration information or to submit a visa application via mail (enclose an SASE), Consular Information Unit, 24 Grosvenor Sq., London W1 1AE ☎ 09055/444-546 for visa information (per-minute charges), 0207/499-9000 main switchboard ⊕ usembassy.org.uk.

TELEPHONES

All U.S. telephone numbers consist of a three-digit area code and a seven-digit local number. Within many local calling areas, you dial only the seven-digit number. Within some area codes, you must dial "1" first for calls outside the local area. To call between area-code regions, dial "1" then all 10 digits; the same goes for calls to numbers prefixed by "800," "888," "866," and "877"—all toll free. For calls to numbers preceded by "900" you must pay—usually dearly.

For international calls, dial "011" followed by the country code and the local number. For help, dial "0" and ask for an overseas operator. The country code is 61 for Australia, 64 for New Zealand, 44 for the United Kingdom. Calling Canada is the same as calling within the United States. Most local phone books list country codes and U.S. area codes. The country code for the United States is 1.

For operator assistance, dial "0." To obtain someone's phone number, call directory assistance at 555-1212 or

occasionally 411 (free at many public phones). To have the person you're calling foot the bill, phone collect; dial "0" instead of "1" before the 10-digit number.

At pay phones, instructions often are posted. Usually you insert coins in a slot (usually 25¢–50¢ for local calls) and wait for a steady tone before dialing. When you call long-distance, the operator tells you how much to insert; prepaid phone cards, widely available in various denominations, are easier. Call the number on the back, punch in the card's personal identification number when prompted, then dial your number.

MAIL & SHIPPING

The main post office is open from 7:30 AM to 9 PM weekdays, 8 AM to 4 PM on Saturday. Lines are often long. There are drop boxes for overnight delivery services all over town and a UPS Store in nearly every strip mall.

Post Offices **Main post office** ⊠ 1001 E. Sunset Rd., Las Vegas 89193 ☎ 702/361-9472. **Major Services** **FedEx** ☎ 800/463-3339. **UPS** ☎ 800/742-5877.

MARRIAGE LICENSES

You can obtain a marriage license at the Clark County Marriage License Bureau. The cost is $55, and both applicants must apply in person. Requirements are the same for U.S. citizens and non-citizens. Blood tests are not required, and there is no waiting period. The bureau is open from Monday through Thursday 8 AM to midnight and from Friday at 8 AM to Sunday at midnight. You can also complete a marriage license online at the bureau's Web site.

Clark County Marriage License Bureau ⊠ 200 S. 3rd St. ☎ 702/455-4415 ⊕ www.co.clark.nv.us.

MEDIA

NEWSPAPERS & MAGAZINES

The morning *Las Vegas Review-Journal* is the largest daily newspaper in Nevada; its Friday entertainment section is called "Neon." The *Las Vegas Sun* is an afternoon daily. It is smaller, but has good local coverage. The *Las Vegas Mercury, City Life,* and *Las Vegas Weekly* are free alternative papers.

Published monthly, *Las Vegas Life* magazine offers fashion, food, entertainment, and feature articles for locals and visitors. The monthly *Vegas* magazine, an offshoot of the popular *Ocean Drive* in Miami, has lifestyle and entertainment news, gossip, and articles on the local club scene. *Cerca*, a quarterly magazine, has scenic photography and information on the region surrounding Las Vegas. Published by the state, the bimonthly *Nevada Magazine* is one of the oldest magazines in the west (since 1936); it has a large section covering Las Vegas events.

RADIO & TELEVISION

Local AM radio stations include **KDWN 720** (talk, news, sports), **KXNT 840** (news, talk), **KBAD 920** (sports), **KNUU 970** (news, talk), and **KENO 1460** (sports, talk).

Among the local FM radio stations are **KNPR 88.9** (National Public Radio news), **KCNV 89.7** (public radio classical), **KOMP 92.3** (rock), **KWNR 95.5** (country), **KKLZ 96.3** (classic rock), **KLUC 98.5** (Top 40), **KJUL 104.3** (classic adult), **KHWY 98/99** (contemporary, highway news), and **KQOL 93.1** (oldies).

The network television stations are **KVBC** (Channel 3, NBC), **KVVU** (Channel 5, Fox), **KLAS** (Channel 8, CBS), **KTNV** (Channel 13, ABC), **KVWB** (Channel 21, cable channel 12, WB) and **KTUD** (Channel 25, cable channel 14, UPN). The public TV station is **KLVX** (Channel 10).

MONEY MATTERS

The prices of typical items in Las Vegas can be gratis or outrageous. For example, you can get a good deli sandwich at one of the rock-bottom casino snack bars (Riviera, Westward Ho) for $2–$3, or you can spend $12 for a skyscraper special at the Stage Deli in the Forum Shops at Caesars. A cup of coffee in a casino coffee shop will set you back $2 to $5, while that same cuppa is free if you happen to be sitting at a nickel slot machine when the cocktail waitress comes by. A taxi from the airport to the MGM Grand goes as low as $10 if you tell the driver to take Tropicana Avenue and there's no traffic, or runs as high as $25 if you take the Airport Connector

and there's a wreck on the freeway. The more you know about Las Vegas, the less it'll cost you.

The Strip is expensive and if you're on a budget then consider having meals at the buffets in downtown Las Vegas, which are generally more of a bargain. For shopping, the locals save money by driving 5 mi south of the Strip to the **Las Vegas Outlet Center** (✉ 7400 Las Vegas Blvd. S ☎ 702/896–5599), where there are 155 shops and you can purchase items such as designer wear at reduced prices. Closer to most tourist areas is **Las Vegas Premium Outlets** (✉ 875 S. Grand Central Pkwy. ☎ 702/474–7500), with more than 120 stores, many of them representing top designers.

Prices throughout this guide are given for adults. Substantially reduced fees are almost always available for children, students, and senior citizens. For information on taxes, *see* Taxes.

ATMS

ATMs are widely available in Las Vegas; they're at every bank and at most casinos, hotels, minimarts, convenience stores, and gas stations as well. In addition, all casinos have cash-advance machines, which take credit cards. You just indicate how large a cash advance you want, and when the transaction is approved you pick up the cash at the casino cashier. But beware: you pay up to a 12% fee in addition to the usual cash-advance charges and interest rate for this convenience; in most cases, the credit card company begins charging interest the moment the advance is taken, so you will not have the usual grace period to pay your balance in full before interest begins to accrue.

CREDIT CARDS

Throughout this guide, the following abbreviations are used: **AE**, American Express; **D**, Discover; **DC**, Diners Club; **MC**, MasterCard; and **V**, Visa.

🔁 Reporting Lost Cards **American Express** ☎ 800/992-3404. **Diners Club** ☎ 800/234-6377. **Discover** ☎ 800/347-2683. **MasterCard** ☎ 800/622-7747. **Visa** ☎ 800/ 847-2911.

NATIONAL PARKS

Four National Parks—Grand Canyon, Zion, Bryce Canyon, and Death Valley—

are within a half-day's drive of Las Vegas, and Lake Mead, a National Recreation Area, and Red Rock Canyon, a National Conservation Area, are even closer. Look into discount passes to save money on park entrance fees. For $50, the National Parks Pass admits you (and any passengers in your private vehicle) to all national parks, monuments, and recreation areas, as well as other sites run by the National Park Service, for a year. (In parks that charge per person, the pass admits you, your spouse and children, and your parents, when you arrive together.) Camping and parking are extra. The $15 Golden Eagle Pass, a hologram you affix to your National Parks Pass, functions as an upgrade, granting entry to all sites run by the NPS, the U.S. Fish and Wildlife Service, the U.S. Forest Service, and the Bureau of Land Management. The upgrade, which expires with the parks pass, is sold by most national-park, Fish-and-Wildlife, and BLM fee stations. A major percentage of the proceeds from pass sales funds National Parks projects.

Both the Golden Age Passport ($10), for U.S. citizens or permanent residents who are 62 and older, and the Golden Access Passport (free), for persons with disabilities, entitle holders (and any passengers in their private vehicles) to lifetime free entry to all national parks, plus 50% off fees for the use of many park facilities and services. (The discount doesn't always apply to companions.) To obtain them, you must show proof of age and of U.S. citizenship or permanent residency—such as a U.S. passport, driver's license, or birth certificate—and, if requesting Golden Access, proof of disability. The Golden Age and Golden Access passes are available only at NPS-run sites that charge an entrance fee. The National Parks Pass is also available by mail and via the Internet.

National Park Foundation ✉ 11 Dupont Circle NW, 6th fl., Washington, DC 20036 ☎ 202/238-4200 ⊕ www.nationalparks.org. **National Park Service** ✉ National Park Service/Department of Interior, 1849 C St. NW, Washington, DC 20240 ☎ 202/208-6843 ⊕ www.nps.gov. **National Parks Conservation Association** ✉ 1300 19th St. NW, Suite 300, Washington, DC 20036 ☎ 202/223-6722 ⊕ www.npca.org.

Passes by Mail & Online National Park Foundation ⊕ www.nationalparks.org. **National Parks Pass** National Park Foundation ✉ Box 34108, Washington, DC 20043 ☎ 888/467-2757 ⊕ www.nationalparks.org; include a check or money order payable to the National Park Service, plus $3.95 for shipping and handling (allow 8 to 13 business days from date of receipt for pass delivery), or call for passes.

PACKING

Ever since the original Frontier Casino opened on the Los Angeles Highway (now the Strip), visitors to Las Vegas have been invited to "Come as You Are." The warm weather and informal character of Las Vegas render casual clothing appropriate day and night. However, there are some exceptions. A small number of restaurants require jackets for men, and some dance clubs have specific requirements such as no sneakers or only dark shoes. If you're making dinner reservations at an upscale spot or considering a visit to a nightclub, call and ask for the dress-code specifics.

While the desert sun keeps temperatures scorching outside in warmer months, the casinos are ice-cold. Your best insurance is to dress in layers. The blasting air conditioning may feel good at first, but if you plan on spending some time inside, bring a light sweater or jacket in case you feel chilly.

Always wear comfortable shoes; no matter what your intentions may be, you cover a lot of ground on foot.

Smarte Carte luggage carts are available at automated stands throughout the airport and parking garage. Cart rental is $3; the machines accept credit cards, currency, and coins. Return the cart to a stand when you're finished for a quarter refund.

In your carry-on luggage, pack an extra pair of eyeglasses or contact lenses and enough of any medication you take to last a few days longer than the entire trip. You may also ask your doctor to write a spare prescription using the drug's generic name, as brand names may vary from country to country. In luggage to be checked, **never pack prescription drugs, valuables, or undeveloped film.** And don't forget to carry with you the addresses of offices that handle refunds of lost traveler's checks. Check *Fodor's How to Pack* (available at online retailers and bookstores everywhere) for more tips.

To avoid customs and security delays, carry medications in their original packaging. Don't pack any sharp objects in your carry-on luggage, including knives of any size or material, scissors, nail clippers, and corkscrews, or anything else that might arouse suspicion.

To avoid having your checked luggage chosen for hand inspection, don't cram bags full. The U.S. Transportation Security Administration suggests packing shoes on top and placing personal items you don't want touched in clear plastic bags.

CHECKING LUGGAGE

You're allowed to carry aboard one bag and one personal article, such as a purse or a laptop computer. Make sure what you carry on fits under your seat or in the overhead bin. Get to the gate early, so you can board as soon as possible, before the overhead bins fill up.

Baggage allowances vary by carrier, destination, and ticket class. On international flights, you're usually allowed to check two bags weighing up to 70 pounds (32 kilograms) each, although a few airlines allow checked bags of up to 88 pounds (40 kilograms) in first class. Some international carriers don't allow more than 66 pounds (30 kilograms) per bag in business class and 44 pounds (20 kilograms) in economy. On domestic flights, the limit is usually 50 to 70 pounds (23 to 32 kilograms) per bag. In general, carry-on bags shouldn't exceed 40 pounds (18 kilograms). Most airlines won't accept bags that weigh more than 100 pounds (45 kilograms) on domestic or international flights. Expect to pay a fee for baggage that exceeds weight limits. Check baggage restrictions with your carrier before you pack.

Airline liability for baggage is limited to $2,500 per person on flights within the United States. On international flights it amounts to $9.07 per pound or $20 per kilogram for checked baggage (roughly

$640 per 70-pound bag), with a maximum of $634.90 per piece, and $400 per passenger for unchecked baggage. You can buy additional coverage at check-in for about $10 per $1,000 of coverage, but it often excludes a rather extensive list of items, shown on your airline ticket.

Before departure, itemize your bags' contents and their worth, and label the bags with your name, address, and phone number. (If you use your home address, cover it so potential thieves can't see it readily.) Include a label inside each bag and **pack a copy of your itinerary.** At check-in, make sure each bag is correctly tagged with the destination airport's three-letter code. Because some checked bags will be opened for hand inspection, the U.S. Transportation Security Administration recommends that you leave luggage unlocked or use the plastic locks offered at check-in. TSA screeners place an inspection notice inside searched bags, which are re-sealed with a special lock.

If your bag has been searched and contents are missing or damaged, file a claim with the TSA Consumer Response Center as soon as possible. If your bags arrive damaged or fail to arrive at all, file a written report with the airline before leaving the airport.

Complaints U.S. Transportation Security Administration Contact Center ☎ 866/289–9673 ⊕ www.tsa.gov.

RESTROOMS

Free restrooms can be found in every casino.

SAFETY

The well-known areas of Las Vegas are among the safest places for visitors in the world. With so many people carrying so much cash, security is tight inside and out. The casinos have visitors under constant surveillance, and hotel security guards are never more than a few seconds away. Outside, police are highly visible, on foot and bicycles and in cruisers. But this doesn't mean you can throw all safety consciousness to the wind. You should take the same precautions you would in any city— be aware of what's going on around you, stick to well-lighted areas, and quickly move away from any situation or people that might be threatening—especially if you're carrying some gambling cash. **When downtown, it's wise not to stray too far off the three main streets: Fremont, Ogden, and Carson between Main and Las Vegas Boulevard.**

Be especially careful with your purse and change buckets around slot machines. Grab-and-run thieves are always looking for easy pickings, especially downtown.

WOMEN IN LAS VEGAS

Apart from their everyday vulnerability to aggressive men, women should have few problems with unwanted attention in Las Vegas. If something does happen inside a casino, simply go to any pit and ask a boss to call security. The problem will disappear in seconds. Outside, crowds are almost always thick on the Strip and downtown, and there's safety in numbers.

Men in Las Vegas need to be on guard against predatory women. "Trick roller" is the name of a particularly nasty breed of female con artist. These women are expert at meeting single men by "chance." After getting friendly in the casino, the woman joins the man in his hotel room, where she slips powerful knockout drugs into his drink and robs him blind. Some men don't wake up.

SENIOR-CITIZEN TRAVEL

Las Vegas is such a bargain town in general that special subsidies and discounts for senior citizens are uncommon. Some casinos give senior citizens special deals through their slot clubs; ask when you join.

To qualify for age-related discounts, mention your senior-citizen status up front when booking hotel reservations (not when checking out) and before you're seated in restaurants (not when paying the bill). Be sure to have identification on hand. When renting a car, ask about promotional car-rental discounts, which can be cheaper than senior-citizen rates.

🛈 Educational Programs **Elderhostel** ✉ 11 Ave. de Lafayette, Boston, MA 02111-1746 ☎ 877/426-8056, 978/323-4141 international callers, 877/426-2167 TTY 🖶 877/426-2166 ⊕ www.elderhostel.org.

SIGHTSEEING TOURS

BOAT TOURS

The *Desert Princess,* a 300-passenger Mississippi River–style stern-wheeler, and *Desert Princess Too,* a 149-passenger Mississippi River–style paddlewheeler, cruise Lake Mead. Tours include 90-minute sightseeing cruises, two-hour dinner cruises, and three-hour dinner and dancing excursions.

🛈 Tour Operators **Lake Mead Cruises** ✉ Lake Mead marina, ☎ 702/293-6180.

BUS TOURS

Gray Line offers city tours, trips to Red Rock Canyon, Lake Mead, and Valley of Fire, and longer trips to the Grand Canyon and Death Valley.

🛈 Tour Operators **Gray Line Tours** ✉ 4020 E. Lone Mountain Rd., Las Vegas 89031 ☎ 702/384-1234 or 800/634-6579.

HELICOPTER TOURS

Helicopters do two basic tours in and around Las Vegas: a brief flyover of the Strip and a several-hour trip out to the Grand Canyon and back.

🛈 Tour Operators **Sundance Helicopters** ✉ 5596 Haven St., Las Vegas 89119 ☎ 702/736-0606 ⊕ www.helicoptour.com.

STUDENTS IN LAS VEGAS

No special discounts or considerations are offered students in Las Vegas. No one under 21 is allowed in the casinos.

🛈 IDs & Services **STA Travel** ✉ 10 Downing St., New York, NY 10014 ☎ 212/627-3111, 800/777-0112 24-hr service center 🖶 212/627-3387 ⊕ www.sta. com. **Travel Cuts** ✉ 187 College St., Toronto, Ontario M5T 1P7 ☎ 800/592-2887 in U.S., 416/979-2406 or 866/246-9762 in Canada 🖶 416/979-8167 ⊕ www.travelcuts.com.

TAXES

Las Vegas and Reno-Tahoe international airports assess a $3 departure tax, or passenger facility charge. The hotel room tax is 9% in Las Vegas.

SALES TAX

The sales tax rates for the areas covered in this guide are: Las Vegas, 7.5%; Arizona, 5.85%; and California, 7.25%.

TAXIS

Las Vegas is heavily covered by taxicabs. You can find cabs waiting at the airport and at every hotel in town. If you dine at a restaurant off the Strip, the restaurant will call a taxi to take you home.

The fare is $3.00 on the meter when you get in, plus $1.80 for every mile. Taxis are limited by law to carrying a maximum of four passengers, and there is no additional charge per person. No fees are assessed for luggage, but taxis leaving the airport are allowed to add an airport surcharge of $1.20. Drivers should be tipped 15% (⇨ Tipping).

🚕 Taxi Companies **Desert Cab** ☎ 702/386-9102. **Whittlesea/Henderson Cab** ☎ 702/384-6111. **Checker/Yellow/Star** ☎ 702/873-2000.

TIME

The states of Nevada and California are in the Pacific time zone. Arizona is in the Mountain time zone. Arizona does not observe daylight saving time.

TIPPING

More so than in other U.S. destinations, workers in Las Vegas are paid a minimum wage and rely on tips to make up the primary part of their income. At restaurants, a 15% tip is standard for waiters; up to 20% may be expected at more expensive establishments. The same goes for taxi drivers, bartenders, and hairdressers. Coat-check operators usually expect $1; bellhops and porters should get 50¢ to $1 per bag. Maids should receive at least 4%–5% of the room-rate total, before taxes, for rooms that cost $100 a night or more. If the room is less than $100 per night, then 3%–4%. If the hotel charges a service fee, be sure to ask what it covers, as it may include this gratuity. A 50¢ or $1 tip per drink is appropriate for cocktail waitresses, even when they bring you a free drink at a slot machine or casino table. On package tours, conductors and drivers usually get $10 per day from the group as a whole; check whether this has already been figured into your cost. For local sightseeing tours, you may individually tip the driver-guide $1 if he or she has been helpful or informative. Tip dealers with the equivalent of your average bet once or twice an hour

if you're winning; slot-machine change personnel and keno runners are accustomed to a buck or two. Ushers in showrooms may be able to get you better seats for performances for a gratuity of $5 or more. Tip the concierge 10%–20% of the cost for a ticket to a hot show. Tip $5–$10 for making dinner reservations or arrangements for other attractions.

TOURS & PACKAGES

Because everything is prearranged on a prepackaged tour or independent vacation, you spend less time planning—and often get it all at a good price.

BOOKING WITH AN AGENT

Travel agents are excellent resources. But it's a good idea to collect brochures from several agencies, as some agents' suggestions may be influenced by relationships with tour and package firms that reward them for volume sales. If you have a special interest, find an agent with expertise in that area; the American Society of Travel Agents (ASTA; ⇨ Travel Agencies) has a database of specialists worldwide. You can log on to the group's Web site to find an ASTA travel agent in your neighborhood.

Make sure your travel agent knows the accommodations and other services of the place being recommended. Ask about the hotel's location, room size, beds, and whether it has a pool, room service, or programs for children, if you care about these. Has your agent been there in person or sent others whom you can contact?

Do some homework on your own, too: local tourism boards can provide information about lesser-known and small-niche operators, some of which may sell only direct.

BUYER BEWARE

Each year consumers are stranded or lose their money when tour operators—even large ones with excellent reputations—go out of business. So check out the operator. Ask several travel agents about its reputation, and try to **book with a company that has a consumer-protection program.** (Look for information in the company's brochure.) In the United States, members of the United States Tour Operators Association are required to set aside funds ($1 million) to help eligible customers cover payments and travel arrangements in the event that the company defaults. It's also a good idea to choose a company that participates in the American Society of Travel Agents' Tour Operator Program; ASTA will act as mediator in any disputes between you and your tour operator.

Remember that the more your package or tour includes, the better you can predict the ultimate cost of your vacation. Make sure you know exactly what is covered, and beware of hidden costs. Are taxes, tips, and transfers included? Entertainment and excursions? These can add up.

Tour-Operator Recommendations American Society of Travel Agents (⇨ Travel Agencies). **National Tour Association** (NTA) ✉ 546 E. Main St., Lexington, KY 40508 ☎ 859/226-4444 or 800/682-8886 🖷 859/226-4404 ⊕ www.ntaonline.com. **United States Tour Operators Association** (USTOA) ✉ 275 Madison Ave., Suite 2014, New York, NY 10016 ☎ 212/599-6599 🖷 212/599-6744 ⊕ www.ustoa.com.

TRAIN TRAVEL

You can't take a train to Las Vegas, but Amtrak can get you there via bus from Los Angeles. You can pick up a timetable at any Amtrak station or request one by mail. Amtrak accepts all major credit cards and personal checks. You can purchase tickets aboard buses; however, an additional charge applies if the ticket office is open at your time of departure.

Amtrak ☎ 800/872-7245 ⊕ www.amtrak.com.

TRANSPORTATION AROUND LAS VEGAS

Though you can get around Las Vegas fine without a car, the best way to experience the city may be to drive it. A car gives you easy access to all the casinos and attractions, lets you make excursions to Lake Mead and elsewhere at your leisure, and gives you the chance to cruise the Strip and bask in its neon glow.

Parking on and around the Strip, although free, is not so easy. You'll have to brave some rather immense parking structures and walk up and down stairs or escalators. Valet parking is available if you're willing

to wait your turn and tip the valets. Taxis are an easy way to go door to door, although the downside is that you can't hail one off the street, so waiting in line at hotels is the only way to get a cab. During busy weekends, the wait can range anywhere from 10 to 30 minutes. Buses don't always run on time and they're frequently crowded. If you're not covering great distances, and when the weather is decent, the best way to get around Las Vegas is on foot or on the monorail.

The monorail, which opened summer 2004, gives Las Vegas an even more Disneyesque look. The monorail stretches from MGM Grand on the south to the Sahara to the north, with five stops in between, and makes the trip in about 14 minutes. To head farther south to Mandalay Bay, walk across the Strip and pick up the small monorail at the Excalibur. To the north, a Downtown monorail extension is in the planning stages, but several years away.

FARES & SCHEDULES

The monorail runs from 8 AM to midnight daily. Fares are $3 for one ride, $5.75 for two rides, $25 for 10 rides, $15 for a one-day pass, and $40 for a three-day pass. You can purchase tickets at station vending machines.

Las Vegas Monorail Company ✉ 3720 Howard Hughes Pkwy., Suite 200 ☎ 702/699-8200 ⊕ www.lvmonorail.com.

TRAVEL AGENCIES

A good travel agent puts your needs first. Look for an agency that has been in business at least five years, emphasizes customer service, and has someone on staff who specializes in your destination. In addition, **make sure the agency belongs to a professional trade organization.** The American Society of Travel Agents (ASTA)—the largest and most influential in the field with more than 20,000 members in some 140 countries—maintains and enforces a strict code of ethics and will step in to help mediate any agent-client disputes involving ASTA members if necessary. ASTA (whose motto is "Without a travel agent, you're on your own") also maintains a Web site that includes a directory of agents. (If a travel agency is also acting as your tour operator, *see* Buyer Beware *in* Tours & Packages.)

🚩 Local Agent Referrals **American Society of Travel Agents (ASTA)** ✉ 1101 King St., Suite 200, Alexandria, VA 22314 ☎ 703/739-2782 or 800/965-2782 24-hr hotline 🖷 703/684-8319 ⊕ www.astanet.com. **Association of British Travel Agents** ✉ 68-71 Newman St., London W1T 3AH ☎ 020/7637-2444 🖷 020/7637-0713 ⊕ www.abta.com. **Association of Canadian Travel Agencies** ✉ 130 Albert St., Suite 1705, Ottawa, Ontario K1P 5G4 ☎ 613/237-3657 🖷 613/237-7052 ⊕ www.acta.ca. **Australian Federation of Travel Agents** ✉ Level 3, 309 Pitt St., Sydney, NSW 2000 ☎ 02/9264-3299 or 1300/363-416 🖷 02/9264-1085 ⊕ www.afta.com.au. **Travel Agents' Association of New Zealand** ✉ Level 5, Tourism and Travel House, 79 Boulcott St., Box 1888, Wellington 6001 ☎ 04/499-0104 🖷 04/499-0786 ⊕ www.taanz.org.nz.

VISITOR INFORMATION

Before you go, contact the city and state tourism offices for general information. When you get there, visit the Las Vegas Convention and Visitors Authority, next door to the Las Vegas Hilton, for brochures and general information. Hotels and gift shops on the Strip have maps, brochures, pamphlets, and free events magazines— *What's On in Las Vegas, Showbiz,* and *Las Vegas Today*—that list shows and buffets and offer discounts to area attractions.

The *Las Vegas Advisor,* a monthly newsletter, keeps up-to-the-minute track of the constantly changing Las Vegas landscapes of gambling, accommodations, dining, entertainment, Top Ten Values (a monthly list of the city's best deals), complimentary offerings, and more, and is an indispensable resource for any Las Vegas visitor. Send $5 for a sample issue.

🚩 City Tourist Information **Las Vegas Convention and Visitors Authority** ✉ 3150 Paradise Rd., Las Vegas, NV 89109 ☎ 702/892-0711 🖷 702/892-2824 ⊕ www.lvcva.com. **Las Vegas Chamber of Commerce** ✉ 3720 Howard Hughes Pkwy., Las Vegas, NV 89109 ☎ 702/735-1616 🖷 702/735-2011. **Las Vegas Advisor** ✉ 3687 S. Procyon Ave., Las Vegas, NV 89103 ☎ 702/252-0655.

🚩 State Tourist Information **Nevada Commission on Tourism** ✉ 401 N. Carson St., Carson City, NV

89701 ☎ 775/687-4322 or 800/638-2328 🖷 702/687-6779.

🚩 Government Advisories **U.S. Department of State** ✉ Overseas Citizens Services Office, 2100 Pennsylvania Ave. NW, 4th fl., Washington, DC 20520 ☎ 202/647-5225 interactive hotline, 888/407-4747 ⊕ www.travel.state.gov. **Consular Affairs Bureau of Canada** ☎ 800/267-6788 or 613/944-6788 ⊕ www.voyage.gc.ca. **U.K. Foreign and Commonwealth Office** ✉ Travel Advice Unit, Consular Division, Old Admiralty Bldg., London SW1A 2PA ☎ 0870/606-0290 or 020/7008-1500 ⊕ www.fco.gov.uk/travel. **Australian Department of Foreign Affairs and Trade** ☎ 300/139-281 travel advice, 02/6261-1299 Consular Travel Advice Faxback Service ⊕ www.dfat.gov.au. **New Zealand Ministry of Foreign Affairs and Trade** ☎ 04/439-8000 ⊕ www.mft.govt.nz.

WEB SITES

Do check out the World Wide Web when planning your trip. You'll find everything from weather forecasts to virtual tours of famous cities. Be sure to visit Fodors.com (⊕ www.fodors.com), a complete travel-planning site. You can research prices and book plane tickets, hotel rooms, rental cars, vacation packages, and more. In addition, you can post your pressing questions in the Travel Talk section. Other planning tools include a currency converter and weather reports, and there are loads of links to travel resources.

LasVegas.com (⊕ www.lasvegas.com) has a partnership with the *Las Vegas Review-Journal,* and it offers travel information and reservations, as does the *Review-Journal's* site (⊕ www.reviewjournal.com).

VEGAS.com (⊕ www.vegas.com) advertises that, in Las Vegas, "it's who you know." Part of the Greenspun Media Group that also publishes the *Las Vegas Sun,* VEGAS.com offers information about and instant booking capabilities for everything from hotels to shows.

One of the oldest sites is **Las Vegas Leisure Guide** (⊕ www.pcap.com), full of hotel, restaurant, and nightlife info. **Las Vegas Online Entertainment Guide** (⊕ www.lvol.com) has listings for hotels and an online reservations system, plus local history, restaurants, a business directory, and even some gambling instruction.

EXPLORING
LAS VEGAS

1

BEST SPOT TO DON A BERET
Atop Paris Las Vegas's Eiffel Tower ⇨*p.18*

RAZZLE-DAZZLE NEON
The Fremont Street Experience ⇨*p.33*

BEST WAY TO CHANGE TIME ZONES
A gondola ride at the Venetian ⇨*p.19*

MOST IMPRESSIVE PLUMBING
Bellagio's dancing fountains ⇨*p.15*

NOT FOR THE FAINT OF HEART
The Stratosphere's observation deck ⇨*p.27*

MOST KITSCH PER SQUARE FOOT
Elvis-A-Rama Museum ⇨*p.24*

Revised and
updated by
Meredith
McGhan

FOR 50 YEARS, up until the early 1990s, the name Las Vegas was synonymous with adult entertainment. It existed for one reason: gambling. Then the city tried to remake itself as a family destination, adding roller coasters, animal attractions, and arcades to its predominantly adult lineup. The strategy didn't really take, as an explosion of topless shows and after-hours nightclubs over the past few years would seem to indicate. But the legacy of Las Vegas's family "experiment" lingers. Fabulous theme hotels such as the Luxor, New York–New York, the Venetian, the Aladdin, and Paris Las Vegas, as well as amusement parks such as Wet 'n Wild and the Adventuredome, provide a minivacation's worth of excitement—no slot machines or blackjack tables required.

Whatever the current state of its on-again, off-again attitude toward families, Las Vegas has never—and probably will never—become a family destination in the sense that Orlando or Cape Cod are. Every year, about 35 million people come to Las Vegas for the traditional reason—to gamble, plain and simple. There are few supermarkets, post offices, video-rental stores, or other conveniences of everyday life on the Strip—just casinos, wedding chapels, gift stores, strip clubs, and discotheques. Las Vegas is a fantasyland—a very adult fantasyland.

The Strip, the 3½-mi stretch of Las Vegas Boulevard South between Russell Road and Sahara Avenue, is the heart of Las Vegas. Its soul is the downtown area north of the Strip, whose core is Fremont Street. By exploring these two areas, you experience both the commercial lifeblood and pioneer spirit of this most flamboyant of American cities.

Getting Your Bearings

It's easy to get around Las Vegas by car. Note, however, that driving up and down the Strip might take only five minutes on a Tuesday morning but could take almost an hour on a Friday or a Saturday night. Parking at the hotel garages on the Strip is free; that's the case downtown as well, if you have your ticket validated by a casino cashier.

Getting around on foot can be a challenge, as distances here are deceiving. Although all the casinos in the center of the Strip, for example, may be within a mile of each other, walking from the street to and around the hotels, especially the large ones, can easily triple that distance. Don't feel like walking? Some of the newer casinos have moving sidewalks, trams, and elevated crosswalks to make it easier to get around on foot. The Strip Trolley, which runs every 15 minutes, is a more convenient means of hotel-hopping, because it picks up and drops off passengers at hotel front doors. The local buses are more frequent, though less convenient to the actual hotels, and usually crowded to overflowing. If an air-conditioned, roomy ride is more to your liking, hop on the sleek, futuristic Las Vegas Monorail, which opened late summer 2004. It travels from the far north end of the Strip, at the Sahara, to Mandalay Bay, stopping at every casino in between and at the Las Vegas Convention Center. The fare is a cheap $3, and the hours are convenient: 8 AM to midnight seven days a week.

We've organized the Strip exploration into three good walks: south, center, and north. A fourth walk covers downtown. Most of the sights in Las Vegas are casinos, so you can start exploring any time of the day

FREEBIES AROUND TOWN

YES, VEGAS BRIMS WITH CASH, GLITZ, and glamour, but that doesn't mean you can't find freebies. It's not impossible to romp around the Strip and the downtown area without spending a dime.

Always free on or near the Strip are the Lied Library, the Lion Habitat at the MGM Grand, M&M World and Gameworks at the Showcase Mall, the Adventuredome at Circus Circus, and the Tropicana Bird Show. Off the walkways from the MGM Grand and Excalibur are a couple of free slot machines, which are good for lots of freebies; chances are you can at least score tickets to the Casino Legends Hall of Fame museum at the Trop. To land coupons for free admission to the Imperial Palace Automobile Museum, look for people handing out flyers in front of the Imperial Palace Hotel & Casino or download a coupon from its Web site, ⊕ www.imperialpalace.com.

If you don't want to plunk down $100 for tickets to the latest production, you can still sample the extravagance of Vegas entertainment from the Strip sidewalk. Catch the Fountains of Bellagio water ballet, Sirens of TI at Treasure Island, or the erupting volcano at the Mirage after dark any night of the week.

Downtown, visit Fremont Street for free slot pulls and roulette spins at many of the casinos. The outdoor Neon Museum exhibits its neon signs along Fremont as well. Head over to the emerging Gateway Arts District and step into the Arts Factory to tour several galleries for free.

or night. But the earlier you set out, the fewer crowds and the less heat (in summer) you face along the way. To see the museums and historical sights, coordinate your tour with hours of operation.

SOUTH STRIP

The southern end of the Strip has received the lion's share of Las Vegas's family boom. In 1989 the only hotel-casino to anchor this part of the Strip was the Tropicana, which had stood alone for more than 30 years. But then came the San Remo and Excalibur (1990), Luxor and MGM Grand (1993), Monte Carlo (1996), New York–New York (1997), and Mandalay Bay (1999). To better manage the expected millions of tourists, these properties joined forces with the county in 1994 to install four overhead pedestrian walkways, complete with escalators and elevators, at a cost of $10 million. These walkways not only make exploring easier, they provide good views (through a protective wire mesh). The intersection of Las Vegas Boulevard and Tropicana Avenue is one of the most magnetic tourist intersections in the world.

Numbers in the text correspond to numbers in the margin and on the Las Vegas Strip map.

If the glitz and neon lights don't scream loud enough that you're in Las Vegas, the **WELCOME TO LAS VEGAS** sign ❶ ► at the southern end of Las Vegas Boulevard will take away all doubts. Be advised—it's difficult to snap photos in front of it without jaywalking, although a median break in front of the sign makes it possible to stop your car there briefly for a very quick photo.

From the sign, drive up the Strip and park in the gigantic garage at **Mandalay Bay Resort & Casino** ❷, the latest and greatest megaresort by the Mandalay Resort Group. Parking your car in Mandalay's garage keeps it out of the brutal summer sun and enables you to take in all of the sights on this part of the Strip. Because this walk winds up about a mile north, you might want to hop on a Strip bus, trolley, or monorail, or jump into a cab to get back to your car. Next door to Mandalay Bay is the **Luxor Resort & Casino** ❸, a perfect pyramid with some 2,500 rooms (plus close to 2,000 more in the stepped towers next to it) and the largest atrium in the world. And next to that is **Excalibur Hotel and Casino** ❹, the white-and-blue, turreted-and-towered, 4,032-room "castle."

Across the Strip from the Excalibur is the **Tropicana Resort and Casino** ❺, with a large, lush swimming pool flanked by rock waterfalls; a water slide; exotic fish, birds, and vegetation; and swim-up blackjack. The **Casino Legends Hall of Fame** museum of Nevada memorabilia has Vegas kitsch from over five decades. If the Vegas legacy has your interest piqued, you may want to wander off the Strip to dig deeper into this town's storied past. Visit UNLV's state-of-the-art **Lied Library** ❻ on the campus off Maryland Parkway. The spacious library, built in 2001, holds more than 1 million books and journals. Don't miss the **Liberace Museum** ❼, 2 mi east of the Strip on Tropicana Avenue. (Take a cab to these two destinations, especially in summer, as they're a bit out of the way.) Back at the Trop, head across the avenue to the **MGM Grand** ❽—with 5,034 rooms, a 171,000-square-foot casino, and a lions' habitat.

Children might want to make a stop at the **Showcase Mall** ❾, next door to the MGM, for **M&M's World** and **Gameworks,** one of the largest arcades in the city. Across the Strip is **New York–New York Hotel and Casino** ❿, with such exact replicas of famous Big Apple landmarks that copyright lawyers had to argue the legality of it all. Next door is **Monte Carlo Resort and Casino** ⓫, a joint venture between Mandalay Resort Group and Mirage Resorts; check out the stunning lobby and European-style casino.

A mile or so east, on Paradise Road, is the **Hard Rock Hotel and Casino** ⓬, which is billed as the "world's only rock 'n' roll casino." It's best to drive from the Strip to the Hard Rock, especially at night, when Harmon Avenue is very dark.

TIMING The southern end of the Strip walk has the largest casinos; a stroll to see them all will take almost a full day. Add another hour each for the side trips over to the Liberace Museum and Lied Library or the Hard Rock Hotel and Casino.

What to See

🕲 ❹ **Excalibur Hotel and Casino.** Before they opened this spectacular property in 1990, the executives of the Circus Circus Resort Group—now the Mandalay Resort Group—visited castles in England, Scotland, and Germany in search of inspiration. The result might be described as "King Arthur does Las Vegas." The pseudo-Bavarian castle, which has been called "the greatest hole in God's own miniature golf course," has plenty of turrets, spires, belfries, a moat, and a 265-foot bell tower. The over-the-top medieval theme is continued inside, with staff members in elaborate royal-court costumes and such place names as the Court Jester's Stage and Sir Galahad's Pub and Prime Rib House.

Downstairs from the 100,000-square-foot casino is **Fantasy Faire Midway,** with carnival games and international gifts. A spin on **Merlin's Magic Motion Machine Film Rides,** which include a spooky roller-coaster ride with Elvira, self-proclaimed Mistress of the Dark, plus a ride with a Greek-mythology theme, and a racetrack, lasts about 5 to 10 minutes.

Upstairs from the casino are shops, theme restaurants, a huge buffet, and a roving Renaissance Faire with jugglers, puppeteers, and magicians.

Families enjoy the *Tournament of Kings* extravaganza in the showroom, and *Thunder from Down Under* is big with bachelorette parties. The Excalibur also has more than 4,000 guest rooms and plenty of ways to win (or lose) a buck. ⊠ *3850 Las Vegas Blvd. S, South Strip* ☎ *702/597–7777 or 800/937–7777* ⊕ *www.excaliburcasino.com* 📧 *Film Rides $4 per ride* ☉ *Fantasy Faire open daily 10–10.*

★ ⓬ **Hard Rock Hotel and Casino.** A haven for the young and hip, the Hard Rock is a high-class rock-and-roll museum, with memorabilia from every rock decade adorning its walls. The multimillion-dollar collection is undoubtedly one of the best on display in the country—you can see everything from Kurt Cobain's guitar to one of Britney Spears's many outfits. And since the Hard Rock is a favorite hiding spot for many current music and film stars, you've got a pretty good chance of bumping into one. Navigating the property is simple: it's completely circular. On the inside of the circle is the small but accommodating gaming floor, and on the outside, various shops, restaurants, and the Hard Rock's intimate concert venue, the Joint. Down one hallway is the Hard Rock's pool area, a tropical beach–inspired oasis with a floating bar, private cabanas, and poolside blackjack—a favorite filming location for MTV and popular TV shows. The logo shop is large, so you won't have to wait in Hard Rock's signature long, slow-moving line to buy a T-shirt. For late-night partying, check out Body English Nightclub. ⊠ *4455 Paradise Rd., Paradise Road* ☎ *702/693–5000 or 800/693–7625* ⊕ *www.hardrockhotel.com.*

★ ❼ **Liberace Museum.** Costumes, cars, photographs, even mannequins of the late entertainer make this museum the kitschiest place in town. In addition to Lee's collection of pianos (one of them was played by Chopin; another, a concert grand, was owned by George Gershwin), you can see his Czar Nicholas uniform and a blue-velvet cape styled after the coronation robes of King George V. Be sure to check out the gift

6 <

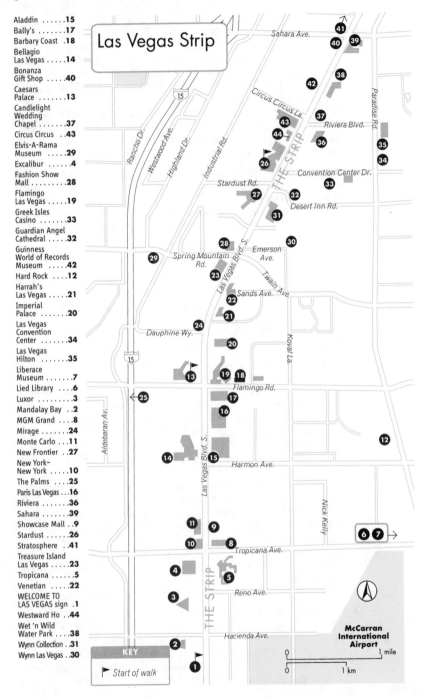

Las Vegas Strip

KEY

► *Start of walk*

McCarran
International
Airport

shop—where else can you find Liberace soap, ashtrays, and other nov-elties? ⊠ *1775 E. Tropicana Ave., East Side* 🕾 *702/798–5595* ⊕ *www.liberace.com* ⌦ *$8* ☉ *Mon.–Sat. 10–5, Sun. 1–5.*

❻ **Lied Library.** The special-collections department of this library of the University of Nevada–Las Vegas has the best collection of materials about Las Vegas and gambling that you can find anywhere. ⊠ *4505 Maryland Pkwy., University District* 🕾 *702/895–2234* ⌦ *Free* ☉ *Mon., Wed., and Fri. 9–5, Tues. and Thurs. 9–9.*

❸ **Luxor Resort & Casino.** In Luxor, the folks at Mandalay Resort Group have built one of the modern wonders of the world—and made sure it could be seen from anywhere in the valley at night. Luxor, a 36-story black glass and bronze pyramid, is made with 13 acres of black glass and topped with a beam that burns brighter than any other in the world. It's composed of 45 xenon lights, and it projects enough light to be visible from space. Standing right at the base of one of the exterior walls and looking up, you get a glimpse of infinity. Inside is the world's largest atrium, with 29 million cubic feet of open space soaring to the building's apex. You get the full impact of the space from the second floor, also known as the Attractions Level.

The "Passport to Adventure" for the entertainment attractions in the Luxor's **Pharaoh's Pavilion** is all-inclusive—it gets you two IMAX movies, "In Search for the Obelisk" 3-D motion simulator ride, the re-production of King Tutankhamen's tomb, and your choice of a virtual roller coaster ride or A&E's movie *The Great Pharaohs*. Stop by the vast two-story video arcade, too.

In the evening, the award-winning Blue Man Group performs an im-provisational, interactive show, in the 1,200-seat Luxor Theater, or adults can see the *Midnight Fantasy* revue in the Pharaoh's Theater.

Luxor has more than 4,000 guest rooms. The rooms in the pyramid build-ing (there are two hotel towers as well) are reached by four "inclina-tors," elevators that travel along the 39-degree incline of the pyramid. ⊠ *3900 Las Vegas Blvd. S, South Strip* 🕾 *702/262–4000 or 800/288–1000* ⊕ *www.luxor.com* ⌦ *Pharaoh's Pavilion attractions $4–$8.95, Passport to Adventure $23.95* ☉ *Pharoah's Pavilion open Sun.–Thurs. 9 AM–11 PM, Fri. and Sat. 9 AM–midnight.*

❷ **Mandalay Bay Resort & Casino.** The 43-story, $950-million Mandalay Bay Resort has 4,766 rooms, including a 400-room **Four Seasons Hotel** on the 36th through 39th floors (with its own parking, entrance, pool, health club, express elevators, restaurants, and meeting area), and the upscale 1,120-suite THEhotel, which opened in 2004. The resort name is a cu-rious one—Mandalay is an ancient inland temple city in Myanmar, the country formerly known as Burma, which has no bay. And while the real Mandalay is in Southeast Asia, the hotel-casino is decked out like a South Seas beach resort, complete with the scent of coconut oil drift-ing through the casino. In fact, there's a 10-acre lagoon complete with a huge wave pool (8-foot waves, roughest waters on the Strip), a ¾-mi-long "lazy river" pool, and a man-made beach where concerts are held

FodorśChoice
★

periodically. The **House of Blues,** a concert venue, nightclub, and restaurant, is also here; the restaurant walls are covered with Louisiana Delta folk art.

The most distinctive attraction at Mandalay Bay is **Shark Reef.** The 105,000-square-foot facility holds some 2 million gallons of seawater housing exotic creatures large and small. The journey begins in temple ruins, where the heat and humidity may be uncomfortable for the humans but is quite nice for the golden crocodiles, water monitors, and tropical fish. Two glass "hallways" allow you to get up close and personal with sea life. Other notable exhibits: a shallow pool offers you a chance to give a one-finger pet to small stingrays, small sharks, and starfish; and jellyfish swim a rhythmic dance in a specially designed environment. The tour saves the best for last—from the bowels of a sunken galleon, watch sharks swim below, above, and around the skeleton ship. Keep an eye out for the fierce-looking hammerhead, and see if you can spot a family of bonnethead sharks—they were born in the Reef in 2003.

This megaresort also houses a 12,000-seat arena complex that hosts major sporting contests, superstar concerts, and special events; a 1,700-seat showroom; a convention center; the Coral Reef Lounge, surrounded by virtual vegetation, rock waterfalls, and lily ponds; the four-story "wine tower" at the signature restaurant Aureole; and rumjungle, one of the hottest nightspots in town. Fans of Swedish supergroup ABBA can see *MAMMA MIA!,* the smash hit musical based on the band's songs. Shows take place in the evenings in the Mandalay Bay Theatre. Check out the unusual collection of shops, including an art gallery and an independent bookstore, in the Mandalay Place mall, which links Mandalay Bay with Luxor. ⊠ *3950 Las Vegas Blvd. S, South Strip* ☎ *702/ 632–7777 or 877/632–7400* ⊕ *www.mandalaybay.com* ✉ *Shark Reef $13.95* ⊘ *Daily 10 AM–11 PM.*

🌙 ❽ **MGM Grand.** With more than 5,000 rooms, the MGM Grand is one of the largest hotels in the world, a self-proclaimed "City of Entertainment" sprawling over 112 acres. The front of the property is adorned with a 100,000-pound bronze lion statue that stands 45 feet tall and sits atop a 25-foot pedestal, making it the largest bronze statue in the United States. Inside is a full half-mile of restaurants, ballrooms, nightclubs, and shops—even a research center for CBS Television, where you can screen potential new shows for parent company Viacom's networks, which also include Nickelodeon and MTV.

The MGM Grand also has a $9-million, 3,000-square-foot **Lion Habitat.** More than 12,000 visitors a day see the lions owned by feline expert and exotic-animal trainer Keith Evans. A see-through tunnel runs through the habitat, allowing you to watch the big cats prowl above and below. The enclosure was designed to replicate the lions' natural habitat as closely as possible and has stone, trees and foliage, four waterfalls, and a pond. The lions are trucked in each day; they really live 12 mi from the MGM Grand on an 8½-acre ranch. Admission is free.

The MGM Grand Garden Arena, a 17,157-seat, 275,000-square-foot venue, attracts big-name performers including the Rolling Stones, Sarah

FIVE TOP STAR-GAZING SPOTS

YOU NEVER KNOW WHEN THE STARS ARE going to come out in the neon city. You might see glamour queens like the Hilton sisters or the who's who of the rock-and-roll crowd, or stumble across the set of a movie or TV show. Here are the best five spots to try for your very own celebrity sighting.

The Palms. The buzz started when the cast of MTV's Real World: Las Vegas stayed here. Britney Spears has been seen dining at N9NE or hopping on stage at Rain for a surprise concert. This is the number-one place to go to see celebs. ⊠ 4321 W. Flamingo Rd., West Side.

The Hard Rock Hotel & Casino. You might catch some of your favorite stars tipping back a few at the Pink Taco or boogying down at Body English. Maybe they're out-of-town celebs playing at the Joint; maybe they're locals like Andre Agassi or Celine Dion who've dropped in for a drink. ⊠ 4455 Paradise Rd.

The Strip. With so many famous faces playing the Strip, it would be a surprise not to see celebrities out and about. Strip performers include Elton John, Gladys Knight, and Wayne Newton. The Strip, as a whole, has been the site of many a movie scene; keep your eyes peeled for cameras and set lights and scope out The Riviera. ⊠ Las Vegas Blvd. S.

Double Down Saloon. Run into members of the Blue Man Group without their makeup here. Comedy Central's Dave Attell filmed a segment of Insomnia here, and you may spot some alternative rockers among the punked-out UNLV students. ⊠ 4640 Paradise Rd.

Fremont Street area. This area was cordoned off during the filming of Ocean's Eleven, but visitors to the neighborhood still caught the occasional glimpse of George Clooney, Julia Roberts, and Brad Pitt strolling around. ⊠ Fremont St., Downtown.

—Meredith McGhan

Brightman, and Britney Spears. It also hosts championship boxing tournaments and special events like the Crown Royal Comedy Soul Festival and the Billboard Music Awards.

After dark, the property brings in both locals and visitors with its two raucous nightclubs, Tabu and Studio 54. The sensual revue *La Femme* is an upscale, adults-only dance performance by 13 French dancers. ⊠ *3799 Las Vegas Blvd. S, South Strip* ☎ *702/891–1111 or 800/929–1111* ⊕ *www.mgmgrand.com* ☉ *Lion Habitat daily 11–10.*

⑪ Monte Carlo Resort and Casino. The *real* Monte Carlo—the Place du Casino in Monaco—is the model for this elegant megaresort. The $350-million hotel-casino is like a sumptuous palace, filled with arches, chandeliers, marble, statuary, and fountains. Note the Gothic glass registration area overlooking the lush pool area—a touch that resort cocreator Steve Wynn dubbed "popular elegance."

In addition to the massive gaming floor and 3,000-plus rooms, the property includes an avenue-style shopping mall called the **Street of Dreams.** There you can find everything from Monte Carlo logo wear to fine jewelry, as well as a number of eateries. Perhaps the most popular restaurant here is the Monte Carlo Brew Pub, with live nightly entertainment, decent pub-style food, and six specialty ales made on the premises. Sports fans especially love the 35 big-screen TVs regularly broadcasting athletic events and the state-of-the-art sound system. Also along the Street of Dreams is a high-tech arcade with more than 60 games.

The resort's most popular attraction—world-class illusionist Lance Burton—performs five nights a week in an opulent, 1,200-seat, $27-million custom-built theater modeled after the opera houses of Europe. ⊠ *3770 Las Vegas Blvd. S, South Strip* ☎ *702/730–7777 or 800/311–8999* ⊕ *www.monte-carlo.com.*

need a break?

Fatburger. Across from the Monte Carlo is this burger joint, where, despite the chain's name, the food is surprisingly healthy: burgers are low in fat and the food is made from all-natural ingredients. Besides, if you're able to grab a window seat, it's a great place for people-watching when you're tired of walking. ⊠ *3763 Las Vegas Blvd. S, South Strip* ☎ *702/736–4733.*

★ ⑩ **New York–New York Hotel and Casino.** When it opened in 1997, the stunning, $460-million complex raised the bar for theme hotels, in Las Vegas and worldwide. The exterior is a mini-Manhattan skyline, complete with a 48-story Empire State Building; a 150-foot Statue of Liberty; and smaller versions of the Chrysler, Seagram, and CBS buildings and the New York Public Library, Grand Central Terminal, and the Brooklyn Bridge. As a poignant tribute to the victims of 9/11, items donated by people from all over the world are being catalogued and preserved on a wrought-iron fence near the model of a New York fireboat. A Coney Island–style roller coaster, the Manhattan Express, encircles the property. The Big Apple flavor continues inside, with an art-deco lobby, a Central Park–theme casino pit, an arcade reminiscent of Coney Island, and a food court patterned after Greenwich Village. And last but not least is ESPN Zone, the mother of all sports cafés, with plush seats for armchair quarterbacks and an arcade filled with sports games.

Roller-coaster aficionados take note: the **Manhattan Express** is a real rocker. While being whisked past great views of the faux New York skyline, you climb 15 stories, dive 75 feet, climb then dive 144 feet, do a 360-degree somersault, twirl through a "heartline twist" (that simulates the sensation one gets in a jet doing a barrel roll), rocket over a dizzying succession of high-banked turns and camel-back hills, and finally zip along a 540-degree spiral before you pull back into the station.

The property wouldn't be a complete homage to New York without a sprinkling of theater. *Another Side of Cirque du Soleil . . . Zumanity* is a 90-minute sensual show about the erotic side of human life. It takes place in the specially constructed **Zumanity Theatre.** Fifty musicians and performers culled from around the world focus on movement, music, acrobatics, and dance to convey their sensual characters. Comedian Rita Rudner performs in the 450-seat **Cabaret Theatre.** Rudner delivers her unique, sophisticated brand of comedy in a deceptively soft-spoken way. ⊠ *3790 Las Vegas Blvd. S, South Strip* ☎ *702/740–6969 or 800/*

693–6763 ⊕ *www.nynyhotelcasino.com* ⊠ *Roller coaster $10* ⊙ *Roller coaster daily 10* AM*–11* PM*, weather permitting.*

⊙ ❾ **Showcase Mall.** This mall has several specialty shops, a movie theater, and Gameworks, a multilevel young-adult arcade.

M&M's World is four stories of fun that will melt in your mouth, not in your hand. The store offers plenty of candy-coated treats (including an **Ethel M. Chocolates** outlet for a more upscale sweet tooth) plus everything from T-shirts to limited-edition lithographs. There's also the **M&M Academy,** with interactive exhibits and a free 3-D movie, *I Lost My M in Las Vegas.*

Gameworks, a joint venture between Steven Spielberg and Sega, more than lives up to its hype—it's the biggest, most boisterous arcade in town. Gameworks has more than 300 arcade-style games, a 21-and-over bar with pool tables and live entertainment, a casual fast-food eatery, and the world's largest free-standing rock-climbing structure. ⊠ *3785 Las Vegas Blvd. S, South Strip* ☎ *702/736–7611 M&M's World, 702/432–4263 Gameworks* ⊠ *M&M Academy free entry; Gameworks free entry, $25 per 2 hrs of play* ⊙ *Showcase Mall and M&M's World Sun.–Thurs. 9* AM*–midnight, Fri. and Sat. 9* AM*–1* AM*. Gameworks Sun.–Thurs. 10* AM*–midnight, Fri. and Sat. 10* AM*–2* AM*. M&M Academy Sun.–Thurs. 10* AM*–6* PM*, Fri. and Sat. 10* AM*–8* PM*.*

❺ **Tropicana Resort and Casino.** The most eye-popping sight here is the 4,000-square-foot stained-glass dome that sparkles above one section of the casino. Be sure to take a look at the lush, 5-acre pool area, where the famous swim-up blackjack game is played. The Tropicana hosts Las Vegas's longest-running show, *Les Folies Bergere,* as well as a great comedy club featuring well-known and up-and-coming comedians.

A must-see at the Trop is the **Casino Legends Hall of Fame.** Portions of the world's largest collection of Nevada casino memorabilia have been displayed at several casinos through the years, but the collection has finally found a permanent home here. Thousands of items are on display, including Las Vegas chips, photographs, movie posters, postcards, slot machines, entertainer contracts and paychecks, menus, album covers, and more. There's a mock-up of a showgirl's dressing room and numerous video monitors run documentaries about the casino implosions, celebrities, hotel fires, and onetime association with organized crime figures— all the iconic people and events that shaped this town's legend. ⊠ *3801 Las Vegas Blvd. S, South Strip* ☎ *702/739–2222 or 800/634–4000* ⊕ *www.tropicanalv.com* ⊠ *Hall of Fame $4; look for free-entry coupons throughout casino* ⊙ *Hall of Fame Sun.–Thurs. 8* AM*–9* PM*, Fri. and Sat. 8* AM*–midnight.*

▶ ❶ WELCOME TO LAS VEGAS. Two blocks south of Hacienda Avenue, at the south end of the Strip, is this welcome sign, a familiar part of the landscape since the early 1950s and quite possibly Las Vegas's most-photographed element. It makes a great photo or video backdrop, but wait for an ebb in the traffic: the sign is on an island in the middle of the boulevard.

CENTER STRIP

This entire part of the Strip is historic. Here you find the Flamingo Las Vegas, which stands on the site of Bugsy Siegel's original Flamingo, as well as Caesars Palace, whose name has been synonymous with opulence for years. Casino mogul Steve Wynn raised even Caesars' high stakes with the 1989 opening of the lush Mirage, but another Wynn creation, the $1.8-billion Bellagio, with its European elegance and gorgeous fountains, set a standard that has yet to be equaled.

a good
walk

Park in the easily accessible garage of **Caesars Palace** ⑬ ▶. It's central to the Strip and, except for the top level, completely covered—just the thing to keep your vehicle's interior from turning into an oven.

From one of Caesars' exits, walk back to the Strip, turn right (south), head to the intersection of Las Vegas Boulevard and Flamingo Road, and use the pedestrian bridges to cross Flamingo. Here, **Bellagio Las Vegas** ⑭ awaits; don't miss its breathtaking fountains.

Now cross to the east side of the Strip to the **Aladdin Resort and Casino** ⑮. Its Desert Passage mall, a fanciful Middle Eastern marketplace, is a must-see. Next door is **Paris Las Vegas** ⑯, with its 50-story, half-size Eiffel Tower. Its sister hotel-casino **Bally's Casino Resort** ⑰ is also right here; enter on a long, moving sidewalk lit by colorful lights and surrounded by fountains.

Across Flamingo Road from Bally's is the **Barbary Coast Hotel and Casino** ⑱, a small, attractive joint wedged between giants. Next is the venerable **Flamingo Las Vegas** ⑲. Its 15-acre water park is one of the nicer pools in town. Next door is the Flamingo's casino annex for low rollers, O'Shea's.

Heading north on the Strip, stop by the **Imperial Palace Hotel and Casino** ⑳, with the **Automobile Museum.** Next door is **Harrah's Las Vegas Casino & Hotel** ㉑, with the Carnaval Court, an outdoor entertainment zone with shops, a bar, and live music. Beyond Harrah's is the **Venetian Resort-Hotel-Casino** ㉒, a meticulously crafted tribute to its namesake city, right down to the 1,800-foot-long canal running down the middle of the **Grand Canal Shops.** The Venetian is also the proud home of the **Guggenheim-Hermitage Museum** as well as a branch of **Madame Tussaud's Celebrity Encounter,** an offshoot of the famous wax museum.

Across the Strip from the Venetian is **Treasure Island Las Vegas (TI)** ㉓. In TI's revamped show, the mysterious and beautiful Sirens of TI battle a band of pirates; music, dance, swordplay, and acrobatics help tell the story. Another Cirque du Soleil show, the incomparable *Mystère*, takes place twice nightly here in a custom-built theater. Next door is the **Mirage Hotel and Casino** ㉔, the $650-million joint that in 1989 kicked off a multibillion-dollar casino construction frenzy that has yet to abate. At the Mirage, volcanoes, rain forests, dolphins, and tigers are found right alongside rows of $100 blackjack tables and $500 slot machines.

A GANGSTER'S PINK LEGEND

T'S A COMMON MISCONCEPTION that Bugsy Siegel introduced gambling to Las Vegas: Siegel no more invented gambling and Las Vegas than Bugs Bunny invented cartoons and Warner Bros. But the gangster was instrumental in paving the way for his business partners from around the country to capitalize on the casino business. Gambling had been legal in Nevada and thriving in Las Vegas for more than 10 years by the time Siegel arrived on the scene.

Benjamin Siegel and Las Vegas were both born in May 1905, Las Vegas in the cruel desert of southern Nevada, and Benny on the mean streets of south Brooklyn. In his early teens Siegel met a street tough named Meyer Lansky, and by the time he was 20 he was a hardened criminal, a shooter in the bootlegging wars that raged in New York during Prohibition. A fearless and reckless soldier, Siegel earned the nickname "Bugsy," which he always hated; no one, not even underworld boss Lansky, called him "Bugsy" to his face.

Throughout the 1920s and '30s, Lansky, Siegel, Charles "Lucky" Luciano, and Frank Costello forged a nationwide coalition of gangsters into an organized-crime syndicate variously known as the Mob, the Mafia, and La Cosa Nostra. Siegel took control of the Mob's gambling, bookmaking, and narcotics-smuggling operations in southern California. When he extended his sphere of influence to Las Vegas, muscling into several downtown casinos in the early 1940s, Siegel instantly recognized the vast potential of the Nevada gambling business.

Siegel's dream was to build and run the classiest resort-casino in the world, and he recruited Mob investors to back him. The project quickly turned into a nightmare, as cost overruns on the Fabulous Flamingo Hotel spiraled out of control, reaching a

healthy (or unhealthy, as it turned out) $5 million. Siegel's investors roundly suspected him of skimming a million or two from the construction costs. And in those days, with that bunch, if you were suspected of dipping into investment capital, you weren't served with a subpoena. If you couldn't make the interest payments on corporate paper, you weren't protected by Chapter 11.

Siegel managed to open the Flamingo on the day after Christmas 1946, even though it wasn't ready (inaugurating a Las Vegas tradition that continues to this day). Although movie stars attended and headliners Jimmy Durante, Xavier Cugat, and Rose Marie performed, the Flamingo flopped. The casino was a magnet for every "crossroader" (casino cheat), "mechanic" (card sharp), and scam artist in town, and it sustained heavy losses. This made Siegel's partners not only unhappy but also suspicious; they took this as further evidence of his embezzlement. The Flamingo closed less than three weeks after it opened, ostensibly to complete construction, but also to make a few adjustments in management.

In June 1947, in the Beverly Hills mansion of Virginia Hill, known as the "Mistress to the Mob," Siegel was shot through a window. He took two slugs, one in the eye, and died as he had lived. He was 42 years old. The murder of Bugsy Siegel remains unsolved to this day.

Ironically, once Siegel had been bumped off, business at the Flamingo boomed—Siegel's gangland assassination had made front-page news across the country, and people flocked to see the house that Bugsy built.

— Deke Castleman

You can exit the Mirage at the south end (near the white tiger habitat) and pick up Caesars' people-mover at its north end; wander through the **Forum Shops at Caesars**, one of the most upscale and original—and profitable—malls in the country to emerge in Caesars' Forum Casino, right by the elevators to the parking garage.

Off the Strip is **The Palms Hotel & Casino** ㉓, famous for its celebrity clientele. From Caesars, drive west 2 mi on Flamingo Road.

TIMING   This walk in the center of the strip is the shortest in terms of outside distance but has the most casinos; the whole circuit can be done in four hours if you're moving right along, five hours at a leisurely pace, and six hours if you take in the auto collection at the Imperial Palace or the Guggenheim museum.

What to See

⑮ **Aladdin Resort and Casino.** The *Arabian Nights* motif is immediately evident in the 50-foot waterfall cascading down a sandstone cliff fronting the $1.4 billion, 2,567-room property. You walk directly inside from the Strip—one of the many elements of the Aladdin designed for convenience—but into a shopping mall rather than a casino.

The **Desert Passage** is a $300-million complex of 135 shops ensconced in minarets, onion domes, and other Moorish architecture. Merchants' Harbor, a North African village with a huge anchored steamer ship, treats mall goers to regularly scheduled thunderstorms. Among the many restaurants in the mall and hotel are a branch of New Orleans's famous Commander's Palace.

Cocktail waitresses in harem garb glide through the 100,000-square-foot casino, which is bedecked with a 36-foot-long Aladdin's lamp. London Clubs International operates a separate casino-within-a-casino, a luxurious hideaway for high rollers, where you find the nightclub Curve. At night, Broadway shows and headliner concerts fill the 7,000-seat Aladdin Theatre for the Performing Arts. The entertainment calendar includes illusionist Steve Wyrick, in the Steve Wyrick Theater, and *Ovation*, a medley of dance, magic, and juggling. ⊠ *3667 Las Vegas Blvd. S, Center Strip* ☎ *702/736–0111 or 877/333–9474* ⊕ *www.aladdincasino.com.*

⑰ **Bally's Casino Resort.** During the day it doesn't look like much, but at night Bally's facade is one of Las Vegas's most colorful: Its Epcot-esque colored lights in green, red, purple, and blue are a throwback to the '60s space age. Four 200-foot moving walkways ferry people between the Strip and the casino—a plus for the footsore. The shopping arcade on the lower level sells everything from fine furs to ice cream. Bally's also hosts the $10-million showgirl spectacular *Jubilee!* ⊠ *3645 Las Vegas Blvd. S, Center Strip* ☎ *702/739–4111 or 800/644–0777* ⊕ *www.ballyslv.com.*

⑱ **Barbary Coast Hotel and Casino.** Decorated with dark woods, stained glass, brass, and crystal, the Barbary Coast evokes turn-of-the-20th-century San Francisco. Downstairs, Drai's is one of Vegas's hottest restaurants. Its after-hours club launched a raft of such Strip spots, but Drai's bar, with its comfortable seating and candlelit red furnishings, captures the opulence of the old Vegas. One of the smallest hotels on the Strip, with only 200 rooms, the Barbary Coast is nonetheless a popular place to stay because of its central location and affordable rates. ⊠ *3595 Las Vegas Blvd. S, Center Strip* ☎ *702/737–7111 or 888/227–2279* ⊕ *www. barbarycoastcasino.com.*

⑭ Bellagio Las Vegas. The $1.8-billion, 3,000-room Bellagio is one of the Fodor'sChoice most opulent and expensive hotel-casinos ever built. Scores of full-★ grown evergreen and deciduous trees line the "shore" (actually, the Strip sidewalk) of the 12-acre lake that fronts the hotel and reflects its Tuscan village architecture.

Stretching 900 feet across Bellagio's lake is a signature outdoor spectacle: the $30-million **Fountains of Bellagio** water ballet, made famous by an appearance in the 2001 remake of *Ocean's Eleven.* More than 1,000 fountain nozzles, 4,500 lights, and 27 million gallons of water combine to dazzle audiences with dancing waters choreographed to music. Some jets launch spray nearly 250 feet in the air. There's a show every 30 minutes from 3 PM (noon on weekends) until about 7 PM, after which the shows run every 15 minutes until midnight. The best view is from the observation deck of the Eiffel Tower, directly across the street.

Walking into the lobby of Bellagio, you're confronted with a fantastic and colorful, 2,000-square-foot glass sculpture called *Fiori di Como,* by famed artist Dale Chiluly. It's composed of more than 2,000 individually blown glass pieces and cost upwards of $10 million.

Beyond the lobby is a 12,500-square-foot conservatory, the **Bellagio Botanical Gardens,** full of living flowers, shrubs, trees, and other plants. All the foliage in the conservatory and throughout the hotel is fresh and live, grown in Bellagio's 5-acre greenhouse, and changes with the seasons.

Through the conservatory is the **Gallery of Fine Art.** Although MGM has sold off most of the gallery's permanent collection (the pieces in the restaurants remain), the gallery remains operational, displaying rotating exhibits arranged with museums, other galleries, and private collectors. Recent exhibits have included 21 masterworks by French Impressionist Claude Monet, loaned to the Bellagio by Boston's Museum of Fine Arts, and the private collection of Steve Martin.

The resort also includes a $75-million showroom where Cirque du Soleil performs its spectacular *O,* and upscale nightclubs Light and Caramel bring in top deejays from around the world. But as elegant as the decor and entertainment in this resort are, the shops nearly outdo them. Bellagio has some of the most exclusive and beautiful stores in the world, including Giorgio Armani, Chanel, Gucci, Prada, and Tiffany & Co. Note: No one under 18 is allowed in Bellagio unless staying at the hotel. ⊠ *3600 Las Vegas Blvd. S, Center Strip* ☎ *702/693–7111 or 888/744–7687* ⊕ *www.bellagio.com* ▣ *Gallery of Fine Art $12* ☉ *Sun.–Thurs. 10–6, Fri. and Sat. 10–9.*

▶ **⑬ Caesars Palace.** A 20-foot statue of Caesar, which stands in front of the Fodor'sChoice driveway to the main entrance, greets visitors to this iconic hotel-casino. ★ Behind him, 18 fountains and 50-foot-high cypress trees adorn the approach to the door. Nearby is a replica of one of Thailand's most popular shrines, with a 4-ton, gold-plated Brahma (the gift of a Thai tycoon). Among the other sculptures that adorn the palatial property is a full-size reproduction of Michelangelo's *David*. The newest jewel in Caesars' crown is the Colosseum, where Celine Dion performs five shows a week. Having undergone major expansions in its long history, Caesars Palace covers a vast area, including two casinos, **Cleopatra's Barge** lounge (which actually sits on water), the **Garden of the Gods** pool area, and numerous restaurants and entertainment venues.

A particular highlight is the ultra-exclusive **Forum Shops at Caesars,** a shopping mall–entertainment complex designed to resemble an ancient Roman streetscape. It houses roughly 100 retailers and eateries, including Abercrombie & Fitch, Emporio Armani, Gucci, Hugo Boss, Louis Vuitton, Virgin Megastore, FAO Schwartz, and Spago. Overhead is a painted sky that changes from airy clouds to stunning sunsets to star-studded nights. The mall also has a number of entertainment options, including two astounding animatronic statue shows. Every hour on the hour, the Festival Fountain and the Atlantis shows spring into action; the former features robotic statues of Bacchus, Pluto, Venus, and Apollo, the latter the royal family of the doomed kingdom of Atlantis. ⊠ *3570 Las Vegas Blvd. S, Center Strip* ☎ *702/733–7900 or 800/223–7277* ⊕ *www.caesarspalace.com* ✉ *Race for Atlantis $10* ☉ *Forum Shops: Sun.–Thurs. 10 AM–11 PM, Fri. and Sat. 10 AM–midnight.*

⑲ Flamingo Las Vegas. Prior to 1946, when Benjamin (Bugsy) Siegel imported Miami luxury to the desert, Las Vegas was still trying to keep alive the last little sliver of the Wild West. But Bugsy was intent on introducing a class joint to the new casino town, a place where his Hollywood buddies and Manhattan partners could gamble legally, where the lure of big-time entertainment would bring the beautiful people to play, and where the ordinary Joe would show up because he wanted to feel like a big shot. Although things didn't work out exactly as Bugsy planned (⇨ CloseUp: A Gangster's Pink Legend), the Flamingo of today is the classy joint that he dreamed of, glitzy and elegant—if relentlessly pink. A highlight of the property is the lovely 15-acre pool park, with pools connected by water slides. The park also includes a wild-animal habitat with a flock of live Chilean flamingos, African penguins, swans, ducks, koi, goldfish, and turtles. All of the animals live on islands and in streams surrounded by sparkling waterfalls and lush foliage. The last remnant of the complex originally built by Bugsy Siegel was torn down, but a monument in the pool park pays respect to the Flamingo's notorious founder.

Bottoms Up, a musical comedy revue, is one of the longest running and least expensive showgirl revues on the Strip. Famed comedy troupe The Second City performs at Second City Theater, along with new comedians and stage veterans from Chicago, Toronto, and Detroit. Gladys Knight also has a show here. ⊠ *3555 Las Vegas Blvd. S, Center Strip* ☎ *702/733–3111 or 800/732–2111* ⊕ *www.flamingolv.com.*

㉑ Harrah's Las Vegas Casino & Hotel. A carnival theme pervades Harrah's, with the festive motif carried throughout to the outdoor Carnaval Court entertainment and shopping area, which occupies a patio near the front entrance. Carnaval Court includes Carnaval Corner, an international food mart; Ragin' Cajun, a Cajun country–inspired gift shop; and the Ghirardelli Chocolate Company. In summer, bands play almost continuously, well into the night.

Harrah's entertainment lineup is a solid attraction. Comedic magician Mac King packs a crowd with his low-key show at the Comedy Cabaret; there's also the Improv Comedy Club for off-the-cuff humor. Clint Holmes performs six nights a week in Harrah's showroom, and both male and female dancers gyrate in the revue *Skintight.* ⊠ *3475 Las Vegas Blvd. S, Center Strip* ☎ *702/369–5000 or 800/427–7247* ⊕ *www.harrahs.com.*

need a break?

Carnaval Court, Harrah's. Bands play a center stage and vendors sell items from colorful booths at this perpetual open air street fair. The food is reasonably priced, and it's right off the sidewalk at Harrah's. Try jalapeño poppers, hot wings, or quesadillas. ⊠ *3475 Las Vegas Blvd. S, Center Strip* ☎ *702/369–5000 or 800/732–2111.*

☝ ⑳ **Imperial Palace Hotel and Casino.** The Imperial Palace is festooned with carved dragons and wind-chime chandeliers and has a distinctly Asian feel. It rests on a postage-stamp-size parcel, so the facilities rise instead of sprawl. On the first floor are the casino and shopping plaza. On the second are the coffee shop and buffet. The third houses the showroom, race and sports book, and meeting rooms. And on the fifth floor are the hotel restaurants.

On the fifth level of the hotel's parking garage (catch the elevator at the back of the casino) is the **Imperial Palace Automobile Museum,** a collection of more than 350 antique, classic, and special-interest vehicles. Because the vehicles are all for sale, the displays change from time to time, but among the cars, trucks, and motorcycles you might see a 1976 Cadillac Eldorado owned by Elvis Presley or the world's largest Duesenberg collection, comprising 25 vehicles built between 1925 and 1937.

Imperial Palace also offers unique entertainment, including *Legends in Concert,* a multimillion-dollar stage production featuring look-and-sound-alike performers portraying stars such as Madonna, the Temptations, Liberace, Ricky Martin, Shania Twain, and, of course, Elvis. ⊠ *3535 Las Vegas Blvd. S, Center Strip* ☎ *702/731–3311 or 800/634–6441* ⊕ *www.imperialpalace.com* 🎟 *Museum $6.95; coupons for free admission are usually handed out in front of hotel-casino or available online* ⊙ *Museum daily 9:30* AM*–11:30* PM.

㉔ **Mirage Hotel and Casino.** When it opened in November 1989, the Mirage launched a decade-long (and counting) building boom the likes of which the world has rarely seen. Every 15 minutes from dusk to midnight, the signature volcano in front of the Mirage erupts, shooting flames and smoke 100 feet above the water below. Just inside the resort's front entrance is a lush rain forest. Palm trees, cascading waterfalls, meandering lagoons, and exotic tropical flora are housed under a 100-foot-high dome, and a 20,000-gallon aquarium provides a stunning backdrop to the front desk.

Fodor'sChoice
★

Behind the Mirage, eight Atlantic bottlenose dolphins live in a 2.5-million-gallon saltwater **Dolphin Habitat**, the largest in the world. The 15-minute tour, which leaves from the large and lush pool area, passes through an underwater observation area and winds up in a video room where you can watch tapes of two dolphin births at the habitat. A gift shop sells dolphin souvenirs, and there's a snack bar next door.

A major attraction at the Mirage is the **Secret Garden of Siegfried and Roy,** a palm-shaded sanctuary for a collection of the planet's rarest and most exotic creatures, including snow-white tigers, white lions, and an Asian elephant. Both attractions are free for children under 11. Danny Gans, impressionist par excellence, performs here as well. ⊠ *3400 Las Vegas Blvd. S, Center Strip* ☎ *702/791–7111 or 800/627–6667* ⊕ *www.themirage.com* ✉ *Secret Garden and Dolphin Habitat $12, Dolphin Habitat alone $5 on Wed. and Thurs.–Sun. after 3* ☉ *Secret Garden Mon., Tues., Thurs., and Fri. 11–5, weekends 10–5; Dolphin Habitat weekdays 11–7, weekends 10–7. Secret Garden closed Wed.*

㉕ **The Palms Hotel & Casino.** Odds are you will spot a star or two at the
FodorśChoice publicity-savvy Maloof family's $268-million hotel-casino. The open-
★ ing party in 2001 packed A- and B-listers into the Palms' bars, restaurants, and casino; Paris Hilton wore a dress made out of $1 million in Palms casino chips. Shortly after, the cast of MTV's *The Real World: Las Vegas* moved into a 2,900-square-foot suite on the 28th floor, spending their evenings moonlighting at mega-nightclub Rain on the casino level of the resort downstairs.

Everything at the Palms seems to ooze cool quotient. Swim-up blackjack is played in the 75,000-square-foot poolside lounge. The pool, painted in lavender, is surrounded by cabanas, patches of grass and sand, and two bars. A three-story, 20,000-square-foot spa has an aromatherapy bar, massages, wraps, and facials. The on-site Hart & Huntington Tattoo Company has inked such high-profile names as Dennis Rodman, Jamie Pressly, and Tony Hawk. Ghostbar, on the 50th floor, has a sweeping, 180-degree view of Las Vegas. Rain nightclub doubles as a rock concert venue. There's also a movie theater and seven restaurants. ⊠ *4321 W. Flamingo Rd., West Side* ☎ *702/942–7777 or 866/942–7770* ⊕ *www.palms.com.*

⑯ **Paris Las Vegas.** This $785-million homage to the City of Lights tries to
FodorśChoice reproduce all the charm of the French capital. Outside are replicas of
★ the Arc de Triomphe, the Paris Opera House, the Hôtel de Ville, and the Louvre, along with an *Around the World in Eighty Days* balloon marquee. Also out front is the Mon Ami Gabi café, offering rare alfresco dining right on the Strip. The main gaming area sits on Monet-style floral carpeting beneath a re-creation of Paris's wrought-iron art nouveau arches. Even the sinks in the restrooms are French porcelain. Be sure to check out the dozen LeRoy Neiman paintings that grace the walls of the high-roller pit. Paris Las Vegas offers several entertainment venues, including Le Théâtre des Arts, a 1,200-seat Parisian-style theater that has hosted everything from French hip-hop groups to a musical version of *The Hunchback of Notre Dame.*

The 50-story **Eiffel Tower,** built almost exactly to a half-size scale, rises above it all; the Eiffel Tower Restaurant is on the 11th floor, and three legs of the tower come right through the casino roof, resting heavily on its floor. A glass elevator ascends to the tower's small observation deck (a caged catwalk) at the 460-foot level. Although you can catch a better, bigger view of the Las Vegas Valley and have more walk-around room at the top of the Stratosphere, the Eiffel Tower offers an incomparable view of mid-Strip. After dark, hang around long enough to catch the dancing-waters show at Bellagio directly across the street. The chic ultralounge on the second story of the premier nightclub **Risqué** has a great view of the Strip's neon lights.

Cobblestone "streets" meander through **Le Boulevard** shopping district, where you can purchase everything from fine jewelry to freshly baked breads and pastries; bread deliverymen ride through on bicycles, singing "Alouette" in operatic voices. Both sweet and savory crepes are sold from a storefront window. ⊠ *3655 Las Vegas Blvd. S, Center Strip* ☎ *702/ 739–4111 or 888/226–5687* ⊕ *www.paris-lv.com* ⊠ *Eiffel Tower $9* ⊙ *Eiffel Tower daily 10 AM–1 AM.*

❷❸ **Treasure Island Las Vegas (TI).** Shifting its focus from a family-oriented clientele to the adult market, Treasure Island has become TI. The buccaneer theme is being phased out in favor of more stylish trappings. The pool area is large and lush, and sits next to a tropical-theme restaurant and bar, Kahunaville. A short tram-ride connects the hotel to the Mirage next door. Treasure Island hosts the Cirque du Soleil production *Mystère,* a spectacular display of strength, dance, acrobatics, and singing.

The free **Sirens of TI** show includes Broadway-caliber dance routines, acrobatics, and a battle between the temptresses of Sirens' Cove and a band of invading pirates. The show debuted in 2003, replacing the earlier battle between two ships. ⊠ *3300 Las Vegas Blvd. S, Center Strip* ☎ *702/894–7111 or 800/944–7444* ⊕ *www.treasureislandlasvegas. com* ⊠ *Sirens of TI free* ⊙ *Sirens of TI performances every 90 min Sun.–Thurs. 5:30–10, Fri. and Sat. 5:30–11:30.*

★ ☾ ❷❷ **Venetian Resort-Hotel-Casino.** The 44-year-old Sands was imploded in 1996 to make room for this $1.5-billion resort complex. This meticulous theme hotel re-creates Italy's most romantic city with reproductions of various Venetian landmarks. From the Strip, you enter through a reproduction of the Doge's Palace, set on a walkway over a 585,000-gallon lagoon. Inside, reproductions of famous paintings with gilded frames adorn a 65-foot dome ceiling above the casino lobby. Hanging behind the front desk is a giant pictorial overview of 17th-century Venice. The geometric design of the marble floor provides an M. C. Escher–like optical illusion of climbing stairs. Renaissance characters roam the public areas, singing opera, performing mime, jesting, even kissing hands.

The centerpiece of the **Grand Canal Shops,** a 90-store mall, is the 1,200-foot-long reproduction of Venice's Canalozzo enclosed by brick walls and wrought-iron fencing. Gondolas (ride for $10 per person, same-day reservations usually required) ply the waterway, steered by serenading gondoliers. The canal ends at a colossal reproduction of St. Mark's Square, authentic right down to the colors of the facades. And it's also worth noting that the Venetian houses Venus—the first new tiki bar to be built in Las Vegas since the Stardust's classic Aku-Aku closed in the early 1980s.

Madame Tussaud's Celebrity Encounter displays more than 100 wax figures, many celebrating Sin City's past—classic Las Vegas crooners such as Tom Jones, Frank Sinatra, and Tony Bennett are among those replicated here.

The main draw at the **Guggenheim-Hermitage Museum** is a 7,660-square-foot "jewel box," whose high-concept iron-oxide walls form part of the Venetian's lobby and display masterworks from the Guggenheim and Hermitage collections. It was designed by Dutch architect Rem Koolhaas, and would be worth seeing even if completely bereft of art. Guided tours are available; periodically, tour guides linger and give minitours for free.

The high-energy *V—The Ultimate Variety Show* has magic, daredevil stunts, comedy, and visual art. ✉ *3355 Las Vegas Blvd. S, Center Strip* ☎ *702/733–5000, 702/642–6440 wax museum, 800/494–3556* ⊕ *www. venetian.com* ✉ *Wax museum $12.50, Hermitage-Guggenheim Museum $15* ⊙ *Wax museum daily 9:30–11; Hermitage-Guggenheim museum daily 9:30–8:30.*

NORTH STRIP

The northern end of the Strip hasn't kept pace with the latest developments of the southern and center parts. In fact, the only large vacant lots on the Strip are in this area. It's here you find the oldest casinos in town, and the quaint architecture of the last century alongside new developments.

But with casino mogul Steve Wynn's reopening of the old Desert Inn as Wynn Las Vegas in 2005, the northern end of the Strip seems poised for a rebirth. Wynn Las Vegas graces the heart of the city, near the Convention Center and across the street from the Fashion Show Mall. The resort includes a championship golf course and meeting rooms designed for both luxury and practicality. Wynn Las Vegas leads a renaissance in the central part of the city. Just consider the luxury condominiums cropping up next to, and across the street from, the venerable Sahara hotel.

a good tour

Park at the **Stardust Hotel and Casino** ㉖ ☞. If you want to keep your car covered, use the Riviera's garage across the street and start and end your tour there.

This is a major trek, with greater distances between the casinos at either end. If you're not up for shin splints or if it's just too hot, consider driving and walking: hit the New Frontier, Fashion Show Mall, and Guardian Angel Cathedral, then the Stardust, Riviera, and Circus Circus on foot; drive to the Convention Center area and then to the Sahara, Bonanza Gift Shop, and Stratosphere.

From the Stardust, walk south on the Strip down to the **New Frontier Hotel and Casino** ㉗, which lures a bustling crowd with good, cheap food, low minimums, and minisuites. Next door to the New Frontier is the **Fashion Show Mall** ㉘, one of four Strip shopping attractions, which has specialty shops, boutiques, and major department stores. A short detour off Fashion Show Drive to Industrial Road (behind the mall) will take you to the **Elvis-A-Rama Museum** ㉙. Return to the Strip via Spring Mountain Road–Sands Road. Across from the Fashion Show Mall on the corner of the Strip and Spring Mountain Road–Sands Road is the site of **Wynn Las Vegas** ㉚. The newest of the luxurious megaresorts for which Steve Wynn is famous is set to open in spring 2005. The **Wynn Collection** ㉛ of fine art is also here on display in the former Desert Inn. East of the Strip on Desert Inn Road is the **Guardian Angel Cathedral** ㉜, a Catholic church that serves the religious needs of many weekend visitors.

The next cross street north of Desert Inn Road is Convention Center Drive, which leads east to Paradise Road. Halfway down Convention Center Drive is the **Greek Isles Casino** ㉝, which has a tribute to the Rat Pack. At the corner of Paradise Road and Convention Center Drive is, logically enough, the **Las Vegas Convention Center** ㉞, one of the largest and busiest convention centers in the country. North of the convention center stands the monumental **Las Vegas Hilton** ㉟. Be sure to check out Star Trek: The Experience. Your best bets for parking are the garages at the Hilton or the Riviera. The walk from the latter isn't unreasonably long, but may be less advisable in summer.

If you head back to the Strip on Riviera Boulevard you come to the **Riviera Hotel and Casino** ㊱, with its fast-food court and snack bar, three production shows, a comedy club, and one of the world's largest casinos. Continuing north on Las Vegas Boulevard, you pass **Candlelight Wedding Chapel** ㊲, the busiest hitching post in town, and the **Wet 'n Wild Water Park** ㊳ before coming to the northern edge of the Las Vegas Strip at Sahara Avenue. There stands the **Sahara Hotel and Casino** ㊴, a venerable attraction, which opened in 1952. You can park in the Sahara's garage or in the oversize lot across the street; there's a covered bridge leading from the lot to the hotel.

Across the Strip from the Sahara is **Bonanza "World's Largest Gift Shop"** ㊵. North of Sahara Avenue starts Las Vegas city proper (south of it is Clark County); four blocks north on the Strip is the megalithic **Stratosphere Casino Hotel & Tower** ㊶, the tallest building west of the Mississippi, with its two high-altitude thrill rides, 1,500 hotel rooms, giant casino, and extensive retail area.

Back down on the Strip is the **Guinness World of Records Museum** ㊷, which is next door to **Circus Circus** ㊸, where the pink-and-white big top covers an almost always crazy scene. Behind Circus Circus is **Adventuredome,** the world's largest indoor amusement park, with a rough roller coaster, flume ride, and kiddie attractions. The small casino next to Circus Circus is **Slots–A–Fun,** which has the least expensive snack-bar food on the Strip, some of the lowest minimums, and—what else?—lotsa slots.

Finally, continue heading south on the Strip to the **Westward Ho** ㊹, which has been billed as the largest motel in the country. Then you arrive back at the Stardust, several hours older but many times wiser in the ways of the gambling capital of the known universe.

TIMING   The North Strip is the longest of the suggested walks, even without the side trip to the Las Vegas Hilton (a leg we recommend you drive). It'll take four to five hours to see everything on the Strip; add another couple of hours to take in the sights on Paradise Road. If you like to shop, you could spend all day taking the tour, browsing in the Fashion Show Mall on one end and the Bonanza Gift Shop and Stratosphere on the other.

What to See

🔟 **Bonanza "World's Largest Gift Shop."** Those who are determined to visit only one gift shop in Las Vegas will want to make it this one. If it's not really the world's largest, it is the biggest and best in town, with an impressive collection of Las Vegas kitsch (this is where you find your life-size Wayne Newton blow-up doll), the most extensive selection of Las Vegas T-shirts and postcards, along with jewelry, gambling supplies, Western memorabilia, film, fudge, and aspirin. ⊠ *2460 Las Vegas Blvd. S, North Strip* ☎ *702/385–7359* ☉ *Daily 8 AM–midnight.*

🔟 **Candlelight Wedding Chapel.** Its central location helps to make this the town's busiest wedding chapel. Couples often line up here waiting to tie the knot (Saturday is especially busy). Anyone can watch a Las Vegas wedding ceremony; just walk in and take a seat. Some weddings take place in the gazebo outside the chapel. ⊠ *2855 Las Vegas Blvd. S, North Strip* ☎ *702/735–4179* 🌐 *www.nos.net/candlelight.*

🔟 🔟 **Circus Circus.** Circus Circus opened in 1968, with the then-unique idea of appealing to the families that showed up in the adult fantasy land of Las Vegas. To this day, Circus Circus remains family central in Las Vegas— enticing to children, surreal to parents weaned on Hunter S. Thompson's *Fear and Loathing in Las Vegas.* Under the pink-and-white big top, the clowns, trapeze stars, high-wire artists, unicyclists, and aerial dancers perform daily every 30 minutes from 11 AM to midnight. Also for the family market, Circus Circus has the only RV park on the Strip.

The **Circus Circus Carnival Midway** has old-time fair games (dime toss, milk can, bushel basket) along with clown-face painting, a video arcade with more than 200 games, fun-house mirrors, corn dogs, and pizza. Many parents park their teens on the midway while they go off to gamble, pull handles, and press buttons downstairs.

Behind the hotel-casino is the **Adventuredome**, a 5-acre indoor amusement park covered by a pink dome. Inside are the world's largest indoor roller coaster, a flume ride, a laser-tag room, bumper cars, four kiddie rides, a carnival midway, an arcade, and a snack bar. The Canyon Blaster roller coaster has two 360-degree loops and a double corkscrew; it's a rough 105-second ride, but quite a thrill. If thrill rides are your thing, also check out the Inverter, 360 degrees of constant G force, and the Fun House Express, an IMAX motion-simulator experience. Designed exclusively for Circus Circus, the Fun House Express uses computer-generated images to portray a fast-paced roller coaster ride through a

GETTING HITCHED IN LAS VEGAS

WHEN WIDE-OPEN GAMBLING was legalized in 1931, Nevada also adopted liberal divorce and marriage laws as part of the strategy to attract tourists. The rules haven't changed: a divorce can still be obtained after only six weeks of residency and a wedding can be arranged without a blood test or a waiting period; once you have a license, a justice of the peace can unite you in marital bliss in five minutes.

Weddings are big business here, to the tune of more than $4 million in marriage licenses alone. To be among the 123,000-plus couples who tie the knot in Las Vegas every year, simply appear at the **Clark County Marriage License Bureau** (⊠ 200 S. 3rd St., Downtown ☎ 702/455–4415) with $55, some identification, and your beloved. It's open between 8 AM and midnight from Monday through Thursday and 24 hours Friday, Saturday, and holidays. New Year's Eve and Valentine's Day are the most popular wedding dates. Even celebrities (including Britney Spears, Bette Midler, Joan Collins, Michael Jordan, and Richard Gere) have found it handy to pop into a chapel for a quick ceremony.

For a no-frills, justice-of-the-peace nuptial ceremony, visit the **Commissioner of Civil Marriages** (⊠ 309 S. 3rd St., Downtown), where a surrogate-J.P. deputy commissioner will unite you in holy matrimony for $35. For flowers, organ music, and photos, head to one of Vegas's renowned wedding chapels, where the average nuptials cost $200 to $700; hotel chapels tend to cost more.

The **Candlelight Wedding Chapel** (⊠ 2855 Las Vegas Blvd. S, North Strip ☎ 702/ 735–4179 or 800/962–1818 ⊕ www. nos.net/candlelight) opened its doors in 1967; it's small, elegant, and churchlike.

Weddings are reasonably priced; the most expensive package costs $500.

The **Little Church of the West** (⊠ 4617 Las Vegas Blvd. S, South Strip ☎ 702/739–7971 or 800/821–2452) is listed on the National Register of Historic Places; the cedar-and-redwood chapel is one of the most famous chapels in Vegas, sitting on an acre of land at the south end of the Strip.

The **Little White Wedding Chapel** (⊠ 1301 Las Vegas Blvd. S, North Strip ☎ 702/ 382–3546 or 800/545–8111 ⊕ www. littlewhitechapel.com), 1 mi north of the Sahara hotel, is where you can get married in a pink Cadillac while an Elvis impersonator croons. The world-renowned chapel is one of only two chapels that offer drive-through weddings (the other is A Special Memory).

Weddings at **Star Trek: The Experience** (⊠ 3000 S. Paradise Blvd., North Strip ☎ 702/697–8750 or 800/774–1500 ⊕ www.startrekexp.com) are held on the bridge of the Enterprise-D from Star Trek: The Next Generation; costumed characters such as Klingon warriors bear witness to the proceedings.

The **Venetian Resort-Hotel-Casino** (⊠ 3355 Las Vegas Blvd. S, Center Strip ☎ 702/414–4280 or 800/883–6423 ⊕ www.venetian.com) offers weddings in a re-creation of St. Mark's Square, on a replica of the Rialto Bridge, or on the Venetian's canal in a gold-and-white gondola. The gondolier sings and passersby applaud loudly, dimming the lines between a real wedding in Venice and this fanciful interpretation.

The **Viva Las Vegas Wedding Chapel** (⊠ 1205 Las Vegas Blvd. S, North Strip ☎ 702/384–0771 or 800/574–4450 ⊕ www.vivalasvegasweddings.com) offers theme weddings ranging from Elvis's Blue Hawaii to Egyptian to Fairy Tale.

spooky world called Clown Chaos. ⊠ *2880 Las Vegas Blvd. S, North Strip* ☏ *702/734–0410 or 800/634–3450* ⊕ *www.circuscircus.com* 🎫 *Adventuredome free, individual rides $2–$5, all-day wristbands $16.95* ⊙ *Amusement park Mon.–Thurs. 10–6, Fri. and Sat. 10 AM–midnight, Sun. 10–8; carnival midway daily 10 AM–midnight.*

㉙ Elvis-A-Rama Museum. The quintessential Elvis experience can be found at this spot on Industrial Road (behind the Fashion Show Mall). The must-see museum (for Elvis fans, at least) houses four of the King's cars, including his purple Lincoln and his 1955 Fleetwood limo. More than 2,000 of Elvis's personal items are on display, including his jewelry, clothing, letters, and records. Every hour an Elvis impersonator croons to fans on a small stage; various impersonators cover different decades of his career. Buy Elvis clocks, key chains, pins, books, and other collectibles in the gift shop. Call the museum to arrange for a free shuttle pickup from any major hotel on the Strip. ⊠ *3401 Industrial Rd., North Strip* ☏ *702/309–7200* ⊕ *www.elvisarama.com* 🎫 *$9.95* ⊙ *Daily 10 AM–7 PM.*

★ ㉘ Fashion Show Mall. With Saks Fifth Avenue, Neiman Marcus, Nordstrom, Dillard's, Robinsons-May, and Bloomingdale's Home as anchor stores, plus boutiques and specialty shops, there's a good possibility that you can find what you're looking for here. A fashion runway, new restaurants, and more airy space are some of the features that are appearing as the mall expands, and a Lord & Taylor is planned for the next phase. A futuristic advertising display, the elliptical "cloud," graces the front of the mall on the Strip. The structure is a 400-foot-long steel canopy. Ads are projected on the cloud above the heads of passersby from 10 AM to 2 PM each day. ⊠ *3200 Las Vegas Blvd. S, North Strip* ☏ *702/369–8382* ⊕ *www.thefashionshow.com* ⊙ *Daily 10–5.*

㉜ Guardian Angel Cathedral. The cathedral often has standing room only on Saturday afternoons, as visitors pray for luck—and sometimes drop casino chips into the collection cups during a special tourist mass. Periodically, a priest known as the "chip monk" collects the chips and takes them to the respective casinos to cash them in. Those staying on the south end of the Strip might find the **Shrine of the Most Holy Redeemer** (⊠ 55 E. Reno Ave. ☏ 702/891–8600) more convenient; it has one Saturday-afternoon and three Sunday masses. ⊠ *336 E. Desert Inn Rd., North Strip* ☏ *702/735–5241* ⊙ *Sat. mass 2:30, 4, 5:15; Sun. mass 8, 9:30, 11, 12:30, 5.*

㉝ Greek Isles Casino. Be transported back to the days when the Rat Pack ruled Las Vegas with the Greek Isles' tribute to Frank Sinatra, Dean Martin, Sammy Davis Jr., and Joey Bishop. The tribute artists—more familiarly known as impersonators—are backed by a 12-piece band. The show takes place in the **Star Theater.** ⊠ *305 Convention Center Dr., North Strip* ☏ *702/952–8000* ⊕ *www.greekislesvegas.com* 🎫 *The Rat Pack Tribute: $56.95, with prime-rib dinner, $79.95.*

☝ ㊷ Guinness World of Records Museum. The Las Vegas version of the best, biggest, and most bizarre has colorful displays, video footage (including clips of elaborate tumbling-dominoes layouts from around the world), and computer data banks of Guinness world records covering sports, science, nature, and entertainment (the most-married man, the largest snowplow). There are models of the world's tallest man and shortest woman and the person with the world's longest human neck. The Las Vegas display alone, which includes information on celebrities married here, the Stratosphere, and Hoover Dam, is worth the price of admission. ✉ *2780 Las Vegas Blvd. S, North Strip* ☎ *702/792–3766* ⊕ *www.guinnessmuseum.com* ☞ *$6* ⊙ *Daily 9–5:30.*

㉞ Las Vegas Convention Center. More than 4 million people attend the more than 1,000 conventions of varying sizes that are held every year in this 3.2-million-square-foot space that's one of the country's largest convention centers. One of the most attractive aspects for conventioneers is its proximity to all the hotels and the airport, and there's a visitors center right off the parking-lot lobby. **Meskerem,** (☎ 702/696–1002) an Ethiopian restaurant inside the center, becomes a nightclub on Saturday nights. A weekly event, the Mess Around, includes belly dancing and movies. ✉ *3150 Paradise Rd., North Strip* ☎ *702/892–0711* ⊕ *www.lasvegas24hours.com.*

㉟ Las Vegas Hilton. Barbra Streisand opened this hotel (then the International) with a four-week gig and was followed by Elvis Presley, who made the Hilton his official Las Vegas venue throughout the 1970s. You can still stay in the Elvis Suite on the 31st floor, where the king of rock and roll resided when he played here. Though the Hilton, which is adjacent to the Las Vegas Convention Center, no longer holds the title of largest hotel in town, it's still a sight to see—best of all by standing at its foot and staring up at the 29-story three-wing tower.

The biggest attraction at the Hilton is **Star Trek: The Experience** (⊕ www.startrekexp.com ☞ $24.99 all-day pass ⊙ daily 11–11), a $70-million museum and 3-D motion simulator ride. Trekkies will go nuts over the museum, which has a Star Trek time line of future history, costumes and props, and video loops from the shows. During the theater–ride, the audience is kidnapped by the Klingons and beamed into the 24th century and onto the bridge of the Starship *Enterprise*; it's up to the crew to get everyone safely back to the 21st-century Hilton. ✉ *3000 W. Paradise Rd., North Strip* ☎ *702/732–5111 or 800/774–1500* ⊕ *www.lv-hilton.com.*

㉗ New Frontier Hotel and Casino. The New Frontier is the oldest hotel-casino on the Las Vegas Strip, beating out the Flamingo by a full five years. In 1942 Hollywood producer D. W. Griffith opened the Last Frontier, the second hotel on the Los Angeles Highway (soon to be known as the Las Vegas Strip). It was sold in 1951 and renamed Last Frontier Village. The original building was torn down and replaced in 1955; the new hotel-casino was named the New Frontier. That structure was torn down and replaced in 1967 and the property was named simply the Frontier. In 1998 it was sold and renamed the New Frontier. (Confused yet?) The vestibule of the Atrium (all-suite) Tower is gardenlike, with a waterfall, creek, and pools. ✉ *3120 Las Vegas Blvd. S, North Strip* ☎ *702/794–8200 or 800/634–6966* ⊕ *www.frontierlv.com.*

36 Riviera Hotel and Casino. Here's a piece of old Las Vegas: the Riviera has been gracing the Las Vegas Strip since 1955, when it became the famous street's ninth resort (it's one of the few of those nine remaining). The Riviera is mostly known for its multitude of lights that brighten up this part of the Strip—and for its entertainment. It's the home of those *Crazy Girls* whose near-bare behinds grace cabs and billboards all over town; *An Evening at La Cage,* whose female impersonators include Joan Rivers look-alike Frank Marino; *Splash,* the only show on the Strip with ice skating; and a popular comedy club. Film buffs may recognize the hotel-casino as the backdrop for dozens of Las Vegas films, including *Casino, Diamonds Are Forever,* and *Austin Powers: International Man of Mystery.* ⊠ *2901 Las Vegas Blvd. S, North Strip* ☎ *702/734–5110 or 800/634–6753* ⊕ *www.theriviera.com.*

39 Sahara Hotel and Casino. The line between old Las Vegas and new is clear at the Sahara. The former Rat Pack haunt manages to encompass both old-school swank and the popular NASCAR Cafe, outfitted for the hottest sports franchise in recent years.

Near the NASCAR Cafe is **Cyber Speedway,** a $15-million virtual reality race car–driving experience, where 3-D motion-simulator rides make audience members feel as though they're driving on the Las Vegas Motor Speedway or the Las Vegas Strip.

The Sahara's signature roller coaster, **Speed—The Ride,** uses magnetic technology to propel riders through a tunnel, around a loop, and in and out of the building at speeds of more than 70 mph. Then you do the entire thing again—backward. Magician Steve Wyrick performs 10 shows a week in the Sahara Theater—each including the appearance of a twin-engine aircraft—for the largest stage illusion in this over-the-top town. ⊠ *2535 Las Vegas Blvd. S, North Strip* ☎ *702/737–2111 or 800/634–6666, 702/737–2750 NASCAR Cafe* ⊕ *www.saharavegas.com* ✉ *Rides $8* ⊙ *Speed—The Ride weekdays 11–10, weekends 10 AM–midnight; Cyber Speedway weekdays 10–10, weekends 10 AM–11 PM.*

▶ **26 Stardust Hotel and Casino.** The Stardust has one of the best facades on the Strip: pink-and-blue neon tubes run down the front of the hotel, leading to a 183-foot tall programmed sign that erupts in bursts of neon stars. On its debut in 1958 the sign was the largest and brightest in Las Vegas, its glow visible for miles. The vision for the Stardust came from mobster Tony Cornero, who in the 1930s ran gambling ships off the southern California coast; he owned a small club out on Boulder Highway and dreamed of building the biggest, classiest casino in town. Cornero didn't live long enough to realize his dream, however; one morning, while shooting craps at the Desert Inn, he had a heart attack, dying with the dice in his hands. Today the Stardust is known for its sports book and has the distinction of exclusively hosting Wayne Newton, "Mr. Las Vegas" himself, in a show-room named for him. ⊠ *3000 Las Vegas Blvd. S, North Strip* ☎ *702/732–6111 or 800/634–6757* ⊕ *www.stardustlv.com.*

---

need a break?

Peppermill Fireside Lounge. Low mirrored ceilings, a sunken lounge area encircling a cozy fireplace, pink-and-blue neon trim, and signature cocktails make this kitschy Vegas institution an ideal place for an afternoon or evening break. Burgers, sandwiches, quesadillas, and salads are on the menu, and portions are huge and ideal for splitting. Try the 64-ounce Scorpion—made with six different liquors—or the popular Elegant Brownie, served in a long-stemmed dish. ⊠ *2985 Las Vegas Blvd. S, North Strip* ☎ *702/735–7635.*

★ ☺ ➍ **Stratosphere Casino Hotel & Tower.** The view from the tower and the thrill rides at the top make it worth the extra effort to get to this hotel-casino, which occupies a sort of no-man's land a few blocks beyond the traditional northern end of the Strip.

The aforementioned view has no peer—you are looking down at Las Vegas from the top of the tallest **observation tower** in the United States, dominating the Las Vegas skyline at 1,149 feet. Although the view is impressive enough during the day, save a trip to the tower for the evening.

High above the Las Vegas Strip are the Stratosphere's three **thrill rides:** the Big Shot, the High Roller, and the X Scream. The Big Shot would be a monster ride on the ground, but being high atop the Stratosphere Tower makes it twice as wild. Four riders are strapped into chairs on four sides of the needle, which rises from the Stratosphere's observation pod (the base of the ride is on the 112th floor). With little warning, you're flung 160 feet up the needle, then dropped like a rock. The whole thing is over in less than a minute, but your knees will wobble for the rest of the day. The High Roller is a roller coaster that, although tame by ground standards, is quite thrilling owing to its perch high atop the tower. The X Scream is a harrowing take on child's play: You see-saw head-first 27 feet over the tower's sides in an open car.

For the less daring, the Stratosphere also has the revolving Top of the World restaurant and lounge, 900 feet above the valley. The restaurant makes a complete revolution once every hour or so, and both offer big views. The shopping plaza between the casino and entrance to the tower houses more than 50 eateries and retail stores. The Strat-O-Fair, at the base of the tower, has a small Ferris wheel and other rides suitable for children, and the new events center periodically hosts concerts. ⊠ *2000 Las Vegas Blvd. S, North Strip* ☎ *702/380–7777 or 800/380–7732* ⊕ *www.stratospherehotel.com* ⊠ *Big Shot $15, High Roller $4, prices include admission to tower elevator; Strat-O-Fair rides $3* ☉ *Rides Sun.–Thurs. 10 AM–1 AM, Fri. and Sat. 10 AM–2 AM.*

➍ **Westward Ho.** The Westward Ho is a rarity on the Strip: a sprawling low-rise motel. With 1,000 rooms (some of them three-room suites), the Westward Ho claims to be the largest motel in the world. It has seven pools and no elevators. The casino is for gamblers, not gawkers, and has a dizzying assortment of slot machines and low-minimum table games. The snack bar is a local favorite, serving a huge strawberry shortcake. ⊠ *2900 Las Vegas Blvd. S, North Strip* ☎ *702/731–2900 or 800/634–6803* ⊕ *www.westwardho.com.*

☺ ➌ **Wet 'n Wild Water Park.** This 26-acre water park provides family-oriented recreation in a 500,000-gallon wave pool, three water flumes, a water

CloseUp

EXCURSIONS WITH THE KIDS

S IN CITY'S AN ADULT PLAYGROUND, but if you're the parent of too-young-to-gamble tourists, you know that the hotel pool will only occupy them for so long. Fortunately, any of the following destinations is sure to be a hit. Also, check out the Side Trips chapter for everything from visiting a Wild West town to scrambling around in Red Rock.

Las Vegas Natural History Museum. The museum has displays of mammals from places such as Alaska and Africa, and has rooms full of sharks (including live ones, swimming in a 3,000-gallon reef tank), birds, dinosaur fossils, and hands-on exhibits. Here kids can walk past a 35-foot-tall Tyrannosaurus rex that lowers its head and roars, see the ichthyosaur Shonisaurus, Nevada's state fossil, and tour the Wild Nevada Gallery, where they can see, smell, and even touch Nevada wildlife. ⊠ 900 Las Vegas Blvd. N, Downtown ☎ 702/384-3466 ☒ $6 for adults, $3 children 3–11 ⊙ Daily 9–4.

Lied Discovery Children's Museum. The Lied (pronounced leed) contains more than 100 hands-on exhibits covering the sciences, arts, and humanities. Children can pilot a space shuttle, perform on stage, or stand in a giant bubble. In the Desert Discovery area for children age five and under, hands-on interactive displays include Boulder Mountain, where children don hard hats and mine soft sculpture boulders in geometric shapes. Also in Desert Discovery is the Baby Oasis, a safe haven for tots who aren't yet walking that has colorful and stimulating props and toys, including a mirrored pull-up bar and a crawling structure of gently inclined ramps. ⊠ 833 Las Vegas Blvd. N, Downtown ☎ 702/382-3445 ⊕ www.ldcm.org ☒ $6 for adults, $5 children 1–17 ⊙ Tues.–Sun. 10–5.

Mountasia Family Fun Center. This amusement park in Henderson has two 18-hole miniature-golf courses, a roller-skating rink, go-carts, bumper-boats, and an arcade with 75 video games. A special $13 package includes unlimited minigolf or roller skating, two rides (bumper boats or go-carts), and five arcade tokens. ⊠ 2050 Olympic Ave., Henderson ☎ 702/454-4386 ☒ $4.50 per ride, 3 rides $11.95, roller skating $5 ⊙ Mon.–Thurs. 3 PM–9 PM, Fri. 3 PM–11, Sat. 11–11, Sun. noon–9.

Scandia Family Fun Center. The center has three 18-hole miniature-golf courses, a video arcade with more than 100 games, 11 batting cages, bumper boats, and the Li'l Indy Raceway for miniature-car racing. You can pay by the ride-activity or purchase an $11.95 Supersaver package (one round of miniature golf, two rides, and five arcade or batting tokens) or a $16.95 wristband (unlimited rides, golf, and 10 arcade or batting tokens). ⊠ 2900 Sirius Ave., West Side ☎ 702/364-0070 ☒ Free admission, individual rides $4.50 each ⊙ Sun.–Thurs. 10–10, Fri. and Sat. 10 AM–midnight.

Zoological–Botanical Park. Five minutes from downtown, you find the last family of Barbary apes in the United States, along with chimpanzees, eagles, ostriches, emus, parrots, wallabies, flamingos, endangered cats (including tigers), and every species of venomous reptile native to southern Nevada. One exhibit features species native to Nevada such as coyotes, golden eagles, and deer; an underwater exhibit stars a 7-foot-long alligator named Elvis. The park has easy-view animal enclosures and a petting zoo with smaller animals. ⊠ 1775 N. Rancho Dr., Rancho Strip ☎ 702/648-5955 ☒ $6.50, $4.50 children 2–12 ⊙ Daily 9–5.

roller coaster, slides, cascading fountains, and lagoons. Showers, changing rooms, and lockers are available, and inner tubes and rafts are for rent. Shops and concession stands sell souvenirs and food. ✉ *601 Las Vegas Blvd. S, North Strip* ☎ *702/737–3819* ⊕ *www.wetnwildlasvegas. com* ✆ *$25.95* ✆ *May–Oct., opens daily at 10 AM, closing times vary.*

③ Wynn Collection. Steve Wynn enjoys two things: building bigger and better resort hotels, and collecting art. While he indulges his first passion on the lot next door—Wynn Las Vegas, a 3,000-room luxury hotel scheduled for completion in 2005—he shares his other joy in a gallery inside one of the former Desert Inn hotel wings. The Wynn Collection is world-class and includes works by Matisse, Van Gogh, and Modigliani, and Picasso's "Le Reve." His collection equals the Guggenheim-Hermitage in quality. ✉ *3145 Las Vegas Blvd. S, North Strip* ☎ *702/733–4100* ✆ *$10* ✆ *Weekdays 10–9, Sat. 10–7, Sun. noon–6.*

③ Wynn Las Vegas. At this writing, casino mogul Steve Wynn's luxury hotel-casino-resort was set to emerge from the old Desert Inn property like the proverbial phoenix in spring 2005. Its 18-hole golf course and opulent rooms herald a revitalization of the North Strip. Built on the site of the old Desert Inn, Wynn Las Vegas will be the first major casino to open on the Strip since the 2000 construction of the Aladdin. 3145 Las Vegas Blvd. S, North Strip.

DOWNTOWN

If you've never traveled north of the Stratosphere Tower, you're missing a vital piece of Vegas legacy: Downtown Las Vegas is where Sin City was born. Las Vegas's first telephone was installed here; its first concrete building was built here (the Golden Gate Casino, opened in 1906 and still going strong); its first train station was at the tip of Fremont Street. And the notorious "Block 16," a block of gambling halls, bars, and legal brothels, remained in business until 1941. That was the last time prostitution was legal within city limits.

The pioneering spirit of those days lives on Fremont Street. Even though the world-famous "Glitter Gulch" was closed to automobiles and transformed into a pedestrian mall in the mid-'90s, the hotels of Fremont still seem like they should have hitching posts in front of them. The lights down here literally turn night to day, and the street's patron saints, the 50-foot-tall neon cowboy Vegas Vic and his gal, Sassy Sally, still welcome all comers with a sincere "howdy." And Fremont Street has one of Las Vegas's most spectacular sights—the four-block long Fremont Street Experience light canopy. The shows that run on it hourly, though a bit corny, are ever-changing and have to be seen to be believed.

The best way to see Fremont Street is to go with its flow—accept the free slot pulls and roulette spins you're offered, watch the shows on the light canopy, shop the weird souvenir stands, accumulate free souvenirs, and enjoy the inexpensive food and drink.

Numbers in the text correspond to numbers in the margin and on the Las Vegas Downtown map.

a good
walk

Two miles north of the traditional northern end of the Strip at Sahara Avenue, Las Vegas Boulevard meets Fremont Street in downtown Las Vegas. Fremont Street runs east from Main Street, which is five blocks west of, and parallel to, Las Vegas Boulevard. At the corner of Main and Fremont is the **Plaza Hotel and Casino** ❶ ▶, one of the most popular casinos for low rollers in town.

The heart of downtown Las Vegas, called Glitter Gulch, is the four-block stretch of Fremont Street that begins at the Plaza. It's where you find the pedestrian mall and high-tech canopy known as the **Fremont Street Experience** ❷. The **Neon Museum** ❸, an outdoor collection of some of the classic neon signs that once adorned the casinos of Old Vegas, lines Fremont. At the mall entrance, on the northeast corner of Fremont and Main streets, is the **Las Vegas Club Hotel and Casino** ❹, with a sports theme and a roomy casino. Walk a block northeast to Main and Stewart for **Main Street Station Casino, Brewery & Hotel** ❺, one of the most aesthetically pleasing casinos in Las Vegas, with its antiques, stained glass, and exquisite workmanship. Take the overhead pedestrian bridge from Main Street Station to the **California Hotel and Casino** ❻, where the clientele is predominantly Hawaiian.

Back on Fremont Street, between 1st and 2nd streets, is the block-long **Binion's Horseshoe Hotel and Casino** ❼, Las Vegas's quintessential old-time gambling den and the scene of some of the most intense action in town. Across 2nd Street is the **Fremont Hotel and Casino** ❽, with a photogenic neon sign outside and the superb Second Street Grill inside.

At Ogden Avenue and 3rd Street is the crowded **Lady Luck Casino and Hotel** ❾, which, with its big picture windows, is the brightest and airiest casino downtown. East two blocks on Fremont Street at the corner of 6th Street is the city's oldest standing casino, the **El Cortez Hotel** ❿, which opened for business in 1941; Bugsy Siegel started his short but memorable Vegas career here.

A two-block stroll south on 7th Street to Bridger Avenue will take you miles from the honky-tonk of downtown and bring you to the everyday life of the **Las Vegas Academy of International Studies, Visual and Performing Arts** ⓫, which, until 1993, was the esteemed Las Vegas High School.

Back on Fremont and 7th streets, walk three blocks west to the 34-story **Fitzgeralds Hotel and Casino** ⓬, the tallest building in Nevada until Stratosphere topped it—by a mere 700 feet. Coming out of the Fitz, walk a few feet west to 3rd Street and cross the street to get to the **Four Queens Hotel and Casino** ⓭, serving downtown low rollers since 1965.

The Four Queens occupies an entire block. If you walk all the way through the casino, you exit at the corner of 2nd and Fremont. Cross 2nd Street and visit the upscale **Golden Nugget Hotel and Casino** ⓮ to see the world's largest gold nugget.

Across 1st Street, atop the Fremont Street Experience logo shop, is **Vegas Vic** ⓯, who's been welcoming people to downtown Las Vegas since 1951. Back at the southeast corner of Fremont and Main is the venerable **Golden Gate Hotel** ⓰. Stripped of a facade that was installed over the original adobe in the mid-1950s, this building has been restored to its early Las Vegas appearance. The **Victory Hotel,** a block south on Main Street, was built in 1910 and retains its original balcony.

If you have a car or want to hop in a cab (don't walk—you pass through a pretty rough area), you can head over to **Cashman Field** ⑰ and the **Old Las Vegas Mormon Fort** ⑱, which are on the same site at the corner of Las Vegas Boulevard North and Washington Street, roughly 2 mi north of downtown. Two miles west of downtown, on Twin Lakes Drive, is the **Nevada State Museum and Historical Society** ⑲.

TIMING If you're staying within the tight confines of the central casino core of downtown, and not straying outside of Ogden Avenue and Fremont Street between Main and 6th streets, you can do a walking tour any time of the day or night and feel perfectly secure. But downtown is a little rough around the edges, so venturing beyond the security of the lights and crowds of the casino center after dark is not recommended. Extra-cautious travelers might want to walk to the Gold Spike (at Ogden Avenue and 4th Street) or the El Cortez (at Fremont and 6th streets) during daylight hours only. In conjunction with the opening of the Fremont Street Experience pedestrian mall, the city and casinos beefed up police (astride mountain bicycles) and security-guard presence in the downtown core, and it now seems safer than ever. But farther afield is still a no-man's-land when the sun is shining on the other side of the world.

This walk is only 8 to 10 city blocks long; all the casinos are small in comparison to those of the Strip, and most are right next to each other. To see everything in detail will take only a couple of hours.

What to See

❼ **Binion's Horseshoe Hotel and Casino.** The late Benny Binion wanted the Horseshoe to be a gambler's haven. So while other casinos have morphed into family attractions, Binion's still holds true to its founder's vision. With low ceilings and an Old Vegas charm, Binion's Horseshoe is a place to lay your money on the table, as many do for a living: Binion's hosts the World Series of Poker, an event that draws professional poker players from all over the world each spring. If you're keen to participate, all you need is a $10,000 ante and a lot of guts. But don't think of making a grab—Binion's also has one of the few remaining displays of guns in a casino in Nevada (including several of Benny's custom-gilt rifles and pistols). ✉ *128 E. Fremont St., Downtown* ☎ *702/382–1600 or 800/237–6537* ⊕ *www.binions.com.*

❻ **California Hotel and Casino.** Although it isn't so very different from most other downtown casinos (low ceilings and old-school charm), there's one quirk about this place: the California is the chief hangout for Hawaiians in Vegas. Though there's no real island theme, this hotel-casino has built a reputation for serving tourists from America's 50th state with enthusiastic hospitality. Saimin is served at the snack bar, the dealers wear Hawaiian shirts, and the carpeting is patterned with tropical flora. Upstairs is a karaoke bar; the later it gets in the evening (and the more inebriated the performers), the more fun it can be. A pedes-

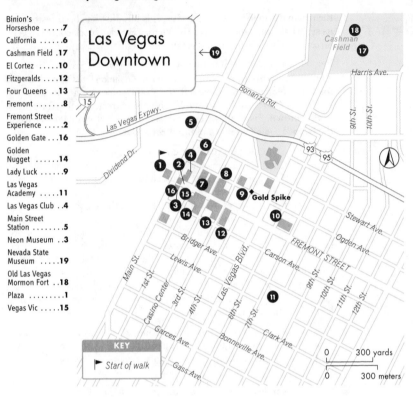

trian bridge connects to Main Street Station across the street, with a few shops on either side. ✉ *12 E. Ogden Ave., Downtown* ☎ *702/385–1222* ⊕ *www.thecal.com.*

⑰ Cashman Field. For a look at Las Vegas's other convention center, which doubles as a sports venue, drive a mile north from Fremont Street on Las Vegas Boulevard. The attractive facility has a 100,000-square-foot exhibit hall, 17,000 square feet of meeting space, and the 2,000-seat auditorium that was used as the courtroom for the trial of Wayne Newton's libel suit against NBC News. ✉ *850 Las Vegas Blvd. N, 2 mi north of its corner with Fremont St., Downtown* ☎ *702/386–7100.*

⑩ El Cortez Hotel. Bugsy Siegel showed up in Las Vegas in 1942 and immediately began to muscle into whatever downtown joints didn't resist him. He started out at the El Cortez, then sold his share and bought into the El Rancho Vegas, then sold that for $1 million, his seed capital to build the Flamingo. Though nothing from that time remains of the other joints, the original El Cortez still stands on the corner of Fremont and 6th streets—including the 60-year-old marquee. Inside, the old wing is delightfully frayed around the edges (contrary to appearances and popular opinion, the carpeting *has* been replaced since it opened) and is a great place to people-watch. The coffee shop serves the last round-the-clock $1 bacon-and-eggs breakfast special in town. The "new" wing, built in the early 1980s, houses the race and sports book, hotel lobby, and Roberta's, one of Las Vegas's great "bargain gourmet" restaurants. ⊠ *600 E. Fremont St., Downtown* ☎ *702/385–5200 or 800/ 634–6703* ⊕ *www.elcortez.net.*

⑫ **Fitzgeralds Hotel and Casino.** It's hard to miss this place. With a sweeping, illuminated rainbow stretched across its front facade, Fitzgeralds is easy to spot along Fremont Street's packed pedestrian mall. Inside, the entire casino is decked out in green, money and otherwise—pieces of the Blarney Stone are on display, direct from Ireland's famous Blarney Castle. Lucky's Lookout (off the Sports Bar) has the only second-floor outdoor balcony along Fremont Street. Arrive early to grab one of the patio lounge chairs and land one of the best spots to see the Fremont Street Experience light-and-sound shows. ⊠ *301 E. Fremont St., Downtown* ☎ *702/388–2400 or 800/274–5825* ⊕ *www.fitzgeralds.com.*

⑬ **Four Queens Hotel and Casino.** In the heart of Fremont Street, the Four Queens' radiating neon rivals the canopy's lightbulb display. Inside, the casino is dark and lushly appointed. A "Big Bertha" slot machine attracts attention at the 2nd Street entrance; at the 3rd Street entrance there's usually a free-pull promotion going on. Otherwise, the Four Queens is typical of the downtown joints: the gambling is the thing. ⊠ *202 E. Fremont St., Downtown* ☎ *702/385–4011 or 800/634–6045* ⊕ *www.fourqueens.com.*

❽ **Fremont Hotel and Casino.** A downtown staple since original owner Sam Levinson switched on its fiery neon back in 1956, the Fremont is a Vegas landmark. It was the first high-rise hotel on Fremont Street. Wayne Newton made his Las Vegas debut here. Even after Boyd Gaming bought the hotel in 1985, the Fremont has remained one of the city's cornerstones. Inside, the old-style casino is reminiscent of many of the other gambling halls downtown, although the neon surrounding the main pit is unique. The poker room walls are graced with interesting Western murals. ⊠ *200 E. Fremont St., Downtown* ☎ *702/385–3232* ⊕ *www.fremontcasino.com.*

★ ❷ **Fremont Street Experience.** In an effort to revive downtown Las Vegas, a partnership consisting of 10 hotels, the city, a privately owned corporation, and the Las Vegas Convention and Visitors Authority created the $70-million Fremont Street Experience, which debuted in 1995. The resulting pedestrian mall is festooned with souvenir stands and cafés, and features live entertainment ranging from mimes to rock bands, but the real attraction is overhead. The sign above this pedestrian mall is the largest electric sign in the world. (The next-largest sign, at the Las Vegas Hilton, is a 50th of its size.) The display is the length of 4½ football fields; the 2.1 million lightbulbs can produce 65,000 colors; the electricity required to run it could power nearly 2,000 homes; 208 speakers operate independently but combine for 540,000 watts of sound—and improvements are underway to beef things up even more. Six-minute light shows are presented on the hour after dark; it takes 31 computers and 100 gigabytes of memory to run the shows, and it's a don't-miss, only-in-Las Vegas experience. ⊠*Fremont St. from Main to 4th Sts., Downtown* ☎ *702/678–5600* ⊕ *www.vegasexperience.com.*

off the beaten path

GATEWAY ARTS DISTRICT – The emergence of the offbeat Gateway Arts District, bounded by South 7th, Main, Bonneville, and Oakey Streets on downtown's eastern edge, is generating excitement among the city's arts community. With a number of funky, independent art galleries in its confines, the area, officially named in 1998, is a growing, thriving cultural hub—a sort of antithesis to the Strip. Trickling into the neighborhood's residences are Las Vegas's alternative artists, musicians, and writers.

An intriguing concentration of antique shops and galleries is found on East Charleston Boulevard and Casino Center Drive, anchored by the **Arts Factory,** which houses several galleries. As part of the neighborhood's First Friday event, a cultural celebration on the first Friday of every month, the Arts Factory hosts art openings and special events. ⊠ *101 E. Charleston Blvd., Downtown* ☎ *702/676–1111* ⊕ *www.theartsfactory.com* ⊠ *Free* ⊙ *Tues.–Sun. 12 PM to 4 PM.*

need a break?

The Icehouse Lounge. The classy yet comfortable neighborhood bar between the Fremont Street Experience and the Gateway Arts District has a full menu and bar, which makes it a perfect end to an evening exploring the city's burgeoning arts culture. On weekends the Icehouse turns into a dance club, with deejays spinning downstairs near the bar and in the lounge upstairs. ⊠ *650 S. Main St., Downtown* ☎ *702/315–2570.*

⑯ Golden Gate Hotel. This is, without a doubt, the city's most historic hotel. It stands proudly, though dwarfed by the high-rises that have been built around it during its 95-year history. The tiny hotel-casino opened in 1906 (as the Hotel Nevada) and not much has changed here since then. Many of the original fixtures are still in place. The inspiration is San Francisco, as evidenced by the large historical photographs. This was the first hotel-casino to introduce the cheap shrimp cocktail to Las Vegas, and its 99-cent wonder is a perennial winner in the *Las Vegas Review-Journal's* annual Best of Las Vegas survey. A piano player entertains the crowds eating the crunchy crustacean cocktails in the deli. ⊠ *1 Fremont St., Downtown* ☎ *702/385–1906* ⊕ *www.goldengatecasino.net.*

⑭ Golden Nugget Hotel and Casino. The Golden Nugget is the classiest joint downtown. Its white marble walls, gold-plated slots, and etched-glass windows stand in stark contrast to the many dark and rustic hotels that surround Fremont Street. The Golden Nugget is also the largest hotel-casino downtown, encompassing 2½ city blocks (including the big parking garage). And it has the biggest and best pool downtown, a concrete courtyard surrounded by the hotel towers, always crowded with sunbathers and swimmers. The most amazing thing about the Golden Nugget, though, is the display of gold nuggets just off the lobby. Here you find the world's largest nugget, the 61-pound "Hand of Faith," along with several dozen other stunning specimens of the precious metal. ⊠ *129 E. Fremont St., Downtown* ☎ *702/385–7111 or 800/634–3454* ⊕ *www.goldennugget.com.*

❾ Lady Luck Casino and Hotel. The Lady Luck started out as Honest John's newsstand in 1964. It's grown a bit since then. The high-rise casino now includes 40,000 square feet of casino space designed specifically for tourists looking to lay their money down. A large neon arch beckons one and all. The prime-rib specials in the coffee shop are locally famous, as is the funbook handed out free to all out-of-town visitors; one of the coupons is good for a free three-minute long-distance phone call from a 1950s English phone booth. ✉ *206 N. 3rd St., Downtown* ☎ *702/477–3000 or 800/634–6580* ⊕ *www.ladylucklv.com.*

⓫ Las Vegas Academy of International Studies, Visual and Performing Arts. This historic structure, the oldest permanent school building in Las Vegas, was built as a high school in 1930 for $350,000. It's a state historical landmark, the only example of 1930s art deco architecture in the city. ✉ *315 S. 7th St., Downtown* ☎ *702/799–7800.*

❹ Las Vegas Club Hotel and Casino. Established in the early 1900s, the Las Vegas Club is a sports-theme casino and hotel. There's not much in the way of entertainment here, but value seekers are sure to appreciate the low-price meals and drinks. It was expanded in the mid-'90s and is now a bit of a maze, covering half a city block. The Las Vegas Club also houses a large private collection of sports memorabilia, some of which is displayed throughout the property. ✉ *18 E. Fremont St., Downtown* ☎ *702/385–1664 or 800/634–6532* ⊕ *www.playatlvc.com.*

★ ❺ Main Street Station Casino, Brewery & Hotel. Downtown's largest and best buffet can be found here, along with the only microbrewery downtown (the Triple 7 Brew Pub, with live entertainment every weekend night). The hotel has a fabulous collection of antiques, artifacts, and collectibles. There are self-guided tours of the collection, which includes Buffalo Bill Cody's private rail car; a fireplace from Scotland's Prestwick Castle; lamps that graced the streets of 18th-century Brussels; and beautiful statues, chandeliers, and woodwork from American mansions of long ago. There's even a piece of the Berlin Wall—in the men's room off the lobby. ✉ *200 N. Main St., Downtown* ☎ *702/387–1896 or 800/713–8933* ⊕ *www.mainstreetcasino.com.*

❸ Neon Museum. A giant neon horseman waves on the corner of Las Vegas Boulevard and Fremont Street. He's the first exhibit in the outdoor museum, a display of neon signs retired from various old Vegas landmarks. Others include the original Aladdin's lamp and the rider on horseback from the Hacienda Hotel. The signs can be seen along Fremont Street, and, at this writing, plans for an indoor venue were in the works. ✉ *731 S. 4th St., Downtown* ☎ *702/229–5366* ⊕ *www.ci.las-vegas.nv.us/neon.html* ⊠ *Free.*

☪ ⓭ Nevada State Museum and Historical Society. Regional history, from the time of the Spanish exploration to the building of Las Vegas after World War II, is the subject of this museum, which also covers the archaeology and anthropology of southern Nevada. It's near the lake in Lorenzi Park, an open space dotted with ponds and home to plants and animals native to the region. ✉ *700 E. Twin Lakes Dr., 2 mi west of corner of Fremont and Main Sts., Downtown* ☎ *702/486–5205* ⊠ *$2* ⊙ *Daily 9–5.*

Old Las Vegas Mormon Fort. Southern Nevada's oldest historical site was built by Mormons in 1855 as an agricultural mission to give refuge to travelers along the Salt Lake–Los Angeles trail, many of whom were bound for the California gold fields. Left to Native Americans after the gold rush, the adobe fort was later revitalized by a miner and his partners. In 1895 it was turned into a resort, and the city's first swimming pool was constructed by damming Las Vegas Creek. Today the restored fort contains more than half the original bricks. Antiques and artifacts help re-create a turn-of-the-20th-century Mormon living room. ⊠ *Washington Ave. and Las Vegas Blvd. N, at Cashman Field, enter through parking lot B, Downtown* ☎ *702/486–3511* ⊕ *www.state.nv.us* ✆ *$2* ◌ *Daily 8:30–4:30.*

Plaza Hotel and Casino. Jackie Gaughan is a Las Vegas legend. He spent time in Nevada during World War II, first in Las Vegas and later in Tonopah, where he trained gunners for the Air Corps' B-17 bombers. He and his wife Roberta (Bertie) and their two sons, the late Jackie Jr. and Michael (who became a casino mogul himself), settled here for good in 1951. He bought a 3% interest in the old downtown Boulder Club on Fremont Street, where the Horseshoe now stands. A short time later he bought a 3% interest in the Flamingo Hotel on the Strip. In 1961 he opened the Las Vegas Club and in 1963 he bought the Cortez. He purchased the Union Plaza Hotel & Casino in 1971 and the Gold Spike Hotel & Casino in 1983. The Plaza sits at the end of Fremont Street, looming over the Fremont Street Experience. It's a sleeper, but it does have low table minimums and great nickel machines, live lounge entertainment, excellent snack-bar food at rock-bottom prices, and a hall of mirrors lining the south staircase. Also here is the largest downtown showroom (one of only three), a second-floor pool deck, and the Center Stage Restaurant, which sits in a dome looking right down the throat of Glitter Gulch. ⊠ *1 Main St., Downtown* ☎ *702/386–2110 or 800/634–6575* ⊕ *www.plazahotelcasino.com.*

Vegas Vic. The famous Las Vegas icon known as Vegas Vic is about the same age as the average Las Vegas visitor. The original version of this well-known landmark was unveiled in 1947, but was replaced by a newer version in 1951. Now Vegas Vic, a 50-foot-tall neon cowboy, stands outside the Pioneer Club, waving to visitors. Vegas Vic's neon sidekick, Sassy Sally, went up across the street in 1980.

CASINOS

2

Updated by
Mike
Weatherford

CONVENTIONAL WISDOM NOTWITHSTANDING, you *can* win in the casinos and many people do. But, as explained in Chapter 9, the odds are riding against you. And that's just for starters. The dazzling lights, the free beer and cocktails, the play money, the absence of windows and clocks, even the oxygen—and, lately, seductive aromas—pumped into the air are all calculated to overwhelm you with a sense of holiday impetuousness that keeps you reaching into your pocket or purse for the green.

Tens of millions of people who *don't* know the odds of, or the strategies for, casino games come to Las Vegas every year, and some of them even win now and then. But let's face it: most people go home with a lighter wallet. Las Vegas casinos make a fortune by taking a big bite out of millions of bankrolls. With table games, casinos keep on average 15% of the cash a player gives for chips; with the slot machines they hold around 25%.

So walk into the casino knowing that the house always has the edge. But who knows, you could beat the odds and walk away a winner. Spend a little time beforehand memorizing the game rules, studying casino etiquette, and taking one of the free gambling lessons offered at most casinos. Then you can join the tables with the all the aplomb of James Bond.

How Not to Go Broke

You should decide before leaving on your vacation how much money you will spend on gambling. This is your gambling bankroll. Gambling newbies are shocked at how quickly the bankroll disappears at the table. As a rule of thumb, a $1,000 bankroll for a weekend trip of gambling lets you bet $5 to $10 a hand at blackjack or play 25¢ slots. That's if you hope to get in five hours of gambling. If you bet $25 a hand at blackjack with the $1,000 bankroll you will most likely run out of money within an hour. ATM or credit card cash withdrawals carry hefty surcharges and should be avoided at all times. A cash advance also leads to you gambling with money you don't have and its devastating consequences.

If you want to shrink the casino's edge over you, take the time to read up on the game strategy in Chapter 9. Then, when you have some idea of the basics, attend the free gambling lessons provided at most major casinos. Even if you think you know the rules, these lessons give you an opportunity to play the game at an actual session and learn the etiquette using practice chips instead of your own cash. Call ahead and get the exact schedule of these free lessons. Most gift shops also sell a small plastic card of a rough strategy for the various games. You can have one in hand as you play your game of choice.

THE CASINOS

This guide progresses as most Las Vegas vacations do, starting with the casinos on the Strip, or Las Vegas Boulevard South, then continuing to the growing ranks of major off-Strip and "locals" casinos (those frequented by area residents). After that come the downtown casinos on and near Fremont Street, then the casinos on the "Boulder Strip" and the "Rancho Strip." The final journey is to the farthest-out casinos in

Getting In & Around Casinos can be confusing places for the first-time visitor. They tend to be large, open rooms full of people who seem to know exactly what they're doing, while you wander around lost. Cameras hung from the ceiling watch your movements, and all the security guards, pit bosses, and dealers seem to be doing the same. Worst of all, there are no signs, announcements, or tour guides to inform newcomers of the rules of behavior. So we'll do that right here.

2

All players must be at least 21 years of age with no exceptions. If you're playing a slot with a child by your side, a security guard will quickly appear (dispatched by casino surveillance) and ask you to leave. But you can walk through the casino with your youngster in tow; as long as you're on the move, you're OK.

Your personal electronic items are also frowned upon in the casino. No electronics, including cell phones, can be used while seated at a casino game. The thick walls of most large casinos block cell phone reception anyhow so you have to walk outside to get a dial tone. In the sports book of the casino, pagers and cell phones cannot be used at all.

Casinos are traditionally camera-shy, but no longer as stringent about no-photography rules that for years protected players; management feared they would get up and leave if a camera was pointed their way. Gambling is now more accepted as a mainstream pastime, and it's hard to separate the gaming floor from the public right-of-way in many a casino. When in doubt, ask a security guard.

Smokers, on the other hand, find casinos a welcome relief. Those who are annoyed by cigarette or cigar smoke will need to find a no-smoking table or slots area. The casinos' smoke permeates clothing quickly.

The security of your person and pocketbook shouldn't be forgotten in the bustle of the casino. Although the casino tries to protect its patrons with omnipresent security cameras and guards, the crowds and distractions overwhelm their vigilance. You probably won't be mugged inside a casino, but theft or short-changing can easily happen. Keep your purse in your lap. Casino chips should not be left on the table under the dealer's protection while you take a quick bathroom break. Recount any chips and cash that casino personnel hand over to you immediately—once you leave the table or cage, you cannot get a mistake corrected. Finally, do not hesitate to request that a security guard escort you to the casino parking lot late at night, especially in downtown Las Vegas.

Joining the Games Almost all casinos offer craps, blackjack, slots, video poker, and roulette. The major casinos will, in addition, have live poker, sports betting, baccarat, keno, and an ever-growing list of table games. Stick to video poker, slots, and roulette if you're nervous about the arcane rules and want a relaxing visit.

Table games, especially blackjack and craps, offer the novice the greatest challenges. However, these games remain two of the most popular in Las Vegas. Free daily lessons at most Strip casinos will warm the tables. The beginner's course will let you belly up to the tables with confidence. Don't hesitate to ask any question you like at the table. If a dealer doesn't answer, or is rude, walk away to another table—or another casino. At some of the smaller and less crowded gambling houses, dealers will take time to orient players to new games. If you're a newcomer to the tables, avoid the larger houses, especially at peak hours, because the personnel may be too busy to help you.

Before you sit down at a table, look at the little placard that announces the betting minimum and maximum. Most casinos offer a range of betting minimums, but the low minimum tables tend to be packed. For example, blackjack tables have minimums of $1 to $500 and maximums up to $10,000. Minimums in casinos on the Strip are generally higher than those of downtown casinos.

Consider also the timing of your casino visit. Las Vegas wakes up around lunchtime, then peaks between 11 PM and midnight. If you arrive at a busy hour, tables may be scarce at the minimums you desire. Weekends are also the busiest time of the week for Vegas as half of California drives in for a quick roll.

Tipping

Tipping is a key element of casino etiquette. Dealers are paid minimum wage at the casinos, and they expect to be tipped when you are winning. It's neither mandatory nor necessary, however, it's only up to your own discretion. Some dealers will "suggest" a tip of 10% of your net win, but this is very generous on your part. Slipping a dealer or change person a chip is like any other tip: a small gratuity for services rendered. This small generosity usually relaxes the dealer, and thus the game, considerably. At most casinos, dealers pool their tips and then split them evenly. So be aware that no matter how much you toke a good dealer, he or she will receive only a percentage. Cocktail waitresses expect $1 for each drink brought to you. Valet parkers should receive $2 or $3.

---

the fast-growing suburb of Henderson. The listings in each area are arranged in alphabetical order. These descriptions are intended to help you find the casinos that will most appeal to you. If you'd like to save time by sleeping where you gamble, Chapter 4 has details on the hotels in which most of these casinos are found. All the casinos have restaurants and most have all-you-can-eat buffets so you can also eat where you sleep and gamble.

The Strip

The Strip casinos, all along Las Vegas Boulevard, are packed in so tight you see nothing when you drive by but one frenetic neon sign on top of another. Strip casinos run the gamut in size and style, from the overwhelming spectacle of the MGM Grand to the small pit at Slots–A–Fun, and from low-roller heaven at Circus Circus to high-roller tension at Bellagio. In general Strip casinos are big and ritzy, with high playing minimums and few comps to give to visitors. (If you're looking for a

$5 blackjack table, you won't find it here; head downtown or visit the "locals" casinos in residential neighborhoods). Strip casinos have even upped their house edge by embracing a "6-to-5" payoff on blackjack instead of the traditional 1½ times the amount of the bet. Nonetheless, the Strip welcomes all comers, no matter what they're wearing. When it comes right down to it, the casinos really care about only one aspect of your attire: that it include a wallet or purse from which you can easily remove your cash.

Aladdin Resort and Casino/Planet Hollywood. The Aladdin was scheduled to change hands and transform into Planet Hollywood, an extension of the movie-theme restaurant chain from the same company controlled by Robert Earl, in 2004. The Aladdin was redeveloped on its original site in 2000 but quickly went bankrupt. The small and generally underwhelming casino has hard-to-find entrances concealed by an elevated sidewalk along the Strip and the labyrinthine Desert Passage mall. Earl's plans make strides to resolve the casino's problematic design, but how soon and in what order is up in the air (the Aladdin name was to stick until at least $90 million of improvement was complete). Two design elements likely won't change: an elevated lounge that overlooks the casino and fills it with live music, and an entirely separate, high-roller casino on the second floor, known as the London Club during the Aladdin era. Table and machine limits upstairs are high, and dealers in tuxes contribute to a James Bond vibe. Parking at the Aladdin involves a wearying walk through the shopping mall, so use the valets if possible. ✉ *3667 Las Vegas Blvd. S, Center Strip* ☎ *702/785–5555 or 877/333–9474.*

Bally's Las Vegas. Bally's owns a huge chunk of one of the most popular intersections in the world—it's across the street from the Flamingo, Caesars Palace, and Bellagio—and it accommodates a perpetually large convention crowd of older players. Despite the prime location, Bally's threatened to become a dormitory annex to flashier sister property Paris, to which it is connected (via a tunnel that replaced the showroom where Dean Martin and Frank Sinatra once performed), until parent company Caesars Entertainment took steps to freshen up Bally's, adding a tequila bar and retro-theme lounge off the casino floor. The 67,000-square-foot casino proper is laid out in an old-fashioned rectangle that offers a good, organized contrast to the busy, heavily themed Paris. The monorail that once connected Bally's to the MGM was incorporated into the larger Strip monorail. If you're trying to park at Bally's, use the Paris garage for a one-minute walk to the casino. ✉ *3645 Las Vegas Blvd. S, Center Strip* ☎ *800/634–3434.*

Barbary Coast Hotel and Casino. The Barbary Coast casino is modeled after late-19th-century San Francisco saloons, with Victorian chandeliers and lamps, tasteful stained-glass signs (including the largest stained-glass mural in the world), and cocktail waitresses who wear garters on their thighs. The Coast is known as a "sweat shop" among blackjack and craps players, meaning the bosses take it personally when you win, but casino table minimums are frequently lower than its larger neighbors. The video poker is playable (the pay schedules are not prohibitive) and the slot club is pretty good, with decent, if not great, cash back and

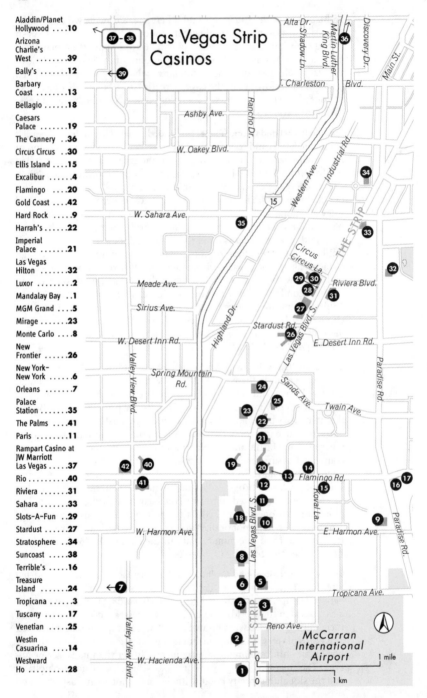

Las Vegas Strip Casinos

benefits. This joint with 680 machines is usually fairly crowded, and it now seems almost unusually small compared to its surrounding neighbors: Caesars Palace, the Flamingo, and Bally's. ✉ *3595 Las Vegas Blvd. S, Center Strip* ☎ *888/227–2279.*

Bellagio Las Vegas. Bellagio is the most opulent and expensive casino ever built anywhere on Earth. It's roomy, luxurious, and filled with a big-money international elite surrounded by gawking tourists. Under its hushed orange canopies you can easily spot a high roller betting $5,000 a hand as if it were pennies. Yet 5¢ slots are tucked in the back corners somewhere for low rollers and excellent blackjack games are offered for serious players; you might even play for $5 per hand before midday. There's also enough room on the floor for a designated craps-table area. The outstanding, large live poker room, famous from the TV poker fad, sees some serious piles of chips in the pot, but you're better off playing video poker almost anywhere else. The race and sports book is super high-tech; each seductive leather seat is equipped with its own TV monitor. Parents take note: those under 18 are unwelcome everywhere within Bellagio, but especially in the casino. ✉ *3600 Las Vegas Blvd. S, Center Strip* ☎ *702/693–7111.*

Caesars Palace. At 129,000 square feet, Caesars is the never-ending casino, and in recent years one of constant transition. Two sprawling wings used to change character from one end of the property to the other, but a gradual remodeling brought most of the casino space into alignment with the faux–ancient Roman theme of the adjacent Forum Shops mall. Much of the original south casino, however, retains its 1966 splendor. The old wing—low ceiling, high stakes—is still where you find the more *serious* older gamblers. The newer Olympic Casino wing, with its high ceiling, soaring marble columns, graceful rooftop arches, and lower limits, embraces the middle market with 5¢ and 25¢ slots. In 2004, 35,000 square feet of connecting casino space, including an aquatic-theme bar with live sea horses, made for easier maneuvering between wings. The Forum Casino, adjacent to the mall, was remodeled to service the 4,000-seat Colosseum where Celine Dion performs. It has a "fast casual" food court, the Cypress Street Marketplace, selling dishes such as pizza and Asian noodles. An outdoor plaza and live entertainment area on top of a new underground parking garage at the south end is geared to pedestrians at the Flamingo Road intersection. The huge race and sports book with its megadisplay must be seen to be believed. Wear your walking shoes and prepare to get lost in this Roman empire which, with its various staircases, was not designed for gamblers with mobility problems. You can even get your picture taken with Caesar, Cleopatra, and the centurion guard. ✉ *3570 Las Vegas Blvd. S, Center Strip* ☎ *877/ 427–7243.*

Circus Circus. Only in Las Vegas would you find a 125-foot high neon sign of a clown sucking a lollipop next to a statue of a nude dancer. And only in Las Vegas could you find Circus Circus, the tent-shape pink casino with live circus acts performing over gamblers' heads. The aging Circus Circus is low-roller and poor-service central, with nickel slots galore amid its 101,000 square feet of casino floor and 2,200 gaming machines. The two must-see attractions here are the slot carousel—20 slots sit on a revolving platform, and players ride in circles as they operate the machines—and the merry-go-round bar, which sits atop the carousel on the midway, with actual carousel horses. Those under 21 can whoop it up in a mezzanine midway of carnival games and circus acts upstairs. The main casino below is low-ceilinged, cramped, and claustrophobic. A coffee shop and a no-frills sports book with individual desktop TVs are set back from the main action. There's a secondary casino with a deli snack bar and pizzeria. ⊠ *2880 Las Vegas Blvd. S, North Strip* ☎ *877/224–7287.*

Excalibur Hotel and Casino. This giant medieval-theme casino offers an immense gaming floor in one continuous room, and the ringing of the Merlin slot machines can become overpowering at times. As the most budget-minded of the three Mandalay Resorts casinos linked by free monorail or pedestrian walkway (to Luxor and Mandalay Bay), it's the place to find $5 blackjack tables and lots of them, in a long straight row that bisects the huge room. There's also plenty of space for a busy poker room that advertises a friendly "kitchen table" game, an expansive sports book with its own circular bar, and even a large keno lounge with a big-screen TV to bide the time between games. The Minstrel Lounge feeds live music into at least a part of the casino, and the Sherwood Cafe is a refueling stop off the casino floor; the other restaurants and child-oriented attractions are either in the basement arcade or on the second floor. The Excalibur is known for a readily available funbook with some good coupons, and there's usually a free-pull promotion going on. The King's Pavilion, a circular bar in the middle of the casino, is a good perch from which to watch the action. ⊠ *3850 Las Vegas Blvd. S, South Strip* ☎ *800/937–7777.*

Flamingo Las Vegas. Modern Las Vegas began here when Bugsy Siegel imported Miami luxury to the desert. Bugsy, of course, wasn't able to hang around long enough to experience the impact of his vision and would no longer recognize any of his original construction, which has been demolished or folded into the larger property. A huge 77,000-square-foot casino services a huge hotel (3,642 rooms). There are more than 70 tables and 2,000 machines in two large gaming areas. The surrounding hotel features are more interesting than the casino proper, which is otherwise surprisingly plain Jane: the sports book is proportionately small, and there is no live music lounge. Like other casinos run by corporate parent Caesars Entertainment, single-deck blackjack players will have to settle for a 6-to-5 payoff on "naturals" unless they're willing to bet $50 or $100 per hand. The Flamingo is not completely devoid of charm, however. Unlike many strip casinos, it's built right up to the sidewalk for easy pedestrian access, and the oval Bugsy's Bar is only a few feet from the tables, letting imbibers vicariously experience the action. The Flamingo as a whole is being gradually remodeled in order to expand its appeal beyond the older crowd with which it has long been associated. A hallway at the casino's north end leads to Jimmy Buffet's Margaritaville nightclub and restaurant. The Irish-theme casino annex next door—the two-story **O'Sheas Casino**—is the place for low rollers, low-limit poker players, and small-time racing and sports bettors. ✉ *3555 Las Vegas Blvd. S, Center Strip* ☎ *800/732–2111.*

Harrah's Las Vegas Casino & Hotel. Carnival music from outside of the Mardi Gras–theme Harrah's will get your heart pumping from far down the sidewalk. The slots are mere feet from the sidewalk, so step inside for a quick look while you're strolling by. Dealers tend to be friendly in this festive purple, green, and gold casino. Harrah's has added some good amenities—the second-floor Range steak house, the outdoor Carnaval Court lounge—around the edges of a property that dates back to 1972. But they haven't changed the main casino, which is still of the low-ceiling, rambling old-Vegas variety. Be prepared to get lost trying to navigate the sprawling, seemingly endless floor of the 86,654-square-foot casino. The indoor La Playa lounge is off to one end and doesn't really contribute to the larger casino atmosphere. There are 70 tables with 13 varieties of games, more than 1,300 reel slots, and 300 video poker games. Blackjack tables are mostly $15 and $25 minimums on weekends. Novelty games such as Caribbean Stud and Boston 5 Stud Poker share table space. Harrah's Total Gold is a nationwide player's club: you can play at any of Harrah's 26 casinos around the United States using a single account number. ✉ *3475 Las Vegas Blvd. S, Center Strip* ☎ *800/634–6765.*

Imperial Palace Hotel and Casino. A blue pagoda-style building with an Asian theme, this house of dragons does a booming business with tour groups. Plan on spending a few minutes finding your way around its 75,000 square feet of gaming space (there are few signs). Except for the 2002 addition of a youthful bar called Tequila Joe's, the Imperial Palace joins the Riviera as the only sizeable Strip properties to still look exactly as they did in the '80s, without any significant facelifts or improvements. However this aging dowager of the Strip is a budget-minded alternative to its hifalutin' neighbors. Table minimums entice low rollers, but the rules generally hurt the player. Perhaps because it's by itself on an upper floor, the race and sports book equipped with 230 individual TV screens is an old favorite on the Strip. The 2002 death of owner Ralph Engelstad created uncertainty as to whether this faded property—which coasts to a large degree on the appeal of its prime location—would perk up or continue its slow fade. The casino did come up with one innovative marketing twist in 2003: Expanding on the image of its "Legends in Concert" show, the IP introduced "Dealertainers" at the blackjack tables, allowing you to try your luck against Elvis or Michael Jackson lookalikes. ✉ *3535 Las Vegas Blvd. S, Center Strip* ☎ *800/634–6441.*

Luxor Resort & Casino. The magnificent bronze-tint pyramid is arguably the most unusual casino in the world, inside and out. Luxor's casino is not only huge, it's also round, so it will take some time to get your bearings. (Orient yourself by looking for periphery landmarks such as the coffee shop, sports book, and lounge.) Comps are tough to come by but, as a Mandalay Resort Group property, Luxor easily transfers your points to its sister properties. You find surprisingly fresh air and a muted noise level as a solid middle-class and black-clad-chic crowd gawk at this eighth wonder of the world. Cool your heels on the free tram to

Mandalay Bay and Excalibur. ✉ *3900 Las Vegas Blvd. S, South Strip* ☎ *888/777–0188.*

Mandalay Bay Resort & Casino. Pagodas and gardens rise out of the vast floors of this Asian-theme newcomer to the ranks of luxury high-roller casinos. Drool at the hordes of fabulous beautiful people and millionaires crowding the tables of this very hip casino, which feels more casual and lively than pretentious counterparts such as Bellagio or the Venetian. Low rollers will be able to find $5 tables on weekdays, but by sunset will have to hop on the monorail to the Luxor or Excalibur to find blackjack tables with less than a $10 or $25 limit. Slot players, however, won't have to search the dark corners to find nickel or quarter machines. The comp program links Mandalay Bay with its sister properties around Las Vegas; play here and then try for freebies at other casinos. Although its wide-open spaces could terrify an agoraphobe, Mandalay Bay is very well organized and its pleasant walkways make wheelchair navigation a breeze. For a break from the action, sit amid the virtual vegetation, rock waterfalls, and lily pond of the Coral Reef Lounge, one of the largest lounges in town. ✉ *3950 Las Vegas Blvd. S, South Strip* ☎ *877/632–7000.*

MGM Grand Hotel and Casino. The MGM has been virtually rebuilt since it first opened with an ill-fated budget family appeal in late 1993. It still tries (perhaps a little too hard) to be something for everyone, but changes from 2002 to 2004 reflect a deepening focus on the business-convention market and a clientele that's either well-heeled or traveling on an expense account. Additions such as the Zuri lounge—a tony martini bar draped in hanging fabric—gradually phased out the original motif of lions and vintage movie photos. In 2003 the "ultralounge" Tabu quickly became the toast of the trendy nightclub crowd. But don't worry, kids, there's still a lion habitat on the casino's west perimeter. The biggest of the Las Vegas casinos, the MGM has a staggering 171,500 square feet of gaming, which include 3,500 slot machines and 165 table games with high minimums (blackjack and roulette mostly starting at $10; you might find a $5 table in the afternoon if you look hard enough). The Strip entrance is slot-heavy, with the Show Bar lounge elevating its bandstand and bands to tower over players. A separate high-roller casino falls in the middle of the long hike to the "restaurant row," Grand Garden arena, and massive sports book with movie-size screens on the east side. You also find symmetrical rows of table games on this end, including poor-odds novelties such as Casino War. It's another good hike from the parking garage to the casino. However, those in a wheelchair will appreciate the spacious aisles and well-spaced slot machines. Search the retail corridor between the hotel and garage for the Strip monorail. ✉ *3799 Las Vegas Blvd. S, South Strip* ☎ *800/929–1111.*

★ **Mirage Hotel and Casino.** The Mirage rang in the modern era of Las Vegas and has held up impressively to competition both from outside and within its own corporate family. The casino has high minimums (such as $500 slots and a plush private pit where the minimum bet is $1,000), ionospheric maximums, and an overall atmosphere of sophisticated fun. Blackjack at the Mirage has some of the best rules of any Strip casino, while single-zero roulette offers the gambler a strong game. The poker room has a stellar reputation for good action, low and high. The look is rainforest rustic: pits are distinguished by separate thatch roofs. There's even a lush tropical garden leading into the main casino to clean your lungs with fresh air. The race and sports book at the south end is full of giant screens that resemble NASA's mission control. The cumulative effect is entirely energizing for a casino. The Mirage's tropical design scheme was partly inspired by the Siegfried & Roy show and their "Jungle Palace" home; despite Roy Horn's near-fatal tiger bite in 2003, the hotel planned to keep the outdoor Secret Garden of Siegfried & Roy animal and dolphin attraction, as well as the white-tiger display near the south exit on the Caesars Palace side. If your feet are tired there's a complimentary slow-moving tram to Treasure Island next door. ⊠ *3400 Las Vegas Blvd. S, Center Strip* ☎ *800/627–6667.*

Monte Carlo Resort and Casino. Modeled after the opulent Place du Casino in Monaco, the Las Vegas version of Monte Carlo replicates its sophistication and opulence with a bright and graciously laid-out casino. The theme elements are unobtrusive and take a background role, however, rather than trying to steal the show as they do at some of the other places. Unpretentious, with a simple flow, the casino is well-organized, considering that it has 2,100 machines and 95 tables quietly serving the mid-level players drawn by the hotel's mid-price room rates. The single-zero roulette wheels are a nice plus here. Points on the One Club card are transferable to other Mandalay Resorts Group properties. ⊠ *3770 Las Vegas Blvd. S, South Strip* ☎ *800/311–8999.*

New Frontier Hotel and Gambling Hall. It's hard to get too excited about a casino that is on borrowed time. The lot is prime real estate for redevelopment as soon as Wynn Las Vegas opens on the former Desert Inn grounds across the Strip. Until the day comes when the New Frontier is imploded, it remains a dingy Western-theme joint for low-rollers, with low-minimum blackjack tables to beckon beginning players. A bingo room, rare for the Strip, occupies a former restaurant on the West side of the property. Beginning live poker lessons are given every day but Sunday. ⊠ *3120 Las Vegas Blvd. S, North Strip* ☎ *800/634–6966.*

New York–New York Hotel and Casino. Enter a fantasy vision of Gotham City, with details such as names on mailboxes and brownstone apartment facades with air-conditioners in the windows. This casino epitomizes Las Vegas's 1990s love affair with intricate themes worthy of a Hollywood backlot. The main casino floor is adorned with artificial trees full of twinkling lights. Space limitations make it more crowded and cramped than other casinos of recent vintage (perhaps a fitting replica of the casino's namesake). Blackjack minimums of $10 to $25 dominate. A remodeled Big Apple Bar almost literally puts bands on a pedestal, towering over the casino floor. Artificial hedges and a fountain set off Gaming on the Green, a separate area for high-limit slots and table games. ⊠ *3790 Las Vegas Blvd. S, South Strip* ☎ *702/740–6969.*

Paris Las Vegas. The spacious and whimsical dazzler of a casino may make you forget that you won't find many breaks here. The casino is all

LAS VEGAS LINGO

BEFORE YOU START *gambling, you'll want to learn some key words in the local language.*

Bankroll. *The amount of cash an individual has to gamble with.*

Black chip. *$100 casino chip, usually black.*

Buy-in. *The amount of cash with which a player enters a game.*

Cage. *The casino cashier station where you can exchange your chips for cash.*

Check. *Another name for a casino chip.*

Comp. *A gift from the casino of a complimentary drink, room, dinner, or show; a freebie.*

Eye. *The overhead video surveillance system and its human monitors in a casino.*

Full-pay video poker. *A video poker game that, if you know perfect strategy, gives you an edge over the casino.*

Green chip. *$25 casino chip, usually green.*

Grind joint. *A gambling house that promotes low table minimums and slot denominations.*

High roller. *A casino customer who plays with a bankroll of $5,000 or more. Some grind joints consider a $1,000 bankroll to be high-roller action; some premium joints require a $10,000 bankroll.*

Hold. *The house profit from all the wagers; what the casino wins.*

Live poker. *Traditional poker games such as seven-card stud that are played against other individuals and not the casino.*

Low roller. *A typical tourist making 25¢ slot machine bets or $1 and $2 table-game bets.*

Marker. *A casino IOU. Players sign markers and get chips at the tables; they then pay off the markers with chips or cash.*

Pit. *A group of tables forming a closed circle on the casino floor. The pit bosses and dealers stand in the middle and serve the customers who sit on the outside. Visitors can't walk into the middle of the pit.*

Pit boss. *The person who supervises the action on the gaming tables.*

Player's card. *A card with a magnetic stripe on it used to track a gambler's activities in a casino. A player's card makes it easy for the casino to rate you and therefore give you comps.*

Rating. *Tracking a gambler's average bet, length of time played, and net loss. Getting rated helps you get comps.*

RFB. *The cream of comps—room, food, and beverage, courtesy of the casino. All you have to do is play $75–$250 a hand for four hours a day.*

Red chip. *$5 casino chip, usually red.*

Shill. *A person employed by the casino to sit at the tables and play games during the less busy hours—with the casino's money. Shills are only used in live poker games.*

Sports book. *The casino area for sports betting.*

Sweating the money. *Pit boss nervousness and anger toward a winning player.*

Table games. *All games of chance such as blackjack and craps played against the casino with the help of a dealer.*

Toke. *A tip (short for token, or token of your esteem). This may be the word you'll hear most often; many of the folks you encounter will be expecting a toke.*

decked out in Gallic regalia, including village facades with arched windows, fake trees, and three massive legs of the 50-story Eiffel Tower replica jutting through the roof and resting on the floor. Game rules are poor for the player; blackjack players frown at the 6-to-5 payoff for a natural. The main casino floor conveys a dreamlike feeling under an artificial pastoral blue sky dotted with white clouds, and the attention to French detail, down to fancy floral wash basins in the Provençal-style bathrooms, adds up to a charming yet classy casino. A live music lounge, Le Cabaret, can be seen and heard in the larger casino. There's even a cobblestone walkway to Bally's, with a mime on the loose and kiosks selling French pastries. As all the dealers say, *bon chance*! ⊠ *3655 Las Vegas Blvd. S, Center Strip* ☎ *800/634-6753.*

Riviera Hotel and Casino. This vaguely French-theme casino is getting a little run-down and dumpy, suffering from lack of new investment in recent years while on the selling block. There's been little follow up to its last interesting addition, a separate slot area on the north side of the building, known as Nickel Town and serviced by a budget snack bar. The main casino is of the low-ceiling, smoke-filled variety (it was used as a '70s setting for the movie *Casino*). It does, however, have a big race and sports book, a convenient fast-food court, nearly 90 table games, betting minimums of mostly $5 and $10, and more than 1,500 slot and video-poker machines. What was once the open LeBistro lounge is now a cabaret for ticketed acts, so there's less energy—or distraction, depending on how one felt about the music—in the casino. ⊠ *2901 Las Vegas Blvd. S, North Strip* ☎ *800/634-6753.*

Sahara Hotel and Casino. The middle-market casino has a clean and unobtrusive Arabian theme. Some of the peripheral changes by bargain-minded 1990s owner Bill Bennett—the buffet, a theater for magic shows—were dubious, but the casino proper has benefited from a lighter, brighter look. The smartest move has been its low-minimum blackjack tables. Instead of trying to keep up with the South Strip, the Sahara went the opposite direction and became the only place on the Strip to offer primarily $1 tables: a dozen of them are nearly full on a typical weekend night, with only one $10 table among them. Full-pay video poker and very generous slot payouts make this casino a good destination for the gambler minimizing the house edge. The friendly player's club and frequent gambling promotions enhance its popularity. In early 2004 the Sahara revived the legacy of its Casbar lounge by booking better-than-average free entertainment. A big, square, "Cheers"-style bar near the small sports book adds to the friendly feel. ⊠ *2535 Las Vegas Blvd. S, North Strip* ☎ *702/737-2111.*

Slots–A–Fun. Slots is a fun little joint to go slumming in without feeling like you're in a slum. As you leave Circus Circus, you are handed a sheet of coupons for free popcorn, 50¢ hot dogs, 99¢ shrimp cocktails, free pulls of a slot machine, and a free gift (usually a key chain). Redeem them at this noisy, smoky, 17,700-square-foot casino next door, where you will find 586 slots and 22 tables offering plenty of $1 and $2 blackjack. ⊠ *2880 Las Vegas Blvd. S, North Strip* ☎ *702/734-0410.*

Stardust Hotel and Casino. The Stardust dates back to the 1950s and has been expanded umpteen times, but now has the subdued atmosphere of a casino that serves primarily as a "dormitory" for more exciting properties. Still, because of its size and sprawling layout, the Stardust never feels overly crowded or claustrophobic. It's a good place to play $2 craps, $5 blackjack, and low-limit poker. The slot club offers excellent perks (especially constant free-room offers). The sports book is the most exceptional part of the casino. It's nationally famous for the "Stardust line," which is usually the first odds posted for upcoming games; for that reason, radio sports talk shows emanate from the Stardust each day. ✉ *3000 Las Vegas Blvd. S, North Strip* ☎ *800/634–6757.*

Stratosphere Hotel Tower and Casino. Good games and a gradual remodeling of the original, unappealing World's Fair theme have made the Stratosphere's 80,000-square-foot casino worth a second look if you were underwhelmed or passed it by on the way to the tower during your original visit. The off-the-beaten-track location forces the casino managers to offer often noticeably better odds at the games. You see signs advertising 98% RETURN ON DOLLAR SLOTS and 100% RETURN ON QUARTER VIDEO POKER. (And no, they can't claim it if it's not true.) One-hundred-times odds at the crap tables, and a single-zero roulette wheel or two give the gambler a good shot at breaking even. The slot club offers frequent promotions, including comps to meals at the top of the tower, with its unparalleled view. Parking at the Stratosphere is easy and unsnarled by heavy traffic. Walking here from other casinos, however, will wear out your feet. ✉ *2000 Las Vegas Blvd. S, North Strip* ☎ *800/998–6937.*

Treasure Island Las Vegas (TI). The jury is still out on Treasure Island's decision to pursue the younger Palms–Hard Rock crowd by nicknaming itself TI and luring Canter's Deli from Hollywood. The distinctive skull-and-crossbones outdoor sign has been replaced, along with all vestiges of the pirate theme indoors. The main casino looks much like that of its corporate big brother, the MGM Grand Hotel: upscale and attractive, yet lacking a specific theme. Even the popular pyrotechnic pirate show outdoors at Buccaneer Bay has been restaged with the new name *The Sirens of TI* to focus on the physical charms of the new female pirate crew. The crowds are still ferocious and create traffic-flow problems in the somewhat cramped casino each time the daily pirate performances end. Race- and sports-betting fans find an oasis in the black leather chairs and desks with individual TV screens found north of the main traffic flow in the sports book. As with most of the MGM Mirage properties, expect $15 table minimums on a Saturday night. A free tram can take you next door to the Mirage. ✉ *3300 Las Vegas Blvd. S, Center Strip* ☎ *800/944–7444.*

Tropicana Resort and Casino. The Trop's background is one of the lushest in town, having had more than 40 years to fill in. Its luxuriant 5-acre water park has swim-up blackjack: yes, you can actually sit in the pool and play 21. Stuff some cash in your swimsuit pocket and when you reach the table, put it into the Trop's money dryer. If you wind up blowing your soggy bankroll, just return to your breaststroke. Indoors, the casino doesn't do as good a job competing with its South Strip neighbors. Its crowded, confusing layout speaks to piecemeal additions and the days when the casinos *wanted* you to wander around lost and confused. But there's an almost quaint nostalgia in the '70s-style crystal chandeliers and the stained-glass dome that runs the length of the main pit. Cardsharps may still want to play here since the blackjack rules shrink the house edge greatly; table minimums usually range $5 to $25. The casino has excellent perks for points accumulated by members of its player's club—in summer it's particularly generous with *Les Folies Bergere* tickets for new sign-ups—and the Casino Hall of Fame displays the largest collection of Nevada casino memorabilia in existence. ⊠ *3801 Las Vegas Blvd. S, South Strip* ☎ *800/634-4000.*

Venetian Resort-Hotel-Casino. Walking from the hotel lobby into the casino is one of the great experiences in Las Vegas: overhead, reproductions of famous frescoes, highlighted by 24-karat-gold frames, adorn the ceiling; underfoot, the geometric design of the flat marble floor provides an M. C. Escher–like optical illusion of climbing stairs. But the pretty pink-and-gold icing of the Venetian is the only plus a gambler will find. The underwhelming gaming area reflects management's focus on the hotel operation and convention industry; you almost get the idea the gaming is there only because people expect it to be. The table-game minimums tend to be high—blackjack starting at $15 on an average weekend night—and with very poor rules for the player. At least there's an open lounge with live music at one end of the casino and a food court not too far from that. A high-limit slot area is nestled into a subdued corner, and the player's club employs an ultra-high-tech tracking system that enables you to comp yourself using your slot club points at any machine in the casino. ⊠ *3355 Las Vegas Blvd. S, Center Strip* ☎ *702/733-5000.*

Westward Ho Motel and Casino. The Westward has something few Strip casinos can offer: parking close to the casino. It also has plenty of low-limit blackjack tables, and the progressive video poker machines are among the best on the Strip. Pit bosses practically throw the buffet comps at players. The casino snack bar has good cheap sandwiches and huge servings of strawberry shortcake if you'd rather pay. ⊠ *2900 Las Vegas Blvd. S, North Strip* ☎ *800/634-6803.*

Beyond the Strip

Arizona Charlie's Hotel and Casino West. It's smoky and generic, more like the tribal casinos spreading across the country than the theme palaces of the Strip; but like most casinos that cater to area residents, Charlie's tries to attract players by offering the best slot club benefits for its 1,600 machines and the best casino coupons that it can—without giving away the store. The video poker has the best schedules available, and the slot club is so straightforward that a printed flyer indicates the number of points that anything in the joint costs. The bingo parlor runs 24 hours a day. Service seems indifferent although the table games have low minimums and average rules. Promotions are continuous; there are three or four good ones almost every day. The buffet is among the cheapest in town (and not bad to boot); play on a double-points day for an hour or so, and you can earn enough points to get it comped. ✉ *740 S. Decatur Blvd., West Side,* ✛ *Take W. Charleston from corner of Charleston and Las Vegas Blvd. about 2 mi, then go right on Decatur Blvd. for ½ mi; the casino is on left* ☎ *800/342–2695.*

The Cannery. A new casino rang in 2003 in a "new" area of town where it has little competition. The Cannery opened north of downtown, near the Las Vegas Motor Speedway, to tap into a fast-growing residential population. It's small compared to the Station Casinos, with 201 hotel rooms and no movie theaters or child care. The payout schedules on the 1,278 gaming machines didn't overly excite slot buffs in the early going either. The casino, however, offers a bright, snappy theme of California in the 1940s and is full of blown-up reproductions of the colorful fruit labels of vintage canning companies. Four attractive restaurants and an unusual indoor-outdoor entertainment venue geared to festivals help justify an out-of-the-way visit. ✉ *4336 Losee Rd., North Las Vegas,* ✛ *Exit I–15 at Craig Rd. and go west, using the Cannery's "smokestack" sign as your guide; casino is on south side of Craig Rd., at Losee Rd.* ☎ *702/399–4774.*

★ **Ellis Island Casino & Brewery.** Busy little Ellis Island put itself on the map with lounge karaoke, of all things, and coffee shop food bargains. It has stood by both—regardless of whether karaoke happens to be fashionable in the outside world—while expanding its casino to include a brewpub, an outlet for locals' favorite Metro Pizza, and a slot club with generous perks that has commanded the loyalty of local players. ✉ *4178 Koval La., Paradise Road* ☎ *702/733–8901.*

Gold Coast Hotel and Casino. Whenever you're at the airport and you see people losing money in the slots, think of the Gold Coast: this casino west of the Strip and west of I–15 was built on airport slot losses. From the mid-1980s, it has charted the course for a whole niche of "locals casinos" focused on the Las Vegas Valley's ever-swelling population. Perhaps because of its head start, the Gold Coast retains the loyalty of residents. It has some of the loosest slots in town, as well as a favorite slot club. It also has a poker room, a bingo parlor, a race and sports book, and a 72-lane bowling center. Most of the gaming space was remodeled top to bottom to step up for competition with the Palms in 2001. The most significant change is an expanded buffet divided into different ethnic cuisines. Like Palace Station, the friendly Gold Coast has low minimums and sizable crowds at times. ✉ *4000 W. Flamingo Rd., West Side* ☎ *888/402–6278.*

FodorśChoice
★ **Hard Rock Hotel and Casino.** Owner Peter Morton made his fortune on a trendy international chain of Hard Rock Cafes (and T-shirts advertising the same), with its rock-and-roll memorabilia and cutting-edge concerts. Slots have guitar-neck handles, blackjack layouts are customized with rock-related art, crap tables are adorned with Grateful Dead lyrics, and rock music pervades the place. It's considered terribly hip by those under 35—actor Ben Affleck and other young Hollywood stars drop their cash at these tables. There's a fun pick-up bar in the middle that's designed for eyeballing the miniskirts walking by. But looking is

a lot more fun than playing here. The dealers at these very poor games are young and good-looking, with a hyperattitude and a concern for carding those under 30. The Hard Rock also has a pool with swim-up blackjack tables. ✉ *4455 Paradise Rd., Paradise Road* ☎ *800/675–3267.*

Las Vegas Hilton. The Hilton's future was in the air after Caesars Entertainment agreed to sell the property in late 2003 for $280 million to Colony Capital, a Los Angeles–based international private investment firm. The main casino is one of the few in Vegas to look essentially as it did in the '70s, when Elvis Presley was the showroom star. Under a chandelier the size of an 18-wheeler, the Hilton's main pit runs down the middle of this conservatively attired casino. The sports "super book" is one of Las Vegas's largest and most elegant (with 46 video screens). Because the Hilton is next door to the Las Vegas Convention Center, many delegates stay here, and they pack the casino at all hours along with some older high rollers. Video poker fans can find excellent games with outstanding cash paybacks. The NightClub is a lounge by day, before the retractable walls close in to make it a dance club at night. The original casino floor is a marked contrast to the only significant change over the years: the SpaceQuest Casino that houses the "Star Trek: The Experience" attraction (which changed its show content to "Borg Invasion" in 2004). It's the most high-tech casino in town and has a far-out space bar. ✉ *3000 Paradise Rd., Paradise Road* ☎ *800/732–7117.*

Orleans Hotel and Casino. A casino that's outrageously popular with Las Vegas residents scored even more points by opening the Orleans Arena in 2003. The arena's easy access and reasonable concession prices instantly boosted attendance for annual shows such as "Disney On Ice." The rest of the Orleans remains a roomy barn of a casino under a high ceiling with scads of full-pay video-poker units among its 3,000 machines, five comfortable bars (and revealing cocktail-waitress uniforms), and hot lounge entertainment. Lots of locals like to leave their children at the Kid's Tyme child-care center, the 70-lane bowling alley, the 18-theater multiplex, or the big arcade and take advantage of the frequent double- and triple-points slot club promotions, cash drawings, and car giveaways. The 23-table poker room is popular, too. A much-needed parking garage opened in 2002. ✉ *4500 W. Tropicana Ave., West Side* ☎ *800/675–3267.*

Palace Station Hotel and Casino. This friendly casino with solid food deals at a number of restaurants is the one that launched Station Casinos as a company that would dominate the locals market. Ironically, the newer properties have siphoned away some of the interest, but the railroad-theme Palace Station has bounced back with a facelift and attractions such as an Irish-theme pub and a comedy club. The knowledgeable gambler will be interested in 10-times odds and good blackjack rules. There are 2,200 video and slot machines, 50 tables, a 600-seat bingo room (the casino got its start as a place called the Bingo Palace), a poker room, and two keno lounges. The Boarding Pass slot club reciprocates with the other properties and lets you march to the head of restaurant and buffet lines. ✉ *2411 W. Sahara Ave., West Side* ☎ *800/634–3101.*

★ **The Palms.** Striated shadows across the ceiling bring to mind palm fronds in this contempo-California style casino. The Palms has mostly succeeded in its bold plan to be a locals casino on the West Side—with a food court, movie theater, and easy garage parking—and hip competition for the Hard Rock Hotel on Paradise Road with the East wing, which houses trendy nightclubs and restaurants. Although its retro design hearkens back to the Sands of the 1950s, the born-in-2001 Palms is also clean and well-ventilated, with slot sections sprinkled comfortably along its length. If you're feeling lucky, get the fortune teller to read your tarot cards and pick a number for you. The Palms does take big bets but the game rules are average. Experts, however, consider the slot club to be among the best in town. A complimentary shuttle bus whisks you to Caesars Palace on the Strip. ✉ *4321 W. Flamingo Rd., West Side* ☎ *866/ 725–6773.*

Rampart Casino at JW Marriott Las Vegas. If the casino seems tiny compared to the Suncoast next door, it's because gambling was originally planned to be only an amenity of a luxurious, upscale resort (which opened as the Regent Las Vegas) that devoted equal attention to golfers, spa aficionados, and older visitors who wanted an "alternative" to Las Vegas. That idea never caught fire, but the casino remains compact, not cluttered. A gorgeous back-lit apricot-color dome decorated with a palm-tree design rises above the pit. Most minimums start at $5 at tables outfitted with plush chairs of outstanding comfort. The roulette wheels are single zero. The sports book is without a doubt the best part: small but elegant, with comfortable couches and picture windows overlooking the lush grounds. The slot club gives you points for anything you buy on the property (including a buffet and a newspaper). This is an excellent place to stop on your way to or from Red Rock Canyon. ✉ *221 N. Rampart Blvd., Summerlin* ☎ *877/869–8777.*

★ **Rio All-Suite Hotel and Casino.** The Brazilian theme of this popular off-Strip hotel originally captured the fancy of locals, but the hotel just kept growing and growing into a sprawling resort now geared more to visitors. The Masquerade Village packs tables and machines underneath a free attraction called the "Masquerade Show in the Sky." Parade floats packed with dancing showgirls circle an overhead, suspended monorail track as dozens of specialty performers sing, dance, mime, and stilt-walk below. Even the cocktail servers are so-called "BevErtainers" that put on a show while they dole out drinks. The Village segues into the older, more traditional casino to the west; in all, there are 1,710 machines and 70 tables throughout the 120,000 square feet of casino space. The player's club at Rio is part of the Harrah's Total Awards Program, which enables you to earn Rio comps at Harrah's locations around the country. With garages on both sides, remembering where you parked the car may be the biggest challenge of the evening. ✉ *3700 W. Flamingo Rd., West Side* ☎ *800/752–9746.*

Suncoast Hotel and Casino. The newest addition to the Coast Resorts family takes all the things that locals love about the Gold Coast and the Orleans, and puts them into an elevated setting—literally, given its hilltop perch, and metaphorically in terms of overall niceness—near the affluent Summerlin area of northwest Las Vegas. The Suncoast has a 16-screen movie theater and a parking garage on its west end, and a 400-seat showroom and a surface lot to the east. In between lie 2,300 gaming machines and 50 table games, all neatly laid out. A 150-seat race and sports book rivals its companion properties' popularity on weekends. ⊠ *9090 Alta Dr., Summerlin* ☎ *702/636–7111.*

★ **Terrible's Hotel and Casino.** The dumpy old Continental Hotel was bought and remodeled into a jam-packed, locals-oriented casino by the Herbst family, who own a network of service stations and car washes, leading humorist Joe Bob Briggs to dub the casino's theme "Convenience Store Moderne." It's not far off the mark: there's a large convenience store next to the slot club sign-up booth, and a plastic statue of Terrible's cowboy mascot and his gas pump rotating above a carousel of slot machines. Table play is limited to seven blackjack tables, one craps game, and one roulette wheel. The big draws here are the generous video poker machines and a slot club offering plenty of deals for the second-floor buffet and coffee shop, which lie next to the 220-seat bingo hall. A bar, sports book, and McDonald's are all bunched in so close together that they look like one McBar. ⊠ *4100 Paradise Rd., Paradise Road* ☎ *702/733–7000.*

Tuscany Hotel & Casino. Beyond elbow room that appeals to the claustrophobic, the only real points of distinction at this business-oriented hotel are some video poker machines with decent pay schedules and the Stars Lounge, outfitted with aluminum siding as a sort of poor man's Coyote Ugly. There's another bar near a tiny sports book, and a casino-level cafe for the hungry. ⊠ *225 E. Flamingo Rd., Paradise Road* ☎ *702/893–8933.*

Westin Casuarina. The former Maxim hotel was gutted and rebuilt as a classy, business-oriented hotel with a small casino. It's cozy but has nothing to offer serious players; the video poker schedules are weak and the blackjack rules favor the house. There's no keno or poker room and only one craps table. For the casual gambler, though, this casino has a great vibe. The best feature is an elevated square bar area with live music and comfortable conversation areas. There's a Starbucks off the casino floor, and a showroom outfitted with plush movie theater-style seats. ⊠ *160 E. Flamingo Rd., Paradise Road* ☎ *702/836–9775.*

Downtown

Fremont Street is the foundation of Las Vegas, and, to some degree, still the place to come for low table minimums, food bargains, a motley street life, and the concentrated explosion of neon lights that made it famous to begin with. However, historic Glitter Gulch has been pummeled from both sides in recent years. The Strip's megaresorts have stolen the dazzle and luster, while the explosion of so-called locals casinos have come in with more inviting casino atmospheres and food bargains that make many of the Downtown properties look faded and second-rate by comparison.

The development of Downtown since 2003 has caused a sort of Dickensian "best of times" and "worst of times." On the plus side are a booming new outlet mall only a few blocks from the Fremont Street casinos and the purchase of the Golden Nugget by dot-com millionaires Tim Poster and Tom Breitling, whose early transitional months of running the casino were documented by TV cameras for a Fox reality series. Also, the Fremont Street Experience updated its four-block canopy light show with a $16.5 million video-display system. On the down side, the historic Binion's Horseshoe went belly-up and closed abruptly in January 2004 for three months. Harrah's Entertainment promptly stepped in to buy the casino but did not plan to operate it, quickly arranging a sale to MTR Gaming Group that was pending at this writing. Also struggling was the Neonopolis shopping center at Fremont Street and Las Vegas Boulevard, a city-subsidized redevelopment project with restaurants, shops, and 12 movie screens.

Downtown at least seemed ripe to benefit from fresh thinking and an infusion of cash, given a new owner for the Four Queens—local bar owner Terry Caudill—and the probable sale of four downtown properties owned by longtime owner Jackie Gaughan. Barrick Gaming Corporation outlined a two-year plan to renovate the Las Vegas Club, Gold Spike, Western, and Plaza casinos, all of which would be expanded with 1,200 hotel rooms, another 1,200 time-share units, and what the company describes as "a themed street to re-create the ambience of the old downtown Las Vegas" in the seven acres surrounding the casinos. Significant investments in these hotels could alter the descriptions below. Fitzgeralds and the Lady Luck also changed hands since 2001, but neither sale resulted in immediate physical improvements.

In the meantime, downtown forges on with 25¢ craps, 50¢ roulette, $2–$3 blackjack, and even 1¢ video poker to accommodate Las Vegas's hordes of beginning and low-stakes players, tinhorns, slummers, and, of course, locals. Soak in the atmosphere and enjoy the neon mascots, Vegas Vic and Vegas Vicky, who still preside over Glitter Gulch. But after dark exercise great care on the sidewalks and parking lots around the Downtown area.

Binion's Horseshoe Hotel and Casino. A historic family legacy came to an abrupt end in early 2004 when Binion's Horseshoe closed for three months, then reopened under new corporate management. For decades, the Horseshoe was the place where serious gamblers came to play. Behind the hotel, by the parking garage, is a 15-foot tall statue of Horseshoe founder Benny Binion, wearing a Stetson and sitting on a horse. A former bootlegger, Binion came to Vegas from Texas in the 1940s and built a joint boasting the highest table limits in the world. In time, the Horseshoe acquired the Mint hotel next door, expanding both its casino floor space and room count while turning a music lounge into the only serious race book downtown. Binion's offspring clashed after his death, and daughter Becky finally lost the hotel because of cash-flow problems. U.S. marshals raided the casino cage, forcing its abrupt closure and subsequent sale. Harrah's Entertainment stepped in with a $50 million offer, but quickly sold the property to MTR Gaming Group, agreeing to run the operation for MTR. Harrah's replaced the carpet and gave the place a good cleaning, but vowed to maintain its unique ambience as much

THE COMP GAME

The word comp—short for complimentary—is perhaps the first bit of Vegas jargon everyone learns. The city was built on the principle of getting at least a little something in return for all those merrily spent gambling dollars. Two of the simplest and most time-honored comps are still very much at play: free drinks for anyone who can stay put in front of a table or machine long enough for the server to return with them (which sometimes can seem very long indeed), and free valet parking at almost every casino.

Beyond these, comps have evolved into a sophisticated system of tracking your play through player's clubs, also called slot cards. When casinos were smaller and unique to Nevada, a pit boss was a gambler's best friend. A sorrowful look often was enough to score a free breakfast or show for those bold enough to ask. Now, a computer chip determines whether you've been a good enough customer to merit a free buffet or sweatshirt. Player's cards track table and machine play and determine through a very democratic system what the casino is willing to give back to all but the high-rolling "rated" players.

The Basic Program

When you insert your card into a machine it begins to track your play and awards you points based on either "coins in" (the total amount you wager) or "coins out" (the total amount you win). A typical club might give you a point for each dollar wagered, and give you $10 cash back for every 100 points. But since casinos aren't fond of giving back even $10, they tempt you to trade in your accumulated points for a higher value in nonmonetary comps like free meals, logo merchandise, or room discounts. Free player's cards and promotional mailings have become a big casino marketing tool, so anyone who plans to gamble for an even an hour could benefit from signing up for a casino club—and there are often "sign-up" bonus points to get you rolling.

Corporate consolidation of the casino industry has resulted in "networked" club cards that keep you from accumulating a stack of plastic cards as you wander the Strip. Harrah's Total Gold card was the first to take the concept nationwide, with one account number good in more than two dozen casinos. Here are the largest Las Vegas corporate entities, the name of their cards, and the casinos where their points are interchangeable:

Caesars Entertainment Connection Card: Bally's, Caesars Palace, Flamingo, Paris Las Vegas (Las Vegas Hilton's sale was pending at this writing).

Harrah's Total Gold: Harrah's Las Vegas, Rio.

Mandalay Resort Group's One Club: Circus Circus, Excalibur, Luxor, Mandalay Bay, Monte Carlo.

MGM Mirage Players Club: Bellagio, MGM Grand Hotel, The Mirage, New York–New York, Treasure Island.

Boyd Gaming Players Gold: California, Fremont, Main Street Station, Sam's Town, Stardust.

Stations Casinos Boarding Pass: Boulder Station, Green Valley Ranch, Palace Station, Santa Fe Station, Sunset Station, Texas Station.

—Mike Weatherford

as possible. The real prize in keeping the Horseshoe name may be its legacy as the home of the annual World Series of Poker in April and May; the final event has a $10,000 buy-in and a $1-million first prize. ✉ *128 E. Fremont St., Downtown* ☎ *800/937–6537.*

California Hotel and Casino. Though the name is California, the motif is Hawaiian: all the dealers wear Hawaiian shirts, the carpet has tropical flowers, the snack bars serve Hawaiian dishes, and many of the customers are in fact islanders. Planeloads of Hawaiian tourists on package tours stay at the hotel and enjoy the Polynesian coffee shop menu and casual and uncrowded casino, which has lots of $3 tables and 5¢ slots. The tourists have made a good choice, too, because the California—part of the Boyd Group that owns the Stardust and Sam's Town—serves up good slots, video poker, and blackjack games. ✉ *12 E. Ogden Ave., Downtown* ☎ *800/634–6255.*

El Cortez Hotel. The oldest standing casino in Las Vegas, the Cortez opened for business on Fremont Street in 1941, when cowboys still rode horses up and down the street. The smelly, old, wood-paneled casino seems little changed from 60 years ago, with locals and desperados cramming the tables. The El Cortez still has great blackjack games, including single-deck blackjack with $3 minimums shrinking the house edge to nothing. Perhaps in an attempt to reduce the "character" quotient, the coffee shop no longer boasts the rock-bottom deals it once was known for. However, Roberta's fine-dining room remains a cherished, not-so-well-kept secret among long-timers. Be careful walking to the El Cortez from Fremont Street after dark. ✉ *600 E. Fremont St., Downtown* ☎ *800/634–6703.*

Fitzgeralds Hotel and Casino. If you don't trust the luck of the Irish, pick up the Fitzgeralds fun book, which always includes a good free souvenir and $3–$4 worth of gambling coupons. This two-story casino comes off as a bit cheesy in most aspects, but does offer a high-tech slot club: you can use your club card to pay for rooms and meals and check your point balance online. Fitzgeralds makes up for its generosity, though, with lousy rules on its table games. There's an outdoor balcony right off the second-floor casino, with lounge chairs and tables, a great place for watching the street life below and the Fremont Street Experience above. ✉ *301 E. Fremont St., Downtown* ☎ *800/634–6045.*

Four Queens Hotel and Casino. If the carnival barkers don't get your attention first, you should know you've found this casino when you walk along Fremont Street and come upon four painted playing cards in the pavement—four queens, in fact. The casino floor conveys a hint of a New Orleans theme and comes off as a little lighter and brighter than some of the downtown hotels of similar age. There are plenty of blackjack tables with mostly $5 minimums, going as low as $3 but seldom higher than $10. An area that once was a music lounge now is a "Nickel Palace." The Four Queens is also known for frequent free-money promotions: walk in, take a free pull on a slot machine, and get a coupon for two free dollar-slot tokens, or pay $21 for 50 spins on the machine of your choice, with a jacket or stuffed animal guaranteed even if you don't win. ✉ *202 E. Fremont St., Downtown* ☎ *800/634–6045.*

Fremont Hotel and Casino. In the heart of Glitter Gulch and adding immeasurably to the light show with its block-long neon facade, the Fremont has been a landmark since it opened in 1956. It has become the least interesting member of its Boyd Group family, however, thanks to crowded aisles, a low ceiling, and a generic atmosphere. Blackjack minimums follow suit: mostly $5 and $10, with few tables for either the low roller or the big shot. The hotel does have one of the oldest and most respected race and sports books, which attracts a lot of gamblers, especially in football season. The Fremont also has a keno progressive that often rises into positive territory—rare for keno. Table game rules are OK, although the Players Gold Club is pretty generous. ⊠ *200 E. Fremont St., Downtown* ☎ *800/634–6182.*

Golden Gate Hotel and Casino. The first structure to house Las Vegas's most historic hotel was built in 1906. Opened as the Hotel Nevada, it was sold to a group of San Francisco investors in 1955; the famous shrimp cocktail, which started a Vegas tradition, dates from then. The Golden Gate's casino is small and crowded, but offers an authenticity that might be just the antidote to the faux-European sameness of the Strip. Ceiling fans beat back the smoke over the tables, where low rollers play $3 to $5 blackjack in a fairly relaxed atmosphere. The crowning touch is the piano player who serenades the deli diners; the sound of tinkling ivories wafts into the pit, making it the only place in town where you can shoot craps to live Scott Joplin or George Gershwin. ⊠ *1 Fremont St., Downtown* ☎ *800/426–1906.*

Fodor's Choice ★ **Golden Nugget Hotel and Casino.** This is the only downtown hotel still elegant enough to draw high ratings and compete with the Strip on most any level of gaming or dining. The hotel left the MGM Mirage family in early 2004, when it was bought by Travelscape founders Tim Poster and Tom Breitling. Their renovation plans play to the young-and-hip; the Zaks restaurant, for example, will be converted into a late-night hangout. It was not known what would become of signature touches such as the gold-plated elevators, pay phones, and slot machines—and the world's largest gold nugget—but it seemed likely that the casino itself would continue to cater to wealthier gamblers. You can find a couple of $5 blackjack tables, but $10 and $25 minimums dominate. One anomaly in the high-roller casino is the race and sports book, which is little more than a tiny lounge next to the music lounge. ⊠ *129 E. Fremont St., Downtown* ☎ *800/634–3403.*

Lady Luck Casino and Hotel. The Lady Luck, at 3rd and Ogden streets across from the Gold Spike, is a bit off the beaten track, but folks are drawn to the rare casino where you can see daylight, thanks to big picture windows that make it the lightest and airiest downtown. There's a small sports book and a lounge that may have the distinction of being the smallest stage for live entertainment in all of Las Vegas. ⊠ *206 N. 3rd St., Downtown* ☎ *800/523–9582.*

Las Vegas Club Hotel and Casino. Downtown juicemen Jackie Gaughan and Mel Exber own this casino, which has been around since day one. It's a typical Glitter Gulch joint, except for the high ceilings, which give

Las Vegas
Downtown
Casinos

it a roomy and airy feeling, and a pervasive sports theme; don't expect a sports version of a Hard Rock Cafe, but the memorabilia all over the walls was innovative for its day. Low limits—mostly $5 tables and quarter machines—and easy comps make this a good choice for budget-minded action. The Las Vegas Club somewhat coasts on the coattails of a reputation it enjoyed for years as a blackjack paradise. It's still known for offbeat games and rules, such as a "suited blackjack" paying two-to-one, and it's winning player loyalty by sticking to the old rules and resisting the "6-to-5" payoff that many of the Strip casinos now have for single-deck blackjacks. You can watch some of the action from a balcony overlooking the casino annex, which includes a small race book equipped with individual TV monitors. ✉ *18 E. Fremont St., Downtown* ☎ *800/634–6532.*

★ **Main Street Station Casino, Brewery & Hotel.** Main Street Station is chock full of antiques, stained glass, bronze bas-reliefs, marble, and wood, wood, wood. It's a pint-size property, connected to the California, a Boyd Group sister property, by an overhead pedestrian bridge. It houses a brewpub that's crowded with downtown workers, as well as the most popular buffet downtown; one that seems almost as large as the casino floor. It's worth a visit for the aesthetics alone, but as long as you're here, there are plenty of machines (live and electronic) to risk your money on. Games are good with 20-times odds on craps and good blackjack rules. ⊠ *200 N. Main St., Downtown* ☎ *800/465–0711.*

Plaza Hotel and Casino. Back in the 1920s, when cowboys rode their horses on Fremont Street and miners came to town to buy grub, the corner of Main and Fremont streets was anchored by the railroad depot. It still is, but today that station has a 1,000-room hotel and giant casino around it. A swanky joint when it capped off Fremont Street in 1971, the Plaza now smells of damp air-conditioning and is frozen in the early '70s, with better days reflected in everything from the retro signage to the chandeliers. The one-man-band entertainer from the nearby stage will keep you chuckling as you play in this smoky low-roller casino. Lots of low-minimum table games are nearby. ⊠ *1 Main St., Downtown* ☎ *800/634–6575.*

Boulder Strip

The Boulder Strip suddenly emerged in 1995 as a destination of its own, competing with downtown and the more famous Strip along Las Vegas Boulevard South. If you're driving to Vegas, the Boulder Strip has some of the nicest facilities at the lowest prices in town, but you certainly need a car to get out there.

Arizona Charlie's East. Headline-grabbing investor Carl Icahn first bought the original West Side Arizona Charlie's (and the Stratosphere), then doubled his investment by acquiring this sputtering Boulder Strip casino, renaming it, and turning it into a twin of the first Charlie's. The higher ceilings in the two-story casino make it roomier than the westside original. Early returns were good enough to warrant a $5 million expansion in 2002. There's a 24-hour bingo room and a 50-seat race and sports book. The Ultimate Rewards Club has both comps and cash-back rewards, and a high-tech tracking system. ⊠ *4575 Boulder Hwy., Boulder Strip* ☎ *702/951–9000.*

Boulder Station Hotel and Casino. Boulder Station is an east-side clone of the popular west-side locals casino, Palace Station. The rich wood, stone, even brick floors; the central luxurious pit framed by big stained-glass murals; the plentiful video-poker machines backed by a good slot club that can be used at all Station properties; and the fast-food counters outside the fine restaurants (serving the same food at half the price) all improve on Palace Station's already successful formula. Kids' Quest, a giant indoor play area off a small satellite pit, makes this the only casino in Las Vegas where parents can play blackjack and watch their children romp at the same time. This is the ultimate indoor playground, 8,000 square feet of fun things to keep youngsters from 6 weeks to 12 years old happily occupied for hours (there's an hourly fee and a time limit). Boulder Station also has a state-of-the-art 11-plex movie theater. ⊠ *4111 Boulder Hwy., Boulder Strip* ☎ *800/683–7777.*

★ **Sam's Town Hotel and Gambling Hall.** The Boulder Strip really began in earnest with Sam's Town. It's a sprawling off-Strip destination for everything imaginable, including an 18-screen movie theater complex and expanded child-care facilities. Sam's motif is touted to be "contemporary western," but sequential remodeling has toned down, if not eliminated completely, most of the red carpet and velvet wallpaper of its cowboy past. The casino is built around a 25,000-square-foot indoor park with animatronic howling wolves, restaurants, and a waterfall under a glass, greenhouse-style atrium. The two-story casino has row after row of 25¢ video-poker machines, a hardwood floor under the pit, and a multipurpose entertainment venue called Sam's Town Live! It also has low-limit table games like 25¢ roulette and $5 blackjack, all under large HDTV screens showing every televised sporting event. For the mid-stakes bettor the great games make Sam's Town a recommended watering hole. If you're driving to Hoover Dam (Boulder Highway is much more picturesque than the freeway), you might stop in on your way. ✉ *5111 Boulder Hwy., Boulder Strip* ☎ *800/634–6371.*

Rancho Strip

In 1990 the Santa Fe opened in the far northwest part of town, one of the fastest-growing areas of the valley. It "owned" the whole northwest for nearly five years, until the Fiesta opened a couple of miles closer to downtown. The Fiesta was so successful that Texas Station opened directly across the street less than a year later. The competition was particularly intense in the video poker, blackjack, and buffet departments until Station Casinos bought the Fiesta and Santa Fe in 2000. Now Rancho Strip is Station's Strip, but the winners, ultimately, are those who patronize the places. A car is mandatory to getting to the Rancho Strip area.

Fiesta Hotel and Casino. Fiesta was a little locals joint with a big, well-deserved reputation, which is probably why Station Casinos bought it. The Fiesta is a popular sports-betting venue, thanks to the drive-up betting window complete with pneumatic tubes and teller call buttons. It has also achieved a reputation among local experts and pros for having the best video poker, a distinction its rivals have aggressively challenged. The bingo hall is mind-bogglingly big. Overall, the table game rules are poor for the player although comps are doled out to all comers. The Fiesta's Festival Buffet is a solid bargain, with its gigantic barbecue fire pit, Mongolian grill, and specialty nights. ✉ *2400 N. Rancho, Rancho Strip* ☎ *800/731–7333.*

Santa Fe Station Hotel and Casino. Santa Fe has a 60-lane bowling alley, a 17,000-square-foot ice-skating rink, a 700-seat bingo hall, and a children's nursery. The big casino—2,000 slot and video-poker machines—generally rams and jams and has one of the largest no-smoking sections in Las Vegas. ✉ *4949 N. Rancho, Rancho Strip* ☎ *702/658–4900.*

★ **Texas Station Gambling Hall & Hotel.** Texas Station is longhorn territory, with Texas-shape brick sidewalks, Lone Star carpeting design, and a revolving mirrored disco ball that looks like an armadillo. Texas Station's Market Street Buffet is one of the best in Las Vegas, with a Texas chile bar and cooked-to-order fajitas. The casino and race and sports book are huge, with video poker galore and all the usual table games. The player's club is one of the best in town: play at Texas Station and redeem your points at any of the Station casinos. Games overall are only OK for the older clientele. A 16-theater multiplex fills the parking lots nightly, and there's a huge indoor playground called Kids' Quest for children from 6 weeks to 12 years old. ⊠ *2101 Texas Star La., Rancho Strip* ☎ *800/654–8804.*

Henderson

Henderson was founded in 1940 as a company town for Basic Magnesium, Inc., a giant production plant built to process magnesium mined in huge quantities from a site in central Nevada for the war effort. The site for the factory was selected for its proximity to the unlimited electricity supplied by Hoover Dam; a town to house 10,000 workers was built alongside the magnesium plant. Since then, the magnesium plant has been subdivided into smaller industrial and chemical factories, but Henderson—like its next-door neighbor Las Vegas—has become one of the fastest-growing communities in the country, thanks to the economic boom in southern Nevada during the 1990s. It's now a vast bedroom community of Vegas and the second-largest city in Nevada. It has a small downtown, a fine local museum, and several major locals casinos.

Casino Montelago. If you have an extra afternoon to kill, take a side trip to masterplanned Lake Las Vegas, the local home of Celine Dion. Casino Montelago sits between condominiums and the Ritz-Carlton Lake Las Vegas, and both its Tenuta Cafe and Tappo sports bar open out to a lakeside retail shopping area with quaint villagelike storefronts. Tappo is the most intriguing element of this invitingly cozy casino. It combines a sports-betting window, grill, and live-music lounge in a multilevel, indoor-outdoor operation. The rest of the small casino includes a table gaming pit with a dozen blackjack tables, two craps tables, and a single roulette table under giant overhead wine barrels. ⊠ *8 Strada Di Villaggio, Henderson* ☎ *702/939–8888.*

Fiesta Henderson. Stations Casinos bought the jungle-theme casino known as the Reserve and remodeled it into a southern-Valley counterpart to the popular Fiesta Rancho. It replicated the Festival Buffet and Garduño's Mexican restaurant, and because it shares slot-club points and privileges with its sister property, it's just as good a spot for video poker as the original Fiesta. ⊠ *777 W. Lake Mead Dr., Henderson* ☎ *702/ 558–7000 or 888/899–7770.*

Fodor'sChoice **Green Valley Ranch Resort.** Under the iron scrollwork of this pleasant green-
★ and-tan Mission-style casino, locals are feted in grand style. The Stations company opened Green Valley for its big bettors, with high limits, excellent service, and swish bars and nightclubs. Check out Whisky Bar, which starts indoors and extends into the pool area and a garden with acres of vineyards, waterfalls, and fountains. Slots players accustomed to the jingle of coins will be disappointed in the paper payouts of the Green Valley machines. A few full-pay video poker machines lurk in the distant corners here. Because this is a Station casino, the player's card transfers to its other properties. If you're seeking hopping nightlife without the traffic of the Strip, stop by Green Valley. The well-organized

parking attendants make finding space stress-free. ✉ *2300 Paseo Verde Pkwy., Henderson* ☎ *888/319–4661.*

★ **Sunset Station Hotel and Casino.** The casino has a Spanish-Mediterranean theme, with ceramic tiles, brick facades, fountains, and wrought-iron balconies. Its size is about standard for a neighborhood joint: 80,000 square feet, with 3,000 slot and video-poker machines, and 50 table games. The video poker is decent, not great, but the slot club is a good one. The middle-market Sunset Station is almost always packed with local players, patrons of the excellent buffet and microbrewery, and residents dropping their children at Kids' Quest, the casino's giant indoor play area, on their way to the movies, or going to a show at the rockin' lounge. (Kids' Quest is for children from 6 weeks to 12 years old; there's an hourly fee and a time limit.) ✉ *1301 Sunset Rd., Henderson* ☎ *702/547–7777.*

WHERE TO EAT

3

Updated by
Heidi Knapp
Rinella

LAS VEGAS HAS—HOWEVER IMPROBABLY—BECOME AMERICA'S hottest restaurant market. Each new megaresort brings its own multiple dining options, with celebrity chefs adding clones of famous signature restaurants and newborn establishments to the mix. And while bargain buffets and coffee shops still abound, the arrival of the superchefs has left its mark on the steak houses and buffets—many of the latter of which have gone upscale. Away from the Strip, the unprecedented population growth in the city's suburbs has brought with it a separate and continuous wave of new restaurants, both familiar chains and independent spots opened by local and nationally based entrepreneurs.

Joining a few gourmet pioneers such as Hugo's Cellar and Andre's, and spurred on by Wolfgang Puck, who tested the desert waters with a local Spago in 1992, a flood of newer restaurants and ever-more-prominent chefs have radically changed the experience of eating in Las Vegas. Status-conscious hotel-casinos now compete for star chefs and create lavish, built-to-order spaces for well-known restaurant tenants. These new establishments rival the upscale restaurants of the country's dining capitals in quality and service.

Among the big-name restaurants in Las Vegas are four Puck outposts spread among three hotels (Caesars Palace, Mandalay Bay, and the Venetian). Other hotels have followed suit. The Bellagio has branches of New York City's famed Le Cirque and Osteria del Circo, along with Jean-Georges Vongerichten's Prime steak house, Julian Serrano's Picasso, Michael Mina's Aqua and Todd English's Olives, an offshoot of the Boston landmark. MGM Grand houses Tom Colicchio's Craftsteak, Mina's Nobhill and Seablue, and Emeril's New Orleans Fish House from Emeril Lagasse. The Venetian has Bouchon from famed French Laundry chef Thomas Keller, Delmonico Steakhouse from Lagasse, and Valentino from Los Angeles überchef Piero Selvaggio. In addition to Puck's Trattoria del Lupo, Mandalay Bay offers Charlie Palmer's Aureole (from New York); China Grill (also from New York); Red Square (from Miami Beach); and Border Grill, an L.A. import run by famed TV chefs the Too Hot Tamales, Mary Sue Milliken and Susan Feniger. The Aladdin's Desert Passage shopping area has the first Commander's Palace outside New Orleans, managed by a member of the famed Brennan restaurateur family. Little Buddha at the Palms is an offshoot of Paris's famed Buddha Bar. And in the planning stages at this writing were restaurants from culinary lions Paul Bocuse, Alain Ducasse, Daniel Boulud, and Hubert Keller as well as up-and-comers Rick Moonen and Bobby Flay.

The restaurant explosion has been partially geared toward satisfying high rollers, who are fed for free as a reward for their often-astronomical bets at the blackjack and baccarat tables, but the city's new reputation as a culinary capital is also drawing attention from those who simply enjoy fine dining. Las Vegas's tendency to do everything to an extreme creates the possibility that too many spectacular restaurants will starve each other, but there's no sign of that yet. Although Sin City's reputation as being recession-proof may be a bit overstated, the city knows how to continually re-invent itself to ensure that the annual average of 35 million visitors—many of them with fat expense accounts—keeps coming.

3

When planning your dining-out excursions in Las Vegas, try to hit at least one or two places off-Strip. You may find that prices are lower—and food quality sometimes just as high—as in the places that cater to tourists. The pace is usually more relaxed, too, and you can often leave your car just steps from the door.

While you're on the Strip, keep your eyes peeled for the legendary bargains; not all Las Vegas establishments have gone highbrow. You can still find a 99-cent half-pound hot dog at Slots–A–Fun and a 99-cent margarita or beer or nickel cup of coffee at the New Frontier to wash it down. Some casino food courts offer high-quality deli-style food instead of the usual fast fare. And check out the crepes window at Paris.

Unless otherwise noted, the restaurants listed in this guide are open daily for lunch and dinner.

Making Reservations
Some restaurants—particularly the most storied, such as Picasso and Renoir—require reservations (and you should make them well in advance). You'd be well advised to call ahead to just about any upscale restaurant, however, to inquire about reservation policies, because waits can be long.

We mention reservations for particular restaurants only when they're essential or not accepted. Book as far ahead as you can, and reconfirm as soon as you arrive. (Large parties should always call to check the reservations policy.) Even if you don't have a reservation at your desired spot, some restaurants may have last-minute cancellations that they'd be happy to fill, so it's worth a shot to call and ask.

What to Wear
The dining dress code, like nearly every other social protocol in Las Vegas, is permissive: As long as you wear your wallet, you're welcome most anywhere. Although the new resorts have inspired more people to dress to impress, you still see flip-flops and cutoffs in the buffet line and cowboy hats in the steak house.

We mention dress only when men are required to wear a jacket or a jacket and tie.

Tipping
A tip of 15%–20% is common practice in Las Vegas restaurants, and in some circumstances you might want to slip the maître d' $5 or $10 for a special table.

	WHAT IT COSTS				
	$$$$	$$$	$$	$	¢
AT DINNER	over $35	$28–$35	$19–$27	$10–$18	under $10

Prices are per person for a main course at dinner.

But even low rollers with thin wallets have plenty of dining options in Las Vegas. Despite the influx of upscale restaurants, you can still find a complete steak dinner for only $4.95 (Ellis Island), a 99¢ shrimp cocktail (Golden Gate), and $2.79 breakfast specials (Arizona Charlie's). And of course, the ever-popular buffet is found in nearly every casino in town.

But crowds at the hotels, long lines at the buffets, and the jangling noise of slot machines prompt some to seek refuge away from the casinos. Venture into the residential areas for a steadily increasing variety of restaurants that satisfy most pocketbooks. Rosemary's, Andre's, the Melting Pot, Tre, Kona Grill, Bonjour Casual French, the Tillerman, and other off-Strip dining rooms satisfy the craving for a civilized meal. And mid-price family eateries (such as Tenaya Creek Restaurant & Brewery, Memphis Championship Barbecue, India Oven, Dona Maria, and Billy Bob's Steak House) offer reliable quality at reasonable prices.

The Strip

American

$$–$$$$ ✕ **Nobhill.** San Francisco cuisine is the star here (but you already knew that), and so is celebrated chef Michael Mina. The menu's emphasis is on seasonal regional favorites such as Gilroy garlic soup, lobster pot pie, cioppino, or sautéed Monterey Bay abalone. A selection of five flavors of mashed potatoes, such as lobster, curry, or basil, is included with dinner, and you can bet the sourdough bread's the real deal. ⊠ *MGM Grand Hotel and Casino, 3799 Las Vegas Blvd. S, South Strip* ☎ *702/891–3110* ▭ *AE, D, DC, MC, V* ✆ *No lunch.*

American/Casual

$$–$$$ ✕ **Bouchon.** Famed French Laundry chef Thomas Keller—widely noted as among the best in the country—opened the stunning, capacious room in the Venezia Tower at the Venetian in 2004. Velvet banquettes, antique light fixtures, and painted tile lend a sophisticated take on French country design. Bouchon's folded brown-paper menu opens to reveal French bistro classics like steak frites, roasted chicken, and Croque Madame. Finish with profiteroles, *pot de créme* (rich little custards), or créme caramel. Breakfast options include sweets from the wondrous bakery. ⊠ *Venetian Resort-Hotel-Casino, 3355 Las Vegas Blvd. S, Center Strip* ☎ *702/414–6200* ▭ *AE, MC, V.*

¢–$$ ✕ **Grand Lux Café.** The Venetian's 24-hour operation is no diner or coffee shop. A member of the same family as the Cheesecake Factory, Grand Lux is an attractive, expansive space in contemporary colors. The menu's all over the place, including such items as Asian nachos, Madeira chicken, and Mongolian steak. And whatever you do, be sure to leave room for the strawberry shortcake or a slice of cheesecake or key lime pie. ⊠ *Venetian Resort-Hotel-Casino, 3355 Las Vegas Blvd. S, Center Strip* ☎ *702/414–3888* ▭ *AE, D, DC, MC, V.*

¢–$$ ✕ **Margaritaville.** Whenever Jimmy Buffett's "Volcano" plays at this casual theme restaurant, a volcano erupts and spews margaritas into oversized blenders. A large window looks out over the Strip and Caesars Palace across the street. The menu includes a cheeseburger in paradise, of course, plus Floribbean favorites such as Bahamian conch chowder,

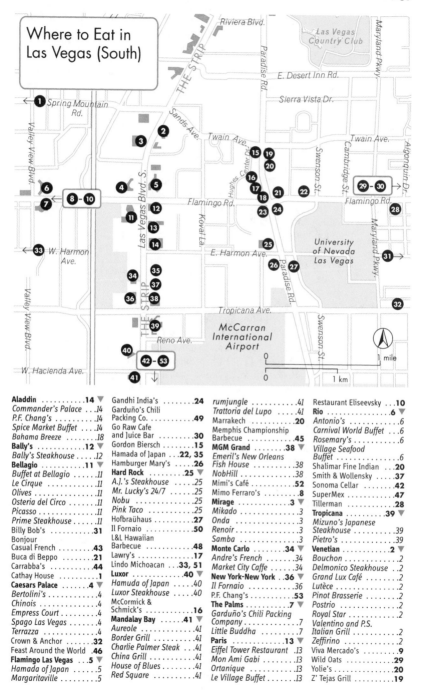

Where to Eat in Las Vegas (South)

Riviera Blvd.

Las Vegas Country Club

THE STRIP

Maryland Pkwy.

Spring Mountain Rd.

Paradise Rd.

E. Desert Inn Rd.

Sierra Vista Dr.

Sands Ave.

Twain Ave.

Twain Ave.

Hughes Center Dr.

Swenson St.

Cambridge St.

Algonquin Dr.

Valley View Blvd.

Las Vegas Blvd. S.

Flamingo Rd.

Flamingo Rd.

Koval La.

W. Harmon Ave.

E. Harmon Ave.

University of Nevada Las Vegas

Maryland Pkwy.

Valley View Blvd.

Paradise Rd.

Tropicana Ave.

Swenson St.

THE STRIP

McCarran International Airport

Reno Ave.

0   1 mile

0   1 km

W. Hacienda Ave.

taro chips, coconut shrimp with orange-marmalade horseradish, and Cuban meatloaf. When it's time for dessert, take the plunge yourself—into a chocolate volcano. ⊠ *The Flamingo, 3555 Las Vegas Blvd. S, Center Strip* ☎ *702/733–3302* ⊟ *AE, D, DC, MC, V.*

🐾 ¢–$ ✕ **NASCAR Cafe.** A model of a vastly overgrown racing car, the Carzilla, hangs suspended over the bar as the crowning centerpiece at this theme restaurant, and TVs all over the restaurant broadcast auto racing (and sometimes other sports). The menu is sprinkled with auto-racing references, too, like the NASCAR burger and collision chicken. Try the chicken pasta, which is linguine with Alfredo sauce and chicken, sugar snap peas, mushrooms, and chunks of ripe tomato. Portions are big, just like Carzilla. Even if you're not a racing fan, it's a fun place to get a quick meal. ⊠ *Sahara Hotel and Casino, 2535 Las Vegas Blvd. S, North Strip* ☎ *702/734–7223* ⊟ *AE, D, DC, MC, V.*

🐾 ¢–$ ✕ **Roxy's Diner.** At this playful replica of a 1950s-era diner, you can dig into mammoth hot-fudge sundaes, sizable burgers, fried catfish, old-fashioned thick milk shakes, blue-plate specials that include meatloaf and chicken-fried steak, and other inexpensive American classics. This joint is always jumping. ⊠ *Stratosphere Hotel Tower and Casino, 2000 Las Vegas Blvd. S, North Strip* ☎ *702/380–7777* ⊟ *AE, D, DC, MC, V.*

Brazilian

$$–$$$ ✕ **Samba Brazilian Steakhouse.** The Mirage's Samba Brazilian Steakhouse presents a lively, colorful, *rodizio* dinner—a parade of rotisserie-style roasted meats, chicken, and fish cooked on skewers and carved table-side, all you can eat. À la carte entrées include roasted herb-crusted halibut and Australian lobster tail. For dessert, try the coconut crème brûlée or chocolate mousse cake. The sparkling open kitchen adds to the room's excitement. ⊠ *Mirage Hotel and Casino, 3400 Las Vegas Blvd. S, Center Strip* ☎ *702/791–7111* ⚲ *Reservations essential* ⊟ *AE, D, DC, MC, V* ☾ *No lunch.*

Buffets

★ $–$$$ ✕ **The Buffet at Bellagio.** In keeping with the resort, this is one of the most beautifully decorated buffet rooms in town. For cozier dining, it's divided into many alcoves, one of which replicates an outdoor café with umbrellas. But the design isn't the main attraction here; even the most discerning foodie should find something to like with selections that include Kobe beef (yes, Kobe beef), roast sirloin of elk, tandoori game hen, steamed clams and mussels, acorn squash ravioli, and white miso soup. The requisite king-crab legs are present as well, and there's quite an array of elaborate pastries—and an in-restaurant bar. ⊠ *Bellagio Las Vegas, 3600 Las Vegas Blvd. S, Center Strip* ☎ *702/693–7111* ⊟ *AE, D, DC, MC, V.*

★ 🐾 $–$$ ✕ **Le Village Buffet.** Let the other buffets touch on international foods; Paris Las Vegas owns the world's foremost cuisine and shows it to advantage at Le Village Buffet. The buffet stations are themed to the regions of France; accordingly, you may find chicken sauté *chasseur* (in a brown sauce of mushrooms, shallots, and white wine) and roasted duck with green peppercorns in Brittany, seafood bouillabaisse in Provence, veal *Marengo* (in olive oil with tomatoes, onions, olives, gar-

BUFFET BONANZA

OH, THOSE SUMPTUOUS, cheap, ever-present buffets. They've long been as much a part of a trip to Las Vegas as stuffing coins into the one-armed bandits.

The birth of the Las Vegas buffet is generally credited to one Beldon Katleman, who bought the El Rancho Vegas (the city's first real resort) in 1947. Katleman was trying to figure out how to keep people in the casino—and, it would follow, spending money in said casino—after the resort's second show of the evening, and came up with the idea for a $1 Midnight Chuck Wagon Buffet. It didn't take long for the other hotels to decide that the loss leader was a great idea, and the idea gradually was expanded into daytime meal options. An enduring tradition was born.

But how times have changed. Those gaming pioneers had no idea how celebrity chefs, following the example (and success) of California institution Wolfgang Puck, would flock to the desert to bring this city a taste of what they'd been doing in New York, San Francisco, New Orleans, Dallas, and Washington.

The star chefs had nothing to do with the buffets, of course. What they did was raise the bar for Las Vegas's professional kitchens—and the expectations of visitors, who still were looking for great all-you-can-eat deals but were no longer satisfied with the steam-table selections of old.

The first "gourmet buffet" opened with the Bellagio, where it fit in with mogul Steve Wynn's plan for a classier joint. Today, the top three buffets in town are generally considered the Bellagio ($24.95 to $31.95 at dinner, $15.95 at lunch), Paris's Le Village Buffet ($24.95 at dinner, $17.95 at lunch), and the Aladdin's Spice Market Buffet ($20.99 at dinner, $14.99 at lunch).

But nearly every resort of any size presents its own version of the classic buffet. One of the lowest-priced is at Circus Circus ($8.99 at dinner, $6.99 at lunch), where the buffet serves an estimated 10,000 daily. Caesars Palace's buffet is at Cafe Lago, where prices are $14 at breakfast and $16 at lunch.

The locals casinos have followed suit; one example is the buffet at the Suncoast, where the breakfast buffet ($4.95) is considered among the best in town. Another is Sam's Town, with its Firelight Buffet ($10.99 at dinner, $6.99 at lunch), which offers steak and fillet nights ($12.99), and a Thursday and Friday seafood and fish fry ($16.99).

Oh, and don't forget the Sunday brunch buffets. Bally's Sterling Brunch ($52.95) is still considered the best in the valley. Other great brunch bets are Paris ($24.95), especially if you like crepes, and Caesars Palace ($21.95 without champagne, $31.95 with unlimited champagne). There's a gospel brunch at House of Blues at Mandalay Bay ($37), jazz brunch Friday through Sunday at Commander's Palace adjacent to the Aladdin ($35, or à la carte), and margarita brunches at Garduno's at the Fiesta ($11.99) and the Palms ($11.99).

Although much about Las Vegas buffets has changed, some things haven't. There are plenty of long lines at peak times. Remember to tip; the suggested minimum is $1 per person. And here's a tip: if you're kind of tricky and very hungry, you sometimes can go toward the end of a buffet serving period (the end of the breakfast hour, say) at some buffets and hang around as they start to put out selections for the next meal, saving a few bucks in the process.

— Heidi Knapp Rinella

lic, and white wine) in Burgundy, smoked salmon salad with fresh dill in Normandy, and braised lamb with Riesling and curry in Alsace. *Raclette* (a dish of melted aged cheese) and the high pile of snow-crab clusters are always popular. For dessert, visit Brittany for dessert crepes or Le Flambe station for bananas Foster and French bread pudding. ⊠ *Paris Las Vegas, 3655 Las Vegas Blvd. S, Center Strip* ☎ *702/946–7000* ⊟ *AE, D, DC, MC, V.*

$–$$ ✕ **Spice Market Buffet.** This buffet in the traffic-challenged Aladdin Resort and Casino is one of the best in town—and one of the best values. It's probably the only one with a Middle Eastern station (in keeping with the Aladdin's theme), with delights such as skewered lamb, basmati rice with lentils and raisins, and tandoori chicken. The Italian station offers stromboli, pizza, chicken scallopini, and macaroni with Gorgonzola cream, while the Asian one has super pot stickers, fried rice, and spring rolls. At this writing, plans to transform the Aladdin into a Planet Hollywood were underway, but how this will affect the buffet remains to be seen. ⊠ *Aladdin Resort and Casino, 3667 Las Vegas Blvd. S, Center Strip* ☎ *702/785–5555* ⊟ *AE, D, DC, MC, V.*

Cajun/Creole

$$–$$$$ ✕ **Commander's Palace.** Although it may lack the gracious Old South atmo-
Fodor'sChoice sphere of the New Orleans institution, this outpost fronting the Strip
★ at Desert Passage manages to replicate every other aspect of the 120-year-old original. That means classics such as turtle soup, shrimp rémoulade, bananas Foster, bread pudding soufflé, and French Quarter beignets; and updated offerings such as Lyonnaise Gulf shrimp with a potato crust and crispy fennel cabbage slaw, or tasso shrimp Henican with crystal hot sauce beurre blanc and five-pepper jelly. Stop in for beignets and chicory coffee for breakfast Monday through Friday, and don't forget the jazz brunch Friday through Sunday. ⊠ *Desert Passage at Aladdin, 3663 Las Vegas Blvd. S, Center Strip* ☎ *702/892–8272* ⊟*AE, D, DC, MC, V.*

★ **$$–$$$$** ✕ **Emeril's New Orleans Fish House.** A stone courtyard, French doors, and faux willow trees grace the entrance to Chef Emeril Lagasse's first Las Vegas dining spot. The original Emeril's is in New Orleans, and that Cajun feeling prevails here as well, with cayenne-color walls, modern metalwork, and black-and-white photos of Louisiana fishermen. A sampling of Emeril's creative dishes includes fried creole-marinated calamari, Hudson Valley foie gras on a peach tart, pan-roasted black bass with tasso hash, creole mustard-glaze redfish and Louisiana cedar-plank campfire steak. Be sure to try the double-chocolate Grand Marnier cake. ⊠ *MGM Grand Hotel and Casino, 3799 Las Vegas Blvd. S, South Strip* ☎ *702/891–7374* ⌫ *Reservations essential* ⊟ *AE, D, DC, MC, V.*

¢–$$ ✕ **House of Blues.** Like the Houses of Blues in other tourist-friendly cities, this one is a gaudy, stylized version of a Delta shack with a deliberately ramshackle look (making it easy to find in the tropical-theme hotel). The HOB compound has a concert hall and the requisite gift shop. Cold beer goes well with just about everything on the menu, from the smoked pork or mesquite-grilled chicken sandwiches to the center-cut pork chop in bourbon sauce or crawfish and shrimp étouffée. ⊠ *Man-*

dalay Bay Resort & Casino, 3950 Las Vegas Blvd. S, South Strip ☎ *702/ 632–7777* ▭ *AE, D, DC, MC, V.*

Caribbean

$$–$$$$ ✕ **rumjungle.** This Mandalay Bay establishment is so hugely popular as a dance club frequented by the see-and-be-seen set that some locals are surprised to learn it even serves food in the evening hours. That's not exactly how it was intended. The intensely themed interior—all waterfalls and fiery displays—was designed with the Brazilian rodizio "fire pit" in mind; a popular choice is the prix-fixe dinner of pork, lamb, chicken, fish, and vegetables served on skewers. Individual entrées include many Caribbean-theme dishes. ⊠ *Mandalay Bay Resort & Casino, 3950 Las Vegas Blvd. S, South Strip* ☎ *702/632–7777* ▭ *AE, D, DC, MC, V* ☉ *No lunch.*

$–$$$$ ✕ **Ortanique.** Chef Cindy Hutson, who became known for her "cuisine of the sun" at her signature Ortanique in Miami, shines a little light on Las Vegas in the walkway between Paris and Bally's. The menu melds flavors from South America, the West Indies, and Asia in such appetizers as jerked chicken, seared foie gras, and West Indian curried crab cakes with papaya coulis and tropical fruit salsa. For the second course, opt for rasta pasta, which is penne pasta topped with sun-dried tomatoes, shiitake mushrooms, and tropically seasoned chicken, all in a cream sauce, or island-spiced, seared ahi tuna with horseradish mashed potatoes. ⊠ *Paris Las Vegas, 3655 Las Vegas Blvd. S, Center Strip* ☎ *702/946– 4346* ▭ *AE, D, DC, MC, V.*

Chinese

$$–$$$$ ✕ **Empress Court.** This venerable upscale Chinese eatery entered a new era when was it relocated to a spot overlooking Caesars' Garden of the Gods swimming pool and the extensive gardens that surround it. Thai, Malaysian, and Indonesian specialties are part of the program, and seafood plays a starring role. Accordingly, some of the sea creatures can be found swimming in the restaurant's tanks until they're ordered. Offerings include abalone and shark-fin soup, Peking duck, and sautéed scallops with macadamia nuts. ⊠ *Caesars Palace, 3570 Las Vegas Blvd. S, Center Strip* ☎ *702/731–7110* ⌂ *Reservations essential* ▥ *Jacket and tie* ▭ *AE, D, DC, MC, V* ☉ *Closed Tues. and Wed. No lunch.*

$$–$$$$ ✕ **Royal Star.** Seafood-oriented dishes are the center of attention in this simple, neutral-tone dining room with lacquered black furniture. Dim sum is the star at lunchtime, when rolling carts offer a quick but quality feast of options such as pan-fried scallion cakes, barbecue-pork puffed pastries, or shrimp-stuffed eggplant. In the evening, you can have lobster or crab fresh from the tank or regional specials such as spicy garlic scallops and six hour spare ribs served over a bed of sautéed spinach. And yes, for the less adventurous there are well-executed versions of familiar dishes such as *kung pao* chicken and orange beef. ⊠ *Venetian Resort-Hotel-Casino, 3355 Las Vegas Blvd. S, Center Strip* ☎ *702/ 414–1888* ▭ *AE, D, DC, MC, V.*

¢–$ ✕ **P. F. Chang's China Bistro.** "Americanized" versions of Chinese classics are served at this high-energy eatery. (⇨ P. F. Chang's China Bistro in Paradise Road) ⊠ *Aladdin Resort and Casino, 3667 Las Vegas*

Blvd. S., Center Strip ☎ *702/785–5555* ⌣ *Reservations not accepted* ☰ *AE, MC, V.*

Contemporary

$$$$ ✕ **Aureole.** Celebrity chef Charlie Palmer re-created his famed New York restaurant for Mandalay Bay. He added a few playful, Las Vegas–style twists: A four-story wine tower, for example, holds 12,000 bottles that are reached by "wine fairies" who are hoisted up and down via a system of electronically activated pulleys. Seasonal specialties on the fixed-price menu might include toasted-corn blini with osetra caviar, saffron scallops with creamed potatoes, and bluefin tuna tartare with a chile-spiced ponzu sauce. For dessert try innovative offerings like decorated lemon custard, cool banana mousse, or pineapple-citrus cheesecake. ⊠ *Mandalay Bay Resort & Casino, 3950 Las Vegas Blvd. S, South Strip* ☎ *702/632–7401* ⌣ *Reservations essential* ☰ *AE, D, DC, MC, V* ⊙ *No lunch.*

$$$$ ✕ **Picasso.** This restaurant is adorned with the artist's original works, and
Fodor'sChoice   you never know just what famous face may be at the next table. Versa-
★   tile chef Julian Serrano prepares innovative takes on the regional cuisines of France and Spain. Appetizers on the seasonal menu might include warm quail salad with sautéed artichokes and pine nuts or poached oysters with osetra caviar and vermouth sauce. Sautéed medallions of fallow deer, slow-roasted short ribs, or roasted Atlantic turbot with carpaccio of potatoes might appear as entrée choices. Dinners are prix-fixe, with four- or five-course menus. ⊠ *Bellagio Las Vegas, 3600 Las Vegas Blvd. S, Center Strip* ☎ *702/693–8105* ⌣ *Reservations essential* 🏛 *Jacket required* ☰ *AE, D, DC, MC, V* ⊙ *Closed Tues. No lunch.*

★ **$$$–$$$$**   ✕ **Spago Las Vegas.** His fellow chefs stood by in wonder when Wolfgang Puck opened this branch of his famous Beverly Hills eatery in the culinary wasteland that was Las Vegas in 1992, but Spago Las Vegas has become a fixture in this ever-fickle city. The café section, which overlooks the busy Forum Shops at Caesars, is great for people-watching; the inside dining room is more intimate. Both menus are classic Puck and include roasted pumpkin ravioli with spinach, endive, and hazelnuts, as well as sautéed giant prawns with steamed bok choy, ginger, and Chinese black beans. ⊠ *Forum Shops at Caesars, 3500 Las Vegas Blvd. S, Center Strip* ☎ *702/369–6300* ☰ *AE, MC, V.*

$$–$$$$ ✕ **Postrio.** In many ways, this location in the Venetian's retail mall is the most elegant of Wolfgang Puck's Las Vegas rooms. Like most Puck places there's an "outdoor" sidewalk café in front of a formal dining room, which is trimmed in rich burgundy and accented with jeweled stained-glass pieces, curved to resemble film strips in a slightly Gaudí-like effect. The familiar Puck pizzas are here, but so are options like a lobster club sandwich or pumpkin ravioli. Dinner emphasizes seafood, including seared black bass with sautéed winter greens and warm lentil vinaigrette. ⊠ *Venetian Resort-Hotel-Casino, 3355 Las Vegas Blvd. S, Center Strip* ☎ *702/796–1110* ☰ *AE, D, DC, MC, V.*

$$–$$$$ ✕ **Red Square.** Theatrical designs, including a long bar made of ice, temper an upscale menu at this Soviet-chic place. For starters, swill a martini made from one of the 100 varieties of vodka and graze on caviar, a crab-stuffed portobello mushroom, or tuna and smoked salmon tartare. Settle into chicken Kiev, lobster and black-truffle fettuccine, or Roquefort-crusted filet mignon for dinner before finishing with the warm chocolate cake or crème brûlée. You can check out the walk-in vodka freezer, in which frequent patrons can rent their own space, if you splurge on an expensive bottle. ⊠ *Mandalay Bay Resort & Casino, 3950 Las Vegas Blvd. S, South Strip* ☎ *702/632–7777* ⚓ *Reservations essential* ▤ *AE, D, DC, MC, V* ☉ *No lunch.*

$$–$$$ ✕ **Pinot Brasserie.** James Beard Foundation Award–winning chef Joachim Splichal and his wife and partner Christine have duplicated their acclaimed Los Angeles Pinot restaurant—an urban-casual bistro with Franco-Californian cuisine. The storefront facade imported from France allows passersby to glimpse diners at their tables and cooks at work. Seafood includes oysters on the half shell (imported from wherever they are the freshest), scallop tartare, Pacific shrimp, and Dungeness crab. Other offerings include sweetbreads, lamb, venison, and poultry. ⊠ *Venetian Resort-Hotel-Casino, 3355 Las Vegas Blvd. S, Center Strip* ☎ *702/735–8888* ▤ *AE, D, DC, MC, V.*

Continental

$$$$ ✕ **Renoir.** The Mirage's showcase for the contemporary Franco-Italian
Fodor'sChoice cuisine of Chef Alessandro Stratta lives up to its name: genuine Renoir
★ paintings decorate the interior. Stratta's cooking is equally artful. The seasonal à la carte menu might include Santa Barbara prawns; roasted breast of pheasant with foie gras, potato, and artichoke confit; pancetta-wrapped veal tenderloin with lentils, arugula, and chanterelles; and braised veal cheeks with Swiss chard, black olives, and creamy polenta. Those who want the full Stratta experience, however, select the five-course tasting menu. ⊠ *Mirage Hotel and Casino, 3400 Las Vegas Blvd. S, Center Strip* ☎ *702/791–7111* ⚓ *Reservations essential* 🏠 *Jacket required* ▤ *AE, D, DC, MC, V* ☉ *No lunch.*

$$$–$$$$ ✕ **Top of the World.** Dining rooms with a view have historically been hard to come by in Las Vegas, but the Stratosphere Casino Hotel & Tower gave the city a striking landmark and a restaurant with stunning views. Rounded, floor-to-ceiling windows at this airy eatery near the top of the 1,149-foot tower give 360-degree views of the Vegas Valley. The entire dining room revolves once each hour. The fare here is standard Continental with a few twists: lobster ravioli, Cajun prime rib, grilled ahi tuna salad, and sandwiches at lunch. There's also a (nonrotating) cocktail lounge for casual sipping. ⊠ *Stratosphere Hotel Tower and Casino, 2000 Las Vegas Blvd. S, North Strip* ☎ *702/380–7711* ⚓ *Reservations essential* ▤ *AE, D, DC, MC, V.*

$$–$$$ ✕ **Pietro's.** You face the difficult choice of which creations to try here: pâté en croûte with lingonberry sauce, coquilles St. Jacques, and Nova Scotia smoked salmon are among the appetizers. Breast of capon Kiev with wild rice and roast duckling à l'orange or Montmorency (flamed with Bing cherries) are among the favored entrées, many of which are prepared tableside by Pietro himself. Among the desserts is crespelle flambe au Cointreau, a lovely light crepe in a buttery orange-flavored sauce, flamed tableside. Pietro's dining room is intimate (only 40 seats), service is exquisite, and tables are adorned with fresh flowers. ⊠ *Tropicana Resort and Casino, 3801 Las Vegas Blvd. S, South Strip* ☎ *702/*

739–2222 ⚑ *Reservations essential* ▤ *AE, D, DC, MC, V* ⊘ *Closed Mon. and Tues. No lunch.*

French

$$$$	✕ **Le Cirque.** This sumptuous restaurant, of the New York City landmark,
Fodor's Choice	is one of Bellagio's best. The mahogany-lined room is all the more op-
★	ulent for its size: in a city of mega-everything, Le Cirque seats only 80. Even with a view of the hotel's lake and its mesmerizing fountain show, you only have eyes for your plate when your server presents dishes such as sea scallops layered with black truffles and wrapped in spinach and puff pastry or black sea bass in crispy potatoes with braised leeks and Barolo sauce. The wine cellar contains more than 1,000 premium selections representing every wine-producing region of the world. ⊠ *Bellagio Las Vegas, 3600 Las Vegas Blvd. S, Center Strip* ☎ *702/693–8100* ⚑ *Reservations essential* ⋔ *Jacket required* ▤ *AE, D, DC, MC, V* ⊘ *No lunch.*

$$$–$$$$	✕ **Lutèce.** Though the famed New York eatery closed its doors in early 2004, Lutèce's legacy lives on at the Venetian. The circular dining room is done in postmodern trappings. The seasonal menu includes appetizers such as sautéed foie gras with chocolate sauce and entrées such as Black Angus sirloin with potato "au four." Those who want to leave the driving to the chef can go with the prix-fixe menu. ⊠ *Venetian Resort-Hotel-Casino, 3355 Las Vegas Blvd. S, Center Strip* ☎ *702/414–2220* ⋔ *Jacket and tie* ▤ *AE, D, DC, MC, V* ⊘ *No lunch.*

$$–$$$$	✕ **Andre's French Restaurant.** This second location of Andre's French
Fodor's Choice	Restaurant serves food that's as excellent as that at the downtown orig-
★	inal, but in a more spectacular room. (⇨ Andre's French Restaurant in Downtown) ⊠ *Monte Carlo Resort and Casino, 3770 Las Vegas Blvd. S, South Strip* ☎ *702/798–7151* ⚑ *Reservations essential* ▤ *AE, DC, MC, V* ⊘ *No lunch.*

★ $$–$$$$	✕ **Eiffel Tower Restaurant.** The signature restaurant of Paris Las Vegas is a room with a view, all right. What's special is not so much the 11-story height as the dramatic perch—about a third of the way up the hotel's half-scale Eiffel Tower replica, with views from all four glassed-in sides. The French-accented menu includes appetizers of cold smoked salmon, sea scallops, and Russian caviar. On the entrée list, you find Atlantic salmon in pinot noir sauce, lobster thermidor, roasted rack of lamb Provençal, and filet mignon in mushroom sauté. ⊠ *Paris Las Vegas, 3655 Las Vegas Blvd. S, Center Strip* ☎ *702/948–6937* ⚑ *Reservations essential* ⋔ *Jacket and tie* ▤ *AE, D, DC, MC, V* ⊘ *No lunch.*

$–$$$	✕ **Mon Ami Gabi.** This French-accented steak house has one of the highest profiles in town; it's the rare restaurant with sidewalk dining on the Strip. For those who prefer a less lively environment, a glassed-in atrium just off the street conveys an outdoor feel, and still-quieter dining rooms are inside, adorned with chandeliers dramatically suspended three stories above. The specialty of the house is steak frites, offered four different ways: classic, au poivre, Bordelaise, and Roquefort. There are fish and poultry dishes as well. ⊠ *Paris Las Vegas, 3655 Las Vegas Blvd. S, Center Strip* ☎ *702/946–7000* ⚑ *Reservations essential* ▤ *AE, D, DC, MC, V.*

Italian

$$$$ ✕ **Valentino and P. S. Italian Grill.** The Italian Grill, the busy front room of this dual restaurant on the Venetian's convention-friendly "restaurant row," has a casual, urban vibe. Choose either appetizer or entrée portions of pasta, or heartier fare such as three-meat lasagna, a rosemary-infused T-bone steak, or a cut of veal. The seasonal dining-room menu offers four meat and four seafood dishes; among them might be Maine scallops with a tomato-horseradish sauce and fresh oregano pesto or roasted chicken breast wrapped in smoked bacon with red-wine sauce, polenta, and spinach. ✉ *Venetian Resort-Hotel-Casino, 3355 Las Vegas Blvd. S, Center Strip* ☎ *702/414–3000* ▭ *AE, D, DC, MC, V* ☾ *Valentino: No lunch.*

$$$–$$$$ ✕ **Terrazza.** This dazzling Italian eatery in Caesars' spectacular Palace Tower has great views of the 4-acre Garden of the Gods pool; you also can dine alfresco on a terrace adjacent to the pool area. Terrazza offers excellent Caesar salads, designer pizzas, mushroom ravioli, lamb, veal chops, and steaks. Imported Italian beers and mineral waters, such as San Pellegrino, are available. ✉ *Caesars Palace, 3570 Las Vegas Blvd. S, Center Strip* ☎ *702/731–7110* ⟴ *Reservations essential* ▭ *AE, D, DC, MC, V* ☾ *No lunch.*

$$–$$$$ ✕ **Onda.** You enter this restaurant through a piano bar opening onto the casino. Beyond the lounge, with its arched, stained-glass ceiling and marble floor, is the restaurant, tucked behind one-way glass. The menu offers seafood choices such as garlic-crusted sea bass and lobster *Milanese* (breaded and pan-fried) as well as traditional pasta dishes such as lasagna, fettuccine Alfredo, and angel-hair pasta with shrimp, garlic, white wine, tomatoes, and bread crumbs. There's roasted chicken and chicken cacciatore, too. ✉ *Mirage Hotel and Casino, 3400 Las Vegas Blvd. S, Center Strip* ☎ *702/791–7111* ⟴ *Reservations essential* ▭ *AE, D, DC, MC, V* ☾ *No lunch.*

$$–$$$$ ✕ **Osteria del Circo.** With its view of the lake, this is one of Bellagio's prime dining spots. The colorful Circo, with its velveteen harlequin-pattern seats and whimsically decorated chandeliers, serves home-style Tuscan food. Among the appetizers are house-cured beef with arugula, Parmesan, and lemon vinaigrette, and a Maine lobster salad with fava beans. The homemade pastas include ravioli with spinach and sheep's milk ricotta in butter-sage or fresh tomato sauce. Caviars by the ounce are offered for dinner, and the extensive wine cellar has selections from every wine-producing region of the world. Circo is a sister restaurant of next-door Le Cirque. ✉ *Bellagio Las Vegas, 3600 Las Vegas Blvd. S, Center Strip* ☎ *702/693–8150* ▭ *AE, D, DC, MC, V.*

$$–$$$$ ✕ **Zeffirino.** Everything—from the tile work to many of the employees— comes straight from Italy, and all who enter here feel Italian, at least for the day. Seafood dominates the menu, which includes sautéed lobster, red snapper, and swordfish steak with herbs. Some dishes, such as the seafood symphony, bring the chef from the kitchen to layer assorted seafood and pasta in heated olive oil tableside. The pasta with pesto is said to have been a favorite of Pope John Paul II when he dined at the original Zeffirino in Genoa (Italy, not Nevada). Desserts include *crema caramella*, tiramisu, and *torta al cioccolato Milanese*. ✉ *Grand Canal*

Shops at Venetian Resort-Hotel-Casino, 3355 Las Vegas Blvd. S, Center Strip ☎ 702/414–1000 ☰ AE, D, MC, V.

$–$$$ ✕ **Market City Caffe.** Recipes passed down through generations are the centerpiece of this lively restaurant owned and operated by a family with successful eateries in southern California. The menu includes such hearty selections as pizzas (such as pizza gamberetto, with shrimp, goat cheese, fresh tomatoes, and pesto), salads (such as insalata di calamari, with calamari, diced tomatoes, capers, and mixed greens), and pastas (such as spaghetti *alla puttanesca*, with a tomato-anchovy sauce). ⊠ *Monte Carlo Resort and Casino, 3770 Las Vegas Blvd. S, South Strip* ☎ 702/730–7967 ☰ AE, D, DC, MC, V.

$–$$$ ✕ **Trattoria del Lupo.** Wolfgang Puck's first Italian eatery is in a rustic-looking dining room with a bar and wine room, an exhibition pizza and antipasto station, and a 20-foot-long communal table. Imaginative traditional and contemporary dishes include fried calamari with spicy tomato; delectable pizzas; linguine with spinach, eggplant, cipollini onions, and roasted garlic; and Alaskan halibut with fennel, potatoes, and heirloom-tomato salsa. For dessert, try the tiramisu cappuccino. ⊠ *Mandalay Bay Resort & Casino, 3950 Las Vegas Blvd. S, South Strip* ☎ 702/740–5522 ⌂ *Reservations essential* ☰ AE, D, DC, MC, V ☉ *No lunch.*

$–$$ ✕ **Bertolini's.** Tables at this sidewalk café inside the Forum Shops at Caesars are set up in the piazza surrounding the Fountain of the Gods. The outside section is noisy; if you want to talk, take a table in the dark, clubby interior, where booths line the black-and-yellow antiqued walls. An open kitchen turns out soups, salads, and wood-fired pizzas; try a wood-fired crab, spinach and artichoke dip to start. Pastas include the musically named rigatoni al telefono. ⊠ *The Forum Shops at Caesars, 3500 Las Vegas Blvd. S, Center Strip* ☎ 702/735–4663 ⌂ *Reservations not accepted* ☰ AE, DC, MC, V.

$–$$ ✕ **Il Fornaio.** Cross the Central Park footbridge inside the wonderfully quirky New York–New York Hotel and Casino and you come to Il Fornaio, a cheery and bright Italian café. You can dine "outdoors" on the patio by the pond and watch the world go by, or opt for a table inside. Cooks in an exhibition kitchen prepare fresh fish, wood-oven pizzas, spinach linguine with shrimp, and gnocchi with sausage, onions, mushrooms, tomato cream sauce, and Parmesan. Very good breads (including ciabatta) are baked twice daily, and you can buy loaves to go. ⊠ *New York–New York Hotel and Casino, 3790 Las Vegas Blvd. S, South Strip* ☎ 702/650–6500 ☰ AE, MC, V.

Japanese

$$–$$$$ ✕ **Mikado.** Only a few steps from the Mirage's casino, this restaurant provides a haven from the gambling madness; request a seat far from the door, near the placid streams, delicate gardens, and soft murals. The menu offers standard Japanese fare: steak, chicken, and shrimp prepared *teppanyaki* (chopped, diced, and sautéed on a hot grill) or tempura style; *yaki-tori* (grilled beef in a thick-noodle soup); plus sushi and sashimi from a sushi bar in the corner. ⊠ *Mirage Hotel and Casino, 3400 Las Vegas Blvd. S, Center Strip* ☎ 702/791–7111 ⌂ *Reservations essential* ☰ AE, D, DC, MC, V ☉ *No lunch.*

★ $–$$$$ ✕ **Hamada of Japan.** Hamada has the most locations of any Las Vegas Japanese restaurant, with several on the Strip for the convenience of visitors. Some are abbreviated versions, but all offer the food that has made Hamada a well-known name here and in Japan. (⇨ Hamada of Japan in Paradise Road) ✉ *The Flamingo, 3555 Las Vegas Blvd. S, Center Strip* ☎ *702/733–3455* ✉ *The Luxor, 3900 Las Vegas Blvd. S, South Strip* ☎ *702/262–4548* ✉ *Polo Towers, 3745 Las Vegas Blvd. S, South Strip* ☎ *702/736–1984* ✉ *Stratosphere Hotel Tower and Casino, 2000 Las Vegas Blvd. S, North Strip* ☎ *702/380–7777* ▭ *AE, D, DC, MC, V* ⊙ *No lunch.*

$–$$$$ ✕ **Mizuno's Japanese Steak House.** Lobster, steak, and chicken entrées are sliced, diced, and grilled at your teppan table by chefs who wield flashy knives and are possessed of witty tongues. Quality teriyaki and seafood dishes are other pluses at this fun Japanese restaurant. ✉ *Tropicana Resort and Casino, 3801 Las Vegas Blvd. S, South Strip* ☎ *702/739–2713* ▭ *AE, DC, MC, V* ⊙ *No lunch.*

Mediterranean

★ $$–$$$$ ✕ **Olives.** Chef–owner Todd English combines the best features of his Boston-area Olives and Figs restaurants in his Las Vegas eatery. The patio overlooking the Bellagio's spectacular lake is perfect for alfresco dining. Among the fare are appetizers of beef carpaccio on crispy Roquefort polenta, portobello picatta, and venison bruschetta. Entrées include crispy-skin duck breast on pumpkin *agrodolce* (with a sweet-sour pumpkin sauce) and a signature butternut squash tortelli. The chocolate falling cake is tantalizing. ✉ *Bellagio Las Vegas, 3600 Las Vegas Blvd. S, Center Strip* ☎ *702/693–8181* ▭ *AE, D, DC, MC, V.*

Pan-Asian

$$–$$$ ✕ **China Grill.** Postmodern architecture and appointments set the stage for Asian dishes with a contemporary accent in this Mandalay Bay restaurant. Start with appetizers such as tempura, sashimi, or broccoli rabe dumplings. The selection of entrées leans toward seafood, with options such as barbecued salmon, but there also are such fusion offerings as green tea–spiced roasted lamb rack with pear jam and roasted vegetables. ✉ *Mandalay Bay Resort & Casino, 3950 Las Vegas Blvd. S, South Strip* ☎ *702/632–7777* ⌦ *Reservations essential* ▭ *AE, D, DC, MC, V.*

$–$$$ ✕ **Chinois.** Yet another Wolfgang Puck creation, Chinois has a Pacific Rim flair. The menu changes daily, but there's a good balance of classic Chinese dishes and more innovative offerings, such as sweet curried beef *satays* (small cubes of meat on a skewer) or a tartare trio for starters, or sweet and sour sesame chicken or basil shrimp for entrées. And there's plenty of sushi. A sophisticated crowd frequents the OPM lounge upstairs, hob-knobbing to hip-hop, salsa, or Top 40 tunes. ✉ *The Forum Shops at Caesars, 3500 Las Vegas Blvd. S, Center Strip* ☎ *702/737–9700* ▭ *AE, D, DC, MC, V.*

Southwestern

★ $–$$$ ✕ **Border Grill.** The hosts of TV's "Too Hot Tamales," Mary Sue Milliken and Susan Feniger, have developed quite a following at their Las Vegas location at Mandalay Bay. Appetizers include green-corn tamales, ceviche, and plantain empanadas; for lunch try the turkey tostada or grilled skirt steak; and for dinner the sautéed rock shrimp, stacked enchilada, or chicken *chilaquiles* (corn tortilla strips saute• ed with vegetables and cheese). Oaxacan mocha cake and key lime pie are among the desserts. ⊠ *Mandalay Bay Resort & Casino, 3950 Las Vegas Blvd. S, South Strip* ☎ *702/632–7394* ▭ *AE, D, DC, MC, V.*

Steak

$$$$ ✕ **Delmonico Steakhouse.** Celebrity chef Emeril Lagasse gives the New Orleans touch to this big city–style steak house at the Venetian. The subdued, modern interior creates a feeling of calm, and friendly but professional staff members set you at ease. Consider the classic steak tartare with Dijon emulsion or the truffle grilled-cheese sandwich with creamy lobster coulis for starters, and entrées such as a roasted double-cut pork chop, Maine lobster, and all manner of steaks. Don't miss the Kahlua chocolate mousse pyramid for dessert. ⊠ *Venetian Resort-Hotel-Casino, 3355 Las Vegas Blvd. S, Center Strip* ☎ *702/733–5000* ⌲ *Reservations essential* ▭ *AE, D, DC, MC, V.*

$$$–$$$$ ✕ **Charlie Palmer Steak.** The whole idea of putting a Four Seasons hotel inside Mandalay Bay was to have a quiet enclave "hidden" within a busy hotel-casino complex. Charlie Palmer got the idea right away. Although his Aureole at Mandalay Bay is ostentatious, the nearby steak house is clubby and understated. The mahogany-lined room off the Four Seasons lobby serves only Black Angus that's been dry-aged for 21 days. There's tuna steak or caramelized chicken for those who don't eat beef. The lounge welcomes the revival of the cigar and has live entertainment on weekends. ⊠ *Four Seasons Hotel, 3960 Las Vegas Blvd. S, South Strip* ☎ *702/632–5120* ▭ *AE, D, DC, MC, V* ☉ *No lunch.*

$$–$$$$ ✕ **Bally's Steakhouse.** The dining room of this traditional steak house feels like a hunting lodge, with a large fireplace and comfortable furnishings. The menu includes sausage-filled mushrooms baked with garlic, spinach, and fontina cheese; Scottish smoked salmon with bagel chips and horseradish crème fraîche; and jumbo pancetta-wrapped sea scallops with fresh-basil relish. Try the aged prime rib or the mesquite-grilled 20-ounce bone-in rib eye with garlic-herb butter. Be sure your dessert pocket is not full—among the magnificently presented sweets is a signature banana cream pie. ⊠ *Bally's Las Vegas, 3645 Las Vegas Blvd. S, Center Strip* ☎ *702/967–4661* ▭ *AE, D, DC, MC, V* ☉ *No lunch.*

$$–$$$$ ✕ **Luxor Steakhouse.** The attractive restaurant, with its classic cherrywood bar and walls, is divided into several rooms and alcoves to afford intimate dining. Whole stuffed artichokes and hearty portobello mushrooms filled with seafood, spinach, and Gorgonzola are among the favorite appetizers. Entrée selections include pesto-crusted Chilean sea bass, fillet of beef Oscar, and live Maine lobster. The steaks are super-aged prime beef in the usual cuts, including filet mignon, porterhouse, and rib eye. ⊠ *Luxor Resort & Casino, 3900 Las Vegas Blvd. S, South Strip* ☎ *702/262–4778* ▭ *AE, D, DC, MC, V* ☉ *No lunch.*

★ $$–$$$$ ✕ **Prime Steakhouse.** Even among celebrity chefs, Jean-Georges Vongerichten has established a "can't touch this" reputation. Prime—with its gorgeous view of the fountains—has become a place to see and be seen at the Bellagio. In a velvet-draped, gold, burgundy, and blue room, choice cuts of beef are presented with mustards and sauces, from the classic béarnaise to the more adventurous tamarind. You can also try signature Vongerichten dishes, such as crab spring rolls with tamarind sauce. ☒ *Bellagio Las Vegas, 3600 Las Vegas Blvd. S, Center Strip* ☎ *702/ 693–8484* ⌔ *Reservations essential* ▭ *AE, D, DC, MC, V* ☾ *No lunch.*

$$–$$$$ ✕ **Smith & Wollensky.** The legendary New York restaurant has been replicated on the Strip, where it's a Las Vegas oddity: a stand-alone restaurant. With hardwood floors and no plush surfaces to soak up the ricocheting sound, it's a raucous place, but that's part of the fun. For steak, try the big Brooklyn porterhouse for two or the "Old Butcher Style" filet mignon. Other specialties include Maryland crab cakes, mustardcrusted tuna, lamb chops, and the famed crackling pork shank with applesauce. Wollensky's Grill, a lively, more casual gathering spot that's open until 3 AM, serves the same menu, as well as sandwiches and pizzas. ☒ *3767 Las Vegas Blvd. S, South Strip* ☎ *702/862–4100* ▭ *AE, DC, MC, V* ☾ *No lunch.*

$–$$ ✕ **Steak House.** Believe it or not, many local residents think this steak house set within the craziness of Circus Circus is among the best. It's totally unlike the rest of Circus Circus; wood paneling and antique brass furnishings adorn a dark, quiet room reminiscent of 1890s San Francisco. A ton of beef—aged 21 days—is displayed in a glassed-in area at one side; the cooking takes place over an open-hearth mesquite grill. Steaks, chops, chicken, and seafood make up the menu, and all entrées are accompanied by soup or salad, fresh bread, and a giant baked potato. ☒ *Circus Circus, 2880 Las Vegas Blvd. S, North Strip* ☎ *702/734–0410* ⌔ *Reservations essential* ▭ *AE, D, DC, MC, V* ☾ *No lunch.*

Downtown

American/Casual

¢–$$ ✕ **Carson Street Cafe.** The Golden Nugget is widely considered one of the gems of Downtown, and the Carson Street Cafe does it proud. The restaurant has a stylish Southern plantation feel and plays host to downtown's movers and shakers during weekday breakfast and lunch hours. Among the breakfast selections are eggs Benedict and the Vegas Experience—banana bread with walnut-cinnamon cream cheese, bananas, kiwi, and strawberries. Old familiars on the lunch and dinner menus include rainbow trout, Southern fried chicken, and slabs of baby-back ribs. ☒ *Golden Nugget Hotel and Casino, 129 E. Fremont St., Downtown* ☎ *702/385–7111* ▭ *AE, D, DC, MC, V.*

¢–$ ✕ **Jillian's.** Jillian's puts the fun in the downtown Neonopolis entertainment complex, with its bowling alley, pool room, and video games, and it's a great spot for watching the goings-on in the eclectic complex outside. The food's more serious, and includes dishes such as the authentic Ybor City cuban sandwich, pot roast, meatloaf, and barbecue ribs. Jumpin' Jack's jambalaya is about as spicy as they come, but the bar offers plenty to put out the fire. For dessert, consider some Southern bread pudding with Southern Comfort–spiked New Orleans sauce. ☒ *Neonopolis, 450 Fremont St., Downtown* ☎ *702/759–0450* ▭ *AE, D, MC, V.*

Where to Eat in Las Vegas (North)

Chinese

$–$$$$ ✕ **Lillie Langtry's.** This restaurant turns out fine Chinese food, but steaks have a starring role as well. The Cantonese dishes include old familiars such as moo goo gai pan and moo shu pork, plus spicier choices such as Szechuan shrimp. The black-pepper steak is a must for charcoal aficionados, and the lemon chicken is a classic. But if you'd rather, you can always go with a 22-ounce porterhouse or a 28-ounce rib eye. Don't miss the dragon-eye fruit for dessert. ⊠ *Golden Nugget Hotel and Casino, 129 E. Fremont St., Downtown* ☎ *702/385–7111* ⌂ *Reservations essential* ☰ *AE, D, DC, MC, V* ☉ *Closed Mon. and Tues. No lunch.*

Contemporary

$$–$$$$ ✕ **Second Street Grille.** Although you find steaks, Chinese roast duck, and Mongolian rack of lamb on the menu, seafood is the specialty here. Daily specials are flown in fresh from Hawaii. For starters try the ahi sashimi or seared sea scallops. For an entrée opt for the cedar-grilled salmon, sautéed soft-shell crab, or whole Thai snapper. The room is dark and intimate; the service is professional but not pretentious; and, best of all, Second Street Grille is relatively unknown in the Las Vegas fine-dining firmament, so you can usually count on same-day reservations. ⊠ *Fremont Hotel and Casino, 200 E. Fremont St., Downtown* ☎ *702/ 385–3232* ⌂ *Reservations essential* ☰ *AE, D, DC, MC, V* ☉ *Closed Tues. and Wed. No lunch.*

Continental

$$$–$$$$ ✕ **Hugo's Cellar.** Every woman receives a red rose at this romantic downtown favorite. Hugo's has been popular with Las Vegas locals since its opening in 1976. The staff is attentive and the narrow, brick-lined room has deep, comfortable booths. Offbeat touches include a hot rock appetizer (you cook marinated meats right at your table on a granite slab that is heated to 500°F) and a salad cart (you design your own salad tableside). Entrées vary from veal T-bone to tasty raspberry chicken to Indonesian-spiced rack of lamb. ⊠ *Four Queens Hotel and Casino, 202 Fremont St., Downtown* ☎ *702/385–4011* ☰ *AE, MC, V* ☉ *No lunch.*

French

$$–$$$$ ✕ **Andre's French Restaurant.** Cynics predicted an early demise for Andre
Fodor'sChoice   Rochat's venture when he opened a classic French restaurant in an ivy-
★   covered 1930s-era home blocks from the bright lights of downtown's famous Glitter Gulch. That was in 1980, and Las Vegans and visiting conventioneers are still savoring his oven-roasted rack of lamb with lentils and pearl onions, fillet of beef in green-peppercorn and cognac cream sauce, and tantalizing soufflés. You also find more updated creations; selections change daily. ⊠ *401 S. 6th St., Downtown* ☎ *702/385–5016* ⌂ *Reservations essential* ☰ *AE, DC, MC, V* ☉ *No lunch.*

Italian

$$–$$$ ✕ **Stefano's.** Tiles from Salerno, graceful hand-blown chandeliers from Venice, and colorful murals produce an island of serenity, and singing waiters (how can you not like a place where the waiters sing "Volare" and "Pepino the Italian Mouse"?) keep things lighthearted in this ristorante named for Las Vegas legend Steve Wynn. The menu includes such standards as prosciutto with melon or mozzarella marinara as well as updated creations such as wide, rippled pappardella noodles in a carbonara sauce, lobster tail Milanese, and scampi Bella Anna. ⊠ *Golden Nugget Hotel and Casino, 129 E. Fremont St., Downtown* ☎ *702/385–7111* ⌕ *Reservations essential* ☰ *AE, D, DC, MC, V* ⊘ *Closed Tues. and Wed. No lunch.*

$–$$ ✕ **Chicago Joe's.** Tucked away in a quiet section of downtown Las Vegas, this modest brick house with lace curtains and faded framed photographs offers a welcome respite from the glitzy casino hustle. Chicago Joe's has been drawing informed tourists and Vegas locals for more than two decades. The marinara sauce, which tops generous portions of pasta, veal, and chicken, has just the right amount of bite. Order "The Works" on any lunchtime sandwich (rib eye, sausage, or meatball) and savor a mound of sautéed green peppers, mushrooms, and onions. Extra napkins are essential. ⊠ *820 S. 4th St., Downtown* ☎ *702/382–5637* ☰ *AE, D, DC, MC, V* ⊘ *Closed Sun.*

Mexican

★ $ ✕ **Doña Maria.** You forget you're in Las Vegas after a few minutes in this relaxed and unpretentious cantina. Stop in on a Wednesday night and you might see a crowd gathered for the *fútbol* game on satellite-provided Mexican TV. All of the combinations and specials are good, but the best play here is to order the enchilada-style tamale (with red or green sauce), for which Doña Maria is justly renowned. You also won't go wrong with the *queso fundido con chorizo* (Mexican-style sports-bar food). ⊠ *910 Las Vegas Blvd. S, Downtown* ☎ *702/786–6358* ☰ *AE, D, DC, MC, V.*

¢–$ ✕ **El Sombrero.** In Las Vegas, where buildings that have been around for just a couple of decades are routinely flattened (sometimes on TV), a restaurant that's been in existence since 1950 is rare indeed. But that's the case with El Sombrero, a small spot downtown. It's not fancy, but the crowds packing in at lunch and dinner—including lots of Mexican expatriates—attest to a deft hand with classics such as enchiladas, tacos, burritos, and the like. The guacamole's homemade, and the *pesole* (pork stew with hominy) is among the best in town. The delicate air-filled *sopaipillas* (deep-fried pastries) make the perfect dessert after a meal of Mexican classics. ⊠ *807 S. Main St., Downtown* ☎ *702/382–9234* ☰ *AE, MC, V* ⊘ *Closed Sun.*

Steak

★ $–$$$ ✕ **Pullman Grille.** It may be close to one end of downtown Las Vegas's Glitter Gulch, but Main Street Station is a quiet island of Victorian elegance, magnified in the Pullman Grille. There's even a Pullman car right in the restaurant; you can retreat to it for a cigar and a port after dinner if you'd like. Dinner leans heavily to steaks, but owing to the Hawaiian clientele of the hotel-casino there are plenty of Asian offerings, too, including a sashimi appetizer of sea-breeze-fresh ahi tuna. Other choices include a seafood medley casserole and succulent lamb chops. ⊠ *Main Street Station, 200 N. Main St., Downtown* ☎ *702/387–1896* ⌕ *Reservations essential* ☰ *AE, D, DC, MC, V* ⊘ *Closed Mon. and Tues. No lunch.*

Paradise Road

American

★ $$–$$$ ✕ **Lawry's The Prime Rib.** In a city famous for low-price prime rib specials, Lawry's is an upscale, art deco–style palace dedicated to the pursuit of excellence in the guise of slow-roasted, aged rib roasts. The dining room, with hardwood floors and plush banquettes, is staffed by waitresses in 1930s-style uniforms and by white-clad carvers, who roll gleaming domed silvery carts up to your table. Atlantic lobster tails and a daily fresh-fish entrée are available for those who don't eat meat. ⊠ *4043 Howard Hughes Pkwy., Paradise Road* ☎ *702/893–2223* ⌂ *Reservations essential* ☰ *AE, MC, V* ⊗ *No lunch.*

American/Casual

$–$$ ✕ **Gordon Biersch Brewing Co.** The Palo Alto import is popular with both singles and the power-lunch crowd. Glassed-off brewing kettles are the design centerpiece as well as the main attraction at the square center bar, which offers specialty brews such as Marzen and Hefeweizen. The menu has one of the city's most creative selections of appetizers, including chile- and ginger-glaze chicken wings and crispy artichoke hearts tossed with Parmesan. Entrées include pastas and wood-oven pizzas, pan-seared ahi tuna, and old-fashioned meatloaf with brown gravy. ⊠ *3987 Paradise Rd., Paradise Road* ☎ *702/312–5247* ☰ *AE, D, DC, MC, V.*

¢–$ ✕ **Mr. Lucky's 24/7.** The hippest casino coffee shop in Las Vegas is inside the Hard Rock Hotel, where banks of slot machines bear the likenesses of Jimi Hendrix and Sid Vicious. Clean, modern lines; light-wood floors; and vintage rock-and-roll posters highlight this bubbly, circular café. You can have vegetable omelets, pizza, or pasta; more filling options include steak, grilled salmon, and baby-back ribs. The garlic mashed potatoes are superb. Insiders ask about the off-the-menu steak special: an 8-ounce New York steak, three grilled shrimp, baked potato, and salad for $7.77. It's open 24 hours, seven days a week—hence the numbers in the name. Beware: the music is loud. ⊠ *Hard Rock Hotel and Casino, 4455 Paradise Rd., Paradise Road* ☎ *702/693–5000* ⌂ *Reservations not accepted* ☰ *AE, D, DC, MC, V.*

Brazilian

$–$$ ✕ **Yolie's.** If you like rodizio served in the fashion of a *churrascaria* (a Brazilian "house of meat"), then this is the place for you. The fixed price of $26.95 ($14.95 at lunch) gets you bread, soup, sides, and all-you-can-eat slices of turkey, lamb, brisket, chicken, sausage, and steak, all grilled over a mesquite-fired, glass-enclosed rotisserie that you can see from the dining room. It's a fun place to eat. ⊠ *3900 Paradise Rd., Paradise Road* ☎ *702/794–0700* ⌂ *Reservations essential* ☰ *AE, D, DC, MC, V* ⊗ *No lunch weekends.*

Caribbean

$ ✕ **Bahama Breeze.** No worries, mon; Bahama Breeze is a casual spot with tropical flavors and flair—a bit of Jamaica, a bit of Cuba, a lot of fun. Signature dishes include the satisfying jerk chicken pasta, with asparagus and mushrooms in an herb cream sauce, as well as such classics as *ropa vieja* (shredded beef stew), steak *churrasco* (barbecue), conch chowder, and black beans and rice. Starters are tropically flavored, too, such as the *tostones con pollo*, in which crispy plantains are topped with chicken and cheese, or Jamaican grilled chicken wings. And watch out for those tropical drinks. ⊠ *375 Hughes Center Dr., Paradise Road* ☎ *702/731–3252* ⌆ *Reservations not accepted* ☰ *AE, D, DC, MC, V* ☺ *No lunch.*

Chinese

¢–$ ✕ **P. F. Chang's China Bistro.** "Americanized" versions of Chinese classics are served at this high-energy eatery. Chinese sculptures and murals are offset by high-tech lighting fixtures and a modern, earth-tone color scheme. The 60-item menu has the basics, like sweet-and-sour pork and barbecued spareribs, or more adventurous options, such as lemon-pepper shrimp and Chang's spicy chicken. Vegetarians will find plenty of noodle, rice, and vegetable dishes at this East-meets-West hot spot. The best—and most popular—dishes on the menu are chicken in soothing lettuce wraps and crispy honey shrimp. ⊠ *4165 S. Paradise Rd., Paradise Road* ☎ *702/792–2207.*

Contemporary

¢–$$ ✕ **Roy's.** Don't worry about fusion confusion here; Roy Yamaguchi practically invented the trend and knows how to do it right. The menu changes daily, but you can expect appetizers such as seared shrimp on a stick with wasabi cocktail sauce or Hawaiian crispy crab cakes in sesame beurre blanc. Entrées might include signature Yamaguchi dishes such as blackened ahi tuna in a spicy hot soy mustard sauce, teriyaki hibachi-grilled salmon with Japanese vegetable salad and citrus ponzu sauce, or roasted macadamia nut mahi mahi in lobster cognac butter sauce. ⊠ *620 E. Flamingo Rd., Paradise Road* ☎ *702/691–2053* ☰ *AE, D, DC, MC, V* ☺ *No lunch.*

Eclectic

¢–$ ✕ **Hamburger Mary's.** A bun choice called You're White Bread might be your first clue that things are different at Mary's; another is a pizza named for Las Vegas's popular mayor Oscar Goodman, with gin-sautéed mushrooms in honor of hizzoner's favorite brew. There are other choices, but burgers are the thing; the Blueboy Burger features bacon-and-blue-cheese dressing. Finish things up with the Hawaiian sweetbread pudding with Captain Morgan spiced-rum sauce, or tiramisu with macadamia nuts. ⊠ *4503 Paradise Rd., Paradise Road* ☎ *702/735–4400* ☰ *AE, D, MC, V.*

¢–$ ✕ **Hofbräuhaus Las Vegas.** Las Vegas upped its kitsch quotient when it imported this offshoot of Munich's most famous brewery. The interior beer garden is the perfect spot to down a Hof brew in those notorious liter mugs, especially on too-hot Vegas evenings. Pair your beer with hearty Bavarian classics, including Wiener schnitzel, goulash, and schweinebraten, or updated dishes such as Caesar salad with pretzel croutons. For dessert, try appel strudel or vanilla ice cream drenched in hot raspberry sauce. They've covered the oopmah here, too: bands brought in from Germany keep things as lively as they are back in München. ⊠ *4510 Paradise Rd., Paradise Road* ☎ *702/853–2337* ☰ *AE, D, DC, MC, V.*

Indian

$–$$ ✕ **Gandhi India's Cuisine.** If you're tired of all of the steak and prime-rib specials offered in town, try this alternative. Gandhi offers dishes from major regions of India; large *thali* platters range from milder North Indian tandoori dishes to spicier versions favored in the country's southern regions. A vegetarian thali includes *samosas* (vegetable fritters), *alu Gobi* (cauliflower and baked potatoes), and *mattar panner* (peas with homemade cottage cheese). Colorful Indian fabrics decorate this airy eatery; there's a small loft for more intimate dining. A buffet lunch is served daily. ⊠ *4080 Paradise Rd., Paradise Road* ☎ *702/734–0094* ⌂ *Reservations not accepted* ▭ *AE, D, DC, MC, V.*

$ ✕ **Shalimar Fine Indian Cuisine.** Las Vegan Wayne Newton is reportedly a frequent visitor to this sedate restaurant just minutes from the Strip. White tablecloths, hanging brass lamps, and taped Indian music provide a comfortable spot for excellent North Indian cuisine. House specialties include eight lamb dishes that can be prepared mild, wild hot, crazy hot, and one-way ticket to the moon, plus marinated seafood and chicken tandoori dishes cooked over a mesquite grill. The weekday luncheon buffet includes 25 different dishes. ⊠ *3900 S. Paradise Rd., Paradise Road* ☎ *702/796–0302* ▭ *AE, D, DC, MC, V* ☻ *No lunch weekends.*

Italian

🐾 **$–$$** ✕ **Buca di Beppo.** Want to really have fun while dining out? Get together a big group of friends and head to Buca di Beppo. While many restaurants aren't particularly welcoming to large groups, Buca di Beppo revels in them. Maybe you can sit in the Pope's room, with the bust of the pontiff on a lazy Susan in the center of the table. Dishes are served family-style—and how; a small Caesar salad can easily serve four. Try the rigatoni Positano, with chicken, eggplant, marinara sauce, and fresh mozzarella; the chicken cacciatore, also billed as "7 pounds of love"; or a Neapolitan-style pizza. ⊠ *412 E. Flamingo Rd., Paradise Road* ☎ *702/ 866–2867* ▭ *AE, D, DC, MC, V* ☻ *No lunch weekdays.*

Japanese

★ **$$–$$$$** ✕ **Nobu.** Chef Nobu Matsuhisa has replicated the decor and menu of his Manhattan Nobu (in the trendy TriBeCa neighborhood) in this sparkling restaurant with bamboo pillars, a seaweed wall, and birch trees. Imaginative specialties include spicy sashimi, caramelized sweet miso–marinated black cod, red-bean and green-tea ice cream, *mochi* balls (ice cream wrapped in sweet rice gelatin), and a warm chocolate soufflé. ⊠ *Hard Rock Hotel and Casino, 4455 Paradise Rd., Paradise Road* ☎ *702/693– 5000* ▭ *AE, D, DC, MC, V* ☻ *No lunch.*

★ **$–$$$$** ✕ **Hamada of Japan.** No matter what type of Japanese food you're in the mood for, you find it here. Hamada of Japan has a teppan room, which offers entrées of the sort found in Japanese steak houses; a sushi bar (which offers a dish called "sushi for beginners"); and a dining room, with a menu that includes teriyaki and tempura dishes, among others. There's a bit of overlap between menus, so if you're seated in the teppan room, you still can order sushi. This location is the flagship and has the best atmosphere of any of the Hamada locations, with a number of Japanese art items and artifacts; it's also the largest, with high ceilings and spacious rooms. ⊠ *365 E. Flamingo Rd., Paradise Road* ☎ *702/733–3005* ▭ *AE, D, DC, MC, V* ☉ *No lunch.*

Mexican

¢–$ ✕ **Pink Taco.** Nothing inside the Hard Rock Hotel is boring, and that goes for this over-the-top take on a Mexican cantina. The food is serviceable but takes a decided backseat to the party scene, which includes a huge four-sided bar, patio doors that open onto the hotel's elaborate pool area, and waitresses in soccer jerseys that are low-cut from every direction. The eyebrow-raising name refers to the grilled salmon taco, one of six special tacos on the menu. ⊠ *Hard Rock Hotel and Casino, 4455 Paradise Rd., Paradise Road* ☎ *702/693–5000* ▭ *AE, D, DC, MC, V.*

Moroccan

$$$ ✕ **Marrakech.** Sprawl out on soft floor cushions and feel like a pampered pasha as belly dancers shake it up in a cozy Middle Eastern–style "tent" with a fabric-covered ceiling and eye-catching mosaics. The prix-fixe feast is a six-course affair that you eat with your hands: shrimp scampi, vegetable salad, lentil soup, Cornish game hen, lamb shish kebab, and the tasty dessert *pastilla,* which is baked phyllo dough layered with apples, peaches, and pecans. Algerian wines flow freely in this upbeat spot where servers wear Moroccan robes and patrons are invited to join the belly dancers if they feel the urge. ⊠ *3900 Paradise Rd., Paradise Road* ☎ *702/737–5611* ▭ *AE, D, DC, MC, V.*

Seafood

★ $–$$$ ✕ **McCormick & Schmick's.** The Portland-based spot has old-tavern charm (complete with stained glass) and offers a huge menu of appetizers, oysters on the half shell, salads, lunch sandwiches, and imaginatively prepared fresh-fish dishes (the selection changes daily). Popular choices are Dungeness crab and artichoke dip with crostinis, Nantucket Bay sea scallops with *persillade* (chopped parsley and garlic), grilled Baja California yellowtail with spicy lemon aioli, and blackened rare Kona Hawaii ahi with wasabi cream. If the weather's pleasant, you can dine on the patio. ⊠ *335 Hughes Center Dr., Paradise Road* ☎ *702/836–9000* ▭ *AE, D, DC, MC, V.*

Southwestern

¢–$ ✕ **Z' Tejas Grill.** This Austin, Texas–based chain first conquered Las Vegas with a spot on the Paradise Road convention corridor, then added a second location in the far west end of town. Both locations offer signature dishes such as catfish beignets, Voodoo Tuna (blackened tuna with spicy soy mustard), ancho-rubbed pork tenderloin, and jerk chicken salad. ⊠ *3824 Paradise Rd., Paradise Road* ☎ *702/732–1660* ▭ *AE, D, DC, MC, V.*

Steak

$$$$ ✕ **A.J.'s Steakhouse.** The Hard Rock Hotel offers a time-machine ride back to Old Las Vegas with this retro-style room that's a tribute to Hard Rock chairman Peter Morton's father, Arnie, a Chicago restaurateur. Behind the oxblood leather front doors lies a dining room decorated with

WHERE TO REFUEL AROUND TOWN

Cook on Wok: *Families seem to appreciate the fresh wok specialties and dinners for four or eight.* ✉ 9255 S. Eastern Ave., East Side ☎ 702/263–8868 ✉ 8380 W. Cheyenne Ave., Northwest Las Vegas ☎ 702/658–8877.

In 'N' Out: *The simple menu of fresh burgers, just-cut french fries, and milkshakes makes this affordable West Coast fast-food joint a cult favorite.* ✉ 2900 W. Sahara Ave., West Side ✉ 4705 S. Maryland Pkwy., University District ✉ 4888 Industrial Rd., West Side ☎ 800/786–1000.

Jason's Deli: *Soups, sandwiches—including hero-style muffalettas and po'boys—and salads star on Jason's extensive menu.* ✉ 3910 S. Maryland Pkwy., East Side ☎ 702/893–9799 ✉ 1000 S. Rampart Blvd., Northwest Las Vegas ☎ 702/967–9008.

Marie Callender's: *Lots of people come for the pies, but Marie's is a good place to get a bargain-price meal.* ✉ 600 E. Sahara Ave., East Las Vegas ☎ 702/734–6572 ✉ 4800 S. Eastern Ave., East Las Vegas ☎ 702/458–2127 ✉ 4875 W. Flamingo Rd., West Side ☎ 702/365–6226 ✉ 3081 N. Rainbow Blvd., West Side ☎ 702/655–8200 ✉ 8175 W. Sahara Ave., West Side ☎ 702/341–0232.

Stuart Anderson's Black Angus Restaurants: *Reliable steaks and quick-in, quick-out service make this a popular neighborhood choice.* ✉ 5125 W. Sahara Ave., West Side ☎ 702/251–9300 ✉ 2025 Village Center Circle, Northwest Las Vegas ☎ 702/341–0767.

1950s-style furniture and photos; there's even a piano bar. Among the appetizers are a gulf shrimp cocktail and smoked Norwegian salmon. Featured steaks include a 20-ounce New York strip sirloin and a 24-ounce prime porterhouse. Alaskan salmon encrusted in horseradish and Hawaiian tuna steak are among the nonbeef options. ✉ *Hard Rock Hotel and Casino, 4455 Paradise Rd., Paradise Road* ☎ *702/693–5500* ⊟ *AE, D, DC, MC, V* ☉ *Closed Sun. and Mon. No lunch.*

Greater Las Vegas

American

$–$$$ ✗ **The Broiler.** Station Casinos has emerged as one of the front-running off-Strip casino organizations; its resorts serve as neighborhood casino outposts of the original Palace Station. Branches of The Broiler, its good, inexpensive steak-and-seafood house, are found at both Palace and Boulder Stations. Both locations have excellent soups, breads, and a salad bar, which set the stage for medium-price mesquite-grilled steaks, veal, and chicken. ✉ *Boulder Station Hotel and Casino, 4111 Boulder Hwy., Boulder Strip* ☎ *702/432–7777* ✉ *Palace Station Hotel and Casino, 2411 W. Sahara Ave., West Side* ☎ *702/367–2411* ⊟ *AE, D, MC, V.*

¢–$$ ✕ **Tenaya Creek Restaurant & Brewery.** Tenaya Creek is a brew pub with a contemporary design and superb customer service. The menu's up-to-date, too—a far cry from the old bar food. It has starters such as fresh crab cakes with green-onion aioli, and filet-mignon-and-vegetable-filled spring rolls. Entrées include North Coast halibut with creamy dill sauce, vodka salmon or prawns pasta, a number of pizzas, and a 28-day-aged sirloin with Black Forest mushroom sauce and truffle oil. ⊠ *3101 N. Tenaya Way, Northwest Las Vegas* ☎ *702/362–7335* ▤ *AE, D, DC, MC, V.*

American/Casual

¢–$ ✕ **Mimi's Cafe.** Mimi's may sound French—a Frenchwoman was the inspiration behind the name of this growing California-based chain—and the furnishings may look French, but the menu is American. For starters, consider a Thai chicken wrap, Cajun popcorn shrimp, or spinach-and-artichoke dip. Entrée choices include barbecued meatloaf, penne with pine nuts and feta, and turkey breast with corn-bread dressing. And don't pass the dessert case without peeking or you might miss the warm triple chocolate brownie or New Orleans bread pudding. ⊠ *1121 S. Fort Apache Rd., Northwest Las Vegas* ☎ *702/341–0365* ⊠ *596 N. Stephanie St., Henderson* ☎ *702/458–0726* ▤ *AE, D, MC, V.*

¢ ✕ **L&L Hawaiian Barbecue.** It's not barbecue as most mainlanders think of it, but L&L is authentic nonetheless and reflects the growing Hawaiian population in Henderson and other parts of the valley. One specialty is the Loco Moco, which is fried eggs on hamburger patties topped with gravy and accompanied by macaroni salad and rice. The plate lunch is the thing here, and comes in many permutations, with macaroni salad and rice. The chicken *katsu* (thinly cut, breaded, and fried) is crisp; the barbecue sauce is island-sweet; and there's Spam on the menu. For filling food at a bargain price, L&L is it. ⊠ *687 N. Stephanie St., Henderson* ☎ *702/433–0240* ▤ *MC, V.*

Barbecue

¢–$$ ✕ **Buckingham Smokehouse Bar-B-Q.** You can smell the barbecue—actually the smoking wood that's used to cook these down-home favorites—the minute you walk in the door, sometimes even before. Buckingham advertises that its beef brisket and pork loin are smoked for 18 hours, and the proof is in the flavor. The baby back ribs are Buckingham's signature piece, but there are plenty of other, less expensive choices, such as the smoked ham, smoked salmon fillet, hot link, pulled pork, and even a hickory-smoked Philly sandwich. For a zesty change of pace, consider the horseradish cole slaw; the sweet-potato french fries are a sweet taste on the side. And for dessert you might want to try a slice of apple pie or pecan pie—maybe à la mode. ⊠ *2341 N. Rainbow Blvd., Northwest Las Vegas* ☎ *702/638–7799 or 702/638–8699* ▤ *AE, D, MC, V.*

¢–$ ✕ **Memphis Championship Barbecue.** Barbecue the old-fashioned way: that's what fans are looking for, and that's what Memphis Championship Barbecue delivers. The owner–founder hails from Murphysboro, Illinois, which apparently is a well-kept secret as a barbecue stronghold, and cooks Memphis-style; hence the name. If you've got a big appetite—or a big family—try Mama Faye's Down Home Supper Dinner for four; you won't go away hungry. Other choices include smoked hot links, barbecued pork shoulder, and catfish. Oh, and on the side, treat yourself to some fried dill pickles. ⊠ *2250 E. Warm Springs Rd., East Side* ☎ *702/260–6909* ⊠ *4379 Las Vegas Blvd. N, North Las Vegas* ☎ *702/644–0000* ⊠ *Santa Fe Station, 4949 N. Rancho Dr., Las Vegas* ☎ *702/396–6223* ☐ *AE, D, MC, V.*

Buffets

$$$ ✕ **Village Seafood Buffet.** Seafood fans flock to the Rio's nautical-theme buffet, complete with American, Mexican, Italian, and Chinese serving stations. At the American station you can load up on seafood salads, snow-crab legs, oysters on the half shell, peel-and-eat shrimp, seafood gumbo, broiled swordfish, oysters Rockefeller, and lobster tails. Then come the ethnic ocean entrées, such as seafood fajitas, cioppino, seafood cannelloni, and kung pao scallops. Try to arrive either early or late, because the Village Seafood Buffet draws the crowds and lines sometimes are long. ⊠ *Rio All-Suite Hotel and Casino, 3700 W. Flamingo Rd., West Side* ☎ *702/252–7777* ☐ *AE, D, DC, MC, V.*

$–$$ ✕ **Carnival World Buffet.** This was one of the first Las Vegas buffets with separate theme areas; the buffets-within-a-buffet serve fresh Mexican, Italian, Chinese, Japanese, American, and other ethnic specialties under one large and colorful roof. Hamburgers and french fries, fish-and-chips, barbecue, sushi, salads, desserts, and more are also available. At this writing, the buffet was undergoing renovations and some of the selection was condensed. ⊠ *Rio All-Suite Hotel and Casino, 3700 W. Flamingo Rd., West Side* ☎ *702/252–7777* ☐ *AE, D, DC, MC, V.*

¢–$ ✕ **Feast Around the World.** The buffet at Green Valley Ranch Resort has a name similar to those at some of Station Casinos' other properties, and the options are somewhat similar, but there's no mistaking that the company has improved its offerings with each new casino. A huge display of fresh produce and the use of natural stone and carefully designed lighting lend a decidedly upscale touch to the entrance hall. Specialty stations include a Mongolian grill, Italian, Mexican, and American, plus a good-size salad bar and a belt-busting selection of pastries. ⊠ *Green Valley Ranch Resort, 2300 Paseo Verde Pkwy., Henderson* ☎ *702/ 614–5283* ☐ *AE, D, DC, MC, V.*

Chinese

¢–$ ✕ **Cathay House.** Cathay House is a bit of a rarity in Las Vegas—a restaurant that has the feel of a mom-and-pop spot, but with a sophisticated atmosphere and a menu that combines the best of both worlds. It's considered one of the best places in town for dim sum; among other local favorites are the flaming pineapple chicken, strawberry chicken, and sautéed crystal shrimp. Save room, too, for moist, flavorful duck prepared in varying styles. ⊠ *5300 W. Spring Mountain Rd., West Side* ☎ *702/876–3838* ☐ *AE, D, MC, V.*

¢–$ ✕ **P. F. Chang's China Bistro.** "Americanized" versions of Chinese classics are served at this high-energy eatery. (⇨ P. F. Chang's China Bistro in Paradise Road) ⊠ *1095 S. Rampart Blvd., Northwest Las Vegas* ☎ *702/ 968–8885* ⊠ *101 S. Green Valley Pkwy., Henderson* ☎ *702/361–3065* ☐ *AE, MC, V.*

Contemporary

$–$$$ ✕ **Rosemary's.** Husband-and-wife chefs Michael and Wendy Jordan established their reputation in Las Vegas with a West Side location that caters to locals, making them the first to prove that good-quality, upscale restaurants could survive off the Strip. Among the signature dishes on the American regional menu are Hugo's Texas BBQ Shrimp with Maytag Bleu Cheese Slaw—a favorite with regulars—plus a starter of crispy veal sweetbreads with lentils and bacon-leek relish. Rosemary roasted lamb, brick chicken, and herb-crusted veal tenderloin are tasty entrée picks. For dessert, try the lemon icebox pie with raspberry sorbet and raspberry coulis. A newer location at the Rio is closer to the tourism corridor. ⊠ *8125 W. Sahara Ave., West Side* ☎ *702/869–2251* ⊗ *No lunch weekends* ⊠ *Rio All-Suite Hotel and Casino, 3700 W. Flamingo Rd., West Side* ☎ *702/362–2033* △ *Reservations essential* ⊟ *AE, D, DC, MC, V* ⊗ *No lunch.*

*Fodor's*Choice
★

¢–$$ ✕ **Roy's.** This suburban Roy's outlet is frequented primarily by locals, which may make it easier to get a late-day reservation. It serves all of the Yamaguchi favorites found at the Roy's in the Paradise Road area. (⇨ Roy's in Paradise Road) ⊠ *8701 W. Charleston Blvd. West Side* ☎ *702/838–3620* ⊟ *AE, D, DC, MC, V* ⊗ *No lunch.*

Eclectic

$–$$ ✕ **The Melting Pot.** Basic fondue and more inventive creations make this chain a forerunner of the fondue trend. Cheese fondue, prepared tableside, comes in four variations; there's the traditional Gruyère and Emmenthaler with white wine or the offbeat spicy fiesta cheddar made with jalapeños. Entrées can be cooked in one of four broths and include boneless chicken breast and medallions of filet mignon; you could also try twin lobster tails or go vegetarian with a plate that includes tofu and artichoke hearts. Finish with any of the nine chocolate fondues. Smooth service and cozy furnishings take the typical frenzied Las Vegas experience down a notch. ⊠ *8704 W. Charleston Blvd., Northwest Las Vegas* ☎ *702/384–6358* ⊟ *AE, D, MC, V* ⊗ *No lunch.*

¢–$ ✕ **J. C. Wooloughan Irish Pub.** What do you get when you build a pub in Ireland, dismantle it, and ship it across the ocean, to be reconstructed in the desert? An Irish pub in a Las Vegas off-Strip resort that looks like a wee bit o' the Emerald Isle. J. C. Wooloughan offers Irish beers and beer blends and lots of Irish foods, both familiar and not-so. Cheek-by-jowl with the corned beef and cabbage, you find Bantry Bay fish cakes, Irish sausage rolls, beef-and-Guinness pie, and all-day Irish breakfast. Finish with the fantastic Aunt Maura's sticky toffee pudding. ⊠ *JW Marriott Las Vegas Casino Resort, 221 N. Rampart Blvd., Summerlin* ☎ *702/869–7777* ⊟ *AE, D, MC, V.*

¢–$ ✕ **Restaurant Eliseevsky.** Talk about an only-in-Las Vegas experience: Slip into this rendition of Uncle Misha's dacha in a strip mall just a few miles from the Strip and you may feel like an extra in *Gorky Park*. The air is thick with smoke and heavy with Russian as expatriates hunch over vodka, cigarettes in hand. Think "Russian cuisine" is an oxymoron? The kitchen makes an honest effort to battle the stereotype with Streletz's Plate, a colorful pastiche of grilled vegetables with garlic, and Gourmand Duck, a duck fillet with grilled oranges and cherry sauce. The familiar pierogi, borscht, blini, or Stroganoff are tasty. ☒ *4825 W. Flamingo Rd., West Side* ☎ *702/247–8766* ▤ *AE, D, MC, V.*

★ ¢ ✕ **Crown & Anchor British Pub.** With its 24-hour service and graveyard specials, Crown & Anchor is uniquely Las Vegas, but most of the food's British, including the steak and kidney pie; Ploughman's Lunch; bangers and mash; and authentic fish and chips. Sandwiches with American and British flavors are plenty, and the nightly specials make this spot even more of a bargain proposition. There are "draught" beers from all over the world and a "British Shoppe" selling "salad cream," Branston Pickle, and the like. If you still doubt the authenticity, know that the trifle is made with Bird's English custard. The decor's decidedly British, and special events add to the fun: on New Year's Eve the celebration starts at the English midnight, eight hours before the Las Vegas one. ☒ *1350 E. Tropicana Ave., East Side* ☎ *702/739–8676* ▤ *AE, D, MC, V.*

French

$–$$ ✕ **Bonjour Casual French.** The hauteur that French restaurants are famous
Fodor'sChoice for is about all that's lacking at Bonjour, which says it's casual and means
★ it. The food at this charming country-French spot is a blend of the classic and the innovative. Among the appetizer offerings are a warm Roquefort-and-pear Napoleon and onion soup gratinée; entrée choices include crusted salmon with spinach, pine nuts, and tarragon sauce, and vegetable ravioli with wild mushrooms and artichokes. A tarte tatin is a fine finish. ☒ *8878 S. Eastern Ave., South Las Vegas* ☎ *702/270–2102* ▤ *AE, D, DC, MC, V* ☉ *Closed Mon.*

$–$$ ✕ **Pamplemousse.** The late singer—and restaurant regular—Bobby Darin chose the name, which means grapefruit in French, on a whim. The dominant color here is burgundy, orchestral music is played over the stereo system, and the food is classic French. Because the entrées change daily, there is no printed menu; instead, the waiter recites the bill of fare. Specialties of the house include roast duckling with cranberry and Chambord sauce and Norwegian salmon with curry sauce. The room is small and popular with the convention trade, so be sure to make reservations as far in advance as possible. ☒ *400 E. Sahara Ave., East Side* ☎ *702/733–2066* ⌂ *Reservations essential* ▤ *AE, D, DC, MC, V* ☉ *Closed Mon. No lunch.*

Indian

$ ✕ **India Oven.** There are a number of good Indian restaurants in Las Vegas, but India Oven stands tall among them. The inside is plain, the outside even plainer. But the location (sort of diagonal from the Sahara Hotel and Casino) makes India Oven easy for visitors to find, and its food makes it a favorite among locals—especially Indians, who make up a large part of the clientele. Tandoori meats and nan bread are prepared in the tandoor oven, and other specialties include lamb korma with cashews, almonds, and raisins, and chicken vindaloo. ☒ *226 W. Sahara Ave., West Side* ☎ *702/366–0222* ▤ *AE, D, MC, V.*

Italian

$–$$$ ✕ **Antonio's.** Inlaid marble floors, a blue-sky dome, and murals depicting Italian scenes decorate this quiet restaurant, which has an open kitchen. The long menu offers well-prepared northern and southern Italian cuisine such as semolina-crusted fillet of salmon, Tuscan *osso buco* (veal shanks braised with vegetables and white wine), lasagna Bolognese, and spaghetti con *aragosta* (lobster). If it's available, order the five-onion soup, served in an onion—and you can ask the waiter for the recipe. Desserts include tiramisu. ⊠ *Rio All-Suite Hotel and Casino, 3700 W. Flamingo Rd., West Side* ☎ *702/252–7737* ⌂ *Reservations essential* ⊟ *AE, DC, MC, V* ⊗ *No lunch.*

$–$$$ ✕ **Mimmo Ferraro's Restaurant & Lounge.** Gino Ferraro's dependable Italian cuisine has been a favorite of Las Vegans since 1985, and now he's passed the baton to his son, Mimmo. The dining room of this casual restaurant is trimmed with black lacquer and pink neon accents. Family recipes are featured, fresh breads and pastas are made on the premises, the wine list is extraordinary, the osso buco is *magnifico,* and Rosalba's tiramisu is *fantastico.* The service is good and prices are moderate, too. ⊠ *5900 W. Flamingo Rd., West Side* ☎ *702/364–5300* ⊟ *AE, D, DC, MC, V.*

$–$$ ✕ **Bertolini's.** If you'd rather avoid the traffic (both vehicular and pedestrian) on the Strip, this is a slightly more sedate outpost of the Forum Shops Bertolini's. (⇨ Bertolini's in The Strip) ⊠ *9500 W. Sahara Ave., West Side* ☎ *702/869–1540* ⌂ *Reservations not accepted* ⊟ *AE, DC, MC, V.*

☾ **$–$$** ✕ **Buca di Beppo.** Buca di Beppo's northwest location brings the same zaniness—and same great family-style, southern Italian food—to the 'burbs. (⇨ Buca di Beppo in Paradise Road) ⊠ *7690 W. Lake Mead Blvd., Northwest Las Vegas* ☎ *702/363–6524* ⊟ *AE, D, DC, MC, V* ⊗ *No lunch weekdays.*

$–$$ ✕ **Il Fornaio.** If you'd rather avoid the hubbub of Il Fornaio's quirky location at New York–New York, this spot is quieter. It still has a similar exhibition kitchen and breads are baked twice daily. (⇨ Il Fornaio in The Strip) ⊠ *Green Valley Ranch Resort, 2197 Paseo Verde Pkwy., Henderson* ☎ *702/614–5283* ⊟ *AE, MC, V.*

$–$$ ✕ **Spiedini Ristorante.** Gustav Mauler, who had long been chef and restaurant developer for the former Mirage Resorts company, struck out on his own with this stylish Italian restaurant. The menu is a contemporary take on traditional favorites. Starters include a sumptuous antipasto platter of scallops and shrimp, brushed with lemon and olive oil. Entrées encompass hand-crafted pastas, a veal chop with arugula and cherry-tomato salad, *osso buco* (veal shanks braised with vegetables and white wine), and a lobster-and-shrimp *fra diavolo* (spicy tomato sauce). Desserts often are deliciously whimsical, as in the case of the pineapple carpaccio with raspberry sorbet. ⊠ *JW Marriott Las Vegas Casino Resort, 221 N. Rampart Blvd., Summerlin* ☎ *702/869–8500* ⊟ *AE, D, DC, MC, V* ⊗ *No lunch.*

¢–$$ ✕ **Carrabba's Italian Grill.** "Chain" may seem like a dirty word to anyone who's especially fond of mom-and-pop Italian joints, but Texas-based Carrabba's manages to put a different spin on things; that's immediately evident when you see the trees on the roof. Relax and enjoy such delights as bruschetta Carrabba (which highlights whatever's best in the market that day), *cozze* in *bianco* (mussels steamed in a lovely white-wine mixture), *tagliarini Picchi Pacchiu* (long, thin ribbon noodles with a crushed-tomato sauce), or *chicken Bryan* (with caprini cheese and sun-dried tomatoes). At dessert time, the tiramisu is equaled only by the Chocolate Dream. ✉ *10160 S. Eastern Ave., Henderson* ☎ *702/990–0650* ✉ *8771 W. Charleston Blvd., West Side* ☎ *702/304–2345* ⌖ *Reservations not accepted* ▭ *AE, D, MC, V* ☾ *No lunch.*

Japanese

★ **$–$$$$** ✕ **Hamada of Japan.** The ever-popular Japanese hot spot has off-the-beaten-path locations frequented by locals and savvy visitors. (⇨ Hamada of Japan in Paradise Road) ✉ *Rio All-Suite Resort, 3700 W. Flamingo Rd., West Side* ☎ *702/252–7777* ✉ *JW Marriott Las Vegas Casino Resort, 221 N. Rampart Blvd., Summerlin* ☎ *702/869–7710* ▭ *AE, D, DC, MC, V* ☾ *No lunch.*

Mediterranean

¢–$$ ✕ **Grape Street Cafe, Wine Bar & Grill.** Grape Street's menu is designed to coordinate nicely with the restaurant's interesting—and not stratospherically priced—wine list. There are salads, sandwiches, pizzas and the like, plus dinner specials such as grilled salmon. Desserts range from austere Stilton and port to positively decadent dark-chocolate fondue. Grape Street is brick-lined, candlelit, and cozy, and there's a patio for pleasant evenings. ✉ *7501 W. Lake Mead Blvd., Northwest Las Vegas* ☎ *702/228–9463* ▭ *AE, D, MC, V* ☾ *Closed Mon.*

Mexican

¢–$$ ✕ **Viva Mercado's.** The explosion of new chain restaurants in suburban neighborhoods makes it easy to forget the charms of the first Las Vegas restaurant to bring a chef's touch to Mexican food. You can get enchiladas and burritos here if you want, and bountiful plates of them at that. More rewarding are the daily specials and fish dishes, such as orange roughy cooked four different ways (including with the ultra-hot *salsa de arbol*), or *banderilla de camaron* (shrimp grilled in garlic, lemon, and pico de gallo). Stucco, fake plants, and tile awnings over rows of booths vaguely suggest an outdoor Mexican plaza, though in a mom-and-pop way compared to the many "theme" and "designed" restaurants around here. ✉ *6182 W. Flamingo Rd., West Side* ☎ *702/871–8826* ⌖ *Reservations essential* ▭ *AE, MC, V.*

$ ✕ **La Barca Mexican Seafood Restaurant.** If you want to eat where Mexicans eat and have no patience for Texas or California twists on Mexican food, this is the place for you. This busy spot inside the otherwise faded Commercial Center doesn't put chips and salsa on the table and the emphasis is on seafood, not gloppy things covered with cheese. Fish and shrimp tacos are the most popular orders, along with the Seven Seas Soup—a mixture of seafood with implied medicinal benefits. The Whaler is a 45-ounce shrimp cocktail that creates an instant party. ✉ *953 E. Sahara Ave., East Side* ☎ *702/792–9700* ▭ *AE, D, DC, MC, V.*

★ ¢–$ ✕ **Doña Maria.** Doña Maria's suburban outpost has the same top-notch, authentic tamales set amidst a more colorful setting. (⇨ Doña Maria in Downtown) ✉ *3205 N. Tenaya Way, Northwest Las Vegas* ☎ *702/656–1600* ▭ *AE, D, DC, MC, V.*

¢–$ ✕ **Lindo Michoacán.** *Lindo* means pretty; Michoacán is a state in central Mexico. Javier Barajas, the congenial owner and host of this colorful cantina named for his native state, presents outstanding specialties that he learned to cook while growing up. Many menu items are named for his relatives, including *flautas Mama Chelo* (corn tortillas filled with chicken). Michoacán is known for its carnitas, so don't miss them. Or try the *cabrito birria de chivo* (roasted goat with red mole sauce). Guacamole is made tableside. Finish with the flan, a silken wonder. Barajas has two other restaurants—Bonito Michoacán and Viva Michoacán—on Decatur Boulevard and Sunset Road, respectively. ⊠ *2655 E. Desert Inn Rd., East Side* ☎ *702/735–6828 or 702/257–6810* ⊠ *3715 S. Decatur Blvd., West Side* ☎ *702/492–9888* ⊠ *2061 Sunset Rd., Henderson* ☎ *702/492–9888* ⊟ *AE, D, MC, V.*

¢–$ ✕ **SuperMex Restaurant & Cantina.** Here's a superlative case of truth in advertising: The California-based SuperMex, a big barn of a place, has a super menu—32 combination plates, plus seven different kinds of burritos in two sizes, combination burritos, salads, tostadas, appetizers, fajitas, tacos, taquitos, and more. You can even get a chiles rellenos burrito or an enchilada with a taco or an enchilada and a tamale or . . . you get the picture. "Extras are extra," the menu says, and you can use them to tailor-make your dish to your tastes. There's even a "lite" menu, for those seeking, say, a whole wheat quesadilla. ⊠ *3460 E. Sunset Rd., Henderson* ☎ *702/436–5200* ⊟ *AE, MC, V.*

Pan-Asian

★ $–$$ ✕ **Little Buddha.** It may sound like a mixed metaphor—an Asian restaurant in Paris—but France's Buddha Bar has achieved world fame for its food and its music. The associated Little Buddha in Las Vegas continues the mystique. The kitchen produces such Pacific Rim wonders as Hawaiian smoked pot stickers, wok-fried salt and pepper calamari and frogs' legs, grilled Asian pork ribs, and curry shrimp in banana leaf. Finish things off with a sweet touch of coconut sticky rice with mango and Florentine crisp or liquid-center chocolate cake with vanilla ice cream. ⊠ *The Palms, 4321 W. Flamingo Rd., West Side* ☎ *702/942–7777* ⊟ *AE, D, DC, MC, V.*

$–$$ ✕ **Mayflower Cuisinier.** You find creative Chinese dishes with Californian, Pan-Asian, and French accents on the menu at this off-Strip eatery. Try the ginger-chicken ravioli, coconut shrimp with sweet chile sauce, sesame-crusted ahi tuna with ginger-Dijon lime sauce, or chicken breast with mushrooms and pineapple in a clay pot. For dessert, consider a delectable trio of crème brûlées flavored with almond, orange, and pineapple-ginger. ⊠ *4750 W. Sahara Ave., West Side* ☎ *702/870–8432* ⊟ *AE, D, DC, MC, V.*

Seafood

$–$$$$ ✕ **The Tillerman.** Its location on Flamingo Road, almost 3 mi east of the Strip, makes the Tillerman a quiet refuge from the casinos. The garden setting also does its part: the restaurant is built around a huge ficus tree growing in the center of the room, under a skylight that's open on hot desert nights. Specialties include linguine with clams, mussels, shrimp, scallops, lobster, white wine, and garlic, and blackened yellowfin tuna with roasted-red-pepper sauce. Up to a dozen fresh-fish selections are offered each night, and the steaks are always done just right, too. ⊠ *2245 E. Flamingo Rd., East Side* ☎ *702/731–4036* ⊟ *AE, D, DC, MC, V* ☉ *No lunch.*

Southwestern

¢–$$ ✕ **Garduño's Chili Packing Co.** The Garduño family imported their restaurants from Albuquerque, along with ongoing shipments of fresh green chiles from Hatch, New Mexico. The chiles are used in many of the spicier dishes; those with more timid taste buds should sample the milder seafood tacos and fajitas that arrive on sizzling iron skillets. The salsa bar has an impressive selection of sauces, the bar an even more impressive collection of tequilas. Meals come with sopaipillas that can be drenched with honey to cool off the chile burn. On Sunday, a margarita brunch is served. The Palms location is the only to serve lunch. ⊠ *The Palms, 4321 W. Flamingo Rd., West Side* ☎ *702/942–7777* ⊠ *Fiesta Hotel and Casino, 2400 N. Rancho Dr., Rancho Strip* ☎ *702/631–7000* ⊠ *Fiesta Henderson Hotel and Casino, 777 W. Lake Mead Dr., Henderson* ☎ *702/558–7000* ▤ *AE, D, DC, MC, V* ⊗ *No lunch.*

¢–$ ✕ **Z' Tejas Grill.** This spacious, attractive location in the Peccole Ranch area serves everything that its Paradise Road sister does, plus Sunday brunch. (⇨ Z' Tejas Grill in Paradise Road) ⊠ *9560 W. Sahara Ave., West Side* ☎ *702/638–0610* ▤ *AE, D, DC, MC, V.*

Steak

$$–$$$$ ✕ **Billy Bob's Steak House.** Big food is the name of the game at the Western-theme Billy Bob's Steak House at Sam's Town. The 28-ounce rib eye is Texas-size, the barbecued brisket could feed a rodeo. And then there's dessert: the chocolate eclairs are a foot long, and the chocolate cake could fill up a good chunk of the Grand Canyon. Sharing is recommended. A porch area adjacent to the bar provides a great view of the Sunset Stampede, the animatronic and laser show in the resort's indoor Mystic Falls Park. ⊠ *Sam's Town Hotel and Gambling Hall, 5111 Boulder Hwy., Boulder Strip* ☎ *702/456–7777* ▤ *AE, D, DC, MC, V* ⊗ *No lunch.*

$$–$$$$ ✕ **Golden Steer.** In a town where restaurants come and go almost as quickly as visitors' cash, the longevity of this steak house, opened in 1958, is itself a recommendation. And while it changed hands a couple of years ago, the tradition continues. Folks still come to this San Francisco–theme restaurant with red leather chairs, polished dark wood, and stained-glass windows for the huge slabs of well-prepared meat. Steak, ribs, and game are particularly popular. Although you wouldn't know it from the outside, the Steer is cavernous. Lots of small, intimate rooms, however, break up the space. ⊠ *308 W. Sahara Ave., West Side* ☎ *702/384–4470* ▤ *AE, D, DC, MC, V* ⊗ *No lunch.*

$$–$$$$ ✕ **Sonoma Cellar.** Sonoma Cellar was one of the first upscale restaurants in a locals casino, and it hasn't lost its verve. It's elegant and serene, with a redwood wine cellar and a cigar lounge. The menu includes, in addition to steaks, such classics as oysters Rockefeller, lobster bisque, and clams casino, and more updated offerings such as Mediterranean shrimp and mesquite-grilled or pan-seared salmon fillet. The details are there, too; don't miss the pretzel rolls. ⊠ *Sunset Station Hotel and Casino, 1301 W. Sunset Rd., Henderson* ☎ *702/547–7898* ▤ *AE, D, DC, MC, V* ⊗ *No lunch.*

Vegetarian

¢–$ ✕ **Go Raw Cafe and Juice Bar.** The name of this vegetarian café refers to the fact that nothing is cooked at temperatures higher than the 100°F-plus it takes to make flat breads and pizza dough. Devotees of living food—as well as vegans and vegetarians—find much to like here. You can make a healthy choice with dishes like basil, tomato, and onion tossed in herbs, olive oil, and pine nuts; or lasagna based on zucchini, spinach, carrots, marinara sauce, and nut "cheese." ⊠ *2910 Lake East Dr., West Side* ☎ *702/254-5382* ✉ *2381 Windmill La. East Side* ☎ *702/450-9007* ▭ *AE, D, MC, V.*

¢ ✕ **Wild Oats Community Market.** Wild Oats has all the stuff you'd expect in the small café of a whole foods market—an extensive salad bar, for example, and smoothies and vegetable juices—but a large helping of the unexpected as well; for example, somebody's enlightened enough to separate vegan dishes (biryani, stuffed tofu pockets) from regular vegetarian (kung pao tofu, traditional slaw) in the deli. Selections include a Reuben sandwich that combines smoked tomato slices with sauerkraut, Swiss cheese, and Thousand Island dressing. ⊠ *7250 W. Lake Mead Blvd., Northwest Las Vegas* ☎ *702/942-1500* ✉ *517 N. Stephanie St., Henderson* ☎ *702/458-9427* ▭ *AE, D, DC, MC, V.*

Reservations

Hotels book up quickly in Las Vegas. The city is filled with people every weekend, and there are even more visitors during holiday weekends, big conventions, and when prizefights and other major sporting events are held here. Make your hotel reservations as far in advance as possible. Overbooking is not common; if you have a reservation, you will get a room.

Call a hotel's toll-free number and ask what package deals it has for your vacation dates. Checking the hotel's Web site is always a good idea as many specials are offered on the Internet only. Another useful guide to bargain rates is the Sunday "Calendar" section of the *Los Angeles Times,* where most Las Vegas hotels advertise.

4

If the hotel reservations clerks continually tell you they're sold out, try the **Las Vegas Convention and Visitors Authority** (☏ 800/332–5333 ☉ Daily 6 AM–9 PM PST) room reservations center, which has access to a good selection of the rooms available for any given day. A good source of available rooms and discounts is the **Las Vegas Reservations Bureau** (☏ 800/831–2754). They may be able to place you in the hotel of your choice.

Prices

In general, rates for Las Vegas accommodations are far lower than those in most other American resort and vacation cities, but the situation is a wacky one indeed. There are a hundred different variables, depending on who's selling the rooms (reservations, marketing, casino, conventions, wholesalers, packagers); what rooms you're talking about (standard, deluxe, minisuites, standard suites, deluxe suites, high-roller suites, penthouses, bungalows); demand (weekday, weekend, holiday, conventions or sporting events in town); and management whim (bean-counter profit models, revenue-projection realities, etc.). When business is slow, many hotels reduce rates on rooms in their least desirable sections, sometimes with a buffet breakfast or even a show included. Most "sales" occur from early December to mid-February and July and August, the coldest and hottest times of the year. Members of casino slot clubs often get offers of discounted or even free rooms, and they can almost always reserve a room even when the rest of the hotel is "sold out."

In the larger hotels, it's generally not possible to haggle over room rates, as in, "Well, will you take sixty dollars for the room, instead of seventy-five?" However, prices change continuously: you can call the same hotel several times within a short span and be quoted several different rates. So you should always ask for a lower-priced room.

WHAT IT COSTS				
$$$$	**$$$**	**$$**	**$**	**¢**
FOR 2 PEOPLE over $200	$150–$200	$100–$150	$50–$100	under $50

All prices are for a standard double room, excluding 10% tax.

The lodgings we list are the cream of the crop in each price category. We always list the facilities that are available, but we don't specify whether they cost extra; when pricing accommodations, always ask what's included and what costs extra. Properties are assigned price categories based on the range between their least and most expensive standard double rooms at high season (excluding holidays). Properties marked ✕▥ are lodging establishments whose restaurants warrant a special trip. Assume that hotels operate on the European Plan (EP, with no meals) unless we specify that they use the Continental Plan (CP, with a Continental breakfast), Modified American Plan (MAP, with breakfast and dinner), or the Full American Plan (FAP, with all meals).

---

on providing an intimate, quiet experience cushioned from the general casino ruckus in town. Luxurious touches extend to the express elevators, pool, health club, recreation area, private parking, and posh restaurants. Guests have full access to the spa and its facilities (⇨ Getting the Spa Treatment). Afternoon tea is served daily in the Verandah lounge. The pampering policy here extends to even the smallest guests: children find a stuffed animal and milk and cookies on their arrival, and pets are welcome. ⌧ *3960 Las Vegas Blvd. S, South Strip 89109* ☎ *702/632–5000* 🖷 *702/632–5195* ⊕ *www.fourseasons.com* ⬎ *338 rooms, 86 suites* ♨ *2 restaurants, room service, in-room data ports, in-room safes, minibars, cable TV with movies and video games, in-room VCRs, pool, gym, hot tub, massage, sauna, spa, steam room, 2 bars, lobby lounge, shops, babysitting, dry cleaning, laundry service, concierge, Internet, business services, meeting rooms, car rental, free parking, some pets allowed, no-smoking floors* ▭ *AE, D, DC, MC, V.*

$$$$ ▥ **Mandalay Bay Resort & Casino.** Upon its opening, Mandalay Bay
Fodor'sChoice   quickly became one of the city's most popular megaresorts. It's a hip,
★   fun, imaginative joint, with some unique elements: a wave pool with 5-foot swells, a million-gallon walk-through aquarium, and a 15,000-seat arena complex that hosts major sporting contests and superstar concerts. The House of Blues operates not only a restaurant and an 1,800-seat concert hall, but the Foundation Room, an exclusive club on the 34th floor that's open to the public on Monday nights. The fabulous rumjungle restaurant turns into the city's trendiest nightclub after 11 PM. The Mandalay Place mall is filled with shops including a wine bar and an independent, brainy, and fun bookstore called the Reading Room. THEhotel is a posh all-suites tower. Guest rooms are spacious, with extra-large beds and separate tubs and showers. ⌧ *3950 Las Vegas Blvd. S, South Strip 89119* ☎ *702/632–7777 or 877/632–7700* 🖷 *702/632–7228* ⊕ *www.mandalaybay.com* ⬎ *3,215 rooms, 1,100 suites* ♨ *11 restaurants, in-room data ports, cable TV with movies, in-room VCRs, 4 pools (1 indoor), health club, hot tub, spa, beach, 7 bars, casino, concert hall, nightclub, showroom, shops, meeting room, no-smoking rooms* ▭ *AE, D, DC, MC, V.*

$$$–$$$$ ▥ **Bellagio Las Vegas.** More than 1,000 fountains erupt in a chore-
Fodor'sChoice   ographed water ballet across a man-made lake at this luxury hotel. There's
★   also an art gallery and one of the most stunning shows on the Strip, Cirque du Soleil's *O*. A breathtaking lobby, an indoor botanical conservatory,

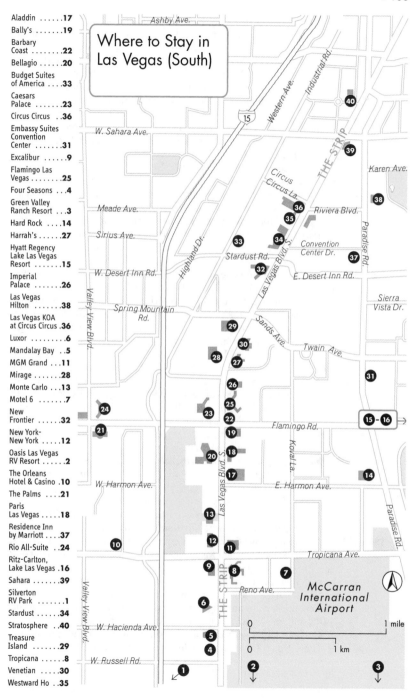

Where to Stay in
Las Vegas (South)

two wedding chapels, an upscale shopping arcade, and the Spa Tower complete the extravagant picture. Bellagio also has one of the best buffets in town, where the wait can sometimes exceed two hours. This is the hardest place in Vegas to land good deals, although it wouldn't hurt to check the hotel's Web site for Internet specials. The rooms are standard size, but continue the opulent theme with luxurious fabrics and Italian marble. Elegant Italian provincial furniture surrounds either a single king bed or two queen beds. Parents take note: no one under 18 is allowed on the property unless they are staying at the hotel—and families with children are encouraged to find lodging elsewhere. ⊠ *3600 Las Vegas Blvd. S, Center Strip 89109* ☎ *888/987–6667* 📠 *702/693– 8546* ⊕ *www.bellagio.com* ↝ *2,602 rooms, 403 suites* ♨ *17 restaurants, ice-cream parlor, patisserie, snack bar, room service, in-room data ports, in-room fax, in-room safes, minibars, cable TV with movies, in-room VCRs, golf privileges, 6 pools, health club, hair salon, hot tub, spa, 7 bars, lobby lounge, lounge, piano bar, casino, nightclub, piano, showroom, shops, dry cleaning, laundry service, concierge, Internet, business services, convention center, meeting rooms, car rental, free parking, no-smoking floors* 🖃 *AE, D, DC, MC, V.*

$$$–$$$$ 🏨 **New York–New York Hotel and Casino.** The resort's facade includes half-size re-creations of the Statue of Liberty, the Empire State Building, the Chrysler Building, and the Brooklyn Bridge. Inside, it's no less thematically realized, with another clever reproduction of a Big Apple icon everywhere you look. The downside is cramped and crowded public areas, just like Manhattan; a long trek from the front desk to some of the towers; and noise from the Manhattan Express roller coaster that loops around the hotel. On the upside, in 2003 Cirque du Soleil opened its new show *Zumanity* here, a sexy addition to Cirque's repertoire on the strip. Rooms are large, some with separate sitting areas and sofas. ⊠ *3790 Las Vegas Blvd. S, South Strip 89109* ☎ *702/740–6969 or 800/693– 6763* 📠 *702/740–6700* ⊕ *www.nynyhotelcasino.com* ↝ *1,920 rooms, 103 suites* ♨ *15 restaurants, café, coffee shop, food court, ice-cream parlor, patisserie, pizzeria, snack bar, room service, in-room data ports, in-room safes, some in-room hot tubs, cable TV with movies, golf privileges, pool, health club, hair salon, hot tub, sauna, spa, steam room, 6 bars, lobby lounge, lounge, piano bar, sports bar, casino, showroom, comedy club, dance club, piano, shops, dry cleaning, laundry service, concierge, Internet, business services, convention center, meeting rooms, car rental, free parking, no-smoking floors* 🖃 *AE, D, DC, MC, V.*

$$$–$$$$ 🏨 **Sahara Hotel and Casino.** The desert oasis theme, established in 1952 when the Sahara opened for business, still remains 50 years later—an eternity in Las Vegas. Like many of its neighbors, the Sahara began as a small motor hotel and grew by adding towers, towers, and more towers. The Sahara's largest expansion doubled the size of the casino, replaced the facade and sign, and added a parking garage. Another $100-million makeover added the NASCAR Cafe and thrill-ride Speed. Rooms are large, with king-size beds and views of either the Strip or Paradise Road. Of the many value properties in Las Vegas, the Sahara offers the nicest rooms, along with such bargains as $1 blackjack tables. ⊠ *2535 Las Vegas Blvd. S, North Strip 89109* ☎ *702/737–2111* or 888/696–2121 🖷 702/791–2027 ⊕ *www.saharavegas.com* 🖵 *1,674 rooms, 26 suites* ⚓ *3 restaurants, coffee shop, room service, in-room data ports, room TVs with movies, pool, hair salon, massage, 2 bars, lobby lounge, casino, video game room, dry cleaning, laundry service, Internet, business services, meeting rooms, free parking, no-smoking floors* 🖃 *AE, D, DC, MC, V.*

$$$–$$$$
Fodor's Choice
★

🏨 **Venetian Resort-Hotel-Casino.** Some of the largest and plushest suites on the Strip are found at this elegant resort. The 700-plus-square-foot guest quarters, richly appointed in modified Venetian style, have a sunken living room with dining table and convertible sofa, walk-in closets, separate shower and tub, three telephones (including one in the bathroom), two 27-inch TVs, and a desk with fax machine. The even posher Venezia tower has 1,013 suites (each has flat-screen 32-inch and 27-inch TVs), a concierge floor, private entrance, fountains, and the restaurant Bouchon. Also on the property are the Guggenheim-Hermitage Museum; a shopping arcade (complete with a replica Grand Canal plied by gondolas); reproductions of Venetian landmarks; and branches of the famous Canyon Ranch SpaClub and Madame Tussaud's Wax Museum. ✉ *3355 Las Vegas Blvd. S, Center Strip 89109* 🕿 *702/414–1000 or 888/ 883–6423* 🖷 *702/414–1100* ⊕ *www.venetian.com* 🖵 *4,049 suites* ⚓ *13 restaurants, 3 cafés, 2 food courts, 2 ice-cream parlors, 2 patisseries, room service, in-room data ports, in-room fax, in-room safes, minibars, cable TV with movies, 3 pools, health club, spa, 4 lounges, casino, showroom, piano, shops, dry cleaning, laundry service, concierge, concierge floor, Internet, business services, convention center, free parking, no-smoking floors* 🖃 *AE, D, DC, MC, V.*

$$–$$$$
🏨 **Aladdin Resort and Casino/Planet Hollywood.** One of the few imploded hotel-casinos to retain its original name, the Aladdin was reborn in 2000 as one of Las Vegas's modern-day megaresorts with a shopping mall and restaurants, but it kept its old *Arabian Nights*–theme. That could all be changing. The Aladdin went bankrupt, and in 2004 the resort was sold and as of this writing was scheduled to become another Planet Hollywood. ✉ *3667 Las Vegas Blvd. S, Center Strip 89109* 🕿 *702/785–5555 or 877/333–9474* 🖷 *702/785–5558* ⊕ *www.aladdincasino.com* 🖵 *2,344 rooms, 223 suites* ⚓ *19 restaurants, room service, in-room data ports, in-room safes, room TVs with movies, 2 pools, health club, spa, 2 bars, 3 lounges, sports bar, casino, nightclub, theater, shops, laundry service, concierge, business services, convention center, free parking, no-smoking floors* 🖃 *AE, D, DC, MC, V.*

★ **$$–$$$$**
🏨 **Bally's Las Vegas.** One of the largest resorts on the Strip—with nearly 3,000 rooms, six restaurants, a showroom, and a 40-store mall—it's clear why Bally's calls itself "a city within a city." The hotel also has a huge casino, separate health spas for men and women, and an attractively landscaped outdoor pool. The large rooms are full of bright, overstuffed furniture, and have great views of Vegas's parade of neon. ✉ *3645 Las Vegas Blvd. S, Center Strip 89109* 🕿 *702/967–4111 or 888/742–9248* 🖷 *702/ 739–4405* ⊕ *www.ballyslv.com* 🖵 *2,567 rooms, 265 suites* ⚓ *6 restaurants, in-room data ports, cable TV with movies, 10 tennis courts, pool, health club, spa, bar, lounge, casino, comedy club, 3 showrooms, shops, concierge, no-smoking rooms* 🖃 *AE, D, DC, MC, V.*

$$–$$$$ ⬚ **Caesars Palace.** The opulent entrance, fountains, Roman statuary, bas-
FodorsChoice reliefs, and roaming centurions all add up to the quintessential Las Vegas
★   hotel. The Forum Shops at Caesars are among the most extravagant in
town. Cleopatra's Barge is a one-of-a-kind lounge floating in an indoor
pool. The hotel also hosts major sporting events and superstars Celine Dion
and Elton John. There's even a rock-climbing wall. The Palace Tower's
spacious rooms have vaulted ceilings and whirlpool baths; smaller rooms
at the front of the Forum Tower have a spectacular view of the Strip. ⊠ *3570*
Las Vegas Blvd. S, Center Strip 89109 ☎ *702/731–7110 or 800/634–6661*
🖷 *702/967–3890* ⊕ *www.caesarspalace.com* ➣ *1,834 rooms, 565 suites*
⚴ *9 restaurants, coffee shop, in-room data ports, cable TV with movies,*
3 pools, health club, spa, squash, bar, 4 lounges, casino, showroom, 2 night-
clubs, theater, shops, dry cleaning, business services, free parking, no-smok-
ing rooms ⊟ *AE, D, DC, MC, V.*

$$–$$$$ ⬚ **Excalibur Hotel and Casino.** The Arthurian theme is omnipresent at
this megaresort, from the casino to the arcade, restaurants, and 20-plus-
shop Renaissance Village (complete with strolling performers). At the
wedding chapel you can tie the knot with all the trappings of King Arthur
and Lady Guinevere. The Excalibur is notable for its good-value accommodations. The standard-size rooms, decorated in bright colors, aren't
spectacular, but the occupancy rate is almost always 100%: don't be
surprised at long lines to check in and crowded public areas. The hotel's
Web site often posts discounted rates for nights months in advance. Try
to get a room that overlooks the Strip, rather than the hotel's back parking lot. ⊠ *3850 Las Vegas Blvd. S, South Strip 89119* ☎ *702/597–7777*
or 877/750–5464 🖷 *702/597–7040* ⊕ *www.excaliburcasino.com*
➣ *4,008 rooms* ⚴ *6 restaurants, 2 pools, 9 bars, casino, showroom,*
shops, meeting rooms, no-smoking rooms ⊟ *AE, D, DC, MC, V.*

$$–$$$$ ⬚ **Flamingo Las Vegas.** The Fabulous Flamingo that opened in 1946, with
everyone from Bugsy Siegel to the janitors dressed in tuxedos, was a swanky
98-room spot with palm trees imported from California. The Flamingo
has changed greatly since then: today its six high-rise towers overlook a
15-acre pool area—one of the largest in town—where the original low-
rise bungalows once stood. The Flamingo is pervasively pink, from the
outside neon sign to the lobby carpeting to the in-room pens and vases.
The pool area is one of the largest and prettiest in town. The spacious
rooms in the towers offer expansive views of the Strip. Bonus: the reg-
istration area is near the elevators, so you won't have to carry your lug-
gage through the casino. ⊠ *3555 Las Vegas Blvd. S, Center Strip 89109*
☎ *702/733–3111 or 800/732–2111* 🖷 *702/733–3353* ⊕ *www.flamingolv.*
com ➣ *3,466 rooms, 176 suites* ⚴ *8 restaurants, in-room data ports,*
in-room safes, room TVs with movies, golf privileges, 4 tennis courts, 3
pools, health club, hair salon, spa, lounge, casino, showroom, shops, busi-
ness services, meeting room, no-smoking rooms ⊟ *AE, D, DC, MC, V.*

☼ **$$–$$$$** ⬚ **MGM Grand Hotel and Casino.** The largest hotel in the world has four
emerald-green towers, three of them 30 stories high, set on 112 acres and
housing more than 5,000 guest rooms, including 700-plus Hollywood-
inspired suites. It's so big that simply entering the parking garage gives
you the feeling of being inside a giant ant farm. Also here are a special-
events arena, a complete day-care facility, a wedding chapel, and a lion

habitat. Rooms are of average size, with a contemporary take on art deco in the decor and picture windows. Bungalow suites in the Grand Tower have plush fabrics, polished wood, and black-and-white Italian-marble bathrooms. The MGM offers airport check-in from 9 AM to 11 PM. ⊠ *3799 Las Vegas Blvd. S, South Strip 89109* ☎ *702/891–1111 or 800/ 929–1111* 🖷 *702/891–1030* ⊕ *www.mgmgrand.com* ⇥ *5,034 rooms* ⚘ *15 restaurants, café, coffee shop, food court, ice-cream parlor, pizzeria, snack bar, room service, in-room data ports, in-room safes, some in-room hot tubs, cable TV with movies, golf privileges, 5 pools, health club, hair salon, hot tubs, spa, 6 bars, 2 lounges, sports bar, cabaret, casino, concert hall, nightclub, shops, dry cleaning, laundry service, concierge, Internet, business services, convention center, meeting rooms, car rental, free parking, no-smoking floors* ▤ *AE, D, DC, MC, V.*

★ **$$–$$$$** 🏨 **Mirage Hotel and Casino.** The $630-million South Seas–theme resort is appropriately named. The property includes a rain forest with 3,000 tropical plants, a habitat for tigers, a 53-foot-long aquarium filled with tropical fish, seven dolphins frolicking in the largest saltwater pool in the world, and a 50-foot waterfall that becomes an exploding volcano after dark. The rooms are immaculate, done in modern tones of gold, taupe, black, and cream. Bathrooms, however, tend to be rather small. Request a room with a view (at check-in, for no extra charge) and enjoy an eye-popping view of the Strip and the volcano. ⊠ *3400 Las Vegas Blvd. S, Center Strip 89109* ☎ *702/791–7111 or 800/627–6667* 🖷 *702/791–7446* ⊕ *www.themirage.com* ⇥ *2,763 rooms, 281 suites* ⚘ *13 restaurants, café, coffee shop, ice-cream parlor, pizzeria, snack bar, room service, in-room data ports, in-room safes, minibars, cable TV with movies, golf privileges, 2 pools, health club, hair salon, hot tub, sauna, spa, steam room, 3 bars, casino, showroom, shops, dry cleaning, laundry service, Internet, business services, convention center, meeting rooms, car rental, free parking, no-smoking floors* ▤ *AE, D, DC, MC, V.*

🕘 **$$–$$$$** 🏨 **Monte Carlo Resort and Casino.** Modeled after the opulent Place du
Fodor's Choice Casino in Monaco, the Las Vegas version of Monte Carlo replicates its
★ fanciful arches, domes, ornate fountains, marble floors, gas-lit promenades, and Gothic glass registration area overlooking the lush pool area. But don't expect high glamour here. Underneath the pseudo-Euro veneer are many family-friendly features: a fast-food court; an inexpensive buffet; a high-tech video arcade; and a water park consisting of adults' and children's pools, a hot tub, and a wave pool and "lazy river" combo. The standard-size rooms are packed with cherrywood furniture and Italian marble. Surprisingly good lodging deals are often found here. ⊠ *3770 Las Vegas Blvd. S, South Strip 89109* ☎ *702/730–7777 or 800/ 311–8999* 🖷 *702/730–7200* ⊕ *www.monte-carlo.com* ⇥ *2,743 rooms, 259 suites* ⚘ *7 restaurants, in-room data ports, cable TV with movies, 3 tennis courts, pool, health club, hot tub, spa, lounge, casino, showroom, shops, meeting room, no-smoking floors* ▤ *AE, D, DC, MC, V.*

★ **$$–$$$$** 🏨 **Paris Las Vegas.** In addition to reproductions of the Arc de Triomphe and the Eiffel Tower, the 2,900-room, $785-million Paris Las Vegas includes a 200-foot-tall sign resembling a hot-air balloon, an in-house parfumerie, a patisserie, and a wedding chapel. Fountains and statues are everywhere. Each spacious room has custom-designed furniture, rich

SPAS FOR SPLURGING

FOLLOWING THE NEWEST TREND in Las Vegas, almost every large Strip hotel offers the poshest pampering in luxury spas. However, you'll pay for the privilege of being indulged, anywhere from $15 to $30 just for a day's admission to use the health club facilities. Skin and hair treatments, massages, and personal training sessions are an additional cost, though many waive the daily facility fee on the day you purchase a treatment. Most spas are open to the public, but some are available only to guests of the hotels in which they are located. All offer luxury touches seldom seen in the average day spa: heated massage tables or exotic treatments from Bali or India. Many offer couples suites and special packages for brides and their bridal parties.

Top Picks

Canyon Ranch SpaClub. At an astounding 65,000 square feet, this outpost of the famed Canyon Ranch in Tucson is one of the best day spas in the country. Besides the usual spa treatments of massages, scrubs, and soaks, you can get a Lifetime Nutrition Consultation ($105), an Acupuncture treatment ($130), or a Stone Massage ($210). The unusual Rasul Ceremony ($160) is a Middle Eastern treatment of herbal steam and medicinal mud in a ornately tiled steam chamber. Weekend warriors love the health club with its large, 40-foot climbing wall, fitness and yoga classes throughout the day, and free lectures from the nutrition, wellness, and exercise physiology departments. An adjoining café serves healthy cuisine. Open to the public; you can buy admission for one, three, or five days. ⊠ Venetian Resort-Hotel-Casino.

Elemis Spa. A departure from the glitz of the Aladdin Resort and Casino, this spa showcases authentic Moroccan furnishings, hanging lanterns, textiles, and

art, all handcrafted and displayed against cinnamon and saffron walls. Inside this medina-like warren, you may await your treatment sipping mint tea in the opulent Moorish Retreat. The changing area has a huge hydrotherapy pool surrounded by tall Moroccan vases. Top-quality spa treatments, however, outshine even these rich surroundings. Try the Well-Being massage ($110) or the Marrakech Ceremony of the Sun, a self-tan treatment after an Exotic Lime and Ginger Salt Glow ($99). Or a Hawaiian Wave Four Hand Massage ($199), consisting of two massage therapists giving a very heavenly tandem massage. There's also a fitness facility with treadmills, recumbent and upright bikes, steppers, and free weights. Open to the public. ⊠ Aladdin Resort and Casino/Planet Hollywood.

Four Seasons. Tiny by local standards, this spa offers the very best in service; every staff member addresses you by name. During traditional Balinese and Javanese body treatments, there are unusual details rarely seen in this town. For example, your path from massage room to bath area during the Bali Spice Ritual ($250) is strewn with rose petals. The meditative JAMU Massage ($175) is offered with a choice of exotic oils made of island fruits, spices, or flowers. A relatively small fitness facility opens onto the pool area with complimentary cabanas. Each cardio machine has its own TV and attendants stand by with water and towels. You also have access to the Mandalay Bay's larger spa and Mandalay Beach. Open to hotel guests only. ⊠ Four Seasons Hotel.

Golden Nugget Spa. More intimate than spas found on the Strip, this downtown spa is a great bargain—an hour-long massage costs only $70, a half-hour $40. The hair salon, gym, and reception area all open onto a pretty tile Palm Court with mirror Palladian doors and a glass-lit arched ceiling. The women's whirlpool bubbles under a cupola painted with a blue sky mural amid relaxing wall murals and pink marble. For a $15 fee, you can use the gym, sauna, whirlpool, and eucalyptus steam room—and that includes your robe, sandals, and even shorts and t-shirts for exercising. ⊠ Golden Nugget Casino.

MGM Grand Spa. Tranquility emanates from a feng shui design, displays of Asian art, and Tibetan rugs. Though one of Vegas's largest, this 29,000-square-foot facility feels private. Attentive attendants proffer trays of juice. Try the Duet Massage ($200), a synchronized massage with two therapists. Or detox your hangover with a Body Cocktail ($60), an exfoliating scrub based on the fragrances of popular cocktails followed by a Vichy shower. The health club facility overlooks the leafy pool complex and has Virtual Reality bikes and Stairmasters. Open to the public. ⊠ MGM Grand Hotel and Casino.

Spa Vita Di Lago. Reminiscent of a classical European spa, the Spa Vita Di Lago is a 30,000-square-foot Tuscan villa at the Ritz-Carlton resort on Lake Las Vegas. Amid acres of cream-color marble, the Spa has luxurious treatments such as the Thermae Spa White Mud ($135), to renew the skin, or a Mint Exfoliation ($70), all marked by the Ritz's unparalleled service. Along with the sauna and whirlpool are a cool plunge pool, refreshing on a blazing desert day; wellness consultations; and free yoga and fitness classes. You can order a meal alfresco in the private, formal, Mediterranean garden or enjoy a very un-Vegas activity, stargazing on the spa's patio. Outdoor activities include mountain biking along lake and mountain trails, kayaking, and guided hikes. Open to the public. ⊠ Ritz-Carlton, Lake Las Vegas.

Spa Mandalay. The 30,000-square-foot space is elegantly appointed with oak lockers and stone floors. Modeled after a Turkish-style bath, the hot, warm, and cold plunges are surrounded by marble and carved-stone fish fountains and plenty of places to lounge. There's also a Quiet Lounge and generous supplies of snacks and toiletries. And, in what must be a first in Las Vegas, the Spa offers yoga on the beach (of the Mandalay Bay wave pool) mornings at 7 AM, March through September. Try the Volcanic Dust Mask exfoliating body treatment ($105) or the Ayurvedic Elemental Balancing massage ($105) using healing herbal oils. Open to the public Sunday through Thursday. ⊠ Mandalay Bay Resort & Casino.

Also Recommended

Aquae Sulis. Some of the most innovative treatments in Las Vegas include a European-style "taking the waters" and a Southwestern hot stone massage. The large fitness facility has daily exercise classes. Open to the public. ⊠ JW Marriott Las Vegas.

Palms Spa. Besides the usual spa treatments, this hip spa offers complimentary tonic shots from the Elixir Bar for energy, calming, or relaxation. Open to the public. ⊠ The Palms.

The Spa at Caesars Palace. While the 6,500-square-foot fitness facility has a rock-climbing wall and a large selection of weight machines, the spa offers luxurious, sometimes exotic, treatments. Open to the public weekdays and Sunday, hotel guests only Friday and Saturday. ⊠ Caesars Palace.

Spa Moulay. Far removed from the Strip, the Hyatt Regency's spa has unusual treatment offerings, including a tandem massage with two masseurs. There's a fitness center and sauna. Open to the public. ⊠ Hyatt Regency Lake Las Vegas Resort.

— Lenore Greiner

French fabrics, and separate marble bath tubs and showers. Request a Strip view and you can see the Bellagio fountains dancing right from your room. Otherwise your room may overlook the pleasant pool area. The fabulous buffet serves dishes from five French regions. ⊠ *3655 Las Vegas Blvd. S, Center Strip 89109* ☎ *702/739–4111 or 888/226–5687* 🖷 *702/946–4405* ⊕ *www.paris-lv.com* 🛏 *2,621 rooms, 295 suites* ♨ *13 restaurants, in-room data ports, in-room safes, cable TV with movies, pool, health club, spa, 7 bars, casino, showroom, shops, business services, meeting room, no-smoking floors* ☰ *AE, D, DC, MC, V.*

$$–$$$$ 🏨 **Treasure Island Las Vegas (TI).** The resort's facade overlooks Siren's Cove, a huge body of water that until mid-2003 was Buccaneer Bay, where American pirates and British sailors flung campy insults at each other and duked it out until the British ship sank. Alas, the fun "argh, mateys" are gone, and four times a night, sexy sirens lure pirates into the cove and taunt them until the pyrotechnics take over. The show's trite, with bad sound, so if you want something more sophisticated and jaw-dropping, see the Cirque du Soleil production *Mystère*, which has a permanent home here. The opulent lobby overlooks the tropical pool and the newly redecorated rooms are modern and inviting, with soft hues, plants in ceramic pots, and marble bathrooms. The pool area is very pleasant, and at night you can have drinks outdoors at the "Kahunaville" tropical nightclub. ⊠ *3300 Las Vegas Blvd. S, Center Strip 89109* ☎ *702/894–7111 or 800/944–7444* 🖷 *702/894–7414* ⊕ *www.treasureislandlasvegas.com* 🛏 *2,665 rooms, 220 suites* ♨ *11 restaurants, café, coffee shop, ice-cream parlor, snack bar, room service, in-room data ports, in-room safes, cable TV with movies, golf privileges, pool, health club, hair salon, hot tub, sauna, spa, steam room, 2 bars, lounge, casino, shops, dry cleaning, laundry service, Internet, business services, convention center, meeting rooms, car rental, free parking, no-smoking floors* ☰ *AE, D, DC, MC, V.*

🖐 **$$–$$$$** 🏨 **Tropicana Resort and Casino.** Although the Tropicana positions itself as an adult-oriented hotel, it's a great place for families. The Trop is a beautifully landscaped hotel-casino, with an especially lush 5-acre pool area, including a meandering swimming pool, waterfalls, and swim-up blackjack. Rooms vary in size, depending on whether you're staying in the Paradise Tower (standard size), one of the Garden rooms by the pool (somewhat larger), or in the rear Island Tower (spacious). All have rattan furnishings and some even have a terrace (again, a plus for families). ⊠ *3801 Las Vegas Blvd. S, South Strip 89109* ☎ *702/739–2222 or 888/826–8767* 🖷 *702/739–2492* ⊕ *www.tropicanalv.com* 🛏 *1,680 rooms, 198 suites* ♨ *5 restaurants, coffee shop, room service, in-room data ports, in-room safes, room TVs with movies, 3 pools, gym, hair salon, hot tubs, spa, 5 bars, lounge, casino, showroom, theater, dry cleaning, laundry service, business services, convention center, airport shuttle, free parking* ☰ *AE, D, DC, MC, V.*

$–$$$ 🏨 **Barbary Coast Hotel and Casino.** The Barbary Coast has one of the most central locations in Las Vegas, across from Caesars and next-door to the Flamingo. It's a small, lively hotel with a Victorian theme. Rooms have brass four-poster beds with canopies, old-fashioned lamps, lacy curtains, etched mirrors, separate eating areas, and good rates. The views are of the Strip or the Flamingo. The number of rooms and suites is limited, so it's not always easy to get a reservation. ✉ *3595 Las Vegas Blvd. S, Center Strip 89109* ☎ *702/737–7111 or 888/227–2279* 🖶 *702/894–9954* ⊕ *www.barbarycoastcasino.com* ⤢ *188 rooms, 12 suites* ♿ *3 restaurants, room service, cable TV with movies, 2 bars, lounge, casino, nightclub, dry cleaning, free parking, no-smoking floors* ☰ *AE, D, DC, MC, V.*

★ **$–$$$** 🖵 **Luxor Resort & Casino.** The 36-story, pyramid-shape hotel-casino is pure Egyptian, Vegas style. Four "inclinators" travel the 39-degree incline of the pyramid to the guest rooms; "hallways" to the rooms overlook the world's largest atrium. Two "step towers," each with almost 1,000 rooms, were later added, making Luxor the second-largest hotel in Las Vegas. Rooms are large and continue the Egyptian motif, with scarabs, palms, ankhs, and hieroglyphics incorporated as design elements. There's a two-level arcade with interactive race cars, small motion simulators, and state-of-the-art video games. A tram connects Luxor with its sister casinos, Mandalay Bay and Excalibur. ✉ *3900 Las Vegas Blvd. S, South Strip 89119* ☎ *702/262–4000 or 800/288–1000* 🖶 *702/262–4452* ⊕ *www.luxor.com* ⤢ *4,040 rooms, 364 suites* ♿ *8 restaurants, coffee shop, ice-cream parlor, in-room data ports, cable TV, 5 pools, gym, hair salon, hot tub, spa, 7 bars, casino, showroom, 3 theaters, shops, meeting room, no-smoking rooms* ☰ *AE, D, MC, V.*

$–$$ 🖵 **Harrah's Las Vegas Casino & Hotel.** A Holiday Inn when it opened in 1973, the flagship of the large Harrah's casino fleet now has an attractive Mardi Gras theme, and there's live entertainment in its outdoor Carnival Court facing the Strip. The rooms are modest, featuring light-wood furniture, brass fittings, blackout drapes, and double soundproof walls. Harrah's is within easy walking distance of such popular resorts as Caesars Palace, the Mirage, and the Venetian. Popular Vegas singer and entertainer Clint Holmes has a long-standing gig here. ✉ *3475 Las Vegas Blvd. S, Center Strip 89109* ☎ *702/369–5000 or 800/427–7247* 🖶 *702/369–6014* ⊕ *www.harrahs.com* ⤢ *2,579 rooms, 164 suites* ♿ *7 restaurants, in-room data ports, pool, health club, hair salon, spa, lounge, casino, showroom, business services, meeting rooms, no-smoking rooms* ☰ *AE, D, DC, MC, V.*

$–$$ 🖵 **Imperial Palace Hotel and Casino.** The Imperial Palace was the first hotel built in Las Vegas around an Asian theme. Standard-size rooms are done in soft beige with a pagoda image and a deep red accent; the "Luv Tub" rooms have a king bed and a Roman bathtub for two. The Imperial houses one of Las Vegas's most popular long-running shows, *Legends in Concert*, as well as Auto Collections, which has more than 250 vintage automobiles on display (all of them for sale). The hotel has two buffets, a wedding chapel, and a spa. The casino has the only multi-tier sports book in Las Vegas, and a Legends Pit with Dealertainers, celebrity lookalike dealers. ✉ *3535 Las Vegas Blvd. S, Center Strip 89109* ☎ *702/731–3311 or 800/634–6441* 🖶 *702/735–8578* ⊕ *www.imperialpalace.com* ⤢ *2,475 rooms, 225 suites* ♿ *10 restaurants, café, coffee shop, room service, cable TV with movies and video games, pool, health club, hair salon, hot tub, spa, steam room, 10 bars, lobby lounge, piano bar, sports bar, casino, nightclub, piano, showroom, theater, video game room, shops, dry cleaning, laundry service, business services, convention center, car rental, free parking, no-smoking rooms* ☰ *AE, DC, MC, V.*

$–$$ **Stratosphere Casino Hotel and Tower.** The tallest observation tower west of the Mississippi (1,149 feet) is the focal piece of this complex, which also includes the world's three highest thrill rides (atop that tall tower), a shopping mall, a showroom and lounge, and a 97,000-square-foot casino. The Top of the World Restaurant and Lounge, perched high over the Strip, slowly rotates for 360-degree views of Las Vegas. Accommodations are standard, with dark purple drapes and matching bedspreads and light-wood furniture. Due to Stratosphere's out-of-the-way location between the Strip and Downtown, room deals abound. ✉ *2000 Las Vegas Blvd. S, North Strip 89104* ☎ *702/380–7777 or 800/998–6937* 📠 *702/739–2448* 🌐 *www.stratospherehotel.com* *2,249 rooms, 195 suites* *11 restaurants, coffee shop, ice-cream parlor, room TV with movies, pool, gym, hair salon, spa, lounge, casino, showroom, shops, no-smoking floors* 💳 *AE, D, DC, MC, V.*

¢–$$ **New Frontier Hotel and Gambling Hall.** While the Frontier of today stands on the same property as the original 1942 hotel, it bears no resemblance to the old place. An Old West motif prevails, but the rooms have been upgraded, and you won't find cacti or branding irons on the walls as in the original. The Atrium Tower has minisuites decorated in earth tones, with separate dining areas and views of the Strip or the Frontier garden area; the center of the 15-story tower is open to the sky. These rooms are some of the best lodging deals in town. ✉ *3120 Las Vegas Blvd. S, North Strip 89109* ☎ *702/794–8400 or 800/421–7806* 📠 *702/794–8327* 🌐 *www.frontierlv.com* *986 rooms, 396 suites* *7 restaurants, coffee shop, pizzeria, in-room data ports, cable TV with movies, 2 tennis courts, pool, hair salon, hot tub, massage, 3 bars, lounge, casino, nightclub, video game room, Internet, business services, meeting rooms, free parking, no-smoking floors* 💳 *AE, D, DC, MC, V.*

$ Fodor's Choice ★ **Stardust Hotel and Casino.** If the interior of the Stardust looks familiar, it's because you've likely seen it in dozens of Hollywood films. Beneath one of the most beautiful neon signs ever to grace the Strip, the Stardust emphasizes slots, low table minimums, and good deals on food. Good room bargains can often be found here, and given its central Strip location between the megaresorts and Downtown, the Stardust is the best option for the budget-minded traveler who wants a comfortable, no-frills room and easy access to the action. "Mr. Vegas" himself, Wayne Newton, has his own theater here. ✉ *3000 Las Vegas Blvd. S, North Strip 89109* ☎ *702/732–6111 or 800/634–6757* 📠 *702/732–6257* 🌐 *www.stardustlv.com* *1,500 rooms, 120 suites* *6 restaurants, snack bar, room service, in-room data ports, refrigerators, cable TV, 2 pools, gym, hair salon, hot tub, spa, 3 bars, 2 lounges, casino, showroom, shops, dry cleaning, laundry service, concierge, Internet, business services, meeting rooms, car rental, free parking, no-smoking floors* 💳 *AE, DC, MC, V.*

¢–$ **Circus Circus.** Circus Circus lives up to its name. Upstairs in the old towers are some of the most garishly appointed guest rooms in Las Vegas: bright red carpets, matching red chairs, and pink walls. The newer tower's rooms are more subdued. The casino attracts so many visitors that drivers find it a major achievement just getting into the parking lot. On a Saturday night the stretch of Las Vegas Boulevard leading up to

Circus Circus is often gridlocked. (If you spend a few minutes learning the back way in, from Industrial Road, you can save yourself much grief.) Nonetheless, Circus Circus is a favorite of families: parents can drop the children off at the midway above the casino to play games or watch the circus acts while they hit the slots; five-minute circus acts are performed every 30 minutes from 11 AM to midnight. The Adventuredome, a 5-acre theme park with a flume ride, a roller coaster, bumper cars, laser tag, and kiddie rides, is directly behind the hotel. You can shop in the Promenade. ⊠ *2880 Las Vegas Blvd. S, North Strip 89109* ☎ *702/734–0410 or 877/224–7287* 📠 *702/734–2268* ⊕ *www. circuscircus.com* ⇨ *3,774 rooms* ☖ *8 restaurants, room TVs with movies, 3 pools, 6 bars, casino, shops, meeting rooms, no-smoking rooms* ⊟ *AE, D, DC, MC, V.*

¢–$ 🏨 **Westward Ho.** The largest motel in the world has hundreds of rooms, six swimming pools, and two casinos. Small rooms are clean and simple, with beige walls and brightly colored furnishings. Beware, on Saturday night this part of town is gridlocked, and returning to your room by car will take considerable time—unless you learn the shortcut from Industrial Road through the Stardust parking lot. Because of its size, location, and deals, it's often crowded with conventioneers, slot-club members, and tournament players. ⊠ *2900 Las Vegas Blvd. S, North Strip 89109* ☎ *702/731–2900 or 800/405–9379* 📠 *702/731–6154* ⊕ *www.westwardho.com* ⇨ *662 rooms, 115 apartments* ☖ *Restaurant, café, room TVs with movies, 6 pools, casino, no-smoking rooms* ⊟ *AE, D, DC, MC, V.*

Beyond the Strip

$$$$ 🏨 **Green Valley Ranch Station Resort, Casino & Spa.** The theme here might just be posh: The lobby, built to resemble an intimate country club, opens up onto cabernet vineyards and a strikingly modern pool with a small, soft-sand beach area. A European day spa has cascading waterfalls and 26 treatment rooms. An outdoor, tree-lined mall called the District extends from the east entrance of the resort. Rooms are spacious, with cherry furniture, plush chairs, and beds with down comforters. The hotel has several excellent restaurants and lounges including Whiskey Sky, a hot spot for the young and the fabulous with huge mattresses strewn about its outdoor patio area overlooking the pool. The casino-resort welcomes pets and even bakes special biscuits for them, served with Fiji water. ⊠ *2300 Paseo Verde, Henderson 89052* ☎ *702/617–7777 or 866/617– 1777* 📠 *702/617–7778* ⊕ *www.greenvalleyranchresort.com* ⇨ *417 rooms, 79 suites* ☖ *7 restaurants, room service, in-room data ports, in-room safes, minibars, cable TV with movies, golf privileges, 4 pools, health club, hair salon, spa, beach, 4 bars, casino, cinema, nightclub, video game room, amphitheater, shops, dry cleaning, laundry service, concierge, Internet, business services, convention center, airport shuttle, free parking, some pets allowed, no-smoking floors* ⊟ *AE, D, DC, MC, V.*

☼ $$$$ 🏨 **Ritz-Carlton, Lake Las Vegas.** Contrary to the Strip experience, the
FodorsChoice Mediterranean-style Ritz is all about rest, playing outdoors, and wan-
★ dering around the quiet little village of MonteLago. The transporting experience begins with the hotel's exterior, done in bright shades of gold

and rust with clay-tile roofs and arched doorways. Inside, large rooms soothe with soft gold, honey, and cream tones and huge, cushy pillows and Frette linens atop feather beds. Plush slippers and robes are provided in the bathrooms. Club Level rooms bump it up a notch with rooms and suites on the Pontevecchio Bridge, which spans Lake Las Vegas. The lounge has panoramic views of the lake and the steep mountains in the distance. Two golf courses flank the Ritz, and you can also kayak, stargaze, fly-fish, take a guided walk or hike, sail, take a yacht cruise or a gondola ride, take yoga and spin classes, rent full-suspension mountain bikes, or wallow in the Spa Vita di Lago (⇨ Getting the Spa Treatment). To gamble, you can walk next door to Casino MonteLago or take the hotel's shuttle to the Strip. For a full dose of luxury, opt for the package that includes a new Mercedes-Benz rental. ⊠ *1610 Lake Las Vegas Pkwy., Henderson 89011* ☎ *702/567–4700 or 800/241–3333* ⊟ *702/567–4777* ⊕ *www.ritzcarlton.com* ⬚ *314 rooms, 35 suites* ⌂ *2 restaurants, in-room data ports, in-room safes, minibars, refrigerators, cable TV with movies, driving range, golf privileges, pool, lake, health club, hair salon, hot tub, spa, beach, dock, boating, marina, fishing, mountain bikes, hiking, volleyball, 2 bars, lobby lounge, piano, children's programs (ages 5–12), dry cleaning, laundry service, concierge, concierge floor, business services, meeting rooms, helipad, some free parking, some pets allowed, no-smoking rooms* ⊟ *AE, D, DC, MC, V.*

$$$–$$$$ 🏨 **Embassy Suites Convention Center.** Business and leisure travelers who crave space stay at this attractive Embassy Suites. Each suite is modern and spacious and comes with separate bedroom and living room with sofa sleeper. There are coffeemakers and Web TV in the suites. In the morning, enjoy your complimentary newspaper over the full breakfast that's included in the room rate. ⊠ *3600 Paradise Rd., Paradise Road 89109* ☎ *702/893–8000* ⊟ *702/893–0378* ⊕ *www.eslvcc.com* ⬚ *286 suites* ⌂ *Restaurant, in-room data ports, microwaves, refrigerators, cable TV, bar, dry cleaning, laundry facilities, meeting rooms, free parking, no-smoking rooms* ⊟ *AE, D, DC, MC, V* ⯐ *BP.*

★ **$$$–$$$$** 🏨 **Hard Rock Hotel and Casino.** It's impossible to forget you're in the Hard Rock, no matter where you go in this rock-fixated joint: even the hall carpeting is decorated with musical notes. The rooms are large and sparsely furnished; some beds have leather headboards, bathrooms have stainless-steel sinks, and the double French doors actually open. The Lagoon pool has a sandy bottom, a water slide, a lazy river, and swim-up blackjack. One of the hippest hangouts for twentysomethings is the fun Pink Taco restaurant and bar, packed to the gills on weekend nights. Be prepared for very crowded (but fun) public areas with plenty of opportunities for people-watching. ⊠ *4455 Paradise Rd., Paradise Road 89109* ☎ *702/693–5000 or 800/693–7625* ⊟ *702/693–5010* ⊕ *www.hardrockhotel.com* ⬚ *583 rooms, 63 suites* ⌂ *5 restaurants, coffee shop, grill, room service, in-room data ports, in-room safes, cable TV with movies, pool, health club, hair salon, hot tub, spa, beach, 3 bars, casino, concert hall, nightclub, shops, concierge, convention center, meeting rooms, free parking, no-smoking floors* ⊟ *AE, D, DC, MC, V.*

★ **$$$–$$$$** 🏨 **JW Marriott Las Vegas Resort, Spa & Golf.** Overlooking two of the city's most popular golf courses and within a few miles of Red Rock Canyon,

LODGING ALTERNATIVES

Apartment & Home Rentals

If you want a home base that's roomy enough for a family and comes with cooking facilities, consider a furnished rental. These can save you money, especially if you're traveling with a group. Home-exchange directories sometimes list rentals as well as exchanges.

If you're staying in Las Vegas for a week or more, you might want to book a motel suite with a kitchenette at a weekly rate. The savings over a daily rate can be as high as 50%, and eating in can also save you plenty on meals. **Budget Suites of America** (☎ 866/877–2000) has seven locations around the city.

Vacation rentals in Las Vegas are not very common since the abundance of inexpensive hotel rooms and all-suite hotels eliminates the demand. But some **vacation home rentals** (⊕ www.vacationrentals.com) are listed on the Internet. **Hideaways**

International (✉ 767 Islington St., Portsmouth, NH 03801 ☎ 603/430–4433 or 800/843–4433 🖷 603/430–4444 ⊕ www.hideaways.com) is another resource; membership is $145.

Hostels

Las Vegas has two hostels. On Las Vegas Boulevard South between downtown and the Strip, **Sin City Hostel** (✉ 1208 Las Vegas Blvd. S ☎ 702/868–0222) is easily accessible, although the neighborhood is not the safest at night. It has 48 beds in men's and women's dorms, a handful of very basic semi-private rooms, shared baths, a communal kitchen and lounge, and a pool. Downtown is **USA Hostels in Las Vegas** (✉ 1322 Fremont St. ☎ 702/385–9955 or 800/550–8958).

the JW is a good escape from the hectic Strip. The combination of elegance and comfort makes it easy to unwind. The Aquae Sulis Spa works all the knots out, and the spacious rooms, which have marble bathrooms with separate whirlpool and shower, are designed to soothe. The hotel provides a complimentary shuttle to the Strip. ✉ 221 N. Rampart Blvd., Summerlin 89145 ☎ 702/869–8777 or 877/869–8777 🖷 702/869–7339 ⊕ www.jwmarriottlv.com ⇱ 463 rooms, 78 suites ♻ 9 restaurants, café, coffee shop, room service, fans, in-room data ports, in-room fax, in-room safes, in-room hot tubs, refrigerators, cable TV with movies and video games, golf privileges, 2 pools, pond, health club, hair salon, spa, steam room, bar, lounge, pub, casino, nightclub, shops, dry cleaning, laundry service, concierge, Internet, business services, convention center, free parking, no-smoking rooms ▭ AE, D, DC, MC, V.

♻ $$–$$$$ 🏨 **Hyatt Regency Lake Las Vegas Resort.** It's 17 mi from the city and a world away on the shores of Lake Las Vegas. Designed to mirror a Moroccan castle, this lovely hideaway is set against the backdrop of hills, a championship golf course, and the sparkling 320-acre lake. Plush rooms continue the Moorish theme with rich earth tones complementing the sweeping views of the lake and desert. There's even a small beach where eight tons of soft, white sand is trucked in every summer. Free shuttle service to the

Strip is provided. ⊠ *101 MonteLago Blvd., Henderson 89011* ☎ *702/ 567–1234* 🖷 *702/567–6067* ⊕ *www.lakelasvegas.hyatt.com* ⇆ *496 rooms, 47 suites* ♿ *2 restaurants, room service, in-room data ports, in-room safes, refrigerators, cable TV with movies, 2 pools, lake, health club, spa, boating, 2 bars, casino, children's programs (ages 3–12), concierge floor, meeting rooms, no-smoking rooms* ⊟ *AE, D, DC, MC, V.*

$$–$$$$ 　🏨 **Las Vegas Hilton.** Though the Hilton, which is adjacent to the Las Vegas Convention Center, no longer holds the title of largest hotel in town, it's still a sight to see—best of all by standing at its foot and staring up at the 29-story three-wing tower. The rooms are spacious, with soft colors, large beds, and telephones in the bathrooms; those on the higher floors have great views of the city. The two-story lounge seats 900, there's a wedding chapel, and the sports book is the largest and busiest in town. There's a fabulous pool area next to a spacious recreation deck with lighted tennis courts for night games. ⊠ *3000 Paradise Rd., Paradise Road 89109* ☎ *702/732–5111 or 800/732–7117* 🖷 *702/732–5834* ⊕ *www.lvhilton.com* ⇆ *2,833 rooms, 124 suites* ♿ *12 restaurants, in-room data ports, in-room safes, cable TV with movies, 18-hole golf course, putting green, 6 tennis courts, pool, health club, hair salon, hot tub, spa, 5 bars, casino, nightclub, showroom, video game room, dry cleaning, laundry service, concierge, airport shuttle, free parking, no-smoking floors* ⊟ *AE, D, DC, MC, V.*

$$–$$$$ 　🏨 **The Palms.** The first true luxury boutique hotel in Las Vegas, the $265
Fodor'sChoice million, 31-floor Palms attracts a younger crowd that keeps the public
　★　 places—lounges, clubs, and restaurants—hopping every weekend night. Rooms are large, opulent, and modern, with some unusual amenities for Las Vegas—such as beds with ultrafirm mattresses, duvets, coffeemakers, and Neutrogena products—and most provide a good view of the city. You don't have to venture far to enjoy the nightlife at the hotel's popular Rain nightclub, and the Hart & Huntington tattoo parlor can give you a permanent Vegas souvenir. ⊠ *4321 W. Flamingo Rd., West Side 89103* ☎ *702/942–7777 or 866/942–7777* 🖷 *702/942–7001* ⊕ *www.palms.com* ⇆ *380 rooms, 45 suites* ♿ *6 restaurants, café, coffee shop, food court, ice-cream parlor, in-room data ports, in-room safes, minibars, cable TV with movies, golf privileges, pool, health club, hair salon, spa, 3 bars, 2 lounges, casino, cinema, nightclub, video game room, children's programs (ages 3–12), dry cleaning, laundry service, concierge, Internet, business services, meeting rooms, car rental, free parking, no-smoking floors* ⊟ *AE, D, DC, MC, V.*

$$–$$$$ 　🏨 **Residence Inn by Marriott.** The town house–style all-suite hotel on nicely landscaped grounds is across the street from the convention center and a short cab ride (1¼ mi) from the Strip. The studios and two-bedroom suites all have kitchens. Curbside parking is a plus. A complimentary continental breakfast is included in the room rate. ⊠ *3225 Paradise Rd., Paradise Road 89109* ☎ *702/796–9300 or 800/331–3131* 🖷 *702/796– 9562* ⊕ *www.marriott.com* ⇆ *144 studios, 48 2-bedroom suites* ♿ *In-room data ports, kitchens, microwaves, refrigerators, room TVs with movies, pool, gym, hot tubs, basketball, volleyball, dry cleaning, laundry facilities, Internet, business services, meeting rooms, free parking, some pets allowed, no-smoking rooms* ⊟ *AE, D, DC, MC, V* ¶◯¶ *CP.*

★ **$$-$$$$** 🏨 **Rio All-Suite Hotel & Casino.** The Rio was the first all-suite hotel-casino in Las Vegas. The striking blue, red, and purple two-tower hotel is just off the Strip and has a Mardi Gras theme, complete with a sandy beach beside the pool and professionally trained singing and dancing cocktail servers who perform several times a day. While suites here don't have separate bedrooms, they're spacious, with extra-large sofas, sitting areas, dining tables, big bathrooms, and floor-to-ceiling windows. The Rio has a large, colorful casino and an excellent seafood buffet. The VooDoo Lounge is a slick nightspot 51 stories above Las Vegas, with an outdoor patio that offers stunning views of the Strip and the city. ⊠ *3700 W. Flamingo Rd., West Side 89103* ☎ *702/777–7777 or 800/752–9746* 🖷 *702/253–6090* ⊕ *www.playrio.com* ⬦ *2,554 suites* ♨ *17 restaurants, 2 coffee shops, ice-cream parlor, in-room data ports, cable TV with movies, 5 pools, gym, sauna, spa, steam room, beach, 4 bars, lounge, pub, casino, dry cleaning, laundry service, concierge, Internet, business services, convention center, free parking, no-smoking rooms* ☰ *AE, D, DC, MC, V.*

$-$$$ 🏨 **The Orleans Hotel and Casino.** With its French Quarter–style green-and-white facade, the 22-story, three-tower Orleans joins the pack of Mardi Gras–theme resorts. It does it well: huge, colorful masks hang from the ceiling of the largest casino floor space in Las Vegas, and playful golds, reds, and greens dominate the vast main area. Standard rooms are done in dark green tones, accented by dark cherrywood furniture. Suites are in purples, pinks, and greens with gold walls and red leather chairs. The hotel is home to the Wranglers, Las Vegas's hockey team, and hosts the Professional Rodeo Cowboys Association rodeo in May. The Orleans bowling alley and Don Miguel's, a Mexican restaurant, are local favorites. ⊠ *4500 W. Tropicana Ave., West Side 89103* ☎ *702/365–7111 or 800/ 675–3267* 🖷 *702/365–7499* ⊕ *www.orleanscasino.com* ⬦ *1,828 rooms, 58 suites* ♨ *13 restaurants, café, coffee shop, ice-cream parlor, room service, in-room data ports, cable TV with movies, pool, gym, hair salon, sauna, spa, steam room, bowling, 6 bars, lounge, pub, wine shop, casino, cinema, concert hall, theater, video game room, shop, children's programs (ages 2½–12), concierge, Internet, business services, convention center, travel services, free parking, no-smoking rooms* ☰ *AE, D, DC, MC, V.*

¢-$$ 🏨 **Sam's Town Hotel and Gambling Hall.** Pioneer gambler Sam Boyd built a small grubstake into one of the largest casino companies in Nevada. His namesake casino hotel has long been a favorite with locals, thanks to liberal slots, plenty of good, inexpensive food, and such amenities as an 18-screen cinema. The standard rooms, done in muted colors such as beige and soft red, are built around a nine-story glass-roof atrium filled with tall live trees, cobblestone paths, and a rock waterfall. This busy hotel is on the Boulder Strip, 6 mi from downtown. ⊠ *5111 Boulder Hwy., Boulder Strip 89122* ☎ *702/456–7777 or 800/634–6371* 🖷 *702/454–8014* ⊕ *www.samstownlv.com* ⬦ *613 rooms, 33 suites* ♨ *8 restaurants, cable TV with movies, pool, hot tub, bowling, 7 bars, lounge, casino, cinema, dry cleaning, laundry facilities, free parking, no-smoking floors* ☰ *AE, D, DC, MC, V.*

☉ **¢-$$** 🏨 **Texas Station Gambling Hall & Hotel.** This place and its four sisters— Palace Station, Boulder Station, Sunset Station, and Green Valley Ranch Station—are primarily casinos–entertainment complexes designed for locals, with friendly odds, fast-food joints, expansive buffets, arcades, and large movie theaters. On the northwest side of Vegas, the Texas has all the action and amenities of many Strip properties. Though not lavishly appointed, rooms are large and comfortable, with separate sitting areas and dining tables. The key perk for families is the Kids' Quest, an 8,000-square-foot multilevel indoor playground and activity center. A free shuttle provides transportation to the Strip. ✉ *2101 Texas Star La., Rancho Strip 89036* ☎ *702/631–1000 or 800/654–8888* 📠 *702/631–8120* ⊕ *www.texasstation.com* 🛏 *200 rooms* ⅃ *5 restaurants, food court, in-room data ports, pool, bowling, lounge, casino, theaters, airport shuttle, no-smoking rooms* ▭ *AE, D, DC, MC, V.*

¢–$ 🖵 **Motel 6.** Welcome to the largest Motel 6 in the United States, with 877 rooms, a pool, and a big neon sign. Rooms here look like those of any other Motel 6, but when travelers think in terms of cheap accommodations, they think of this chain, so it tends to get booked up fast. ✉ *195 E. Tropicana Ave., Paradise Road 89109* ☎ *702/798–0728* 📠 *702/798–5657* ⊕ *www.motel6.com* 🛏 *607 rooms* ⅃ *Room TVs with movies, pool, laundry facilities, some pets allowed, no-smoking rooms* ▭ *AE, D, DC, MC, V.*

¢ 🖵 **Budget Suites of America.** A nearby alternative to the Westward Ho is this sprawling complex on the corner of Industrial and Stardust roads. Every room here is a minisuite with a living-dining room, a small separate bedroom, and a full kitchenette; the TV is mounted on a swivel between the living room and bedroom. Weekly rates offer a good discount; rooms on the second and third floors are the least expensive and are even cheaper if you bring your own sheets and towels. ✉ *1500 Stardust Rd., West Side 89109* ☎ *702/732–1500 or 800/752–1501* 📠 *702/732–2656* ⊕ *www.budgetsuites.com* 🛏 *639 suites* ⅃ *Kitchens, cable TV, tennis court, pool, gym, 4 spas, laundry facilities, free parking, some pets allowed* ▭ *AE, MC, V.*

Downtown

$–$$$ 🖵 **Four Queens Hotel and Casino.** This prominent downtown hotel at the hub of the Fremont Street Experience has contemporary rooms, a coffee shop that is one of the least expensive in the downtown area, and the secluded, gourmet Hugo's Cellar, a longtime local favorite that's still one of the better restaurants on Fremont. ✉ *202 E. Fremont St., Downtown 89101* ☎ *702/385–4011 or 800/634–6045* 📠 *702/383–0631* ⊕ *www.fourqueens.com* 🛏 *648 rooms, 42 suites* ⅃ *5 restaurants, coffee shop, ice-cream parlor, pizzeria, room service, in-room data ports, some in-room safes, cable TV with movies, 4 bars, pub, wine bar, casino, video game room, shop, meeting rooms, car rental, free parking, no-smoking floors* ▭ *AE, D, DC, MC, V.*

★ $–$$$ 🖵 **Golden Nugget Hotel and Casino.** The best hotel downtown, the Golden Nugget was transformed by Steve Wynn from a simple gambling hall into an elegant jewel. New owners, who took over in 2003, plan to keep it that way. Red rugs flow over white marble, leading you to the lobby with faux-marble columns, etched-glass windows, and fresh flowers in gold-plated vases. Almost everything here is gold (or, more accurately, brass-plated)—the telephones, the slots, the elevators. The well-kept rooms are modern and comfortable, though the bathrooms are considerably smaller than those at the newer hotels on the Strip. The Nugget's Spa Tower has 27 opulent duplex suites, some with a personal room-service waiter. The pool is the biggest one downtown, and the old poker room's been reinstated. ✉ *129 E. Fremont St., Downtown 89101* ☎ *702/385–7111 or 800/634–3454* 🖷 *702/386–8362* ⊕ *www. goldennugget.com* ⬅ *1,805 rooms, 102 suites* ⚿ *5 restaurants, café, coffee shop, snack bar, room service, in-room data ports, in-room safes, cable TV with movies and video games, pool, health club, hair salon, spa, 3 bars, lounge, casino, showroom, dry cleaning, laundry service, concierge, Internet, business services, meeting rooms, car rental, free parking, no-smoking floors* 🖃 *AE, D, DC, MC, V.*

¢–$$ 🎰 **Lady Luck Casino Hotel.** The two towers of this hotel are across the street from each other, connected via a glass-enclosed pedestrian bridge on the third-floor level. Lady Luck has large rooms with white walls and half-windows that look out on mountains or city. There are also 115 junior suites and 385 "senior" suites for the Lady's many high rollers, who stay here because the casino has some of the least demanding criteria for comps. ✉ *206 N. 3rd St., Downtown 89101* ☎ *702/477–3000 or 800/634–6580* 🖷 *702/477–3002* ⊕ *www.ladylucklv.com* ⬅ *623 rooms, 115 suites* ⚿ *4 restaurants, café, coffee shop, snack bar, room service, refrigerators, cable TV with movies, pool, exercise equipment, bar, lounge, casino, showroom, dry cleaning, laundry service, concierge, meeting rooms, some free parking, no-smoking rooms* 🖃 *AE, D, MC, V.*

¢–$$ 🎰 **Las Vegas Club Hotel and Casino.** The sports theme prevails everywhere but in the guest rooms. The small rooms in one tower are Southwest-style. In the other tower they're flowery. Tiny half windows overlook Fremont and Main streets. The hotel's newer tower houses 186 rooms, three restaurants, and a casino annex. The Barrick Gaming Corporation, which took over in March 2004, is upgrading the Club's looks and building a walkway to a sister property, the Plaza Hotel and Casino. ✉ *18 E. Fremont St., Downtown 89109* ☎ *702/385–1664 or 800/ 634–6532* 🖷 *702/387–6071* ⊕ *www.vegasclubcasino.net* ⬅ *401 rooms, 9 suites* ⚿ *3 restaurants, snack bar, in-room data ports, in-room safes, cable TV with movies, 3 bars, casino, video game room, laundry service, Internet, meeting room, airport shuttle, free parking, no-smoking floors* 🖃 *AE, DC, MC, V.*

$ 🎰 **Main Street Station Casino, Brewery & Hotel.** Filled with antiques, collectibles, and memorabilia, the elegant, Victorian-style casino is brimming with things to look at, including Theodore Roosevelt's Pullman railroad car, dropped-dome chandeliers from the El Presidente Hotel in Buenos Aires, and a section of the Berlin Wall in the men's bathroom. Early American furnishings complement rosy walls in guest rooms. Make sure to get one on the south side of the building, facing Main Street—it's hard to get away from the noise of I–15 on the north side. There's a free shuttle service to the Strip. ✉ *200 N. Main St., Downtown 89101* ☎ *702/387–1896 or 800/713–8933* 🖷 *702/386–4466* ⊕ *www.mainstreetcasino.com* ⬅ *420 rooms* ⚿ *3 restaurants, in-room data ports, in-room safes, cable TV with movies, lounge, pub, casino, meeting rooms, free parking, no-smoking floors* 🖃 *AE, DC, MC, V.*

Where to Stay in
Las Vegas (North)

¢–$ 🛏 **Binion's Horseshoe Hotel & Casino.** Though the Horseshoe has been
on shaky ground since patriarch Benny Binion's death, closing for three
months in early 2004, Harrah's Entertainment partnered up with MTR
Gaming Group to purchase and operate the hotel, sprucing up the place
while keeping its original flair. The modern and medium-size west-side
rooms are done in light colors, and the east-side rooms reflect the Western style of the original Horseshoe. The outdoor pool is on the roof.
The steak house (on the 24th floor, reached by a glass elevator) is enor-
mously popular. ⊠ *128 E. Fremont St., Downtown 89101* ☎ *702/
382–1600 or 800/937–6537* 🖷 *702/384–1574* ⊕ *www.binions.com*
🖙 *366 rooms* ⌂ *Restaurant, coffee shop, room TV with movies, pool,
2 bars, casino, no-smoking rooms* ⊟ *AE, D, DC, MC, V.*

¢–$ 🛏 **El Cortez Hotel.** The El Cortez is a slice of historic Las Vegas: it's one
of the only downtown hotels to retain its original 1940s facade. There
are two floors of tiny rooms, each with twin beds, a small TV, and a
narrow window with a view of Fremont Street. Take a room in the tower,
if you can: they're newer, larger, and only a little more expensive. ⊠ *600
E. Fremont St., Downtown 89109* ☎ *702/385–5200 or 800/634–6703*
🖷 *702/474–3626* ⊕ *www.elcortez.net* 🖙 *287 rooms, 10 suites* ⌂ *Restaurant, coffee shop, in-room data ports, cable TV, 3 bars, casino, free parking, no-smoking floors* ⊟ *AE, D, DC, MC, V.*

¢–$ 🏨 **Fitzgeralds Casino Hotel.** The old-Vegas–style 34-story hotel was the tallest building in Nevada for 15 years, until it was eclipsed by the Stratosphere Tower. Bright, recarpeted hallways lead to clean and comfortable rooms done in fall colors; the Fitz is gradually replacing the somewhat seedy dark-green room carpets. Upper floors get grand views of the valley, while lower rooms look out onto the Fremont Street canopy or an industrial scene. Take in the light show from the Fitz's outdoor balcony, the only one under the Fremont canopy. ⊠ *301 E. Fremont St., Downtown 89101* ☎ *702/388–2400 or 800/274–5825* 🖷 *702/388–2181* ⊕ *www.fitzgeralds.com* ➥ *624 rooms, 14 suites* ఉ *5 restaurants, café, cafeteria, in-room data ports, in-room safes, cable TV with movies, pool, hot tub, 3 bars, lounge, sports bar, cabaret, casino, dry cleaning, concierge, Internet, business services, convention center, car rental, some free parking, no-smoking rooms* ⊟ *AE, D, DC, MC, V.*

¢–$ 🏨 **Plaza Hotel and Casino.** The Plaza anchors Fremont Street and could be seen in the center of nearly every photo of the street before the canopy of the Fremont Street Experience was built. Rooms are almost always available, even during big conventions. Be sure to ask for one overlooking Fremont Street; otherwise you have a view of the railroad tracks. Rooms are medium-size, with bright bedspreads. There's a showroom (the largest downtown) and a wedding chapel on the premises. ⊠ *1 Main St., Downtown 89101* ☎ *702/386–2110 or 800/634–6575* 🖷 *702/382–8281* ⊕ *www.plazahotelcasino.com* ➥ *1,037 rooms* ఉ *3 restaurants, room TV with movies, 4 tennis courts, pool, gym, hair salon, lounge, casino, showroom, laundry facilities, meeting rooms, no-smoking rooms* ⊟ *AE, D, DC, MC, V.*

¢ 🏨 **Gold Spike Hotel and Casino.** The hotel is billed as "Las Vegas as it used to be," with penny slots and video poker, 40¢ live keno, and $2 blackjack tables. Small, plain double rooms have twin beds, a nightstand, a TV, and a view of East Ogden Avenue. A suite adds a four-poster bed, couch, and balcony. All rates include breakfast. ⊠ *400 E. Ogden Ave., Downtown 89101* ☎ *702/384–8444 or 800/634–6703* 🖷 *702/384–8768* ⊕ *www.goldspikehotelcasino.com* ➥ *107 rooms, 3 suites* ఉ *Coffee shop, room TVs with movies, lounge, casino, no-smoking rooms* ⊟ *AE, D, DC, MC, V* ⍾ *BP.*

RV Parks & Campgrounds

Las Vegas is an RVer's dream. The city offers thousands of hookups, some next to casinos, some tucked away in private resorts. Nearby options are limited if you plan to camp, however. Only a small number of places allow tent camping, but with numerous state and national parks within an hour of the city, it's possible to find a place to pitch the pup tent.

🏕 **Boulder Lakes.** Near Sam Boyd Stadium, Boulder Lakes is a good hike from the Strip. But this RV park is more for people looking to spend some serious time in Vegas than those who want to just hang out for a weekend. With monthly rates and numerous perks—including a playground, a clubhouse, three spas, and a ballroom—Boulder Lakes is designed for extended stays. Pets are allowed. ⊠ *6201 Boulder Hwy., East Side 89122* ☎ *702/435–1157* 🖷 *702/435–1125* ➥ *417 sites* ఉ *Flush* *toilets, full hookups, drinking water, guest laundry, showers, public telephone, general store, play area, swimming (pools)* 🖭 *$18–$20* ▭ *MC, V.*

⚠ **Las Vegas KOA at Circus Circus/Circusland RV Park.** The only RV park right on the Strip, Circusland makes for easy access to Las Vegas's main drag. The only problem: like Circus Circus, the casino it's attached to, Circusland tends to fill up quickly, often running at capacity on weekends and holidays. Pets are welcome, and there's also a pet run. ✉ *500 Circus Circus Dr., North Strip 89109* ☎ *702/733–9707 or 800/562–9707* 🖷 *702/696–1358* ⟿ *399 sites* ♿ *Flush toilets, full hookups, dump station, drinking water, guest laundry, showers, public telephone, 2 general stores, swimming (pool)* 🖭 *$14–$25* ▭ *AE, D, DC, MC, V.*

⚠ **Oasis Las Vegas RV Resort.** As much a resort as a place to park the mobile kingdom, Oasis Las Vegas is a plush, well-landscaped RV park with 701 sites and lots of amenities—including a pool and its own clubhouse. Just minutes from the Strip—there's even a shuttle that runs from Oasis to the heart of casino row—as well as within walking distance of the Las Vegas Outlet Mall, Oasis is perfectly situated to enjoy the neon without feeling overpowered by it. Just make sure to make your reservations early. Though Oasis Las Vegas is the area's largest RV park, it tends to fill up during holiday weekends and winter months. Pets (except pit bulls) are allowed. ✉ *2711 W. Windmill La., South Las Vegas 89123* ☎ *702/260–2000 or 800/566–4707* 🖷 *702/263–5160* ⟿ *701 sites* ♿ *Flush toilets, full hookups, dump station, drinking water, guest laundry, showers, public telephones, general store, swimming (pool)* 🖭 *$32–$36* ▭ *AE, D, MC, V.*

⚠ **Sam's Town RV Park.** There are two separate RV locations, one on Boulder Highway, just to the east of the casino, and one just north on Nellis Boulevard. Both offer the standard amenities, as well as shuttle service to the Strip. Both allow pets. Given Sam's Town's guaranteed price of $18, these are the cheapest spots in town. They also now have telephone and cable TV hookups at each site. ✉ *5111 Boulder Hwy., Boulder Strip 89122* ☎ *702/454–8055 or 800/634–6371* 🖷 *702/456–5665* ⟿ *499 sites* ♿ *Flush toilets, full hookups, drinking water, guest laundry, showers, public telephone* 🖭 *$20* ▭ *AE, D, DC, MC, V.*

⚠ **Silverton RV Park.** Like the casino it's named for, the Silverton RV Park is all about down-home charm. Just to the southwest of the Strip, the park has telephone and cable hookups for every stall. There's Internet access, a playground, and basketball and tetherball courts. When the urge hits, there's a shuttle to the Strip. Pets are allowed. ✉ *3333 Blue Diamond Rd., South Las Vegas 89139* ☎ *702/263–7777 or 800/588–7711* 🖷 *702/897–4208* ⊕ *www.silvertoncasino.com* ⟿ *324 sites* ♿ *Flush toilets, dump station, drinking water, guest laundry, showers, grills, general store, play area, pool* 🖭 *$27–$31* ▭ *AE, D, DC, MC, V.*

NIGHTLIFE & THE ARTS

5

Updated by
Mike
Weatherford

THE VERY NAME "LAS VEGAS" HAS BEEN synonymous with a certain style of showbiz entertainment ever since Jimmy Durante first headlined at Bugsy Siegel's Fabulous Flamingo Hotel in 1946 and *Minsky Goes to Paris* introduced topless showgirls at the Dunes in 1957. In those days the lounges gave up-and-coming performers a chance to polish their acts on their way to the showrooms; the camaraderie and informality lent an anything-can-happen-here-tonight air to the entertainment. Through the years the Entertainment Capital of the World has weathered a number of changes in its stage presentations, policies, and prices, but one thing has remained consistent for the past 50 years—doing things big with as much attention called to the doing as possible.

Headliners such as Tom Jones, Gladys Knight, Wayne Newton, and George Carlin still pack the traditional showrooms. Extravagant revues such as *Les Folies Bergere* and *Jubilee!* continue to stage up to 12 shows a week, with outrageous sets, costumes, variety acts, and song and dance. Young and exuberant shows such as *Blue Man Group* and Cirque du Soleil's *O* and *Mystère* have modernized the spectacle, while illusionists such as Lance Burton and comedians such as Carrot Top became stars in their own right. Female and superstar impersonators, "dirty" dancers, comedians—all perpetuate the original style of razzle-dazzle entertainment that Las Vegas has popularized for the world.

Some traditions have changed, however. Many shows deliberately avoid nudity and foul language. Some even encourage parents to bring their children along by offering special prices for youngsters (usually in the summer months). And the dinner show has mostly gone the way of the mink stole, unless you count the utensil-free "medieval style" dining at Excalibur's "Tournament of Kings." But everything is cyclical; topless "girlie" shows have made a comeback in recent years, and it's safe to say Las Vegas entertainment now is all things to all people.

In the not-so-old days, the shows were loss leaders, much as the buffets are today: they were intended to draw patrons who would eventually wind up in the casino. Admission prices were dirt-cheap, and the programs were fairly short. Nowadays, it will cost you at least $60 to see Newton or Gladys Knight, as much as $225 (before taxes and service charges) for Celine Dion, and $150 for any seat on the lower level of the big production *O*. Yet many of the smaller shows have much lower prices. Bargain-hunters have learned to look to afternoon shows, such as Tropicana magician Rick Thomas or the Flamingo's campy burlesque revue *Bottom's Up,* as ways to hold ticket prices around the $20 line.

There are several kinds of shows in Las Vegas. What used to be known as the "big room headliners" are a vanishing breed, and so are the old table-and-booth showrooms where they used to perform. But you can still find a few of the old names, along with a new generation of "resident headliners"—singer Clint Holmes and impressionist Danny Gans—who keep the tradition alive. The big-production spectaculars also remain a Las Vegas trademark, presenting little or no language barrier to the city's large numbers of international tourists. But the classic "feather show"—90 minutes of song, dance, topless showgirls, specialty

Reserved-Seat Ticketing

Most hotels have switched over to reserved-seat ticketing through corporate networks such as Ticketmaster. Many Internet-savvy travelers now pick their seats and purchase tickets for some attractions online well before their visits. In fact, it's advisable to do so for the hotter shows, such as Gans and the Cirque du Soleil productions.

5

Ticketmaster. Most of the showrooms and concert venues in town are part of Ticketmaster, making it possible for you to buy tickets for many Las Vegas shows at your hometown Ticketmaster outlet or through the company's Web site. Las Vegas's **Tower Records** (✉ 4580 W. Sahara Ave., West Side) is conveniently located for ticket buyers. ☎ *702/474–4000* ⊕ *www.ticketmaster.com.*

unlvtickets.com. The notable holdout from Ticketmaster is the Thomas and Mack Center on the University of Nevada–Las Vegas (UNLV) campus. The center hosts Runnin' Rebels basketball, concerts, and special events such as TV-theme children's productions. Tickets can be purchased online, by phone, or at the arena itself. ☎ *702/739–3267 or 866/388–3267* ⊕ *www.unlvtickets.com.*

Allstate Ticketing and Tours. Allstate operates box offices all over town, most prominently in casinos without a show of their own. It sells tickets for almost every casino show except the two Cirque du Soleil productions. It's important to know that Allstate works on a system in which producers pay commissions for each ticket sold, which may prejudice a ticket broker's enthusiasm about a particular show. The lesser shows sometimes offer the highest commissions. ☎ *800/ 838–9383* ⊕ *www.showtickets.com.*

Closed or In-House Ticketing

Other shows have reserved seats but "closed" or "in-house" ticketing networks operate more on a first-come, first-served basis. On weekends it can be tough getting in to see the top names and production revues. Your chances of getting a seat are usually better when you're staying—and gambling—at the hotel. If you plan on spending a fair amount of time at the tables or slots, call VIP Services or a slot host and find out what their requirements are for getting a comp, tickets that have been withheld, or a line pass (that allows you to go straight to the VIP entrance without having to wait in line with the hoi polloi). Then be sure to have your play "rated" by the pit boss when you gamble, in order to qualify for the privileges.

Maître d' Seating

Computerized ticketing and customer preference for reserved seats have all but eliminated the once-frightening realm of maître d's (who assigned the seats at the door) and captains (who show you to your seats). The Imperial Palace's *Legends in Concert* remains the only show in a mid- to large-size room that still operates on the fabled system, though it should come as no surprise that sometimes a little cash can upgrade seating even in rooms with assigned seating. To ensure a good seat, arrive early and discreetly toke the maître d' (with bills or chips the denomination of which he can readily see); $5 is usually sufficient.

acts, and special effects—has taken a backseat to the stylized eye candy of Cirque du Soleil, or the avant-garde stunts of the Blue Man Group. Foreign visitors are on equal footing because you don't have to understand English to enjoy them, yet domestic audiences don't feel anything is missing. The same is true for a number of burlesque-derived revues that still rely on the topless showgirl or dancer, whose blatant charms can be appreciated in any language.

The Strip also broke down the walls that used to exist between old-school Las Vegas headliners and contemporary concert attractions. The casinos conformed to the modern concert industry by building arenas—the MGM Grand Garden, Mandalay Events Center, and Orleans Arena—and music clubs such as the House of Blues at Mandalay Bay. Las Vegas is now a mandatory tour stop for top-name stars of all ages and musical genres. The boldest step to date was taken in March 2003, when Celine Dion opened a three-year commitment to a 4,000-seat venue at Caesars Palace, staying in one place while her fans do the "touring." Elton John recognized a good thing when he saw it, and signed on to perform during many of Dion's vacation weeks.

The latest Las Vegas converts, however, are the young singles who may not buy a ticket for any conventional show. In the latter half of the '90s, the Strip became a nightlife capital, drawing favorable comparisons to Ibiza, Spain, among "clubbers" worldwide. A wave of large dance clubs, such as the Luxor's Ra and the Hard Rock Hotel's Baby's (now Body English), was followed by a trendy new batch of cozier "ultra lounges" such as the MGM Grand's Tabú.

Finding Out What's Going On

Information on shows, including their reservation and seating policies, prices, suitability for children (or age restrictions), and smoking restrictions, is available by calling or visiting the box offices. It's also listed in several local publications. The *Las Vegas Advisor* (⊠ 3687 S. Procyon Ave., Las Vegas 89103 ☎ 800/244–2224) is available at its office for $5 per issue or $50 per year; this monthly newsletter is invaluable for its up-to-the-minute information on Las Vegas dining, entertainment, gambling promotions, comps, and news. You can also pick up free copies of *Today in Las Vegas* and *What's On in Las Vegas* at hotels and gift shops.

The *Las Vegas Review-Journal,* the city's morning daily newspaper, publishes a tabloid pullout section each Friday called "Neon." It provides entertainment features and reviews, and showroom and lounge listings with complete time and price information. The "Neon" section is sold separately for a quarter in some news boxes along the resort corridor. The *Review-Journal* maintains a **Web site** (⊕ www.reviewjournal.com), where show listings are updated each week. The *Las Vegas Sun,* the city's afternoon daily paper, also has a **Web site** (⊕ www.vegas.com) with the latest details.

Three alternative weekly newspapers are distributed at retail stores and coffee shops around town and maintain comprehensive Web sites. They usually offer more detail on the nightclub scene and music outside the realm of the casinos: **Las Vegas Mercury** (⊕ www.lasvegasmercury.com), **Las Vegas Weekly** (⊕ www.lasvegasweekly.com), and **Las Vegas City Life** (⊕ www.lasvegascitylife.com).

ENTERTAINMENT

Afternoon Shows

Las Vegas has become a wider-reaching and more family-friendly destination. But at the same time, evening show prices have broken into the triple-digits. These factors are sometimes at odds with one another and help explain a host of afternoon shows that hold their ticket prices around the $20 mark. The following are the most proven and popular.

Bottom's Up. Comedian Breck Wall has been a fixture on the Strip since 1964, when his Dallas-based comedy troupe first offered Las Vegas a campy hour of blackout sketches and burlesque humor that may have inspired TV's *Laugh-In.* (Wall says Rowan & Martin used to catch the show when they were working in town.) No joke is too old or raunchy for the only daytime topless show. ⊠ *Flamingo Las Vegas, 3555 Las Vegas Blvd. S, Center Strip* ☎ *702/733–3333* 🎟 *$15* ⊙ *Mon.–Sat. 2 PM and 4 PM.*

⏱ **The Illusionary Magic of Rick Thomas.** It's a rare afternoon show to offer big production value, and Thomas generates repeat business by offering outsize illusions at bargain prices. Once dismissed as a poor man's Siegfried & Roy for his use of white tigers, Thomas's stage is now one of the few places to see such creatures in action. ⊠ *Tropicana Resort and Casino, 3801 Las Vegas Blvd. S, South Strip* ☎ *702/739–2222* 🎟 *$21–$26* ⊙ *Mon.–Sat. 2 PM and 4 PM.*

⏱ **Mac King.** This comic magician keeps the payroll small; the only "ex-
FodorsChoice otic animal" is a goldfish that pops out of his mouth at an unexpected
★ moment. King stands apart from the other magic shows on the Strip by offering a one-man hour of low-key, self-deprecating humor and the kind of "close-up" magic that often requires more skill than the "cabinet tricks" of the larger shows. ⊠ *Harrah's Las Vegas Casino & Hotel, 3475 Las Vegas Blvd. S, Center Strip* ☎ *702/369–5111* 🎟 *$18.65* ⊙ *Tues.–Sat. 1 PM and 3 PM.*

Comedy Clubs

Even when Las Vegas wasn't the hippest place to catch a musical act, it was always up-to-the-minute in the comedy department. From Shecky Greene to Chris Rock, virtually every famous comedian has worked a Las Vegas showroom or lounge. While the franchised comedy club boom of the 1980s went bust in most cities, the Strip still has at least four dependable comedy clubs, all with multiple-act formats featuring top names on the circuit. Cover charges are in the $25 range, but two-for-one coupons are easy to come by in freebie magazines and various coupon packages.

Comedy Stop. There are two shows each night at this 400-seat club. Three comedians perform during each show. The price of admission includes two drinks. ⊠ *Tropicana Resort and Casino, 3801 Las Vegas Blvd. S, South Strip* ☏ *702/739–2714* ☉ *Nightly 8 and 10:30.*

The Improv. Comedy impresario Budd Friedman oversees the bookings for this 300-seat showroom in the old bingo hall on the second floor of Harrah's. The Improv is dark on Monday night, and drinks are not included in the admission price. ⊠ *Harrah's Las Vegas Casino & Hotel, 3475 Las Vegas Blvd. S, Center Strip* ☏ *702/369–5111* ☉ *Tues.–Sun. night 8:30 and 10:30.*

Laugh Trax. This 300-seat club at the locals-friendly Palace Station undercuts the price of its Strip competitors but adds a one-drink minimum and bills only two comedians for each program. ⊠ *Palace Station Hotel and Casino, 2411 W. Sahara Ave., West Side* ☏ *888/464–2468* ☉ *Tues.–Thurs. night 7:30; Fri. and Sat. 7:30 and 10.*

Riviera Comedy Club. Steve Schirripa was a doorman, then manager of this long-running comedy room before he found larger fame as Bobby Bacala on *The Sopranos.* He still has a hand in booking the talent. Two shows run each night of the week in the cozy 375-seat club. ⊠ *Riviera Hotel and Casino, 2901 Las Vegas Blvd. S, North Strip* ☏ *702/794–9433* ☉ *Nightly 8:30 and 10:30.*

Evening Revues

⟳ ***American Superstars.*** This upstart impersonator show made *Legends in Concert* pick up its energy level by challenging it with rollicking tributes to pop stars such as Ricky Martin and Christina Aguilera. Both shows are better for the competition. ⊠ *Stratosphere Hotel Tower and Casino, 2000 Las Vegas Blvd. S, North Strip* ☏ *702/380–7711* ▱ *$33* ☉ *Sun.–Tues. 7 PM, Wed., Fri., and Sat. 7 PM and 10 PM.*

Fodor'sChoice ***Blue Man Group: Live at Luxor.*** The New York–based troupe launched its
★ fourth and largest production at the Luxor just before it became ready for prime-time in a series of high-profile computer processor commercials. Three men in utilitarian uniforms, their heads bald and gleaming from cobalt blue greasepaint, prowl the stage committing twisted "science projects" that are alternately highbrow and juvenile. A civil-engineering lesson might be followed by marshmallow spitting. A seven-piece band plays angular spaghetti Western music to complement the Blue Men's signature percussion instruments made from PVC pipe. ⊠ *Luxor Resort & Casino, 3900 Las Vegas Blvd. S, South Strip* ☏ *702/262–4400* ⊕ *www.blueman.com* ▱ *$79–$90* ☉ *Nightly 7 and 10; additional show Sat. 4 PM.*

Crazy Girls. The Americanized, low-rent version of the Crazy Horse Cabaret in Paris is a topless club experience within the safe confines of the hotel. The Riviera imported the show long before Vegas returned to its "Sin City" image, but that doesn't make it the front-runner: cheap production values give other "girlie" shows the upper hand. ⊠ *Riviera Hotel and Casino, 2901 Las Vegas Blvd. S, North Strip* ☏ *702/794–9433* ▱ *$45–$53* ☉ *Fri.–Wed. 9:30 PM.*

An Evening at La Cage. This durable female-impersonator show has been guided since 1985 by Frank Marino, whose campy take on Joan Rivers provides the live voice to introduce lip-synch musical tributes, including the likes of Tina Turner, Cher, and Reba McEntire. ⊠ *Riviera Hotel and Casino, 2901 Las Vegas Blvd. S, North Strip* ☎ *702/794–9433* 🖳 *$47–$58* ⊙ *Wed.–Mon. 7:30 PM.*

Les Folies Bergere. The singing male host of this classic French topless revue tells audiences the Folies is the oldest show in America that's still running. It has been at the Tropicana since 1959, and its survival is almost a miracle, considering the city's zeal for imploding its past. The painted flats and dance segments such as the "Can-Can" show their age compared to newer, high-tech competition, but the hotel preserves the show with some degree of pride. New segments added in 2003 and 2004 rightfully put more of an emphasis on the dancers than the faded trappings, adding fresh costumes and more current (recorded) music. It would, perhaps, benefit from a cheekier attitude. But there's an argument for playing it straight, now that the Strip has only two classic revues complete with singers, dancers, a juggler, and, of course, showgirls in feathers. Only the late show is topless. ⊠ *Tropicana Resort and Casino, 3801 Las Vegas Blvd. S, South Strip* ☎ *702/739–2411* 🖳 *$52–$62* ⊙ *Mon., Wed., Thurs., and Sat. 7:30 PM and 10 PM; Tues. and Fri. 8:30 PM.*

Jubilee! This is the last place to experience the over-the-top vision of Vegas showman Donn Arden—who produced shows on the Strip from 1952 until his death in 1994—and to sample the "class" (or kitsch) Vegas of old. A cast of 80 or more performs in a theater with 1,100 seats, but the gargantuan sets and props steal the show: the sinking of the *Titanic* and Samson destroying the temple. It's still the best vehicle for showgirls parading about in the largest spectacle of feathers and bare breasts you've ever seen, even if attempts to freshen some of the segments middle out between retro nostalgia and a modern reinvention of the form. Baz Luhrmann, where are you? ⊠ *Bally's Las Vegas, 3645 Las Vegas Blvd. S, Center Strip* ☎ *702/739–4567* 🖳 *$56–$72* ⊙ *Sat.–Thurs. 7:30 PM and 10:30 PM.*

La Femme. The MGM Grand Hotel wooed Paris's Crazy Horse Cabaret to Las Vegas by offering to remodel a lounge into a near-spitting image of the French institution. After years of hosting knockoffs such as *Crazy Girls*, the original girlie show is by comparison a classy affair in which symmetrically matched, naturally endowed women are expertly choreographed and "painted in light" for a succession of humorous or erotically mimed vignettes. ⊠ *MGM Grand Hotel and Casino, 3799 Las Vegas Blvd. S, South Strip* ☎ *702/891–7777* 🖳 *$59* ⊙ *Wed.–Mon. 8 PM and 10:30 PM.*

☾ **Lance Burton: Master Magician.** When Roy Horn's tiger bite suddenly put Siegfried & Roy out of business in October 2003, the reigning kings of magic became David Copperfield and Burton, a nice guy from Kentucky who worked his way up the ranks from specialty act to star. While Copperfield still performs only about half his annual schedule on the Strip, Burton is a year-round attraction in an opulent 1,200-seat Victorian theater that makes a splendid long-term home. He's a charmer with the ladies, and works youngsters into the show like no other act on the Strip. Unfortunately, the small magic—the sleight of hand and close-up tricks that earned him the prestigious Gold Medal from the International Brotherhood of Magicians—is lost from way up in the balcony. Still, the major illusions, such as making cars disappear, are downright stunning. ⊠ *Monte Carlo Resort and Casino, 3770 Las Vegas Blvd. S, South Strip* ☎ *702/730–7777* ◧ *$66–$72* ☉ *Tues.–Sat. 7 PM with additional 10 PM shows on Tues. and Sat.*

◔ **Legends in Concert.** The durable *Legends* rotates impersonations of Madonna, Liberace, Tom Jones, and others, with the Elvis Presley finale the only nonvariable rule. This show launched an unfortunate slew of copycats, but maintains its own quality. There's no lip-synching and always a band. ⊠ *Imperial Palace Hotel and Casino, 3535 Las Vegas Blvd. S, Center Strip* ☎ *702/794–3261* ◧ *$40* ☉ *Mon.–Sat. 7:30 PM and 10:30 PM.*

★ ◔ **Mamma Mia!** The musical phenomenon parked on the Strip for an open-ended, "sit-down" run in early 2003. A local cast adds its own charm to the Las Vegas edition that is presented uncut, with an intermission, as it is in other cities and tour stops. The '70s pop hits of ABBA are woven into a traditional musical comedy about a bride-to-be who uses her wedding to deduce which of her mother's past suitors is her father. The soapy, sitcom plot attracts a largely female audience. ⊠ *Mandalay Bay Resort & Casino, 3950 Las Vegas Blvd. S, South Strip* ☎ *702/632–7580* ◧ *$71–$93* ☉ *Mon., Wed., Thurs., and Sat. 7 PM, Fri. 8 PM, Sat. 10:30 PM, Sun. 5 and 9 PM.*

MGM Cirque du Soleil show. At this writing, there were few details on the massive, yet-to-be named Cirque du Soleil show set to replace *EFX* sometime in 2004. The Asian-theme show takes Cirque into the realm of theater with a linear storyline, spinning a tale in which two brothers battle each other after taking separate sides in the war of good versus evil. Cirque's traditional acrobatics are incorporated into mind-blowing displays of martial arts, puppetry, fire, and multimedia effects. Even the seating configuration and set designs done by Mark Fisher, who designed tours for U2 and the Rolling Stones, were billed as an unusual departure for Las Vegas. ⊠ *MGM Grand Hotel and Casino, 3805 Las Vegas Blvd. S, South Strip* ☎ *702/891–7777.*

Midnight Fantasy. This is the most "innocent" and tamest of the midsize topless shows. Though it has energetic choreography and eye-catching costumes, it plays more like a theme-park revue, to no complaints from the mainstream couples—heavy on room guests from Mandalay Resorts hotels—who support this Luxor show. ⊠ *Luxor Resort & Casino, 3900 Las Vegas Blvd. S, South Strip* ☎ *702/262–4400* ◧ *$33* ☉ *Tues., Thurs., and Sat. 8:30 PM and 10:30 PM, Wed. and Fri. 10:30 PM, Sun. 8:30 PM.*

★ ◔ **Mystère.** Even though the Strip has continually reinvented itself since Cirque du Soleil's new age circus opened in 1993, the years have not diminished it as the premier family show in town and a memorable experience. From the moment you enter the big top, you are intimately involved with this show. "Flounes" (clowns) mingle and fool with the audience as it's seated, and roving "devils" make trouble even before the show begins. The music is rousing and haunting, the acrobatics chilling, and the dance numbers inspiring. The usual circus-type distractions are kept to a minimum, and there are no animals. Although Cirque du Soleil's *O* and *Zumanity* have since conquered Las Vegas and expectations are high for the fourth production at the MGM Grand Hotel, *Mystère* has retained an audience by keeping the spectators close to the action and the human achievements in the spotlight. ⊠ *Treasure Island Las Vegas, 3300 Las Vegas Blvd. S, Center Strip* ☏ 702/894–7722 🎫 $95 🕐 *Wed.–Sun. 7:30 PM and 10:30 PM.*

★ **A New Day.** Las Vegas was built on star power, but Celine Dion pioneered a new concept for Las Vegas entertainment by promising to stay put for three years, letting fans "tour" to see her in the 4,000-seat Colosseum built for her in front of Caesars Palace. Divisive ticket prices topping out at $225 are somewhat at odds with *O*- and *Mystère*-cocreator Franco Dragone's attempt to extend the show's appeal beyond diehards with 50 dancers and a lavish revue. The distractions tend to compete with the star, and it sometimes becomes a game of "Where's Waldo?" to find her on a 120-foot-wide stage that's too big by a third. But the show's still innovative and undeniably spectacular in places, such as her signature song "My Heart Will Go On," set against giant-screen film footage of the moon in orbit. ⊠ *Caesars Palace, 3570 Las Vegas Blvd. S, Center Strip* ☏ 702/474–4000 🎫 $87.50–$225 🕐 *Wed.–Sun. 8 PM.*

FodorsChoice **O.** More than $70 million was spent on Cirque du Soleil's theater at Bellagio, and on the liquid stage that takes over as the real star of the show.
★ *O* is the pronunciation of *eau*, French for water, and water is everywhere—1.5 million gallons of it, 12 million pounds of it, contained by a "stage" that, thanks to hydraulic lifts, can change shape and turn to dry land in no time. The intense and nonstop action by the show's acrobats, aerial gymnasts and trapeze artists, synchronized swimmers, divers, and contortionists takes place above, within, and even on the surface of the water, making for a stylish spectacle that manages to have a vague theme about the wellspring of theater and imagination. Even if the deeper themes elude you, so much is going on that you may be exhausted from trying to see everything. ⊠ *Bellagio Las Vegas, 3600 Las Vegas Blvd. S, Center Strip* ☏ 702/693–7111 🎫 $93–$150 🕐 *Fri.–Tues. 7:30 PM and 10:30 PM.*

The Second City. Shoehorning itself onto a Strip filled with stand-up comedy clubs, Chicago's ensemble comedy institution is a breath of fresh air. It has the class and polish of a theatrical revue but isn't afraid to go for the cheap or lowbrow when there's a good laugh to be had. Five performers write and perform sketches (some of which lampoon the many easy targets of Las Vegas) but also pull audience members into improvisational games in Bugsy's Celebrity Theatre. ⊠ *Flamingo Las Vegas, 3555 Las Vegas Blvd. S, Center Strip* ☏ 702/733–3333 🎫 $35 🕐 *Thurs.–Tues. 8 PM and Thurs.–Sun 10:30 PM.*

Skintight. This "equal opportunity" topless show includes a dynamic male front man, Darryl Ross, and male dancers along with women in the chorus. ✉ *Harrah's Las Vegas Casino & Hotel, 3475 Las Vegas Blvd. S, Center Strip* ☏ *702/369–5111* 🎫 *$55* ⊙ *Mon.–Wed. 10:30 PM, Fri. 10 PM and midnight, Sat. 10:30 PM, Sun. 7:30 PM and 10:30 PM.*

Splash. The original show made one in the 1980s but has long been eclipsed by such spectaculars as *O* and *Mystère*. The name is a bit of a misnomer now, since the water is frozen; the trademark tank was removed in 1999 to shift the focus to ice-skating, pop-star impersonations, and variety acts that occasionally get the adrenaline pumping. *Splash* used to be live MTV. Now it's just for channel surfers. ✉ *Riviera Hotel and Casino, 2901 Las Vegas Blvd. S, North Strip* ☏ *702/794–9301* 🎫 *$60–$75* ⊙ *Sat.–Thurs. 8 PM and 10:30 PM.*

🕓 **Tournament of Kings.** One of Las Vegas's most unusual big shows takes place in a dirt-floor arena, with the audience eating a basic dinner (warning: no utensils) and cheering fast horses, jousting, and swordplay. It's a wonderful family show—especially for pre-adolescents, who get to make a lot of noise. ✉ *Excalibur Hotel and Casino, 3850 Las Vegas Blvd. S, South Strip* ☏ *702/597–7600* 🎫 *$39.95* ⊙ *Nightly 6 and 8:30.*

🕓 **"We Will Rock You."** The U.S. debut of the *Mamma Mia!*–style musical using the song catalog of Queen was set to play at Paris Las Vegas starting in September 2004. British humorist Ben Elton helms the satirical tale of a future where rock-and-roll is outlawed and pop music is computer-generated until a certain Galileo leads a revolt. ✉ *Paris Las Vegas, 3655 Las Vegas Blvd. S, South Strip* ☏ *800/634–6753.*

Zumanity. Cirque du Soleil deliberately raised eyebrows by announcing its third Las Vegas show would turn away from the family market to indulge in a racy, near-naked exploration of sexuality. The end product also followed the lead of Baz Luhrmann's movie *Moulin Rouge* by fusing Cirque acrobatics with European cabaret and English music hall tradition. The result is a mixed bag that attracts a young-adult demographic. The more conventional comedians, strippers (male and female), and drag-queen host Joey Arias founder against the familiar feats of derring-do spiced up with erotic sizzle. ✉ *New York–New York Hotel and Casino, 3790 Las Vegas Blvd. S, South Strip* ☏ *866/606–7111* 🎫 *$65–$105* ⊙ *Tues.–Sat. 7:30 and 10:30.*

Showrooms

Resident Headliners

The turn of the new century took Las Vegas back to one of the traditions from its past. The success of impressionist Danny Gans—not to mention the hassles of post-terrorism air travel—opened the doors to a wave of "resident headliners" who live in Las Vegas and perform on a year-round schedule comparable to the revues (as opposed to visiting headliners such as the Moody Blues, Huey Lewis, or Tom Jones, who stay anywhere from three nights to two weeks).

Clint Holmes, Rita Rudner, and even a certain fellow named Wayne Newton all bet that show goers were tired of special effects and ready to re-embrace the "down front" performing tradition that put Las Vegas on the map.

★ **The Amazing Johnathan.** The crackpot comedian and almost-magician draws warm bodies to the Riviera through strong word of mouth and heavy exposure on cable TV. The bellicose, belligerent Johnathan isn't afraid to draw a little (fake) blood as he tortures both his dingbat stage assistant and a hapless audience volunteer, who changes each night but never fails to spend an inordinate amount of time onstage. ⊠ *Riviera Hotel and Casino, 2901 Las Vegas Blvd. S, North Strip* ☎ 877/892–7469 ⊑ *$47–$58* ⊙ *Fri.–Wed. 10 PM.*

★ **Clint Holmes (Harrah's).** Harrah's wagered that Danny Gans–style lightning would strike twice when it backed a relative unknown, and strong word-of-mouth brought Clint Holmes deserved acceptance. The singer has only one distant hit single to his name: the uncharacteristic "Playground in My Mind" from 1973. But his endearing persona and his jazzy way with self-penned songs or baby-boomer pop standards (he prefers 1970s-era material to the Sinatra classics) allow him to pull off the seemingly impossible task of becoming a new-generation crooner who isn't a retro throwback to the swing era. The musical ensemble who back him is uniformly strong and enthusiastic. ⊠ *Harrah's Las Vegas Casino & Hotel, 3475 Las Vegas Blvd. S, Center Strip* ☎ 702/369–5111 ⊑ *$66* ⊙ *Mon.–Sat. 7:30 PM.*

★ **Danny Gans: Man of Many Voices (Mirage).** The impressionist (and former baseball player) pulled off a near miracle in Las Vegas, coming in from the trade show and convention circuit as a "no name" and becoming one of the hottest tickets in town. This talented impressionist leaves 'em standing and cheering every night, after performing upwards of 60 characters—everyone from Gerald Ford and Kermit the Frog to Dean Martin and Homer Simpson. Gans is also a singer, dancer, musician, and comedian, and fronts a band that provides musical mimicry. With a show that plays more like a one-man theatrical revue than a nightclub act, Gans lacks spontaneity but pushes emotional buttons. ⊠ *Mirage Hotel and Casino, 3400 Las Vegas Blvd. S, Center Strip* ☎ 702/791–7111 ⊑ *$100* ⊙ *Tues.–Thurs. and weekends 8 PM.*

★ **Gladys Knight (Flamingo).** The R&B legend is a longtime Las Vegas resident but kept her show mostly on the road before settling into an open-ended run at the Flamingo in 2002. Her warm personality unites a range of song choices—not all of them her own hits—and older brother Bubba becomes a comic stage foil to make up for the other missing Pips. ⊠ *Flamingo Las Vegas, 3555 Las Vegas Blvd. S, Center Strip* ☎ 702/733–3333 ⊑ *$68–$79* ⊙ *Tues.–Sat. 7:30 PM.*

★ **Penn & Teller (Rio).** After years of doing at least a third of their shows in Las Vegas, eccentric comic magicians Penn & Teller finally took residency in the Rio's gorgeous Samba Theatre, a 1,500-seat auditorium with opulent chandeliers and original artwork in the lobby. Penn's verbal overkill and the duo's flair for the grotesque make them an acquired taste for many, but what once was a fringe act now has become almost mainstream for the new Las Vegas. Their magic is unusual and genuinely baffling, and their comedy provocative and thoughtful, albeit blasphemous. ⊠ *Rio All-Suite Hotel and Casino, 3700 W. Flamingo Rd., West Side* ☎ *702/777–7776* ⊠ *$77* ☉ *Wed.–Mon. 9 PM.*

★ **Rita Rudner (New York–New York).** It's rare to be a female comedian in Las Vegas and rarer still to offer a "clean" act that's still insightful in its look at domestic life and female obsessions. The folding chairs in the so-called Cabaret Theatre are nothing to write home about, but Rita gets the job done for an intimate evening of soft-spoken wit. ⊠ *New York–New York Hotel and Casino, 3790 Las Vegas Blvd. S, South Strip* ☎ *702/740–6815* ⊠ *$54* ☉ *Mon., Wed., and Thurs. 8 PM, Fri. 9 PM, Sat. 7 PM and 9 PM.*

The Scintas (Rio). The Buffalo, New York, quartet of three siblings and a drummer possesses a warm charm that helps sell routines that hearken back to the era of the "show band," where every member had double-threat comic and musical duties. The Scintas lay on the schtick pretty thick, but have a loyal, mostly older fan base for an act that can perhaps be described as Wayne Newton meets the Smothers Brothers. ⊠ *Rio All-Suite Hotel and Casino, 3700 W. Flamingo Rd., West Side* ☎ *702/252–7776* ⊠ *$60* ☉ *Fri.–Wed. 7:30 PM.*

Wayne Newton (Stardust). The years have punished his now-raggedy voice, but Mr. Las Vegas, the Midnight Idol, the King of the Strip still knows how to turn on the charm. A homegrown phenomenon, he has been performing here since his teens. On stage Newton gives it the Al Jolson treatment, working and sweating his way through a leisurely two hours—singing, telling jokes, and playing the guitar, violin, and trumpet. Whatever one thinks of his diminished vocal ability or the corn-pone, no one would dispute the fact that he knows how to entertain his audience. Seeing him in this appropriately aged showroom (which once housed the *Lido de Paris*) is as much a part of the experience of visiting Las Vegas as gambling and a trip to Hoover Dam. ⊠ *Stardust Hotel and Casino, 3000 Las Vegas Blvd. S, North Strip* ☎ *702/732–6325* ⊠ *$60* ☉ *Sat.–Thurs. 8 PM.*

Headliners Showrooms

Who would have thought the day would come when the traditional headliner room was an endangered species on the Strip? Part of it is due to the previously mentioned effect of the concert industry shifting the action to venues such as the House of Blues. A few rooms do still host a rotating roster of names, but much of the action has switched to the locals scene away from the Strip proper, with one-night concerts or weekend engagements replacing extended stays.

Hilton Theater. Once famous as the home base for Elvis Presley, this large showroom with a balcony has since been converted to theater seating. The pending sale of the Hilton had it marking time in 2004, booking concert attractions such as Kenny Rogers and Sinbad on the weekends, and impersonator tributes to Elvis and the Beatles on the weeknights. ⊠ *Las Vegas Hilton, 3000 Paradise Rd., Paradise Road* ☎ *702/732–5755.*

Hollywood Theatre. Tom Jones, Paul Anka, and Carrot Top are among those who make regular visits to this contemporary update of the classic showroom at the MGM Grand, which eliminates the long tables to improve sight lines but keeps the booths. The sound system in the 650-seat venue is among the best in town. ⊠ *MGM Grand Hotel and Casino, 3799 Las Vegas Blvd. S, South Strip* ☎ *702/891–7777.*

Orleans Showroom. Theater seating and a super-wide stage (designed to lure TV production) highlight this 800-seat room slightly west of the Strip at the Orleans, which has proven popular with both locals and visitors. Frequent headliners include Neil Sedaka, Bill Medley, and Debbie Reynolds. ⊠ *Orleans Hotel and Casino, 4500 W. Tropicana Ave., West Side* ☎ *702/365–7075.*

Suncoast Showroom. The Suncoast is a locals-oriented casino from the Gaughan family that built the Gold Coast and Orleans. While the latter are only a couple of miles away from the Strip, the Suncoast is a determined drive 15 mi or so west of the tourist corridor in Summerlin. A handsome 400-seat showroom with a classic old-Vegas feel was a risk that paid off, drawing strong local support for acts ranging from Tower of Power to Bobby Rydell. The showroom made a 2004 push to redefine itself primarily as a jazz room, with the likes of Ramsey Lewis and Jean Luc Ponty. ⊠ *Suncoast Hotel and Casino, 9090 Alta Dr., Northwest Las Vegas* ☎ *702/365–7075.*

Theatre Ballroom. The Golden Nugget once closed its upstairs cabaret, leaving downtown short on entertainment, but the cozy 400-seat room reopened in late 2000 and new tiered seating was added in early 2003, creating a classy downtown venue for both headliners and revues. ⊠ *Golden Nugget Hotel and Casino, 129 Fremont St., Downtown* ☎ *702/796–9999.*

Venues

In addition to the hotel showrooms and theaters, Las Vegas has four large multipurpose arenas for both concerts and sports, and several smaller performance venues.

The Strip

Aladdin Theatre for the Performing Arts. The 7,000-seat concert hall was spared the wrecking ball when the old Aladdin was destroyed; the new Aladdin—which was set to become Planet Hollywood in 2004—was built to surround it. Since Las Vegas does not have its own municipal theater, the Aladdin often hosts touring companies for Broadway musicals such as *Les Misèrables.* ⊠ *Aladdin Resort and Casino, 3667 Las Vegas Blvd. S, Center Strip* ☎ *702/785–5555.*

Colosseum at Caesars Palace. The sound is stunning even when the sightlines are strained at this 4,100-seat auditorium. The $95 million theater was built mainly to house 200 annual performances of Celine Dion's *A New Day.* Elton John later signed on to do at least 75 shows over three years, and big names such as Jerry Seinfeld and Gloria Estefan have squeezed into the schedule. The walls are padded with fiberglass and the 115 speakers are clustered for "severe directionality" to

THE LOUNGE EVOLUTION

TRENDS ARE FICKLE IN VEGAS. *Take lounges, which, once the hub of the hip, plummeted to the dregs of popular culture, then resurged with a vengeance, even spawning upscale spin offs. Now the word "lounge" encompasses both the old cliché, an open casino hangout where a trio in matching sequined vests warbles Top 40 covers, and the trendy spot where everyone lines up to pay $8 a drink and rubberneck for a glimpse of a celebrity.*

The lounge came into its own as an all-night party in the early 1950s, when stars like Louis Prima, the Treniers, and the Mary Kaye Trio kept gamblers energized until dawn. Casino employees—showgirls, pit bosses—wired from their late-night shifts joined the mix, packing out the 5 AM shows. The hot ticket was Chinese food at the Sands, a far cry from the chic nightclubs and busy sports bars lining the Strip today.

The '70s was a rough time for lounge lovers. On the casino front, slot machines became all the rage, and casino managers cut down the size of the free lounges to create more floor space for the lucrative machines. Pop culture turned to rock-and-roll, and suddenly the Vegas music scene, former home to legends like the Rat Pack, was the punch line of the music industry. "Lounge singer" became synonymous with Bill Murray's cheesy "Nick the Lounge Lizard," who crooned the theme to Star Wars on Saturday Night Live.

But Vegas is a town that reinvents itself, and lounges are no exception. Movies like Swingers spun the city back around to its '50s cool image, and lounges became an ironic spot to hang out for people in the know. Even that reviled lounge music made a comeback on the Strip as tribal casinos and legalized pockets of gaming around the country made casino gambling

by itself less unique. People missed the tinselly Vegas. Once again, like the old days, they line up early to snag seats for a hot act, like Jimmy Hopper at Bellagio's **Fontana Lounge** *(☎ 702/693–7111) a singer who's more popular than many headlining stars. Hipsters descend on* **Peppermill Fireside Lounge** *(☎ 702/369–5000). And the outdoor lounge* **Carnaval Court** *sits unapologetically off the sidewalk in front of Harrah's Las Vegas.*

The latest lounge makeover is a wave of so-called "ultra lounges," which combine aspects of a cocktail lounge and a larger dance club. Cool Gen-Xers looking for an alternative to the confetti-falling-from-the-ceiling megaclub scene drop their cash on pricey drinks at places like **Risque** *(☎ 702/946–4589) at Paris Las Vegas or* **Shadow** *(☎ 702/731–7990) at Caesars Palace. Tables at these posh cribs often come with a hefty "bottle service" price tag: you can reserve a seat if you dish out anywhere from $100 to $250 for a bottle of wine or liquor at a lounge like* **Tabu** *(☎ 702/891–7183) at the MGM Grand Hotel and Casino or* **OPM** *(☎ 702/369–4998) in the Forum Shops at Caesars Palace.*

— Mike Weatherford

equalize the acoustics in every area of seating. The two balconies can seem distant from the ridiculously wide 120-foot stage, but a 40-foot video screen, billed as the world's largest, improves the views. ✉ *Caesars Palace, 3750 Las Vegas Blvd. S, Center Strip* ☎ 877/427–7243.

★ **House of Blues.** This nightclub-concert hall hybrid at Mandalay Bay is the seventh entry in this chain of successful intimate music clubs. An electic choice of performers takes the stage almost nightly; past acts include Al Green, Bo Diddley, and Seal. ✉ *3950 Las Vegas Blvd. S, South Strip* ☎ 702/632–7600.

Mandalay Bay Events Center. With a capacity of 8,000 to 11,000, this venue is slightly smaller than the city's other two large arenas, the MGM Grand Garden and the Thomas and Mack Center. A consumer-friendly management leans toward holding the line against heart-stopping ticket prices for concerts. Each summer, **Mandalay Beach** offers weekly general-admission concerts in the hotel's lushly landscaped pool and beach area. ✉ *Mandalay Bay Resort & Casino, 3950 Las Vegas Blvd. S, South Strip* ☎ 702/632–7777.

MGM Grand Garden. The biggest concert names, including Bruce Springsteen and Britney Spears, tend to headline here. But to secure the acts with adult appeal, such as Cher and Jimmy Buffett, the MGM has a reputation for outbidding the rival arenas, then passing the costs along to fans in the form of triple-digit ticket prices. It holds from 12,000 to 15,200 people. ✉ *MGM Grand Hotel and Casino, 3799 Las Vegas Blvd. S, South Strip* ☎ 702/891–7777.

Away from the Strip

For those who venture off the Strip, the Station Casinos family caters more to locals, with mid-level concert acts at reasonable prices. These small showrooms have hosted everyone from Toby Keith to Keith Sweat, and from Merle Haggard to Jerry Vale.

Club Madrid. Sunset Station was built after sister property Boulder Station enjoyed success with concert acts, and Club Madrid was designed as a hybrid lounge–concert venue with room to seat 500 people. ✉ *1301 E. Sunset Rd., Henderson* ☎ 702/547–7777.

The Joint. Big-ticket attractions usually found in arenas—the Rolling Stones, the Eagles, and Sting—as well as smaller acts more often matched to a 1,200-capacity club play this venue inside the Hard Rock Hotel and Casino. ✉ *4455 Paradise Rd., Paradise Road* ☎ 702/693–5000.

Orleans Arena. An incredibly popular casino for locals further boosted its likeability quotient when it opened a new arena in May 2003. No matter that it was the fourth in a 3½-mi area. The Orleans Arena opened strong by luring Disney on Ice and the Ringling Bros. and Barnum & Bailey Circus away from the Thomas and Mack Center, and the National Horse Show Indoor Championships away from its longtime home at Madison Square Garden in New York. The casino also signed a professional hockey team, the Las Vegas Wranglers, as the anchor tenant. Padded seats, free parking, and reasonable concession prices add to the appeal of a venue that seats about 7,600 for concerts. ✉ *4500 W. Tropicana Ave., West Las Vegas* ☎ 702/284–7777.

The Railhead. This comfortable venue in Boulder Station started as an open casino-lounge that occasionally hosted ticketed concerts. It has since become an enclosed club that comfortably seats 660 people, perfect for a diverse range of mid-level concert acts like Dave Mason, B. J. Thomas, or Motley Crue screamer Vince Neil. ⊠ *4111 Boulder Hwy., Boulder Strip* ☎ *702/432–7777.*

Sam's Town Live! The Railhead in Boulder Station got some competition with the arrival of this smartly designed concert and convention hall with retractable seating at Sam's Town Casino. ⊠ *5111 Boulder Hwy., Boulder Strip* ☎ *888/464–2468.*

Thomas and Mack Center. Since the MGM Grand and Mandalay Bay both built their own concert and sporting arenas, this center on UNLV's campus has come to rely on more sporting events such as the National Finals Rodeo. It holds anywhere from 7,000 to 18,000 people. There's now a smaller "field house" that connects to the main arena: the **Cox Pavilion** has hosted concerts for 2,000 to 4,000 people. ⊠ *Tropicana Ave. at Swenson St., University District* ☎ *702/739–3267.*

UNLV Performing Arts Center. Like the Thomas and Mack Center, this complex is also on the UNLV campus but tends to stage more genteel events. It's divided into the 400-seat **Judy Bayley Theatre,** which hosts ballet and plays, and the 1,800-seat **Artemus Ham Concert Hall.** ⊠ *4505 S. Maryland Pkwy., University District* ☎ *702/895–2787.*

NIGHTLIFE

Bars & Lounges

The Strip

The lounges of the Las Vegas casino-hotels were once places where such headliners as Frank, Dean, and the gang would go after their shows, taking a seat in the audience to laugh at the comedy antics of Shecky Greene or Don Rickles or to enjoy the music of Louis Prima and Keely Smith. Now the lounges have been mostly reduced to small bars within the casino, where bands play Top 40 hits in front of small crowds of people pie-eyed from the slots (The Lounge Evolution CloseUp). Virtually every casino has such a spot; all you need to do is buy a drink or two and you can listen to the music all night long. A few lounges—the Las Vegas Hilton and Boardwalk among them—have computerized lighting and larger dance floors, making them as much a small dance club as live music club. Some of the nicest are at Paris Las Vegas, the Tropicana, the Stratosphere, Mandalay Bay, and the Orleans.

The turn of the 21st century, however, brought an explosion of hybrid nightspots aiming for the middle ground between dance club and conversational lounge.

Caramel. The owners of the Bellagio's dance club, Light, opened Caramel as a warm-up, wind-down, or distinct alternative to the larger club. The sweet name is backed up by martinis served in signature chocolate and caramel-coated chilled glasses. ✉ *Bellagio Las Vegas, 3600 Las Vegas Blvd. S, Center Strip* ☎ *702/693–7111.*

Carnaval Court. Harrah's has the rare outdoor lounge to take advantage of the Strip's parade of street life. Misters cool the scene in the summertime, and performing "flair bartenders" juggle bottles to the awe of customers. ✉ *Harrah's Las Vegas Casino & Hotel, 3475 Las Vegas Blvd. S, Center Strip* ☎ *702/369–5000.*

Coyote Ugly. Barmaids in tight clothes break into choreographed bartop dances intended to make Hooter's look like a church picnic at this noisy joint. Patrons line up to savor this reincarnation of the 2000 movie's title nightspot, which has galvanized aluminum siding, old license plates, and an impressive bra collection adorning the bars. ✉ *New York–New York Hotel and Casino, 3790 Las Vegas Blvd. S, South Strip* ☎ *702/740–6330.*

Drai's. Once the tony restaurant's tables are cleared away after evening dining hours, the wild scene inside Drai's is closer to a full-bore dance club than a lounge. ✉ *Barbary Coast Hotel and Casino, 3595 Las Vegas Blvd. S, Center Strip* ☎ *702/737–0555.*

★ **Fontana Lounge.** The bar inside the Bellagio is styled like a 1940s-era supper club and has a spectacular view of the dancing water shows outside. ✉ *Bellagio Las Vegas, 3600 Las Vegas Blvd. S, Center Strip* ☎ *702/693–7111.*

Fodor'sChoice **Ghostbar.** Perched on the penthouse level of the Palms, Ghostbar has a ★ glassed-in view of the city from its white, '60s-mod furniture. An outdoor deck is cantilevered over the side of the building, with a Plexiglas platform that allows revelers to look down 450 feet below. ✉ *The Palms, 4321 W. Flamingo Rd., West Side* ☎ *702/942–7777.*

Mist. The partners behind the Bellagio's Caramel room opened a similar room off the casino floor of Treasure Island. The "Munchie Menu" includes the Pooh Bear, a peanut-butter-and-jelly sandwich on banana nut bread. ✉ *Treasure Island Las Vegas, 3300 Las Vegas Blvd. S, Center Strip* ☎ *702/894–7111.*

OPM. The second floor of Wolfgang Puck's Chinois restaurant in the Forum Shops at Caesars is a two-room club with an elevated catwalk perch for those who want to peek down on the mall traffic below. Some Sunday nights have a lesbian and gay format. ✉ *Forum Shops at Caesars, 3500 Las Vegas Blvd. S, Center Strip* ☎ *702/369–4998.*

Red Square. It's easy to forget there's a Russian restaurant behind this lounge, which functions as a virtually self-sufficient nightspot. The hook is the limitless vodka selection and the front bar that's made of a flat panel of ice to keep your choices at a cool sipping temperature. ✉ *Mandalay Bay Resort & Casino, 3950 Las Vegas Blvd. S, South Strip* ☎ *702/632–7777.*

Risqué. The distinction between "ultra lounge" and dance club blurs at this sizable second-floor room that holds around 700 people. Views from the six individual balconies take in both the Strip and the Bellagio foun-

CloseUp

BEST SWIM-UP BARS

When Las Vegas's hold on casino gambling was far more autonomous, pool attendants could have been wearing shirts that said "Get Back In There" when they began folding up deck chairs. But now that the city shares the casino experience with the rest of the country, casino executives have started to see the pool area as more of a revenue point. For years, the *Tropicana* kept the (tiki lawn) torch burning for a resort image that dated back to 1953, when a creative Sands publicist staged a photo of swimmers crowded around a floating craps table. Now it's just one of several places to literalize the concept. Here are the top picks:

The Hard Rock Hotel. The hotel's expansion added more amenities to capitalize on the popular pool area, including the Palapa Lounge. An island cabana houses both a bar and blackjack. ⊠ 4455 Paradise Rd. ☎ 800/675–3267.

Mandalay Bay. The hotel's Moorea Beach Club allows topless sunbathing on its overstuffed daybeds by sunlight, and converts into a poolside nightclub after dark. ⊠ 3950 Las Vegas Blvd. S ☎ 877/632–7800.

The Palms. The Hard Rock Hotel's arch-rival, The Palms, has a sound system, lighting, and fog effects that were built into the pool area known as the Skin Pool Lounge. Poolside blackjack by day gives way to aquatic go-go girls as the area segues into a nightclub after dark. ⊠ 4321 W. Flamingo Rd. ☎ 866/725–6773.

The Tropicana. At the pool's bar, the original swim-up blackjack game still runs between Memorial Day and Labor Day as the conversation piece of a 12,000-square-foot main pool area. ⊠ 3801 Las Vegas Blvd. S ☎ 702/739–2222.

tain show across the street, but if you're not a VIP, your best chance of scoring one is on a weeknight. Famous corporate faces such as Bill Gates have been known to charter the separate Salon Privé, which includes its own deejay setup and big round furniture fixtures that look a lot like beds. The Sunday night *Vamps* burlesque revue attempts to draw locals. ⊠ *Paris Las Vegas, 3655 Las Vegas Blvd. S, Center Strip* ☎ 702/946–4589.

Shadow. Caesars Palace converted one of its traditional lounges into Shadow, thus named because of the seemingly naked women dancing behind scrims in silhouette. ⊠ *Caesars Palace, 3570 Las Vegas Blvd. S, Center Strip* ☎ 702/731–7990.

Tabú. The high-tech touches of a big dance club combine with the coziness of a lounge here. A former Cirque du Soleil lighting designer created "murals" of light that change depending on the perspective of the viewer. Square tables double as "canvases" for projected images and as makeshift dance floors once the music steps up a notch or two around midnight. ⊠ *MGM Grand Hotel and Casino, 3799 Las Vegas Blvd. S, South Strip* ☎ 702/891–7183.

V Bar. The founders of New York's Lotus and Los Angeles's Sunset Room launched this small hot spot inside the Venetian, starting the "cool bar" trend in Las Vegas. As competition heated up around the Strip, the V Bar responded by relaxing the dress code (on weeknights, at least) and going for more of a casual, Los Angeles rock-and-roll vibe. ⊠ *Venetian Resort-Hotel-Casino, 3355 Las Vegas Blvd. S, Center Strip* ☎ *702/733–5000.*

Venus Lounge and Tiki Bar. The retro design of this spot in the Venetian's retail mall appeals to "Cocktail Nation" nostalgists, though the club has since repositioned itself to have a more mainstream appeal. ⊠ *Venetian Resort-Hotel-Casino, 3355 Las Vegas Blvd. S, Center Strip* ☎ *702/414–4870.*

Away from the Strip

Outside the realm of the big casinos, the Las Vegas bar scene is dominated by so-called "video poker taverns," named for the 15 video poker machines they are legally allowed to have. Most are generic, but there are exceptions.

Crown & Anchor Pub. If you dig the wave of faux Irish pubs sweeping the casinos but want something a bit less contrived, this friendly British-style pub not far from the Strip is the best of the bunch. ⊠ *1350 E. Tropicana Ave., University District* ☎ *702/739–8676.*

Double Down Saloon. For the boho crowd, there's this deliberately down-scale bar, with a jukebox blasting everything from Patsy Cline to classic punk. Fans of the place include filmmaker Tim Burton. (Don't bother checking it out before midnight, though.) ⊠ *4640 Paradise Rd., Paradise Road* ☎ *702/791–5775.*

Gordon Biersch Brewing Co. Also a full-scale restaurant, this brewpub caters to Las Vegas's new breed of white-collar workers. ⊠ *3987 Paradise Rd., Paradise Road* ☎ *702/312–5247.*

Icehouse Lounge. Downtown regained a bit of sparkle with the arrival of this two-story, retro nightspot. It looks as though it's a rescued-and-restored building, but it's actually a ground-up construction replacing a dive bar. The open, South Beach–inspired design, with an upstairs balcony and dozens of blown-up vintage Vegas photos, is accented by an almost ridiculous number of plasma TV screens. ⊠ *650 Main St., Downtown* ☎ *702/315–2570.*

J. C. Wooloughan Irish Pub. In order to create the proper environment for serving Guinness, Bass, and Harp, the entire exterior of the pub was constructed in Dublin, then shipped to Las Vegas. The crowd is yuppie-leaning after work, then gets more casual and more diverse as the evening wears on. There's live music (usually Celtic rock bands) Wednesday through Saturday nights, but the bands are treated more as incidental additions than as the main attraction. ⊠ *JW Marriott Las Vegas Casino Resort, 221 N. Rampart Blvd., Summerlin* ☎ *702/869–7777.*

Peppermill Fireside Lounge. Many of those who come to Sin City looking for a bit of classic Vegas leave disappointed, finding the frequently swinging wrecking ball has left behind little but massive, movie-set-like resort-casinos to dominate the landscape. But, benign neglect has preserved this shagadelic lounge, attached to a freestanding coffee shop across from the Stardust Hotel, where *Vega$* private eye Dan Tanna could hob-nob with either Austin Powers or "The Ladies Man." ⊠ *2985 Las Vegas Blvd. S, Center Strip* ☎ *702/735–7635.*

Dance Clubs

Dance clubs have been the Strip's biggest entertainment innovation of the past few years. Hotels, tired of watching their guests hop a cab to off-Strip nightspots, built fantasy-theme dance palaces that only establishments with unrestricted budgets could create. Cover charges have correspondingly crept into the $10 to $20 range—and don't be surprised to find that, even in these "enlightened times," men will pay more than women to get in. Although that level of capital investment gives these clubs a longevity their New York counterparts don't enjoy, dance clubs are still a fickle, fleeting enterprise by nature.

Each club sets its own dress code, but all clubs enforce a fairly rigorous one: no T-shirts, ball caps, or tennis shoes, and no logos that could be affiliated with gangs. Prepare for frustration, depending on the whim of the doorman, if you try to argue for the validity of designer tennis shoes or pullovers without a collar. How much you paid for them doesn't seem to matter.

The Beach. Life is one nonstop fraternity bash at this two-story club designed to look like a South-of-the-Border party barn. Still known for a less-restrictive dress code than those imposed by the hotels, the Beach partners up with local radio stations for theme promotional nights. Its location also keeps it very in tune with big conventions and trade shows across the street at the Las Vegas Convention Center. It's open nightly at 10. ⊠ *365 Convention Center Dr., Paradise Road* ☎ *702/731–1925* ⊕ *www.beachlv.com.*

Bikinis. Since Las Vegas is a city where innovation is followed by imitation, the Rio swiped pages from both the Beach and Coyote Ugly to create this "year-round indoor beach bash" in late 2002. The 14,000-square-foot club augments its theme with water tanks, Jacuzzis, and "exhibition showers." Thursday is the featured "Bikini Nation" ladies night and bikini contest. ⊠ *Rio All-Suite Hotel and Casino, 3700 W. Flamingo Rd., West Side* ☎ *702/777–6582.*

Body English. An increasingly competitive nightclub environment motivated the Hard Rock Hotel to close its Baby's club in early 2004 and remodel it with a new name and interior design. The basic features of the club are likely to remain: its partially underground location, accessed by elevator, and an antechamber with a low ceiling, stone walls, and a tiny dance floor giving way to the main room. ⊠ *Hard Rock Hotel and Casino, 4455 Paradise Rd., Paradise Road* ☎ *702/693–5000.*

Club Rio. Wraparound video screens, a big stage, and a large dance floor make this pioneering dance club inside a casino a perennial standby. To combat the loss of novelty as newer clubs open in other casino-hotels, Club Rio has embraced Latin pop and house music to make Thursday's

Latin Libido its signature night. If the dance floor gets too hot, over-head misters cool everyone down. It's open Wednesday through Sunday from 10:30 PM. ⊠ *Rio All-Suite Hotel and Casino, 3700 W. Flamingo Ave., West Side* ☎ *702/777–7977.*

Curve. The Aladdin pulled victory from the jaws of defeat when it turned part of the underutilized London Club on the second floor of the casino into a busy nightspot. It's a large club with the feel of a small one, thanks to separate rooms with different music and an outdoor balcony with a view of the Strip for those in need of a little fresh air. The club's status was uncertain in the changeover from the Aladdin to the new Planet Hollywood name and management. ⊠ *Aladdin Resort and Casino–Planet Hollywood, 3667 Las Vegas Blvd. S, South Strip* ☎ *702/ 290–9582* ⊕ *curvelasvegas.com.*

Light. Nightclub entrepreneur Andrew Sasson brings his celebrity connections to the Bellagio nightclub that matches the upscale (pricey) image and celebrity appeal of the larger hotel. This 600-capacity room at the Bellagio emphasized the exclusivity of its 40 reserved tables and expensive "bottle service" in the early going, but it's also open to those of average means. The party begins here nightly from 9:30 PM. ⊠ *Bellagio Las Vegas, 3600 Las Vegas Blvd. S, Center Strip* ☎ *702/693–8300* ⊕ *www.lightlv.com.*

FodorsChoice **Ra.** Luxor's $20-million hot spot is still the most fancifully designed of ★ Las Vegas clubs, with a theme park–style interior inspired by the "Egyptian-deco" futurism of the sci-fi movie *Stargate.* Bands sometimes take to the center stage; dancers gyrate in cages. The club spotlights visiting deejays from other cities and its signature night is Wednesday's "Pleasuredome." Collared shirts for men are required. It's open Wednesday through Saturday from 10:30 PM. ⊠ *Luxor Resort & Casino, 3900 Las Vegas Blvd. S, South Strip* ☎ *866/725–8967* ⊕ *www.ralv.com.*

Rain in the Desert. The club by Michael Morton and Scott DeGraff got tons of free publicity in 2002–03 as a major setting for MTV's *The Real World.* The round, 1,500-capacity nightclub and concert house is equipped with dancing waters, video projections on a 40-foot high water curtain, and occasional blasts of fire. Perhaps because the Palms shares ownership with the Sacramento Kings, the club even includes "skyboxes" for rent. Thursday is the signature night, "Drenched." In summer the action expands to the adjacent pool area for Skin, a "pool lounge" with the same management. ⊠ *The Palms, 4321 W. Flamingo Rd., West Side* ☎ *702/938–9999* ⊕ *www.rainatthepalms.com.*

rumjungle. Disney-style lines have trailed from this Mandalay Bay version of a Brazilian paradise since the day it opened. The "fire wall" out front beckons club goers into a wild 20,000-square-foot room with waterfalls, dancing girls on platforms above the 85-foot-long bar, giant conga drums, and even aerialists attached to trapezelike harnesses. The house, hip-hop, and Latin music keep the dance floor hoppin'. It's open Thursday through Saturday from 11 PM. ⊠ *Mandalay Bay Resort & Casino, 3950 Las Vegas Blvd. S, South Strip* ☎ *702/632–7408.*

Studio 54. This tri-level, 22,000-square-foot dance club inside the MGM Grand Hotel and Casino took over the area where a cheesy lion's mouth once welcomed you, leaving the steel beams in place for a stark industrial look. The club can sustain itself on weekends with MGM traffic alone, so Tuesday became the signature night with EDEN: "Erotically Delicious Entertainers Night." It's open from 10 PM Tuesday through Saturday. ⊠ *MGM Grand Hotel and Casino, 3799 Las Vegas Blvd. S, South Strip* ☎ *702/891–7254.*

Whiskey Bar. Rande Gerber, the entrepreneur better known to some as "Mr. Cindy Crawford," banked on the popularity of his "Whiskey"-named clubs in other cities to lure celebrities and club-hoppers to Green Valley Ranch, a suburban casino several miles from the Strip. The main room still offers a picture-window view of the distant lights from its elevated perch. The club appeals to a slightly older demographic and sets the dance floor off in a separate room. During fair-weather months, the club expands outdoors to include the entire landscaped pool area. ⊠ *Green Valley Ranch Resort, 2197 Paseo Verde Pkwy., Henderson* ☎ *702/614–5283* ⊙ *Nightly from 5 PM.*

Gay & Lesbian Nightlife

Las Vegas was never known for gay tourism, partly because the dance club scene in its infant days was smaller and so inclusive of gay patrons there was no need to draw distinctions. Things have changed rapidly in the past few years. Now there are quite a few bars and nightclubs catering to different segments of the community, and a new branch of the gay-oriented restaurant chain Hamburger Mary's. The all-gay **Blue Moon Resort** (⊕ www.bluemoonlv.com) has 45 rooms near Sahara Avenue and Interstate 15.

Most gay and lesbian nightlife is concentrated into two areas of town. The most prominent is near the intersection of Naples Drive and Paradise Road, just north of the airport and near the Hard Rock Hotel and Casino. The other is the area in and around Commercial Center, one of the city's oldest shopping centers, on East Sahara Avenue, just west of Maryland Parkway. Expect cover charges to be around $10 for dance clubs on weekends.

For a more complete list, pick up a copy of the *Las Vegas Bugle* gay monthly or check the listings in *Fodor's Gay Guide to the USA.*

Eagle. Away from the mainstream Vegas gay corridors is a more rustic bar best known for its "Underwear Nights" on Wednesday, Friday, and Saturday (those in their skivvies drink free). ⊠ *610 E. Naples Dr., Paradise Road* ☎ *702/794–2310* ⊕ *www.freezonelv.com.*

Flex. A smaller, more neighborhood-oriented bar–club for men, this place sometimes has floor shows, contests, and entertainment. ⊠ *4371 W. Charleston Ave., West Side* ☎ *702/385–3539.*

Freezone. A mix of men and women congregate at this bar with a dance floor, pool table, and video poker. Each night brings a different theme: Ladies night is Tuesday, the "Boy'z Night" male revue on Thursday, and the "What a Drag!" show is Friday and Saturday. ⊠ *610 E. Naples Dr., Paradise Road* ☎ *702/794–2310* ⊕ *www.freezonelv.com.*

Gipsy. The oldest, largest, and most famous alternative dance club in Las Vegas is within walking distance of the Hard Rock Hotel and Casino. Predominantly a male club, it has always welcomed the open-minded regardless of sexual preference. However, competition from new mainstream nightclubs has taken a little of the edge off its crossover appeal outside the gay community. The club stays busy nonetheless, with nightly drink specials, "Retro Wednesdays," and the "Illusions" drag show on Sunday and Thursday. ⊠ *4605 Paradise Rd., Paradise Road* ☎ *702/731–1919.*

Goodtimes. The location of this bar and dance club with a 600-square-foot floor should appeal to campy senses of humor: it's in the same strip mall as the Liberace Museum. ⊠ *1775 E. Tropicana Ave., East Side* ☎ *702/736–9494.*

Hamburger Mary's. Party from morning to morning at this branch of the restaurant–club, which has a Sunday brunch at 10 AM and wilder events in the evenings. Drop in for the beefcake contest on Wednesday, the "Boys Gone Wild" Saturday night, the Friday evening ladies night and wet T-shirt contest, or local bands on Sunday. ⊠ *4503 Paradise Rd., Paradise Road* ☎ *702/735–4400.*

Las Vegas Lounge. If you want to see something really different, catch the nightly shows (except Sunday) in this offbeat room billed as the city's premier transgender bar. ⊠ *900 E. Karen Ave., East Las Vegas* ☎ *702/737–9350.*

Spotlight Lounge. Play to your mood here. Feeling frisky? Watch the male strippers writhe to music. For something a bit more subdued, opt for offerings like video poker and barbecues. ⊠ *957 E. Sahara Ave., East Side* ☎ *702/696–0202.*

Tramps. Amidst the glut of bar–club combinations in the Hard Rock Hotel and Casino area is this hot spot for bargain drink prices and theme events most nights. ⊠ *4640 Paradise Rd., Paradise Road* ☎ *702/735–3888* ⊕ *www.trampslasvegas.com.*

Live Music

Country & Western

Dylan's Dance Hall & Saloon. Once known as Rockabilly's, this Boulder Highway honky-tonk is the spiritual heart of Las Vegas country music. It's open only on Friday and Saturday from 7 PM. ⊠ *4660 Boulder Hwy., Boulder Strip* ☎ *702/451–4006.*

Gilley's Dancehall Saloon & Barbecue. This institution, which Mickey moved from Texas to Las Vegas, has less live music than deejayed line dancing, but it's country's home on the Strip. It's now the chief claim to fame for the faded New Frontier Hotel. The club is open Thursday through Saturday from 6 PM for dancing, but the restaurant is open nightly for dinner. ⊠ *New Frontier Hotel and Gambling Hall, 3120 Las Vegas Blvd. S, South Strip* ☎ *702/794–8434.*

Jazz

Jazzed Cafe and Vinoteca. The best bet away from the Strip is this fun room that's decorated as a bold piece of living pop art. It seats about 40 for dinner but stays open past the dinner hour as a cozy spot for live music. ☒ *8615 W. Sahara Ave., West Las Vegas* ☎ *702/233–2859.*

Las Vegas Jazz Society. Call for information on concerts in parks and municipal library theaters. ☎ *702/313–6778* ⊕ *vegasjazz.org.*

Rock

Cooler Lounge. A dumpy little bar in a rundown shopping center makes the perfect counterpoint to the themed, homogenized clubs on the Strip. The genres and bands change every night of the week; the music doesn't get going until 10. ☒ *1905 N. Decatur Blvd., West Side* ☎ *702/368–0750* ⊕ *www.coolerlounge.com.*

Huntridge Theatre. Before the arrival of the Hard Rock Hotel and House of Blues, a former movie theater built in 1945 gave Las Vegas locals a chance to see early career performances by the likes of Courtney Love, Beck, and Smashing Pumpkins. The corporate clubs put it out of business for a time, but the Huntridge reopened in late 2002 with an ambitious schedule to be a haven for local bands and breaking national acts. ☒ *1208 E. Charleston Ave., East Side* ☎ *702/678–6800* ⊕ *www.thehuntridge.com.*

Strip Clubs

Strip clubs are a major industry in Sin City, but no one knew how big until the FBI's "Operation G-Sting" rocked the city in 2003 with a political corruption scandal. The probe led Jaguars and Cheetah's owner Michael Galardi to plead guilty on charges that he paid between $200,000 and $400,000 to elected county officials in exchange for actions that benefited his clubs. The investigation left the ownership and possible future of some clubs, including Jaguars, in the air. Beyond the legal crackdown on the clubs and the conduct permitted within, a shakeout also seemed possible given the "super-sizing" of major clubs—Jaguar's, Sapphire, and Treasures—at the expense of smaller ones. Zoning still restricts most clubs to industrial areas off the Strip, but an upscale trend has caused most of them to institute cover charges of $5 to $20. The real money is made on the table dances continuously solicited inside. Most of them cost $20 per song.

Newer clubs seem to succeed by sacrificing their liquor license in exchange for full nudity. Let your own preferences be your guide, but remember that the Palomino Club in North Las Vegas is the only place where you can have both. Otherwise, the choice is between booze and g-strings or soft drinks and full nudity.

Club Paradise. Its location—directly across the street from the Hard Rock Hotel and Casino—has been a plus for this place. It was also one of the first local clubs to embrace the "gentleman's club" boom of the 1990s. Once a run down place called the Pussycat Lounge, it renovated, changed its name, suited its bouncers in tuxedos, and put computerized lighting over the stage. ☒ *4416 Paradise Rd., Paradise Road* ☎ *702/734–7990.*

Jaguar's Gentlemen's Cabaret. The Las Vegas topless club reached new heights of ambition in 2002 with the opening of this two-story, 25,000-square-foot building that claims to host 200 dancers on even an average night. A stylish interior intensifies the general "upscale" trend for these clubs. ⊠ *1531 Las Vegas Blvd. S, Downtown* ☎ *702/385–8987.*

Little Darlings. This is the largest of the total nudity clubs with no alcohol, for those who have their priorities. ⊠ *1514 Western Ave., West Las Vegas* ☎ *702/366–1141.*

Olympic Garden. Right on the northern edge of the Strip, this is one of the busiest, most easily located jiggle joints in town. It was the first to install several "pod" stages to take the place of the single stage found in older clubs. A separate room has male revues for the ladies. ⊠ *1531 Las Vegas Blvd. S, Downtown* ☎ *702/385–9361* ⊕ *www.ogvegas.com.*

Palomino Club. One of the oldest strip clubs in the area, it's grandfathered into North Las Vegas zoning codes, which means it's allowed to have both a full bar and full nudity. The Palomino combines the generations by keeping its old "burlesque" stage downstairs, while upstairs the dancers perform on miniplatforms and solicit private dances. ⊠ *1848 Las Vegas Blvd. N, North Las Vegas* ☎ *702/642–2984.*

Sapphire. The owners of this club claimed to spend $26 million in late 2002 for the bragging rights of proclaiming their club the "largest adult entertainment complex in the world." A defunct athletic club was remodeled to dedicate 40,000 square feet to topless dancing, complete with 13 second-floor "skyboxes." Dancers descend a ramp to a clear, elevated main stage that towers over the floor. ⊠ *3025 S. Industrial Rd., West Side* ☎ *702/796–6000* ⊕ *www.sapphirelasvegas.com.*

Spearmint Rhino. The national chain got a late start in Las Vegas and didn't hit the city until 1998. It grew fast, recently expanding the original location by 18,000 square feet; it's also the rare topless club to offer lunch, including pizza, burgers, and steak sandwiches. ⊠ *3340 S. Highland Dr., West Las Vegas* ☎ *702/796–3600.*

Treasures. The latest mega-club, costing an eye-popping $7.5 million, opened in late 2003 with an eye toward the high-end customer. A gourmet dining room inside the front entrance is in the works, as well as a separate VIP club-within-a-club on the second floor. Dennis Rodman gave the place some unintended publicity when he crashed his motorcycle out front. ⊠ *2801 Westwood Dr., West Las Vegas* ☎ *702/ 257–4475.*

THE ARTS

Although known more for theatrical spectacles than serious theater, Las Vegas does have a lively cultural scene. The groups listed below offer full seasons of productions each year. The **Allied Arts Council** (⊠ 3750 S. Maryland Pkwy., East Side ☎ 702/731–5419) can provide a detailed schedule of local theater, dance, music, and fine-arts exhibits.

Ballet

Nevada Ballet Theatre. The city's longest-running fine-arts organization (this being Las Vegas, it only dates from 1973) stages three to five productions each year, anchored by an annual December presentation of *The Nutcracker*. Bruce Steivel is artistic director for the troupe, and most performances are held in UNLV's Judy Bayley Theatre. ✉ *4505 S. Maryland Pkwy., University District* ☎ *702/243–2623 or 702/895–2787* ⊕ *www.nevadaballet.com.*

Classical Music

Las Vegas Philharmonic. Formed in 1998, the Philharmonic is conducted by Hal Weller, formerly of the Flagstaff Symphony Orchestra. The Philharmonic performs at Artemus Ham Hall on the UNLV campus. ✉ *4505 S. Maryland Pkwy., University District* ☎ *702/258–5438 for schedule information, 702/895–2787 for tickets* ⊕ *www.lasvegasphilharmonic.com.*

Film

The second half of the 1990s saw an explosion of multiplex construction in Las Vegas—there are 20 theaters and more than 150 screens in town, a surprising number of them attached to casinos. There's even an eight-theater multiplex on the Strip. Several theaters are conveniently located.

Boulder Cinemas. The 11-screen facility is at the Boulder Station. ✉ *Boulder Station Hotel and Casino, 4111 Boulder Hwy., Boulder Strip* ☎ *702/ 221–2283.*

Brenden Theatres at the Palms. The Palms took a run at the nearby Orleans by opening its own theater with 14 screens, each with stadium seating featuring rocking-chair-style seats with armrests that can be raised to convert them into love seats. There's also an IMAX screen that runs both special-format films and large-screen versions of regular releases. ✉ *Palms, 4321 W. Flamingo Rd., West Side* ☎ *702/507–4849.*

Century 18. The most popular theater in Las Vegas addressed its only real shortcoming when the Orleans built a parking garage in 2002. ✉ *Orleans Hotel and Casino, 4500 W. Tropicana Ave., East Side* ☎ *702/227–3456.*

Century 18 Sam's Town. Just down the road from the Boulder Station, Sam's Town has high-back seats, with alternating rows of rockers and love seats with movable arm rests. ✉ *5111 Boulder Hwy., Boulder Strip* ☎ *702/547–7469.*

� **Crown Theatres Neonopolis.** A 14-screen theater is a major component of the struggling, $100-million Neonopolis downtown revival project. The theater does its part, with convenient underground parking, wall-to-wall screens, and digital sound, with 6 out of 14 screens THX-certified. ✉ *Neonopolis, 1st St. and Las Vegas Blvd. S, Downtown* ☎ *702/383–9600.*

� **Luxor IMAX Theatre.** Luxor has multiple daily screenings of movies created for the giant screens of the 70mm IMAX process. Films available in this format usually have appealing scientific or natural-history subjects, such as travel on a space shuttle or explorations of the Grand Canyon, but lately have expanded into more purely entertaining attractions such as *Matrix Revolutions* and *Beauty and the Beast.* ⊠ *Luxor Resort & Casino, 3900 Las Vegas Blvd. S, South Strip* ☎ *702/262–4629.*

Showcase 8. The only movie theater on the Strip is in the Showcase Mall, next to the MGM Grand. It's a great break from the slots for nearby hotel guests but the hidden parking garage is a real challenge for those who for some reason might choose to visit by car. ⊠ *3785 Las Vegas Blvd. S, South Strip* ☎ *702/221–2283.*

Theater

Away from the Strip, a booming community theater scene caters to the area's many new residents, retirees in particular, who are looking for a low-cost alternative to the pricey shows. With the exception of UNLV, Las Vegas Little Theatre, and Nevada Theater Company, most don't have their own performance spaces and instead rent municipal auditoriums for their productions.

Jade Productions. This senior-citizen–oriented group focuses on revues themed around Broadway composers or stars. ☎ *702/263–6385* ⊕ *www.jadepro.com.*

Las Vegas Little Theatre. Las Vegas's oldest community theater has branched out from its base of Neil Simon comedies to more wide-ranging productions such as *A Few Good Men* and *What the Butler Saw.* ⊠ *3850 Schiff Dr., West Side* ☎ *702/362–7996* ⊕ *www.lvlt.org.*

Nevada Theater Company. This company has come on strong in recent years, moving into a former video store and presenting more adventurous efforts, such as *Hedwig and the Angry Inch.* ⊠ *2928 Lake East Dr., The Lakes* ☎ *702/873–0191* ⊕ *www.nevadatheatreco.org.*

University of Nevada–Las Vegas Theater Department. UNLV brings in outside professionals and holds community-wide auditions for a full season of productions each academic year. Most performances are held in the Judy Bayley Theatre on campus. ⊠ *4505 S. Maryland Pkwy., University District* ☎ *702/647–7469 for schedule information, 702/985–2787 tickets.*

SPORTS &
THE OUTDOORS

6

BEST PLACE TO TAKE A HIKE
50 mi of trails at Mt. Charleston ⇨*p.159*

HUM "HAPPY TRAILS"
Horseback riding at
Bonnie Springs Ranch ⇨*p.160*

BEST REASON TO PACK A COWBOY HAT
National Finals of Rodeo ⇨*p.162*

HIPPEST WAY TO HAVE A BALL
Bowling at an off-Strip casino ⇨*p.153*

BEST PLACE TO PULL YOURSELF UP
Rock climbing in Red Rock Canyon ⇨*p.161*

DON'T-MISS LINKS
Bear's Best golf course ⇨*p.156*

Updated by
Mark Anderson

THE PLAYFUL SPIRIT OF LAS VEGAS, epitomized in its casinos, is also very much alive in its sports. With more than 50 golf courses (roughly half public or semiprivate), Las Vegas hosts several prestigious tournaments that include a $1-million stop on the PGA tour. Many boxing superstars— Muhammad Ali, Sugar Ray Leonard, Thomas Hearns, George Foreman, Mike Tyson, and Evander Holyfield—have faced each other in a Las Vegas ring. Las Vegas also hosts the 51s triple-A minor-league baseball team and the Runnin' Rebels college basketball team. The Las Vegas Motor Speedway is one of the largest Indy-style racetracks in the country; every March, the Las Vegas 400, a NASCAR Winston Cup race, attracts more than 120,000 spectators to the largest sporting event held in Nevada.

And if you'd rather do it yourself, there are more than 300 sunny days a year and many opportunities: a flat valley for jogging, walking, and biking; surrounding mountains for hiking, bouldering, climbing, and skiing; a fantastic collection of tennis courts; swimming in hotel pools; and boating and fishing in one of the world's great lakes. Most locals-oriented casinos now have snazzy bowling alleys. And in how many other cities in the world can you go horseback riding in the desert in the morning, and alpine skiing in the afternoon?

Auto Racing

Las Vegas Motor Speedway. The NASCAR circuit makes an annual stop at this 1½–mi superspeedway in the UAW–DaimlerChrysler 400. The event attracts the state's largest spectator crowd, which fills the 140,000 seats for the early March race. The Earnhardt Terrace, a grandstand that provides an additional 22,000 seats, was added in 2004 and honors racing legend Dale Earnhardt, who died at the Daytona 500 in 2001. Winners have included such drivers as Jeff Gordon, Matt Kenseth, Mark Martin, Sterling Marlin, and Jeff Burton. The second-tier Busch Series races the day before NASCAR, and the NASCAR Craftsman Truck Series race is held here in September.

The Speedway is part of a larger racing complex that includes a ⅜–mi paved oval known as the Bullring, road courses, a dirt track, a motocross, and a drag strip. And if you want to know what it feels like to travel at 160 mi per hour firsthand, you can attend one of four driving schools. One of the schools is for those interested in motorcycles. Students can ride along with a professional driver who takes the car inches from the wall or test the course solo.

If you attend a race, buy tickets in advance and plan on arriving early and staying late. Traffic lanes have been widened around the Speedway, but the wait can still test anyone's patience. ⊠ *7000 Las Vegas Blvd. N, Northeast Las Vegas* ☎ *800/644–4444* ⊕ *www.lvms.com* ☒ *Ride-along program $79; additional racing packages up to $2,000* ☉ *Daily 9–5; track tours every hr.*

Ballooning

Several hot-air balloon companies can take you up, up, and away in their beautiful balloons. The balloon season runs from October through

April, depending on the local thermals, though some companies fly year-round. The flights start just before sunrise or sunset, when the air is stillest (you have to get up very early in the morning in summer so as not to land too long after the sun rises). Most balloon businesses ask for reservations (held by a credit-card number) a week in advance. The Las Vegas Balloon Classic, which takes place in October, attracts more than 100 balloons from all across the West.

The Little White Chapel in the Sky. This outfit does hot-air-balloon weddings in a 12-passenger basket (the largest basket in town). You have to plan on a three-day window for getting married, since wind conditions are so variable. A wedding package starts at $650 for the couple, with the cost rising (so to speak) from there: $150 per additional guest; $250 for photography or videotaping; and more for flowers, cake, and music. ⊠ *1301 Las Vegas Blvd. S, Downtown* ☎ *702/382–5943.*

Nevada High. Champagne is included in the cost ($125 per person) of your one-hour flight with this company that emphasizes safety. They also offer instruction in flying hot-air balloons, in their balloons or yours. ☎ *702/873–8393.*

Baseball

FodorsChoice **Las Vegas 51s.** The triple-A Pacific Coast League team used to be the
★ Las Vegas Stars. But when the parent team switched from the San Diego Padres to the Los Angeles Dodgers, the team adopted a more distinctive and publicity-generating name, taken from nearby Area 51, rumored home of UFO and mysterious military activity. The 51s play at **Cashman Field** (⊠ 850 Las Vegas Blvd. N, Downtown ☎ 702/386–7200), the field where professional baseball made its Las Vegas debut in 1983.

Basketball

Runnin' Rebels. The hottest tickets in town during the school year were once the basketball games of the former NCAA champions at the University of Nevada–Las Vegas. But since head coach Jerry Tarkanian was fired in the early 1990s, the Rebels—and their ticket sales—have cooled off considerably. Charlie Spoonhour coached most of the 2002–03 season before resigning for health reasons in February. Lon Kruger signed a five-year contract to take over the program beginning in the 2004–05 season. Games take place at the **Thomas and Mack Center** (⊠ 4505 S. Maryland Pkwy., University District ☎ 702/739–3267) on the UNLV campus.

Biking

Because the summer heat is intense, the best times to bike in this area are fall and spring. The winter is often warm enough to brave the outdoors on two wheels, but in summer, unless you get up at first light, it's too bloody hot. Wherever you ride, whatever the season, carry lots of water.

Las Vegas Valley has a handful of good, long rides. One popular trip is the jaunt out to Red Rock Canyon on West Charleston Boulevard; it's

11 mi from the Rainbow Boulevard intersection to the Red Rock Visitors Center. The road has a good shoulder, or dedicated bike paths, the whole way. Once there, you can continue around Red Rock Canyon's moderately difficult 13-mi scenic loop (the road is one-way).

Another good ride is between the entrance to Red Rock Canyon and the city park in the small settlement of Blue Diamond, just under 8 mi south on Highway 159. The road has good shoulders and long gentle grades with flat recuperation stretches.

A third possibility is a ride out on Boulder Highway through Henderson. It's best to start east of Tropicana Avenue; there's a shoulder the whole way. If you turn around before climbing up and over Railroad Pass, the round-trip is a little less than 40 mi.

Mountain biking is limited primarily to Mt. Charleston and the Bristlecone Trail, accessible at the top of the Lee Canyon ski area parking lot. It's a 6-mi loop and climbs 1,400 feet. Another popular mountain-biking locale is Cottonwood Valley. To get there, take the Blue Diamond exit off I–15 south of Las Vegas, head west for 6 mi, and turn off at the sign. You drive another ½ mi to the PACK-IN PACK-OUT sign, then ride on a 14-mi loop. Any bike store in town can give you a map to the place.

Escape the City Streets. A convenient store that rents bikes, Escape is on West Charleston Boulevard almost halfway between downtown and Red Rock Canyon. Most folks drive to the store, park there, rent their bikes, and pedal out the rest of the way to Red Rock and back (30 mi round-trip). Bike rentals range from $28 to $50, with both hybrid bikes (fat slick tires) and mountain bikes available. For a fee, Escape will also deliver bikes to your hotel or motel and pick them up again ($12 each way). Tours are available. ⊠ *8221 W. Charleston Blvd., West Side* ☎ *702/838–6966.*

Las Vegas Scooters. If you don't want to pedal, rent a scooter. Rentals are available by the hour, half-day, or full day. ⊠ *3735 Las Vegas Blvd. S, South Strip* ☎ *702/736–8633.*

Boating

FodorsChoice
★
Lake Mead National Recreation Area. All water sports in the Las Vegas area are centered on Lake Mead. The entrance fee of $5 per vehicle is good for five days, and there are lake use fees of $10 per vessel. ☎ *702/293–8907* ⊕ *www.nps.gov/lame.*

OUTFITTERS &
INFORMATION
Get It Wet. You can rent personal watercraft such as small motorboats (complete with water-ski equipment), Jet Skis, and inner tubes here. ⊠ *661 W. Lake Mead Dr., Henderson* ☎ *702/558–7547.*

Lake Mead Resort and Marina. You can rent motorboats (and water-ski equipment) here by the hour or day. ⊠ *322 Lakeshore Rd., Boulder City* ☎ *702/293–3484.*

Bowling

WHERE TO BOWL
Bowling (and movie theaters) have gone from a novelty to something that locals almost expect at an off-Strip casino. Several casinos have bowl-

ing facilities that are open 24 hours a day. And because most facilities were built since the mid-'90s, they include the most up-to-date equipment (automatic scoring, video score screens, and the like), shoe rental, a pro shop, a snack shop, a bar and lounge, and cocktail service. At most places the prices are the same all the time, though at one or two prices rise a nickel or dime a game on weekends. It's a good idea to call for public bowling hours before you go, since bowling leagues are a major rage in Las Vegas, and the alleys can be closed to the public for hours at a time, especially on weekday evenings.

Castaways Hotel, Casino, and Bowling Center. With 106 lanes, this is the world's largest bowling alley. (Although given its size, it's surprisingly quiet.) Its pseudo-tropics atmosphere is a charming throwback to another era. ⊠ *2800 E. Fremont St., Boulder Strip* ☎ *702/385–9153.*

Orleans Hotel and Casino. The Orleans is in a working-class neighborhood, and its 70-lane bowling center sees lots of traffic, but its not-far-off-the-Strip location also makes it a popular spot for visitors. ⊠ *4500 W. Tropicana Rd., West Side* ☎ *702/365–7111.*

Santa Fe Station Hotel and Casino. Santa Fe Station is a locals casino, but it's one of the area's most polished, and that's reflected in its bowling center. The 60-lane bowling facility has the Frameworx scoring system, which has an instant-replay function. ⊠ *4949 N. Rancho Dr., Rancho Strip* ☎ *702/658–4995.*

Suncoast Hotel and Casino. Reflecting its upscale Summerlin neighborhood, the bowling center at the Suncoast, with 64 lanes, is designed to provide every high-tech toy for bowlers. ⊠ *9090 Alta Dr., Northwest Las Vegas* ☎ *702/636–7400.*

★ **Texas Station Gambling Hall and Hotel.** This 60-lane alley was the first to declare itself a nightclub hybrid, adding fancy lights and a booming sound system for a "cosmic bowling" concept that's since been initiated at the Gold Coast and Suncoast as well. It draws a youngish crowd, so if you like to party while you bowl, this one is for you. ⊠ *2101 Texas Star La., Rancho Strip* ☎ *702/631–1000.*

ON THE SIDELINES **Castaways Invitational Bowling Tournament.** The Professional Bowling Association's oldest competition takes place in Las Vegas at the **Castaways Hotel and Casino** every January.

Boxing

Championship boxing came to Las Vegas in 1960, when Benny Paret took the welterweight title from Don Jordan at the Las Vegas Convention Center. Since then most of boxing's superstars have fought here. A title match draws the well-heeled and the well-known from all fields—and brings out the high roller in everyone. Spectators willingly fork over $200 to $1,500 a seat to watch two guys pummel each other, then hang around the casinos laying down chips for the rest of the evening, sometimes for the rest of the week. Major fights are usually held at Mandalay Bay, Caesars Palace, the MGM Grand, or the Thomas and Mack

Center. To learn about upcoming boxing events, look for the fight odds posted in the race and sports book of any casino.

Caesars Palace. For the most comprehensive fight listings, check Caesars' Web site (⊕ *www.caesarspalace.com.*).

Fishing

Floyd Lamb State Park. Tule Lake is a good place to catch rainbow trout (summer) and catfish (winter). The park is open 8 AM to 7 PM in summer, until 5 in winter. ✉ *9200 Tule Springs Rd., North Las Vegas* ☎ *702/486–5413.*

Lake Mead. Fish for largemouth and striped bass, channel catfish, crappie, bluegill, and various types of trout. The lake is stocked with a half-million rainbow trout regularly, and at least a million fish are harvested every year. You can fish here 24 hours a day, year-round (except for posted closings). If you plan to catch and keep trout, be mindful that a trout stamp is required. ⊕ *Write to 601 Nevada Hwy., Boulder City 89005* ☎ *702/293–8907 or 702/293–8990.*

Lorenzi Park. A good spot to cast your line in Las Vegas itself is the pond at Lorenzi Park, which is stocked with rainbow trout in the winter and channel catfish in spring and summer; the park is open 7 AM to 11 PM. ✉ *3333 Washington Ave., West Side* ☎ *702/229–6297.*

A license is required for fishing in Nevada. You can purchase one at any local sporting-goods store, or the sporting-goods sections of Kmart and Wal-Mart. Nevada nonresident licenses are $12 a day or $51 for the year; a trout stamp is an additional $10, and a second pole is $10.

Blue Lake Bait and Tackle. Sure you're going fishing, but you can't snag 'em with patience alone. Stop here for bait and lures sure to entice the elusive denizens of Lake Mead. ✉ *5485 E. Lake Mead Blvd., Las Vegas* ☎ *702/452–8299.*

Las Vegas Fly Fishing Club. Desert fishermen are a special breed. Contact the Las Vegas Fly Fishing Club for more information on fishing in the Las Vegas area. ✉ *Box 27958, Las Vegas, NV 89126-1958* ☎ *702/ 451–9296.*

Sandy Cove Bait Store. You know you're getting close to the lake when you reach the Sandy Cove and see rods, reels, bait, and other fishing supplies in the middle of all that desert sand. ✉ *5225 E. Lake Mead Blvd., East Side* ☎ *702/459–2080.*

Football

Las Vegas Gladiators. The Gladiators, an arena football team, play home games at the **Thomas and Mack Center** (✉ 4505 S. Maryland Pkwy., University District ☎ 702/739–3267).

UNLV Rebels. Spectator interest couldn't have been lower for UNLV's Division 1A, Mountain West Conference football team during the years when the men's basketball team was a national power. Attention shifted somewhat to the football Rebels when John Robinson came on board as coach. Home games are held at **Sam Boyd Stadium** (⊠ 7000 E. Russell Rd., East Side ☎ 702/739–3267).

Golf

With an average of 315 days of sunshine a year and year-round access, Las Vegas's top sports recreation is golf. It's no accident that there are more than 50 golf courses in the Las Vegas area and more opening every year. The peak season is from October through May. In June through September only mad dogs and Englishmen are out in the noonday sun, and early-morning starting times are most heavily in demand.

Reservations for tee times can be made up to a week in advance (one or two days are sufficient at some courses, and a select few allow reservations up to three months in advance). Starting times for same-day play are possible, but you're given the first available time. All courses have pros, pro shops, practice facilities, club rentals, and clubhouses. Watch out for the hustlers who hang around the resort courses looking for an easy mark.

No matter where you're staying in the Las Vegas Valley, there are plenty of courses. The closest to the Strip is Bali Hai Golf Club, just south of Mandalay Bay. There are plenty of others in the city and in communities such as Summerlin, Green Valley, and Lake Las Vegas. If you want to make a little bit of a drive, you can head to Boulder City or Primm. Most hotel concierges will help you reserve tee times.

WHERE TO GOLF **Arroyo Course at Red Rock Country Club.** The breathtaking Red Rock mountains surround the only public course at Red Rock Country Club. The Arnold Palmer–designed course has tough water hazards. Greens fees are $155 Monday through Thursday, $185 Friday through Sunday. ⊠ *2250C Red Springs Dr., Summerlin* ☎ *866/934–4653.*

Bali Hai Golf Club. Inspired by the South Pacific, the 18-hole Bali Hai, with its 2,500 palm trees and 7 acres of water, is reminiscent of a tropical island. The entrance is a mere 10-minute walk from Mandalay Bay—making it the only course within easy walking distance of the Strip. The clubhouse comes complete with a pro shop, restaurant, and a bevy of tropical plants to round out the tropical-paradise theme. Hefty greens fees begin at $245 mid-week, going up to $295 on weekends; ask about twilight specials that are $169 during the week and $199 on weekends. ⊠ *5150 Las Vegas Blvd. S, South Strip* ☎ *702/450–8170.*

Fodor's Choice ★ **Bear's Best Las Vegas.** Replicas of the best 18 holes from Jack Nicklaus–designed courses in the Southwest and Mexico (such as the PGA West course in La Quinta, California, and Castle Pines in Colorado) are in one place at Bear's Best. If the course isn't tantalizing enough or if the greens fees are too steep, the clubhouse might be worth the drive to see all the Nicklaus memorabilia that adorns Jack's Place. A 3,000-square-foot dining area doubles as a banquet hall, and a 5,000-square foot pavilion provides beautiful views of the mountains and the Strip. Greens fees are $195 during the week and $245 on weekends. Summer rates are lower.

✉ *11111 W. Flamingo Rd., Summerlin* ☎ *702/804–8500 or 866/385–8500* ⊕ *www.bearsbest.com.*

The Falls Golf Club. Tom Weiskopf designed this beautiful but difficult course. Waterfalls on the 11th and 17th holes are set against the surrounding desert and mountain vistas. The 12th through 14th holes could become Las Vegas's version of Augusta National's famed Amen Corner. Greens fees are $240 on weekdays and $260 on weekends. Twilight rates are $150 weekdays and $170 weekends. ✉ *101 Via Vin Santo, Henderson* ☎ *702/740–5258 or 877/698–4653.*

Las Vegas National Golf Club. Las Vegas's most historic course has five difficult par-3s and finishes with a killer 550-yard par-5 hole. During the 1996 Las Vegas Invitational, Tiger Woods played here on his way to claiming his first PGA Tour title, and Mickey Wright won two of her four LPGA Championships on this course. Greens fees are $125 during the week and $150 on weekends, with the summer rates dropping to $75 and $90, respectively. ✉ *1911 E. Desert Inn Rd., East Side* ☎ *702/734–1796* ⊕ *www.lasvegasnational.com.*

Painted Desert Golf Club. The eighth hole at this 18-hole course designed by architect Jay Morrish is challenging, and four par-5s measuring at least 500 yards make for exciting play. The course design is tailored to the desert scenery (hence the name). Fees are $79 during the week and $109 on weekends. ✉ *5555 Painted Mirage Rd., Northwest Las Vegas* ☎ *702/645–2568.*

Paiute Golf Resort. You can play three Pete Dye–designed courses here: Wolf, Snow Mountain, and Sun Mountain. Snow Mountain fits most skill levels and was ranked by *Golf Digest* as Las Vegas's best public-access course. Sun Mountain is a player-friendly course but is more challenging than Snow Mountain largely because of its difficult par-4s. Six of those holes measure longer than 400 yards, but the best is the par-4 No. 4 that is 206 yards over water. Snow Mountain has wide fairways, but also has its share of challenges, especially if you stray into the treacherous rough. Wolf, with its island hole at No. 15, is the toughest of the three and one of the most difficult in the area. Snow Mountain and Sun Mountain are $85 to $165, and Wolf is $100 to $195. ✉ *10325 Nu-Wav Kaiv Blvd., Northwest Las Vegas* ☎ *702/658–1400 or 800/711–2833* ⊕ *www.lvpaiutegolf.com.*

Reflection Bay Golf Club. Fifteen miles from the Strip and minutes from the Hyatt resort, the Jack Nicklaus–designed Reflection Bay has a beautiful location fronting Lake Las Vegas, with 10 mi of lakefront beach. La Chandele Restaurant in the elegant clubhouse has a large patio overlooking the lake. Weekday greens fees are $240 and $260 on weekends. Twilight rates are $150 weekdays and $170 weekends. ✉ *75 Monte-Lago Blvd., Henderson* ☎ *702/740–4653.*

Rhodes Ranch Golf Club. One of the better-conditioned courses in the Las Vegas Valley, Rhodes Ranch isn't an overpowering course. The average hacker can play without feeling intimidated, but there are enough challenges for a low handicapper—numerous water hazards, difficult bunkers, and less-than-even fairways. Greens fees are $130 Sunday through Thursday and $160 Friday and Saturday; twilight rates are $70 and $80, respectively. ✉ *20 Rhodes Ranch Pkwy., West Side* ☎ *702/740–4114 or 888/311–8337.*

Rio Secco Golf Club. Tiger Woods tees off at this Rees Jones–designed course when he's in town (his former coach, Butch Harmon, has an on-site golf school). You battle quick greens and difficult breaks, so be sure you don't get caught above the hole. The 7,332-yard course has six holes atop plateaus, six in even-lying desert, and six in steep canyons. Some experts believe the No. 2 hole—a 435-yard par-4 with a dogleg right, a short landing area, and a shot into a bunkered green—to be the best in the Las Vegas Valley. Greens fees are $250 for guests of the Rio All-Suite Hotel & Casino and $300 for Southern Nevada residents. ✉ *2851 Grand Hills Dr., Henderson* ☎ *888/867–3226.*

Royal Links Golf Club. Similar to Bear's Best, this course replicates the best of the British Open holes. You can play "The Road Hole" from the famed St. Andrews and "The Postage Stamp" from Royal Troon. It's a rare chance to play links golf without having to cross an ocean, and the Las Vegas weather usually has far more sunshine and warmth. Also on-site is Stymie's Pub. Greens fees are $135 for weekday twilight, $155 for weekend twilight, $225 for weekdays, and $250 for weekends. ✉ *101 Via Vin Santo, Henderson* ☎ *702/740–5258 or 877/698–4653.*

Shadow Creek Golf Club. This $52-million club is owned by MGM Mirage. One of the most exclusive golf courses in the country, it's a stomping ground for high-caliber celebrities and high rollers. Contrary to popular belief, mere mortals *can* get one of 6 to 12 daily tee times here—if they're staying at any of the MGM Mirage resorts. A round of 18 holes costs $500 and includes a personal caddie and round-trip limo transfers. Check with your concierge at the following hotels: MGM Grand, New York–New York, the Mirage, Golden Nugget, Bellagio, and Treasure Island. ✉ *3 Shadow Creek Dr., North Las Vegas* ☎ *702/791–7111.*

Siena Golf Club. If you want more of a local flavor, this course is well-maintained and challenging, but you may not feel completely taxed at the end of your round. The fairways aren't flat, but neither are they overly intimidating. Even so, the 97 bunkers and greens with big breaks can make any golfer nervous. The best hole may be the 159-yard par-3 No. 5, an island green with bunkers on each side. Rates are $139 on weekdays and $169 on weekends. ✉ *10575 Siena Monte Ave., West Side* ☎ *702/566–7618 or 800/470–4622.*

TPC/The Tournament Players Club at the Canyons. The PGA manages this 18-hole championship layout complete with elevation changes, steep ravines, and a canyon lake. The course is one of the venues for the Las Vegas Invitational, a stop on the PGA Tour. Fees are $195 during the week and $250 on weekends. ✉ *9851 Canyon Dr., Summerlin* ☎ *702/ 256–2000.*

ON THE **Las Vegas Invitational.** October brings this annual golf tournament,
SIDELINES with top PGA golfers competing for high stakes. Now that the Desert
★   Inn is closed, the tournament is held at the Tournament Players Club

at Summerlin and Tournament Players Club at the Canyons. ☎ *702/ 242–3000.*

Health Clubs

Most big hotels have health clubs, and most charge hefty admission fees, even for guests. **Bally's, Caesars, Flamingo, Harrah's, Imperial Palace,** and the **Riviera** have separate facilities for men and women; the **Las Vegas Hilton, Luxor, Mandalay Bay, MGM Grand, Monte Carlo,** and **Tropicana** are coed. All of the above are open to the public; hotel guests and nonguests pay the same fee, generally $10–$25 per day. The health club at the Bellagio is for hotel guests only, and even then the daily fee is $25.

Las Vegas Athletic Club. There are four facilities around the city. Each offers large and clean workout areas and plenty of equipment, along with racquetball courts, indoor pools, big Jacuzzis, coed steam rooms, saunas, Nautilus and free weights, aerobics classes, tanning, massage, and snack bars. The fee is $15 per day or $35 per week. ✉ *1070 E. Sahara Ave., East Side* ☎ *702/733–1919* ✉ *5090 S. Maryland Pkwy., East Side* ☎ *702/795–2582* ✉ *3830 E. Flamingo Rd., East Side* ☎ *702/451–2526* ✉ *5200 W. Sahara Ave., West Side* ☎ *702/364–5822.*

Hiking & Walking

You do a lot of walking in Las Vegas. The distance from one end of the Strip to the other looks deceptively short on a map, but it's 4 mi from Stratosphere at the north end to Mandalay Bay at the south end. Though the terrain is perfectly flat, often you're not wearing proper footwear, or the sun is more ferocious than you think, or the wind is whipping harder than you realize, and usually the distances are farther than you bargained for. Fatigue, overheating, and blisters are common on the Strip. Be prepared for walking more than you're probably used to during your Las Vegas visit: train a little before you arrive, bring comfortable walking shoes (and moleskin), and either carry water and snacks, or remember to buy them along the way.

For dyed-in-the-wool hikers and climbers, Las Vegas is a year-round draw. Within an hour of the city center are literally hundreds of trails, paths, and bouldering routes around Red Rock Canyon, Lake Mead National Recreation Area, Valley of Fire State Park, and Mt. Charleston Wilderness Area. Where you wind up hiking, bushwhacking, bouldering, and/ or climbing usually depends on the season.

The best books on hiking in the area are *Hiking Las Vegas* and *Hiking Southern Nevada,* both by local mountain man Branch Whitney and both published by local publishing company Huntington Press (☎ 800/244–2224 ⊕ www.huntingtonpress.com). Each book contains 60 trails within 60 minutes of the Las Vegas Strip; there are hikes for everyone from rank beginners to mountain goats.

FodorśChoice ★ **Mt. Charleston.** In summer, hikers escape the heat by traveling 45 minutes up to Mt. Charleston, where the U.S. Forest Service maintains more than 50 mi of marked hiking trails for all abilities. Trails vary from

¼-mi long (the Robber's Roost and Bristlecone Loop trails) to the extremely strenuous 10-mi North Loop Trail, which reaches the Mt. Charleston summit at 11,918 feet; the elevation gain is 3,500 feet. There are also plenty of intermediate trails, along with marathon two-, three-, four-, and five-peak routes only for hikers who are highly advanced (and in peak physical condition). The Mt. Charleston Wilderness Area is part of the Toiyabe National Forest; for information, contact the **U.S. Forest Service** (✉ 2881 S. Valley View Blvd., Suite 16, Las Vegas, NV 89103 ☎ 702/873–8800 ⊕ www.fs.fed.us).

🔄 **Red Rock Canyon Recreation Area.** In winter, when downhill and cross-country skiing are the outdoor activities of choice on Mt. Charleston, hikers head to Red Rock, which encompasses 197,000 acres of Bureau of Land Management recreation lands. Like Mt. Charleston hiking, Red Rock Canyon hiking has many options, including short discovery trails for children and all-day routes up the sandstone to various mountain peaks. Note that there are only 35 mi of maintained trails at Red Rock, and it's extremely easy to get lost; search-and-rescue teams, including helicopters, are dispatched regularly to find lost hikers. People are also hurt or killed occasionally in falls. It's imperative to know where you're going (and how to get back!) and what you're doing before you set out to conquer the Aztec sandstone of Red Rock Canyon. Make sure someone else knows where you're going, and when you're expected to return. For guided group hikes in Red Rock Canyon, contact the Southern Nevada chapter of the **Sierra Club** (☎ 702/392–7136). ✉ *W. Charleston Blvd., West Side* ☎ *702/363–1922* ⊕ *www.redrockcanyon.blm.gov.*

Horseback Riding

★ 🔄 **Bonnie Springs Ranch.** A little past Red Rock Canyon (18 mi from the Strip), Bonnie Springs offers one-hour guided rides at the base of the Spring Mountains, within the canyon. The rides cover 3 to 4 mi round-trip and cost $25. The ranch also offers a four-hour excursion to see wild horses for $130, including meal; and a sunset ride for $135, including meal. Note that no children under six are allowed. ✉ *1 Bonnie Springs Ranch Rd., West Side* ☎ *702/875–4191* ⊙ *Rides set out at 9, 10:15, 11:30, 12:45, 2, and 3:15. Two rides are added in summer at 4:30 PM and 5:45 PM.*

🔄 **Sagebrush Ranch.** Sagebrush offers one- and two-hour guided rides as well as breakfast and dinner trail rides. The one-hour ride is $25, the two-hour ride is $50. The breakfast ride includes a big hot meal cooked and served around a campfire ($99); dinner is an all-you-can-eat steak feast ($139). The ranch caters to families, and riding helmets are provided. The rides head up into the Spring Mountains, where the landscape looks like something straight out of a John Wayne movie. ✉ *12000 West Ann Rd., North Las Vegas* ☎ *702/645–9422.*

Jogging

You can spot many joggers at dusk on the wide sidewalks south of the Mandalay Bay, running parallel to the airport and the Bali Hai golf course.

However, it gets noisy on the boulevard and somewhat polluted. A little calmer are the jogging trails that run around the Las Vegas Hilton. The most pleasant time to hit the streets of Las Vegas, especially in the hot months, is early in the morning. You can also jog at Red Rock Canyon: the 2-mi Moenkopi Loop begins and ends at the visitor center; the Willow Springs Trail is a 3-mi circuit.

University of Nevada–Las Vegas. Your best bet for jogging in Las Vegas is UNLV's regulation track (Bill Cosby's favorite hangout when in town), from which you can see the Strip in the distance as you run without inhaling exhaust fumes. ✉ *4505 S. Maryland Pkwy., University District* ☎ *702/739–3011.*

Racquetball

Several places in Las Vegas have racquetball courts that are open to the public for a fee.

Las Vegas Athletic Club. There are courts at this and four other locations; the fee is $15 per day for nonmembers, or $35 weekly. This Athletic Club is open 24 hours a day and the others are open 7 AM to 8 PM. ✉ *1070 E. Sahara Ave., East Side* ☎ *702/733–1919.*

YMCA. The local branch issues daily passes for its facilities, which include a jogging track. Passes are $10. ✉ *4141 Meadows La., West Side* ☎ *702/877–7200.*

Rafting

Black Canyon, just below Hoover Dam, is the place for river-running near Las Vegas. You can launch a raft here on the Colorado River year-round. The 11-mi run to Willow Beach on the Arizona side is reminiscent of rafting the Grand Canyon, with its vertical canyon walls, bighorn sheep on the slopes, and feeder streams and waterfalls coming off the bluffs. The water flows at roughly 5 mph, but some rapids, eddies, and whirlpools can cause difficulties, as can head winds, especially for inexperienced rafters.

U.S. Bureau of Reclamation. If you want to go rafting in Black Canyon on your own, you must apply for a $5 permit. Permits are issued immediately. The bureau will also send a list of guides and outfitters. Launches take place every morning at 8:30 AM and 10 AM. ✉ *Box 60400, Boulder City, NV 89006* ☎ *702/293–8204.*

Rock Climbing

FodorsChoice **Red Rock Canyon Recreation Area.** The best places to climb in the area
★ are among the Calico Hills in Red Rock Canyon. This is a year-round international rock-climbing destination, with more than 1,500 known routes up the sandstone-limestone escarpment (Todd Swain's *Red Rocks Select* details many of them). There's a $5 per vehicle entrance fee to the park. ✉ *W. Charleston Blvd., West Side* ☎ *702/515–5138* ⊕ *www. redrockcanyon.blm.gov.*

OUTFITTERS &
INFORMATION **Desert Rocks Sports.** Indoor and outdoor equipment are available, and the knowledgeable salespeople will happily advise you on routes. ✉ *8201 W. Charleston Blvd., West Side* ☎ *702/254–1143.*

Powerhouse Climbing Center. Beginner to advanced rock climbers hone their climbing skills indoors on these simulated rock walls. ✉ *8201 W. Charleston Blvd., West Side* ☎ *702/254–5604.*

★ **Sky's the Limit.** Half-day ($180) and full-day ($280) private lessons or private guided hikes are available; Sky's the Limit also has two-day classes ($260). All equipment is provided. Sky's the Limit also has the largest indoor climbing facility in the state. ☎ *702/363–4533.*

Rodeo

FodorsChoice **National Finals of Rodeo.** When the rodeo comes to town in December,
★ the casinos showcase country stars and the fans dress in Western gear. The NFR, said to be the Super Bowl of professional rodeo, offers more than $2 million in prize money. It's held at the Thomas and Mack Center on the UNLV campus. ☎ *702/895–3011.*

Scuba Diving

The creation of Lake Mead flooded a huge expanse of land, and, as a result, sights of the deep abound for scuba divers. The old Mormon town of St. Thomas, inundated by the lake in 1938, has many a watery story to tell. Wishing Well Cove has steep canyon drop-offs, caves, and clear water. Ringbolt Rapids, an exhilarating drift dive, is for the advanced only, and the Tennis Shoe Graveyard, near Las Vegas Wash, is one of many footholds of watery treasures. The yacht *Tortuga,* doomed and said to be haunted, rests at 50 feet near the Boulder Islands, and Hoover Dam's asphalt factory sits on the canyon floor nearby. The boat *Cold Duck,* in 35 feet of water, is an excellent training dive. In summer, Lake Mead is like a bathtub, reaching 85°F on the surface and staying at about 80°F down to 50 feet below the surface. Divers can actually wear bathing suits rather than wet suits to do some of the shallower dives. Visibility averages 30 feet to 35 feet. The National Park Service has designated an underwater trail at Boulder Beach, near the Pyramid Island Causeway; just follow the buoys. Be aware that Lake Mead's level has dropped because of low snowfall in the Rockies. This has had some effect on diving conditions; St. Thomas, for example, is now only partially submerged.

OUTFITTERS &
INFORMATION **American Cactus Divers.** American Cactus has scuba diving courses and issues certificates. ✉ *3985 E. Sunset Rd., East Side* ☎ *702/433–3483.*

Desert Divers Supply. Certified divers can rent masks, fins, boots, wet suits, tanks, and regulators. ✉ *5720 E. Charleston Blvd., East Side* ☎ *702/ 438–1000.*

Neptune Divers Scuba Center. Neptune Divers rents scuba equipment and offers lessons. ✉ *231 Sun Pac, East Side* ☎ *702/564–5253.*

Skating

☺ **Crystal Palace.** There are three Crystal Palace roller- and ice-skating rinks in the area. Each has a large skating floor, rentals (you can also bring your own skates or blades), a snack bar, an arcade, a youth hockey clinic, and plenty of public skating time. ⊠ *3901 N. Rancho Dr., North Las Vegas* ☎ *702/645–4892* ⊠ *4680 Boulder Hwy., Boulder Strip* ☎ *702/458–7107* ⊠ *9295 W. Flamingo Rd., West Side* ☎ *702/253–9832.*

★ ☺ **Santa Fe Station Ice Arena.** This professional ice-skating arena has 17,000 square feet of ice and 1,200 seats. This is not only the one ice-skating rink at a casino in the country, it's also the only professional-level indoor ice-skating rink in the state. Instruction, skate rentals, and public skating hours are all available here; Little League and semi-professional hockey teams compete at the Santa Fe as well. ⊠ *4949 N. Rancho Dr., Rancho Strip* ☎ *702/658–4900.*

Skiing & Snowboarding

★ ☺ **Las Vegas Ski and Snowboard Resort.** Southern Nevada's skiing headquarters is a mere 47 mi northwest of downtown Las Vegas. Depending on traffic and conditions, it can take as little as an hour to go from a 70°F February afternoon on the Strip to the top of a chairlift at an elevation of 9,500 feet. "Ski Lee," as it's affectionately known (for its site in Lee Canyon), is equipped with three double chairlifts, a ski school, a half pipe and terrain park, a ski shop, rental equipment, and a day lodge with a coffee shop and lounge. Clothing rentals are even available for those who left their parkas in Poughkeepsie. There are 40 acres of groomed slopes: 20% of the trails are for beginners, 60% are intermediate, and 20% are advanced runs. The longest run is 3,000 feet, and there's a vertical drop of more than 1,000 feet. You know you're at the closest ski resort to Las Vegas when you see the slope names: Blackjack, High Roller, Keno, the Strip, Bimbo 1 and 2, and Slot Alley. The lifts are open from about Thanksgiving to Easter for skiing. Lift-ticket rates are $30. To get here, take U.S. 95 north to the Lee Canyon exit (Hwy. 156), and head up the mountain. A telephone call will get you **snow conditions** (☎ 702/593–9500); driving conditions can be had through the **local road report** (☎ 702/486–3116). ⊠ *Mt. Charleston, Hwy. 156* ☎ *702/646–0008.*

Swimming

Most hotels and motels have outdoor pools that are open from about mid-March through October. While hotel pools used to be an afterthought, they've been getting better and better. The pool at the Flamingo, for example, is actually a series of pools connected by water slides, and Mandalay Bay's pool has a beach. Other cool pools are at the Hard Rock Hotel, the Palms, Caesars Palace, the Tropicana, Bellagio, the Mirage, and the MGM Grand. For lake swimming, make the 30-mi drive to Lake Mead.

Public Pools. There are several in town; two are convenient for visitors. **Baker Swimming Pool** (⊠ 1100 E. St. Louis Ave., East Side ☎ 702/229–

6395) is open June through August. The **Municipal Pool** (✉ 430 E. Bonanza Rd., Downtown ☎ 702/229–6309), built in the late '90s, is open year-round and is a reasonable walk from Fremont Street hotels.

YMCA. The Y is across the street from the large Meadows Mall and has a full-size indoor pool with separate children's pool. It reciprocates with YMCA memberships in other cities. ✉ *4141 Meadows La., West Side* ☎ *702/877–7200.*

Tennis

Las Vegas has an abundance of tennis courts, many of them lighted for evening play. The Flamingo, New Frontier, MGM Grand, and Riviera have tennis courts where the public is welcome, though hotel guests take priority. At the New Frontier, there's no charge for hotel guests.

Bally's Casino Resort. Eight courts are open to the public for a $10–$15 (per hour, per person) court fee. ✉ *3645 Las Vegas Blvd. S, Center Strip* ☎ *702/739–4111.*

Sunset Park. Court rentals are $3 per person per hour during the day, $5 per person per hour at night. Racket stringing, sales, and other supplies also are available. ✉ *2601 E. Sunset Rd., East Side* ☎ *702/455–8200 or 702/260–9803.*

SHOPPING

7

Revised and
updated by
Lenore Greiner

WORLD-CLASS SHOPPING IN VEGAS? Yes, among the scads of kitsch and Elvis memorabilia (looking for a piece of the King's pillowcase?), there's also the *ne plus ultra* from Cartier and Yves St. Laurent. The square footage in the Forum Shops at Caesars alone is the most valuable retail real estate in the country; bankrolls are dropped there as readily as on the gaming tables. It's the variety of options that has pushed Las Vegas near the ranks of New York, London, or Rome: You may tote home a vintage slot machine or Lenôtre chocolates from the only place in the United States where you can buy them (at Paris Las Vegas, in case you're salivating). You might start to think those darn casinos only get in the way of your shopping safaris.

Strip shopping malls take their themes to extremes: you can stroll along a Venice canal at the Venetian or traverse North African trade routes at the Aladdin. Most Strip hotels offer expensive dresses, swimsuits, jewelry, and menswear; almost all have shops offering logo merchandise for the hotel or its latest show. Inside the casinos, the gifts are elegant and expensive. Outside, all the Elvis clocks and gambling-chip toilet seats you never wanted to see are available in the tacky gift shops. Beyond the Strip, Vegas shopping encompasses such extremes as a couture ball gown in a vintage store and, in a Western store, a fine pair of Tony Lamas leftover from the town's cowboy days. Shoppers looking for more practical items can head for neighborhood malls, supermarkets, shopping centers, and specialty stores. And to avoid the stratospheric prices on the Strip, shoppers not averse to driving a bit can find the same high-ticket items at lower prices at the town's factory outlet malls.

Shopping Neighborhoods

South Strip

The south end of the Strip, from the famous and much-photographed WELCOME TO LAS VEGAS sign to the always traffic-filled Tropicana Avenue, offers fewer chances to max out your credit card than the Strip's center. However, like slot machines and free drinks, places to spend your money can be found just about anywhere in Vegas—if you know where to look. On the east side of this section of the Strip are gas stations, tourist centers, fast-food restaurants, and a few incidental motels and casinos. Prime examples of Vegas's theme and upscale resorts, **Mandalay Bay** and **Luxor,** inhabit the west side. At the intersection of Tropicana Avenue and Las Vegas Boulevard, informally known as the Four Corners, four major hotels are visual juxtapositions of old and new Vegas. The **Excalibur** and **Tropicana** refuse to yield to the encroachment of the newer, slicker properties; they face, respectively, **New York–New York,** with its big-city spires and mini Brooklyn Bridge, and the **MGM Grand,** with its emerald-green building and brass lion. North of the MGM Grand, the **Showcase Mall** offers sweet temptations.

The hotels occupying the south end of the Strip offer the typical upscale shops found in most of the major hotels, albeit with different themes and ambiences. You can easily spend outrageous sums on clothes, jewelry, luggage, and other luxury items. Mandalay Bay has stores, expensive restaurants, an art gallery, and a gourmet coffee shop. A must-see store

BLITZ TOURS

Shopping in Vegas means schlepping across millions of retail square feet in huge hotel-casino and outlet malls. So lace up your walking shoes and get ready to put your plastic through its paces by following these shopping itineraries. They're arranged by special interest; exact addresses can be found in this chapter's store listings.

Around the World

Why shop Italy and France, Manhattan and Beverly Hills, Cairo and the South Seas when it's all on the Strip? Start with a visit to the **Grand Canal Shoppes at the Venetian** for the top fashion, art, and jewelry. Don't miss **Burberry, Lladró,** or **Ca' d'Oro.** Be sure to visit **Il Prato** for Venetian masks and **Ripa di Monti** for delicate art glass. Jump on the monorail or walk south on the Strip to continue this Italian state of mind at the Bellagio's **Via Bellagio,** a world-class shopping promenade where **Prada, Gucci,** and **Giorgio Armani** reign.

Then head across the street to stroll along **Le Boulevard at Paris Las Vegas.** This Parisian shopping lane claims the **Lenôtre** café, the only place in the country that sells the famous Lenôtre chocolates. For Parisian designs, **La Boutique by Yokohama de Paris** carries Celine.

Traverse North African trade routes at the **Desert Passage at the Aladdin** next door, taking in the exotic surroundings, including belly dancers and thundering rainstorms. Take the monorail to the MGM Grand and hump your shopping bags across the street to the **Luxor** for a visit to Egypt. Stop at **Treasure Chamber** to pick up a real Egyptian artifact.

Outlet Malls

You need a car to cram all this shopping into one day, but if you're without, there's a shuttle from the MGM Grand to the Primm outlet.

Start downtown at the **Las Vegas Premium Outlet Mall** for designer names that aren't often found at outlets, such as **Dolce Gabbana** and **A/X Armani Exchange.** Check out **Samsonite Black Label,** which sells a European clothing line (not luggage).

Gather your bags and drive south on the Strip 2½ mi to the **Las Vegas Outlet Center,** an indoor mall. Here you find brand names such as Billabong, Danskin, and Jones New York as well as Mikasa, Samsonite, and Fossil. Hop on I-15 for a 30-minute drive to Primm for a grand finale at **Fashion Outlets Las Vegas.** This is designer heaven with St. John Knits, Escada, Versace, Burberry, and a Neiman Marcus Last Call. Be sure to breeze through the Banana Republic and Gap outlets.

is the **Bali Trading Company**; reminiscent of a South Seas island market, it offers an assortment of unusual gifts. As long as you're at Mandalay Bay, don't miss the chance to see the **House of Blues.** The outside of the restaurant and bar is made up of eye-popping "garbage" art: everything from bottle caps to mirror shards has been used to create its eclectic exterior. Buy music, books, hot sauce, and T-shirts at the souvenir shop. A free tram runs between Mandalay Bay, Luxor, and Excalibur.

Suspended between Mandalay Bay and Luxor is the **Mandalay Place Mall**, a 100,000-square-foot skybridge with 41 stores and four restaurants. New-to-Vegas options include fashion-forward **GF Ferre, Nike Golf,** and Nevada's first **Urban Outfitters.**

Talking camels greet you at the entrance of the **Giza Galleria** at Luxor. The galleria shops are worth a look-see, especially the **Treasure Chamber,** where you can purchase real Egyptian artifacts, and the **Cairo Bazaar,** designed to look like an open market with canvas-covered carts of merchandise. Upstairs from the Luxor casino is a faux minicity with the inevitable souvenir shops. A walkway takes you from the Middle East to the medieval—the Excalibur. Most retail offerings here aren't too noteworthy.

The Tropicana offers very little shopping fun. New York–New York does not measure up to its namesake, but does have some places to shop and eat in **SoHo Village** and on the second-floor mezzanine. The MGM Grand's cavernous **Studio Walk** includes more places to eat than places to shop, but more stores can be found at the lower-level **Star Lane Shops.**

Keep an eye out for **Hawaiian Marketplace,** which at this writing was set to open in 2004 on the Strip between the **Aladdin** and **Tropicana** hotels. This $140-million, 80,000-square-foot Polynesian-theme shopping complex was inspired by the famous International Market Place in Waikiki. A 17-foot statue of King Kamehameha towers over a jungly atmosphere, where you can wander past grass shack kiosks, restaurants, and tiki statues. **Wynn Las Vegas,** scheduled to open across the Strip from the Fashion Show mall sometime in 2005, promises even more shopping riches.

Center Strip

The best shopping on the Strip can be found in its midsection, from Harmon Avenue to Spring Mountain Road. Here are some of the most extravagant shopping experiences in the world. Where else on earth can you explore exotic North African bazaars, stroll through a Parisian shopping lane, cross the street to visit the elegant boutiques of international designers, then traverse the short distance to ancient Rome?

Occupying corners of the intersection of Flamingo Road and Las Vegas Boulevard, **Bellagio** and **Caesars Palace** create a shopper's dream of shoes, handbags, evening wear, jewelry, art, and more—all within a two-block radius. Not many Strip hotels can compete with the posh **Via Bellagio** promenade. Shoppers at Bellagio enjoy a nearly child-free spending spree: no children under the age of 18, except those of registered hotel guests, are allowed on the property. Caesars rules the retail market with the **Forum Shops at Caesars** and **The Appian Way,** where you can purchase everything from lingerie to linguine.

Just south of this power duo, the battle for your gold card continues. The 13 shops of **Le Boulevard** at **Paris Las Vegas** mimic a Continental shopping excursion. However, Paris's next-door neighbor, the **Desert Passage at the Aladdin,** presents an exotic experience, almost beating out the changing-sky ceiling and animatronic shows at the Forum Shops at Caesars. The Desert Passage, with over 140 retail shops and eight restaurants, reconstructs the ancient trade routes through Spain, North Africa, India, a port on the Arabian Sea, and a mysterious Lost City.

Across the Strip and just north of the **Monte Carlo Resort Hotel and Casino** stands a convenient **CVS Pharmacy** that's open 24 hours, like the rest of the Strip. Here, you can develop photos or buy a show ticket as well as fill a prescription.

A mile north of the Flamingo Road intersection, on the corner of Sands Avenue and Las Vegas Boulevard, are the sumptuous **Grand Canal Shoppes** at the **Venetian.** The usual assortment of stores can be found just south at **Harrah's,** but the hotel also has a nice outdoor mall with a Ghirardelli's chocolate store, a liquor store (one of the few on the Strip), a deli, and lots of places to sit. Concerts and other events are held on the covered stage.

Across the street from the Venetian, the **Mirage** and **Treasure Island (TI)** have a smattering of shops. Visiting TI is more fun; not only do you get to see a pirate battle, but the shops have names such as **The Candy Reef** and **Captain Kids.** On the corner of Spring Mountain Road and the Strip is the **Fashion Show Mall.** The two-story complex has 250 retail shops, including eight department stores, and frequent high-tech fashion shows on the Great Hall's retractable runway.

North Strip

The Fashion Show Mall marks the end of serious mall shopping, but lots of little places along the last stretch of the Strip sell cheap and varied Las Vegas souvenirs such as key chains, shot glasses, and magnets. For totally tacky one-stop souvenir shopping, go to **Bonanza,** the "World's Largest Gift Shop," at the corner of Sahara Avenue. As for hotel shops, other than the regular logo gift stores and newspaper stands, choices are limited. **Circus Circus** has a 40,000-square-foot promenade with the usual eateries and souvenir shops.

Shopping opportunities grow sparse between Sahara Avenue and downtown Las Vegas. Past the Stratosphere Hotel you end up among Vegas's seedier establishments: small motels, pawn shops, bail bond offices, and adult video stores. The older, stand-alone wedding chapels also populate this end of Las Vegas Boulevard. If you're close by and need film, money, or a quick meal, **Walgreens, Wells Fargo,** and fast-food establishments are just before Charleston Boulevard.

Paradise Road

The **Deep Space 9 Promenade** in the **Las Vegas Hilton's** *Star Trek Experience* has a collection of Star Trek souvenir shops, including the **Admi-**

ral Collection, where you can buy actual props from the Star Trek television shows. Pick up a Vulcan lute or the same phaser Captain Kirk screamed into. High rollers take note—Klingon warrior uniforms cost only $12,000.

Downtown

The **Fremont Street Experience** is a four-block downtown pedestrian mall covered by a spectacular canopy featuring 2.1 million lights. Do a little shopping in hotel-casinos that line the street, or browse the kiosks scattered throughout the outdoor mall for trinkets, jewelry, T-shirts, and more. Depending on your taste, you can have a fancy coffee or a half-yard of beer (the beer is cheaper and it's served in a tall hard-plastic glass that makes a nifty souvenir). For a one-of-a-kind shopping experience, visit Fremont Street during the nightly light-and-sound shows. The shows begin at 6 PM and continue every hour on the hour until midnight. But don't expect to chat while you browse—the accompanying music reaches near-deafening volume.

Maryland Parkway

Travel in either direction on any of the major streets that intersect Las Vegas Boulevard and you find a number of neighborhood strip malls with grocery, department, and specialty stores. However, a mile east of the Strip is a shopping destination popular with locals: Maryland Parkway. The best shopping areas are at the intersections of Maryland Parkway with Flamingo Road and with Tropicana Avenue, where there are numerous strip malls and stores, including national chains such as **Big & Tall, Best Buy, Marshalls, Target,** and **Tower Records.** There's also a diverse group of businesses across from the **University of Nevada–Las Vegas** campus, on Maryland Parkway between Flamingo Road and Tropicana Avenue. Most of these places appeal to young college students: you can pick up vintage fashions at **Buffalo Exchange,** buy gourmet coffee, grab a burger or taco, rent a video, make copies, drink beer, and even get a tattoo. One of Nevada's largest malls, **Boulevard Mall,** is at the corner of Maryland Parkway and Desert Inn Road.

Chinatown Plaza

On Spring Mountain Boulevard (about 2 mi west of the Fashion Show Mall), just off Valley View Boulevard, the two-story **Chinatown Plaza** shopping center is made up of restaurants, Asian food markets, gift shops, art stores, jewelers, and florists. Check out the **Snack House** for Asian delectables and unusual drink concoctions.

Sunset Road & Green Valley Parkway, Henderson

Henderson is one of the fastest-growing cities in Nevada. Minutes away from the Strip, it offers big-time shopping in small-town surroundings. In the last three years the popularity of the area around the intersection of Sunset Road and Green Valley Parkway has resulted in the addition of two hotels, three restaurants, and a bank. To get to this trendy little spot, go south on Las Vegas Boulevard until you reach Sunset Road. Turn east and travel about 5 mi. Several shopping centers line either side of the street; stop and shop if you want, or keep driving until you reach Green Valley Parkway. Before the stoplight, on the left side, is a small shopping center with an **Albertson's** grocery store as well as an assortment of eating establishments and shops. After the stoplight, on the right side of the street, is **Green Valley Plaza.** It has numerous stores, including **Agave,** which has hand-blown glass and other unique gifts; and **Natural Clothing Co.,** which sells imported clothing and jewelry. You also find **Trader Joe's,** a huge specialty foods store, an inexpensive all-you-can-eat Chinese food buffet, and a discount shop where greeting cards are half the regular price.

On the left side of Sunset Road is **Town Center.** This complex includes a movie theater, several restaurants, a pet store, ice-cream parlors, and a grocery store. The front center of the complex has an outdoor seating area; in summer, outdoor concerts and other events are held here. A fountain with dancing spigots of water entertains tired shoppers. Several fast-food chain restaurants dot both sides of Sunset Road. The street officially ends at the next stoplight, but if you travel through it you enter a series of business complexes. Turn left at the first "street" and then right at the stoplight to find **Ethel M. Chocolates Factory,** Henderson's most popular store.

Sunset Road & Stephanie Street, Henderson

In Henderson the corner of Sunset Road and Stephanie Street has scads of shopping options in a fairly new area. On North Stephanie Street, you find lots of fast-food places and chain restaurants, but you can also get fresh bread and meats at **Wild Oats,** a gourmet grocery. There's a nice **Barnes and Noble** bookstore sharing space with a **Starbucks.** And many national chain stores such as **Petco, Ross Dress for Less, Old Navy, Circuit City,** and **Target** are also here. **Galleria At Sunset,** a two-story mall with more than 130 stores, occupies the northeast corner of Sunset Road and Stephanie Street. Across the street from the mall is a favorite locals hotel-casino, Sunset Station, which has a movie theater, child care, and several eateries. If you continue east, you see delis, casinos, boutiques, pawn shops, clothing stores, and Highway 95 (take the highway north to return to the Strip). For a more unusual shopping experience, head for **Ron Lee's World of Clowns** (south on Stephanie Street to Warm Springs Road, turn left).

Malls & Department Stores

★ **Appian Way at Caesars.** Not to be confused with the Forum Shops at Caesars, these marble halls are centered around an exact replica of Michelangelo's David in Carrera marble. The upscale shops include **Cartier** and **Cuzzens** for fine menswear. ✉ *Caesars Palace, 3570 Las Vegas Blvd. S, Center Strip* ☎ *702/896–5599* ⊕ *www.caesars.com.*

Boulevard Mall. You see places to shop all along Maryland Parkway, but this one, with 150 stores, has the greatest single concentration of retailers. Less expensive than its counterparts on the Strip, the mall is anchored by **Macy's, Sears Roebuck, Dillard's, Marshalls,** and **JCPenney** department stores. The food court offers mostly fast-food choices; for more leisurely meals away from the mall's hustle and bustle try **Applebee's** or the **International House of Pancakes,** both in separate buildings in the mall's parking lot. Stroller rentals are available; they're dispensed

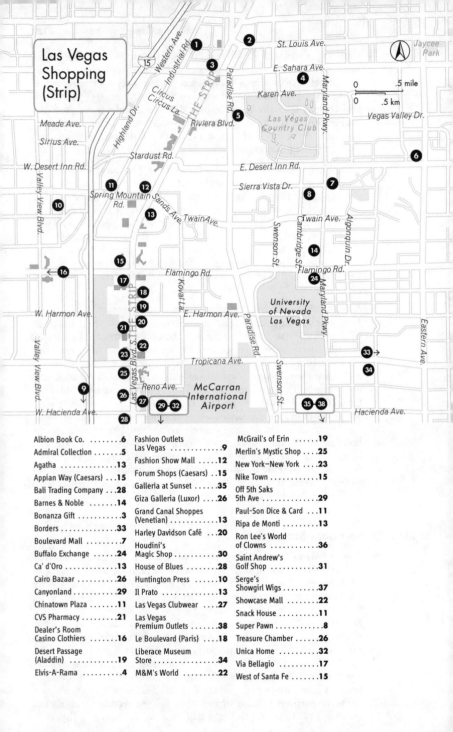

Las Vegas Shopping (Strip)

from automatic machines for $3. ⊠ *3528 Maryland Pkwy., East Side* ☎ *702/732–8949* ⊕ *www.blvdmall.com.*

Fodor'sChoice
★
Desert Passage at the Aladdin. Inspired by the ancient trade routes through Spain, North Africa, and India, the 475,000-square-foot Desert Passage has more than 130 retail stores and 14 restaurants. The circular shopping center surrounds the 7,000-seat Aladdin Theatre of the Arts. Kiosks look like just-opened tents; watch belly dancers and other performers as you peruse the many fine shops. Be sure to watch the storm clouds gather every hour (and half hour Friday through Sunday) at the Merchant's Harbor. A gentle desert thunderstorm washes in and then passes quickly through the port as you sip espresso at the **Merchant's Harbor Coffee House** (sorry, no hookahs). The entrance to the **Endangered Species** store is guarded by a life-size stuffed gorilla. If you prefer your stuffed animals a bit more tame, you can create your own teddy bear at the **Build-A-Bear Workshop.** Other offerings include **bebe, Jhane Barnes, Tommy Bahama,** and **Eddie Bauer.** Desert Passage competes easily with the Forum Shops for upscale clothing boutiques: **Ann Taylor Loft, Hugo/Hugo Boss, Betsey Johnson,** and **White House/Black Market.** Head over to **Sephora** for a makeover. Jewelry lovers have 16 fine stores to browse through, including **Clio Blue Paris, Joli-Joli,** and **Gioia: The Art of Jewels.** For home accessories, check out **Chiasso, Illuminations, Sur La Table,** and **McGrail's of Erin.** Among the restaurants, the **Commander's Palace** is a Sin City branch of the Louisiana landmark and the **Oyster Bay Seafood and Wine Bar** serves fresh oysters, fried calamari, and fish-and-chips. Las Vegas is one of only two U.S. cities that can claim the **Blue Note Jazz Club.** ⊠ *3663 Las Vegas Blvd. S, Center Strip* ☎ *702/866–0703 or 888/800–8284* ⊕ *www.desertpassage.com.*

Fodor'sChoice
★
Fashion Outlets Las Vegas. This outlet mall is definitely worth a shopping safari to nearby Primm, about a half hour west on I–15. Here you find many of the same superstars as on the Strip with prices as much as 75% less. And you don't often see these stores represented at an outlet mall: **Burberry's, Williams Sonoma Marketplace, St. John,** and **Versace Company Store. Last Call from Neiman Marcus** stocks designer labels as well as their private labels. And there are the usual outlet-mall suspects: **DKNY, Banana Republic, Polo Ralph Lauren,** and the **Gap.** A shuttle service runs daily from the MGM Grand and New York–New York, costing $13 each way. Call 702/874–1400 for reservations. ⊠ *32100 Las Vegas Blvd. S, Primm* ☎ *702/874–1400.*

★
Fashion Show Mall. After a dramatic expansion, this mall totals 2 million square feet of retail space, outdistancing every other mall on the Strip. The Fashion Show, next to the New Frontier, is hard to miss due to its signature architectural element: The Cloud is a 400-foot-long steel shade structure upon which images are projected. The well-maintained mall includes an 11,000-square-foot food court and the Great Hall, a fashion-show venue with an 80-foot-long retractable catwalk. Not everything is overpriced—the two-story building contains 300 shops, anchored by eight department stores: **Neiman Marcus, Saks Fifth Avenue, Macy's, Robinsons–May, Bloomingdale's Home, Nordstrom, Lord & Taylor,** and **Dillards.** You do find many of the same stores that are at the casino malls, such as **Louis Vuitton,** but there's also a smattering of different fare, such

as a great shoe store, **Stiletto,** and the only bookstore on the Strip, **Waldenbooks.** Stroller rentals are $5. ✉ *3200 Las Vegas Blvd. S, North Strip* ☎ *702/369–8382* ⊕ *www.thefashionshow.com.*

FodorśChoice
★
Forum Shops at Caesars. Resembling an ancient Roman streetscape, this shopping extravaganza is replete with immense columns and arches, two central piazzas with fountains, and a cloud-filled ceiling displaying a sky that changes from sunrise to sunset over the course of three hours (perhaps inspiring shoppers to step up their pace of acquisition when it looks as if time is running out). The Festival Fountain (in the west wing of the mall) puts on its own show every hour on the hour daily starting at 10 AM: a robotic, pie-eyed Bacchus hosts a party for friends Apollo, Venus, and Mars, complete with lasers, music, and sound effects; at the end, the god of wine and merriment delivers a sales pitch for the mall. The "Atlantis" show (in the east wing) is even more amazing: Atlas, king of Atlantis, can't seem to pick between his son, Gadrius, and his daughter, Alia, to assume the throne; for eight minutes, the royal family struggles for control of the doomed kingdom amid flame and smoke. If you can tear yourself away from the animatronic wizardry, you find both familiar and unusual shops. The upscale and excellent include clothiers **Christian Dior, Gianni Versace, Gucci,** and jewelers **Bulgari, Judith Leiber** (for jewel-like handbags), and **M. J. Christensen.** And more luxe is on the way: a **Harry Winston** jewelry salon opens in late 2004. Check out the **Virgin Megastore** for music, movies, or entertainment-oriented books, and the **Planet Hollywood Superstore** for namesake teeshirts, sweatshirts, key chains, and the like. Restaurants include **Caviarteria, La Salsa, Spago,** and **Chinois.** You can glide into the Forum from the Strip on a moving sidewalk. The mall is open late (until 11 Sunday through Thursday, until midnight Friday through Saturday). ✉ *Caesars Palace, 3500 Las Vegas Blvd. S, Center Strip* ☎ *702/893–4800* ⊕ *www.caesars.com.*

Galleria at Sunset. This 140-store mall in Henderson, on the northeast corner of Sunset Road and Stephanie Street, sits directly across from the popular locals hotel-casino Sunset Station. Anchored by **Dillard's, Robinsons–May, JCPenney, Galyan's,** and **Mervyn's California** department stores, the two-level shopping complex has vaulted skylights, sparkling fountains, and huge palm trees. The food court has mostly fast-food fare, with two exceptions; **Edo Japan** stir-fries to order, and the **Bourbon Street Grill** offers New Orleans–style edibles. Several restaurants can be found on the perimeter of the mall, but **Chevy's,** a Tex-Mex restaurant and bar, and **Red Robin,** a burger joint, are inside the Galleria. Strollers are available for $4; they must be returned within three hours. ✉ *1300 W. Sunset Rd., Henderson* ☎ *702/434–0202* ⊕ *www.galleriaatsunset.com.*

FodorśChoice
★
Grand Canal Shoppes at the Venetian. The most elegant shopping complex on the Strip is laid out along walkways bordering indoor re-creations of Venice's Grand Canal and St. Mark's Square. For $12.50 per person, gondolas transport shoppers through the canals. Among the stores, **Burberry, Lladró,** and **Pal Zileri** have luxe shopping. Two must-see stores are **Il Prato,** which sells unique Venetian collectibles such as Carnevale masks, stationery sets, and glass pen and inkwell sets, and **Ripa de Monti,** which has luminescent Venetian glass. **Canyon Ranch Living Essentials** has

cookbooks, body products, and spa robes from Arizona's famous Canyon Ranch spa. Hit the **Krispy Kreme** in the food court to satisfy your sweet tooth, or visit **The Coffee Bean & Tea Leaf** for a caffeine lift (the Ultimate, an ice-blended coffee drink made with chocolate-covered espresso beans, is to die for). Other dining options include Wolfgang Puck's **Postrio** and the northern Italian fare of **Canaletto**. The mall is open late (until 11 Sunday through Thursday, until midnight Friday through Saturday). ⊠ *Venetian Resort-Hotel-Casino, 3355 Las Vegas Blvd. S, Center Strip* ☎ *702/733–5000* ⊕ *www.venetian.com.*

Las Vegas Outlet Center. Just a few miles from the Strip's most exclusive and expensive shopping areas is one of the country's largest discount malls. About 3 mi south of Tropicana Avenue on Las Vegas Boulevard South you can immerse yourself in 580,000 square feet of shopping choices. **Jones New York** and **London Fog** are among the 155 stores selling clothing, jewelry, toys, shoes, beauty products, housewares, accessories, sportswear, souvenirs, and more at discount prices. The mall has two food courts and a full-size carousel. **Off 5th Saks Fifth Avenue** occupies the majority of space at **Las Vegas Outlet Center Annex,** a small separate building on the south side. ⊠ *7400 Las Vegas Blvd. S, South Las Vegas* ☎ *702/896–5599* ⊕ *www.LasVegasOutletCenter.com.*

Las Vegas Premium Outlets. Rarely seen outlets of some heavy fashion hitters, such as **Dolce & Gabbana, Coach, St. John Company Store, Brooks Brothers Factory Store,** and **A/X Armani Exchange,** are part of the upscale mix at this 435,000-square-foot, racetrack-shape downtown outlet mall, which stands on the grounds of the old Union Pacific rail yards. Among the 120 shops are names you can find at your own mall, but with better discounts: **Carters, Quicksilver, Naturalizer,** and **Crabtree & Evelyn.** This is one of the few outdoor malls in town, and there's plenty of shade as well as misting towers to keep you cool in the hot Las Vegas desert. The mall runs a $1 shuttle from points downtown. ⊠ *875 S. Grand Central Pkwy., Downtown* ☎ *702/474–7500* ⊕ *www. premiumoutlets.com/lasvegas.*

Le Boulevard at Paris Las Vegas. Petite by Vegas standards, this Parisian shopping lane has many Gallic delights. The **Lenôtre** café is the only place in the United States where the famous Lenôtre chocolates are sold. The café also has fresh French pastries and coffee. **La Boutique by Yokohama de Paris** has Parisian designer wear from Celine, among others, and Fendi watches. **Le Journal** is the place to pick up your jaunty French beret. ⊠ *Paris Las Vegas, 3655 Las Vegas Blvd. S, Center Strip* ☎ *702/946–7000* ⊕ *www.parislasvegas.com.*

★ **Mandalay Place.** Here's a twist on Vegas mall gimmicks: a 100,000-square-foot skybridge that spans the gap between Mandalay Bay and Luxor. Stores are geared toward the well-to-do. The first-ever **Nike Golf** sells men's and women's sportswear for the greens as well as Tiger Woods golf shoes and Nike One golf balls. Practice your swing with Nike irons and drivers. The swanky **The Art of Shaving** is a high-roller "barber spa" and upscale grooming emporium, with items such as gold-plated or sterling silver three-blade razors, gold-plated brush stands, and after-shave masks. **Samantha Chang,** who carries cashmere loungewear and high-end Italian and French lingerie, opened her flagship store in the United

States. The first Strip outpost of the cool local boutique **Musette** carries hot brands such as Juicy Couture. **Davidoff** is an upscale tobacconist. ✉ *Mandalay Bay Resort & Casino, 3950 Las Vegas Blvd. S, South Strip* ☎ *702/632–7777.*

Showcase Mall. Right next to the MGM Grand, this mall is worth a visit, especially for kids. **M&M's World** is a rollicking, four-story homage to the popular candy. Logo merchandise includes stuffed toys and sheets, and you can buy any type of M&M candy here. Better yet, create your own custom bag (all blue! only red! plain and peanut together!)—huge dispensers with every color and every type line one wall of the fourth level. The flagship store of **Ethel M. Chocolates,** the famous local chocolatier, has gourmet chocolates including divine truffles and assorted gift boxes. **Everything Coca-Cola** offers collectibles, gifts, and Coke. You can sip a Coke float at an old-time soda fountain or buy a vintage Coke vending machine. Steven Spielberg had a hand in creating the high-tech **Gameworks** arcade. There's a multiscreen cinema and the **Grand Canyon Experience,** in case you can't make it to the real natural wonder. ✉ *3785 Las Vegas Blvd. S, South Strip* ☎ *702/740–2525.*

★ **Via Bellagio.** Steve Wynn spared no expense to create Bellagio, so be prepared to spare no expense shopping at its exclusive boutiques. Via Bellagio is a long passage lined with elegant stores such as **Yves Saint Laurent Rive Gauche, Prada, Chanel, Giorgio Armani, Gucci, Hermès, Moschino,** and **Tiffany&Co.** Bellagio's upscale restaurants include **Prime Steakhouse, Aqua,** and **Le Cirque.** Dine on the balcony at **Olives,** right in the promenade, and get the best seat for watching the Fountains of Bellagio (otherwise known as the dancing waters). Here, there's child-free shopping, except for the children of hotel guests. ✉ *Bellagio, 3600 Las Vegas Blvd. S, Center Strip* ☎ *702/693–7111* ⊕ *www.bellagiolasvegas.com.*

Specialty Shops

Books

GENERAL Las Vegas has a full complement of national bookstore chains, though only the Waldenbooks at the Fashion Show Mall is directly on the Strip.

Barnes & Noble. ✉ *2191 N. Rainbow Blvd., North Las Vegas* ☎ *702/631–1775* ✉ *3860 Maryland Pkwy., East Side* ☎ *702/734–2900* ✉ *8915 W. Charleston Blvd.,, West Side* ☎ *702/242–1987.*
B. Dalton. ✉ *Boulevard Mall, 3860 S. Maryland Pkwy., East Side* ☎ *702/735–0008* ✉ *Galleria at Sunset Mall, 1300 W. Sunset Rd., Henderson* ☎ *702/434–1331.*
Borders Books and Music. ✉ *2190 N. Rainbow Blvd., West Side* ☎ *702/638–7866* ✉ *2323 S. Decatur Blvd., West Side* ☎ *702/258–0999* ✉ *1445 W. Sunset Rd., Henderson* ☎ *702/433–6222.*
Waldenbooks. ✉ *Fashion Show Mall, 3200 Las Vegas Blvd. S, North Strip* ☎ *702/733–1049.*

DISCOUNT Used bookstores are as easy to find in Las Vegas as video-poker machines. If you venture out into the greater metro area, you inevitably find one stashed among the many strip malls and neighborhood shopping centers.

TWO SURE
BETS IN LAS VEGAS.

Play it smart at the area's two outlet centers,
featuring large collections of designer and name brands
at great savings, only minutes from the Strip.

LAS VEGAS PREMIUM OUTLETS®

Hit the designer jackpot at this upscale outdoor center located just north of the Strip. Experience 120 fabulous designer and name brand outlets, including:

A|X Armani Exchange, Adidas, Ann Taylor Factory Store, Banana Republic Factory Store, Brooks Brothers Factory Store, Dolce & Gabbana, Guess, Kenneth Cole, Lacoste, Liz Claiborne, MaxStudio.com, Nike Factory Store, Polo Ralph Lauren Factory Store, Samsonite, Theory, Tommy Hilfiger Company Store and more.

LAS VEGAS OUTLET CENTER®

You and your family will love this indoor outlet center located at the south end of the Strip. Shop 130 of the most popular name brand outlets, featuring:

Billabong, Bose, Carter's, Danskin, Etienne Aigner, Harry and David, Jones New York Country, L'eggs Hanes Bali Playtex, Lenox, Liz Claiborne, Mikasa, Nike Factory Store, OshKosh, Reebok, Samsonite, Skechers, Tommy Hilfiger Company Store, Waterford Wedgwood, Wilsons Leather Outlet and more.

Las Vegas PREMIUM OUTLETS®

Las Vegas, NV • (702) 474-7500
I-15, Exit 41B-Charleston Blvd.
www.premiumoutlets.com/lasvegas
Open Daily

Las Vegas OUTLET CENTER

Las Vegas, NV • (702) 896-5599
Las Vegas Blvd. South to Warm Springs Rd.
www.LasVegasOutletCenter.com
Open Daily

Albion Book Company. Albion is a 10-minute drive from the Strip, in the Von's shopping center on the corner of Eastern Avenue and Desert Inn. The majority of space in the voluminous bookstore, which takes in about 6,000 books a month, is devoted to hardcovers on almost every possible topic in fiction and nonfiction. First-edition books and rare finds occupy a corner in the front of the store; mass-market paperbacks can be found in the back. ⊠ *2466 E. Desert Inn Rd., East Side* ☎ *702/792–9554.*

Book Magician. One of the oldest bookstores in Las Vegas has been in the business for 20 years. With more than 150,000 in-stock titles, it's also one of the largest. The store carries many genres, including a few comics, but its specialties are science fiction and metaphysics. ⊠ *2202 W. Charleston Blvd., #2, West Side* ☎ *702/384–5838.*

SPECIAL **Gambler's Book Club.** GBC is the world's largest independent book store
INTEREST specializing in books about 21, craps, poker, roulette, and all the other games, as well as novels about gambling, biographies of crime figures, used books and magazines, and anything else that relates to gambling and Las Vegas. Call for the jam-packed free catalog. ⊠ *630 S. 11th St., Downtown* ☎ *702/382–7555 or 800/522–1777* ⊕ *www.gamblersbook.com.*

Huntington Press. This small-press publisher produces some of the best books about gambling and Las Vegas. You can buy books, software, and handheld games at its offices, just two blocks north of the Rio (less than 1 mi from the Strip). ⊠ *3867 S. Procyon Ave., West Side* ☎ *702/ 252–0655* ⊕ *www.huntingtonpress.com.*

Psychic Eye Book Shop. Inside the innocuous strip-mall facade are all sorts of esoteric books, lucky talismans, tarot cards, and candles. Get a psychic reading or an astrological chart on where to place your bets. ⊠ *6648 W. Charleston Blvd., East Side* ☎ *702/255–4477.*

Clothing for Children

Though the casino-hotel malls and area shopping centers have the usual children's clothing stores such as **Gap Kids** and **Gymboree,** you can find some great gifts for kids at the shops below.

Desert Brats. Little girls will find their inner showgirl in these frothy creations with feathers and sequins. ⊠ *Desert Passage at the Aladdin, 3663 Las Vegas Blvd. S, Center Strip* ☎ *888/800–8284.*

Harley Davidson Café. The café's retail store is the spot to outfit kids with a Harley Hog Cap, flight jacket, or Captain America teeshirt. ⊠ *3725 Las Vegas Blvd. S, Center Strip* ☎ *702/740–4555.*

Clothing for Men

You can't walk into the shopping areas of the Strip's hotels without stumbling on high-end men's clothiers. If the price tags on the Strip are too stratospheric, the outlet malls have brand names for less, such as Tommy Hilfiger, Eddie Bauer, and DKNY.

Bernini. This Rodeo Drive–based men's clothier has five branches in Las Vegas, three at Caesars Palace alone. The Forum Shops has a Bernini shop and a Bernini Collections, and the Appian Way shops inside the casino have a Bernini Couture. All purvey the very best menswear and some even offer bespoke suits. The Bernini Collezioni at MGM Grand sells Brioni, Canali, Versace, Hugo Boss, and Zegna. There's a less expensive Bernini Sport at the Stratosphere. ⊠ *Forum Shops at Caesars, 3500 Las Vegas Blvd. S, Suite B13, Center Strip* ☎ 702/893–7786 ⊠ *Appian Way at Caesars, 3570 Las Vegas Blvd. S, Center Strip* ☎ 702/ 731–9786 ⊠ *MGM Grand Hotel and Casino, 3799 Las Vegas Blvd. S, Space 6, South Strip* ☎ 702/798–8786 ⊠ *Stratosphere Hotel Tower and Casino, 2000 Las Vegas Blvd. S, North Strip* ☎ 702/471–7786.

ESPN Zone SportsCenter Studio Store. Increase the cool quotient with official ESPN and ESPN Zone merchandise, including sportswear. ⊠ *New York–New York Hotel and Casino, 3790 Las Vegas Blvd. S, South Strip* ☎ 702/933–3776.

Giorgio Armani Boutique. This elegant store displays the simplicity of the Armani suit as well as signature sportswear, shoes, and accessories. ⊠ *Via Bellagio, 3600 Las Vegas Blvd. S, Center Strip* ☎ 702/893–8327.

Hugo Boss. Be prepared to be confused. Called Hugo/Hugo Boss at the Desert Passage and Boss/Hugo Boss at the Forum Shops, both have different owners and both carry styles off European and New York runways. ⊠ *Forum Shops at Caesars, 3500 Las Vegas Blvd. S, Center Strip* ☎ 702/696–9444 ⊠ *Desert Passage at the Aladdin, 3663 Las Vegas Blvd. S, Center Strip* ☎ 702/732–4272.

Versace Jeans Couture. Casual and fashion-forward jeanswear are the objects of desire here. ⊠ *Forum Shops at Caesars, 3500 Las Vegas Blvd. S, Center Strip* ☎ 702/796–7332.

Clothing for Women

Vegas shopping can send the most jaded shopper into ecstasy. Prepare to find a great selection of women's wear at area hotel-casino malls and outlet centers. Your favorite national chain store or designer boutique will have a Vegas outlet. In fact, name a designer and you should find a signature shop in this town.

Ann Taylor Loft. The Loft offers value-price career and casual designs for women with more relaxed lifestyles. ⊠ *Desert Passage at the Aladdin, 3663 Las Vegas Blvd. S, Center Strip* ☎ 702/732–3348.

bebe. Fashionistas love this boutique's stock of dresses, jeans, and separates. ⊠ *Fashion Show Mall, 3200 Las Vegas Blvd. S, North Strip* ☎ 702/ 892–8083 ⊠ *Desert Passage at the Aladdin, 3663 Las Vegas Blvd. S, Center Strip* ☎ 702/892–0406.

Burberry. The luxury British brand has its famous trench coat and rain gear as well as hot fashion accessories. ⊠ *Grand Canal Shoppes at the Venetian, 3355 Las Vegas Blvd. S, Center Strip* ☎ 702/735–2600.

DKNY. Up to the nanosecond fashion from this New York designer collection is worth a test-drive. ⊠ *Forum Shops at Caesars, 3500 Las Vegas Blvd. S, Center Strip* ☎ 702/650–9670.

Gucci. If you must drop a grand on a pair of loafers, come here. Though the salespeople's noses are definitely turned up, the Gucci reputation prevails. ⊠ *Forum Shops at Caesars, 3500 Las Vegas Blvd. S, Suite C1, Center Strip* ☎ 702/369–7333 ⊠ *Via Bellagio, 3600 Las Vegas Blvd. S, Center Strip* ☎ 702/732–3900.

Judith Leiber. These bejeweled handbags qualify as fine jewelry, with prices in the thousands of dollars to match. ⊠ *Forum Shops at Caesars, 3500 Las Vegas Blvd. S, Suite G11, South Strip* ☎ 702/792–0661.

Las Vegas Clubwear. At a loss on what to wear for your debut at Rain? Throw on the hip clothes here, such as beaded tops and furry hats, to cruise past the velvet rope. A deejay spins on the weekends and a disco ball dangles in the middle of the store to get you in the clubbing groove. ✉ *3999 Las Vegas Blvd. S, Center Strip* ☎ *702/262–1669.*

Last Call from Neiman Marcus. Score irresistible discounts on designer clothing as well as gifts, furniture, and men's clothing at this department store outlet. ✉ *Fashion Outlets Las Vegas, 32100 Las Vegas Blvd. S, Primm* ☎ *702/874–2100.*

Marshall-Rousso on Park Avenue Collections. This shop has a fine selection of resortwear, shoes, and accessories. ✉ *New York–New York Hotel and Casino, 3790 Las Vegas Blvd. S, South Strip* ☎ *702/798–1981.*

Off 5th Saks Fifth Avenue Outlet. Don't miss drop-dead low prices on a large selection of upscale casual and formal designerwear. ✉ *Las Vegas Outlet Center, 7680 Las Vegas Blvd. S, South Las Vegas* ☎ *702/263–7692.*

Talulah G. Celebrities and socialites converge at Vegas fashionista Meital Granz's trendsetting boutiques to scour her handpicked styles. ✉ *Fashion Show Mall, 3200 Las Vegas Blvd. S, North Strip* ☎ *702/737–6000.*

Versace Jeans Couture. Score trendy jeanswear and tops, including sexy Italian leather jeans. ✉ *Forum Shops at Caesars, 3500 Las Vegas Blvd. S, Center Strip* ☎ *702/796–7332.*

VINTAGE ★ **The Attic.** No other used-clothing store in the world compares. Thick with incense and booming with club music, the two-story building is filled with an eclectic selection of shirts, shoes, pants, hats, jewelry, halter tops, prom dresses, evening wear, and feather boas, as well as furniture and collectors' items. Fans of 1960's and '70's styles should especially love it. ✉ *1018 S. Main St., Downtown* ☎ *702/388–2848* 🖷 *702/388–1047* ⊕ *www.theatticlasvegas.com.*

Buffalo Exchange. This is a must-stop for the terminally hip. The very extensive collection of great vintage clothing at reasonable prices makes for satisfying shopping. You also find great recycled discards and, since we all could use the help, lots of suggestions from the friendly staff. ✉ *4110 S. Maryland Pkwy., East Side* ☎ *702/791–3960.*

Food & Drink

♻ **Ethel M. Chocolates Factory and Cactus Garden.** The "M" stands for Mars, the name of the family (headed by Ethel in the early days) that brings you Snickers, Milky Way, Mars Bars, Three Musketeers, and M&Ms. More than 1,000 people come daily to watch the candy-making at this fancy chocolate factory and to taste free samples in the adjoining shop. A 2½-acre cactus garden contains more than 350 species of succulents and desert plants that are very colorful during spring flowering. Nine other Ethel M. stores are scattered about at casino-hotels and even at the airport. ✉ *2 Cactus Garden Dr., Henderson* ☎ *702/458–8864* ⊕ *www.ethelm.com.*

Le Cave. After selecting your French imported wines, pâtés, and cheeses, you can buy the Limoges chinaware upon which to grandly dine. ✉ *Paris Las Vegas, 3655 Las Vegas Blvd. S, Center Strip* ☎ *702/946–7000 Ext. 64339.*

★ ♻ **M&M's World.** On the Strip about a half block from the MGM Grand, this four-level candy store shares its complex with Gameworks, the

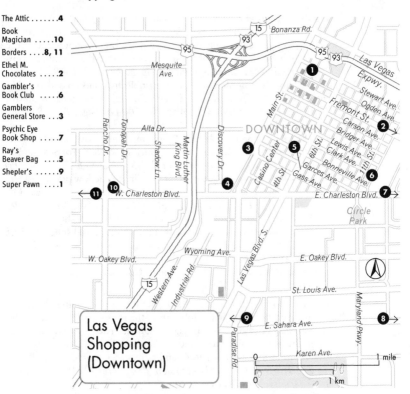

Las Vegas
Shopping
(Downtown)

Coca-Cola logo shop, and Ethel M's. This popular tourist attraction is usually crowded; it's not easy to maneuver strollers and wheelchairs around the displays. Be sure to catch their 3-D movies even if you're not a kid. ✉ *Showcase Mall, 3785 Las Vegas Blvd. S, South Strip* ☎ *702/458–8864.*

☺ **Rocky Mountain Chocolate Factory.** This chocolate store and ice-cream parlor, in the Las Vegas Outlet Center, has a nice selection of boxed chocolates and assorted items that make ideal gifts for chocolate lovers. ✉ *Las Vegas Outlet Center, 7400 Las Vegas Blvd. S, South Las Vegas* ☎ *702/361–7553.*

Snack House. Asian snack foods, dried fruit, and nuts make this Chinatown Plaza shop a popular stop. ✉ *Chinatown Plaza, 4255 Spring Mountain Blvd., West Side* ☎ *702/247–9688.*

Teuscher's Chocolates. The tempting Swiss chocolates and a coffee bar make for a delightful way to gather energy for more shopping. ✉ *Desert Passage at the Aladdin, 3663 Las Vegas Blvd. S, Center Strip* ☎ *702/ 866–6624.*

Gifts & Souvenirs

★ ☺ **Admiral Collection.** Trekkies will salivate over this collection of Federation merchandise: watches, uniform belt buckles, Klingon black robes, model ships cast in pewter, even a Starfleet Academy diploma. But the exciting offerings are the actual Paramount props for sale dating from the original series that began the Star Trek saga. These very rare collectibles include Dr. McCoy's medical kit for $1,300 or a $5,000 life-size Borg Queen. And, since resistance is futile, be sure to catch Borg Invasion 4-D. ⊠ *Las Vegas Hilton, 3000 Paradise Rd., Paradise Road* ☎ *888/697–8735.*

Bali Trading Company. One of Mandalay Bay's most unusual stores, this is a good place to shop for such gifts as rain sticks and omnariums (semi-enclosed, self-sufficient aquariums), island-style clothing, and South Seas art. ⊠ *Mandalay Bay Resort & Casino, 3950 Las Vegas Blvd. S, South Strip* ☎ *702/632–6123.*

★ **Bonanza "World's Largest Gift Shop."** Across the street from the Sahara Hotel, Bonanza is the city's best souvenir store. It may not, in fact, be the world's largest, but it's the town's largest. And while it has most of the usual junk, it sells some unusual junk as well. It's so huge that you won't feel trapped, as you might in some of the smaller shops. And it's open until midnight. ⊠ *2460 Las Vegas Blvd. S, North Strip* ☎ *702/ 385–7359.*

Cairo Bazaar. Designed to look like an ancient Egyptian open market, this shop in the Luxor's Giza Galleria is filled with canvas-covered carts selling perfume bottles, papyrus art, jewelry, and trinkets. ⊠ *Luxor Resort & Casino, 3900 Las Vegas Blvd. S, South Strip* ☎ *702/632–6123.*

Canyonland. A big rock fountain gives this place at Las Vegas Outlet Center an "outdoor" feel. It offers decorative items, including Southwest-style accessories, jade statues, miniature fountains, wind chimes, and cedar trinket boxes. ⊠ *Las Vegas Outlet Center, 7400 Las Vegas Blvd. S, South Las Vegas* ☎ *702/361–6682.*

★ **Canyon Ranch Living Essentials.** Canyon Ranch is famous for its focus on total wellness, and you find all of the accessories for a healthy makeover—from yoga gear and body products to books and videos—in its boutique. Canyon Ranch's outpost in Las Vegas, the Canyon Ranch Spa Club, is on the second floor of the Venetian. The elevator right next to the shop will take you to the Spa Club and its restaurant. ⊠ *Grand Canal Shoppes at the Venetian, 3377 Las Vegas Blvd. S, Center Strip* ☎ *702/ 414–3636.*

House of Blues. Buy music, books, hot sauce, and T-shirts at the souvenir shop in the popular bar–restaurant at the Mandalay Bay hotel. Rest for a bit in the comfortable chairs in the shop's alcove: read a book about the blues or look out the shop's windows into the restaurant. ⊠ *Mandalay Bay Resort & Casino, 3950 Las Vegas Blvd. S, South Strip* ☎ *702/ 632–7600.*

★ **Il Prato.** Il Prato saves you a shopping foray to Venice, where the original pricey boutique stands. The Vegas outpost offers the same authentic gifts crafted by Italian artisans, such as tooled-leather journals and photo albums, glass-tip quills, wax-seal kits, miniatures, and paintings. And, just as in Venice, there's a huge collection of traditional Carnevale masks here. A back room offers a comprehensive collection of Ferrari collectibles, such as scale models and racing flags. ⊠ *Grand Canal Shoppes at the Venetian, 3377 Las Vegas Blvd. S, Center Strip* ☎ *702/733–1201.*

Les Memories. A Francophile's fantasy, this shop stocks Diptyque candles, Provençal kitchenware, and French-milled soaps. ⊠ *Le Boulevard at Paris Las Vegas, 3655 Las Vegas Blvd. S, Center Strip* ☎ *702/ 946–7000 Ext. 64329.*

McGrail's of Erin. This one-of-a-kind shop devoted to things Irish is found in an unlikely spot—the Desert Passage at the Aladdin. Buy a bit of the Blarney stone, Celtic jewelry, figurines, and apparel shipped all the way from Ireland. ⊠ *Desert Passage at the Aladdin, 3663 Las Vegas Blvd. S, Center Strip* ☎ *702/732–8810.*

Merlin's Mystic Shop. A life-size figure of Merlin hunched over a selection of crystal figurines sets the tone for this Excalibur gift shop. The eclectic collection includes glow-in-the-dark stickers, 3-D sand pictures, and a skull-shape toilet-brush holder. A palm reader can predict your gambling luck Thursday through Sunday. ⊠ *Excalibur Hotel and Casino, 3850 Las Vegas Blvd. S, South Strip* ☎ *702/597–7251.*

Ripa di Monti. Exquisite Venetian glass creations—including smaller items, like magnets and key chains, as well as the more elaborate vases and figurines—are sold at this store, one of the Grand Canal Shoppes at the Venetian. It's one of Las Vegas's must-see shops. Buy glass-bead necklaces and earrings or a bowl of glass fruit for your dining-room table. ⊠ *Grand Canal Shoppes at the Venetian, 3377 Las Vegas Blvd. S, Center Strip* ☎ *702/733–1004.*

★ **Treasure Chamber.** Bring home a piece of Egypt (and a lighter wallet). This shop sells real and faux Egyptian artifacts, art, and jewelry in the Luxor's Giza Galleria. Some pieces are more than 2,000 years old. ⊠ *Luxor Resort & Casino, 3900 Las Vegas Blvd. S, South Strip* ☎ *702/ 730–5932.*

Home Furnishings

National chains can be found in most Vegas malls, but be sure to hit Las Vegas Outlet Center for reduced prices on brand names such as **Waterford Wedgwood, Springmaid, Corning-Revere, Mikasa, Pfaltzgraff, Lenox,** and more.

Sur La Table. Culinary aficionados and home chefs love the table linens, kitchen tools, and specialty foods. ⊠ *Desert Passage at the Aladdin, 3663 Las Vegas Blvd. S, Center Strip* ☎ *702/732–2706.*

Unica Home. Feast your eyes on contemporary home furnishings and totally cool, sometimes wacky offerings, such as a chew toy that looks like stick. Check out the Campbell soup can lamp or the Settegiorni appointment book with the months and days in French, Italian, German and English. Unica is across I–15 from the Las Vegas Premium Outlet Mall. ⊠ *7540 S. Industrial Ave., Suite 501, East Side* ☎ *702/ 792–0661.*

West of Santa Fe. One of the Forum Shops, West of Santa Fe carries home accessories, Native American collectibles, and a large selection of silver jewelry. ⊠ *Forum Shops at Caesars, 3500 Las Vegas Blvd. S, Center Strip* ☎ *702/737–1993.*

Williams Sonoma Marketplace. All the kitchen witchery of its catalog and stores are sold here at deep discounts. ⊠ *Fashion Outlets, 32100 Las Vegas Blvd. S, Primm* ☎ *702/874–1780.*

Jewelry

Most malls and shopping centers on and off the Strip have jewelry stores, including such national chains as **Ben Bridge, Gordon's, Lundstrom, Whitehall Co.,** and **Zales.** More exclusive jewelers can be found in several of the Strip hotels, most notably Bellagio and the Venetian.

Agatha. Chunky, hip, and affordable jewelry—gold and silver bracelets, necklaces, earrings, and even hair clips—is sold here. ⊠ *Grand Canal Shoppes at the Venetian, 3355 Las Vegas Blvd. S, Suite 2010, Center Strip* ☎ *702/369–0365.*

Ca' d'Oro. This is the premier jewelry shop on the Strip—perhaps in all of Las Vegas. Not surprisingly, it's one of the many unique, elegant stores in the Grand Canal Shoppes at the Venetian. The store is made up of several boutiques, among them the only Damiani boutique in the United States and one of only six Charriol boutiques in the country. UnoAerre, Charles Krypell, and Silvio Hidalgo offer jewel and enamel settings in platinum and 18-karat gold. Lovers of fine watches will find numerous brands, including Ebel, Omega, Tag Heuer, and Bertolucci. The Katherine Baumann purses, studded with Swarovski crystals and other gems, are carried by stars and celebrities to the Oscar and Emmy awards. ⊠ *Grand Canal Shoppes, 3355 Las Vegas Blvd. S, Center Strip* ☎ *702/ 696–0080.*

Tiffany & Co. Browse through a full selection of Tiffany's timeless merchandise as well as the exclusive jewelry designs of Elsa Peretti, Paloma Picasso, and Jean Schlumberger. ⊠ *Via Bellagio, 3600 Las Vegas Blvd. S, Center Strip* ☎ *702/693–7111.*

Only in Las Vegas

Dealers Room Casino Clothiers. If you've caught the gambling spirit and want to go home in a white shirt, black pants, and a big red bow tie, this place will be happy to sell you dealer's duds. ⊠ *4465 W. Flamingo Rd., West Side* ☎ *702/362–7980* ⊠ *3507 S. Maryland Pkwy., East Side* ☎ *702/732–3932.*

Elvis-A-Rama Museum Store. You may feel ecstatic shopping here if you're an Elvis fan; if not, you might wonder at the decline of our civilization. The store stocks such finds as an Elvis doll (the Army years), an Elvis lunch box, aviator sunglasses, and a swatch of his pillowcase. There are many CDs, videos, and photos; even his furniture is for sale. ⊠ *3401 Industrial Rd., Wet Side* ☎ *702/309–7200.*

Fodor'sChoice ★ **Gamblers General Store.** There's a big collection of gambling books, such as *"Craps for the Clueless,"* as well as poker chips, green-felt layouts, and slot and video-poker machines. Warning: the highly collectible vintage slots cost $2,000 and up. They'll make sure your state allows the type of slot machine you want before you buy. You can buy used casino card decks here but only after they've been re-sorted and repackaged by guests of the Nevada state penal system. It's eight blocks south of the Plaza Hotel on Main Street. ⊠ *800 S. Main St., Downtown* ☎ *702/382–9903* ⊕ *www.gamblersgeneralstore.com.*

☺ **Houdini's Magic Shop.** Magicians are hot in Vegas and it's no surprise that Houdini's corporate headquarters is in town. There are ten branches with all the tricks and gags—nearly one in every casino-mall. ⊠ *Grand*

Canal Shoppes at the Venetian, 3355 Las Vegas Blvd. S, Center Strip ☎ 702/796–0301 ⊕ www.houdini.com ✉ Desert Passage at the Aladdin, 3663 Las Vegas Blvd. S, South Strip ☎ 702/314–4674 ✉ MGM Grand Hotel and Casino, 3799 Las Vegas Blvd. S, South Strip ☎ 702/736–2883 ✉ Circus Circus, 3645 Las Vegas Blvd. S, Center Strip ☎ 702/836– 6594 ✉ Houdini's Factory Store, 6455 S. Industrial Rd. #L, South Strip ☎ 702/798–4789 ✉ New York–New York Hotel and Casino, 3790 Las Vegas Blvd. S, South Strip ☎ 702/740–6418 ✉ Forum Shops at Caesars, 3500 Las Vegas Blvd. S, South Strip ☎ 702/866–0010 ✉ Showcase Mall, 3785 Las Vegas Blvd. S, Center Strip ☎ 702/597–0285 ✉ Tropicana Resort and Casino, 3801 Las Vegas Blvd. S, South Strip ☎ 702/597–3104 ✉ Bally's Las Vegas, 3645 Las Vegas Blvd. S, South Strip ☎ 702/967–4303.

The Liberace Museum Store. The store stocks the maestro's CDs and videos, jewelry and, in case you're running low, his signature candelabras. ✉ 1775 E. Tropicana Ave., East Side ☎ 702/798–5595 ⊕ www.liberace.org.

Paul-Son Dice & Card Inc. Want some authentic casino dice and chips? This store supplies the casinos and also sells retail. The company also designs and produces chips, gaming table layouts, and other tools of the trade—in case you're thinking of going into the business. ✉ 1700 Industrial Rd., West Side ☎ 702/384–2425.

★ **Ray's Beaver Bag.** This place defies description as Vegas's most bizarre shop. As a supplier for pre-1840s mountain man re-enactors, it goes beyond moose milk, beeswax candles, black powder, and buffalo jerky. Even if you don't trap or fur trade, poke around the muzzle guns and bearskins and you may find a 1960s Indian trade blanket or a unique 4-foot-long beaded, fringed elk-skin pipe bag made by a Native American craftsman. ✉ 727 Las Vegas Blvd. S, Downtown ☎ 702/386–8746.

☺ **Ron Lee's World of Clowns.** Every kind of clown item known to man is sold at this bizarre shop. They make clown figurines on the premises, and there's a self-guided factory tour as well as a café. Clown clothing, accessories, and assorted other clown stuff line the walls in the tour area, which is touted as a Clown Museum. There's also a branch at Desert Passage. ✉ 330 Carousel Pkwy., Henderson ☎ 702/434–1700 ✉ Desert Passage at the Aladdin, 3663 Las Vegas Blvd. S, Center Strip ☎ 702/ 889–8710 ⊕ www.ronlee.com.

★ **Serge's Showgirl Wigs.** If you always wished for the sleek tresses of those showgirls (or female impersonators), head to this Vegas institution. The largest wig store in the world can transform you into a Renaissance angel or Priscilla Presley on her wedding day. After checking out Serge's celebrity wall of fame, head for their wig outlet directly across the parking lot. ✉ 953 E. Sahara Ave., East Side ☎ 702/732–1015.

Pawn Shops

Las Vegas is a great place to pick up cheap televisions, watches, and cameras pawned by locals feeding video poker habits or visitors who need extra cash to get home.

Super Pawn. There are 25 locations around town, but the following locations are the most convenient for those staying on the Strip or downtown. ✉ *126 S. 1st St., Downtown* ☎ *702/384–2686* ✉ *515 E. St. Louis St., East Side* ☎ *702/792–2900.*

Sporting Goods & Clothing

Nike Town. This multilevel Nike theme park features booming "Just Do It" videos and giant swoosh symbols amid the latest cool technology in athletic shoes displayed in glass cases. Flashy and crowded, it's full of salespeople running around with two-way radios. On the second floor, the swoosh info desk has the scoop on local sporting events, bike races, and hiking spots. ✉ *Forum Shops at Caesars, 3500 Las Vegas Blvd. S, Center Strip* ☎ *702/650–8888.*

Saint Andrew's Golf Shop. In the Callaway Golf Center at the south end of the Strip, this shop is part of a 45-acre state-of-the-art practice, in-struction, and learning center. There's a branch at the Forum Shops at Caesars. ✉ *Callaway Golf Center, 6730 Las Vegas Blvd. S, South Strip* ☎ *702/897–9500* ✉ *Forum Shops at Caesars, 3500 Las Vegas Blvd. S, Center Strip* ☎ *702/837–1234.*

Toys & Games

Build-A-Bear Workshop. The store's motto is "Where Best Friends Are Made" . . . if your best friend is a soon-to-be stuffed animal. Choose a furry friend, take it to a stuffing machine (you work the pedals!), and pick out a cloth heart to put inside. An employee sews it up, then it's off for an air bath and brushing. If you don't want your new best friend to go out into the world naked, you can dress it in tiny clothes, shoes, and accessories. Don't forget to fill out the stats for the birth certificate; all friends go home in a cardboard house. ✉ *Desert Passage at the Al-addin, 3663 Las Vegas Blvd. S, Center Strip* ☎ *702/836–0899* ⊕ *www. buildabear.com.*

Western Shops

Shepler's. Cowboys (and cowgirls) can get their Wranglers and Stetsons here as well as Western decor and accessories. ✉ *4700 W. Sahara Ave., West Side* ☎ *702/258–2000* ✉ *3025 E. Tropicana Ave., East Side* ☎ *702/898–3000* ⊕ *www.sheplers.com.*

SIDE TRIPS FROM LAS VEGAS

8

Updated by
Heidi Walters

A FAVORED BUMPER STICKER IN RURAL NEVADA READS: "Eat Nevada lamb—10,000 coyotes can't be wrong." The same goes for adventuring into the incredibly diverse Southwest region surrounding the bright city bauble of Las Vegas: tens of millions of adventurers can't be wrong. They seek the infamous heat and lore of Death Valley and delightedly find horizon-to-horizon flowers, hot springs, nights dark and star-strewn, and the deepest silence they've ever known. They dutifully drive to the Grand Canyon to peer over the edge, and discover a vast record of time in the colorful rock layers. They drive north, only wanting to escape the city for a spell, and end up sitting in a sun-flooded diner talking to a crusty cowpoke.

The only trick is knowing when to get out of the city, and how. In general, go north, or high into the mountains, in summer; and stay low in the deserts in winter (unless, of course, you must see what it's like to be in Death Valley when it's 130°F, or you want to get cold and snowy). As for leaving Las Vegas, it's pretty easy once you get onto the freeways, especially if you're heading north or south. But be aware that weekend traffic, especially on I-15, can imitate a parking lot both leaving and entering the city. Leave extra early, or travel mid-week, if possible. Conversely, weekday traffic within the city can be murderously slow during morning, noon, and late-afternoon rush hours. Because the city continues to grow, roads are constantly being improved or built; your best bet is to ask locals for new travel options and tips on construction delays.

Dining and lodging price ranges in this chapter refer to the charts in Chapters 3 and 4.

LAKE MEAD AREA

Southeast of Las Vegas sits Boulder City, prim, languid, and full of historic neighborhoods, small businesses, parks, greenbelts—and not a single casino. Over the hill from town, enormous Hoover Dam blocks the Colorado River as it enters Black Canyon. Backed up behind the dam is incongruous, deep-blue Lake Mead, the focal point of water-based recreation for southern Nevada and northwestern Arizona and major water supply to seven Southwest states. The lake is ringed by miles of rugged desert country. The breathtaking wonderland known as Valley of Fire, with its red sandstone outcroppings, petrified logs, petroglyphs, and hiking trails, is along the northern reach of the lake. And all of this is an hour or less from Vegas.

en route

In the city of Henderson you can stop at the **Clark County Heritage Museum** (⊠ 1830 S. Boulder Hwy., Henderson ☎ 702/455–7955 ☎ $1.50 ⊙ Daily 9–4:30). A chronological history of southern Nevada includes exhibits on settler life, early gambling, and nuclear testing. Other attractions include a restored bungalow from the 1920s, built by a pioneer Las Vegas merchant; a replica of a 19th-century frontier print shop; and buildings and machinery dating from the turn of the 20th century.

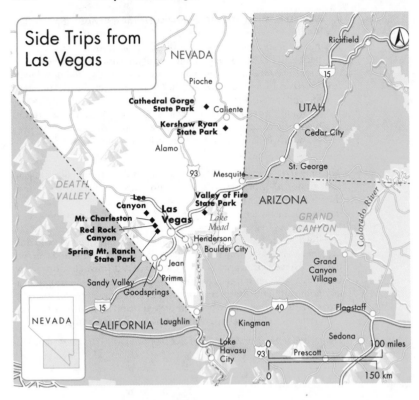

Side Trips from
Las Vegas

More than 200 bird species have been spotted among the system of
13 ponds at the 140-acre **Bird Viewing Preserve** (✉ 2400 B Moser
Dr., Henderson ☎ 702/267-4180 ✆ Free ⊙ Daily 6 AM–3 PM). The
ponds are a stop along the Pacific flyway for migratory waterbirds,
and the best viewing times are spring and fall. The ponds also harbor
hummingbirds, golden eagles, peregrine falcons, tundra swans,
cormorants, ducks, hawks, and herons.

*Numbers in the margin correspond to numbers on the Lake Mead
Area map.*

Boulder City

❶ *25 mi southeast of Las Vegas via U.S. 93.*

In the early 1930s Boulder City was built by the federal government
to house 5,000 construction workers on the Hoover Dam project. A
strict moral code was enforced to ensure timely completion of the dam,
and to this day, the model city is the only community in Nevada in
which gambling is illegal. Note that the two casinos at either end of
Boulder City are just outside the city limits. After the dam was completed, the town shrank but was kept alive by the management and

maintenance crews of the dam and Lake Mead. Today it's a vibrant little Southwest town.

★ Be sure to stop at the historic **Boulder Dam Hotel**, built in 1933. On the National Register of Historic Places, the 22-room bed-and-breakfast hotel once was a favorite getaway for notables, including the man who became Pope Pius XII and actors Will Rogers, Bette Davis, and Shirley Temple. The **Boulder City/Hoover Dam Museum** (☎ 702/294–1988 ⊕ www.bcmha.org ☞ $2 ⊙ Mon.–Sat. 10–5, Sun. noon–5) occupies the second floor of the hotel. The museum has artifacts relating to the workers and construction of Boulder City and Hoover Dam. ⊠ *1305 Arizona St.* ☎ *702/293–1309* ⊕ *www.boulderdamhotel.com.*

The **Boulder City Chamber of Commerce** is a good place to gather information on the Hoover Dam and sights around town. ⊠ *465 Nevada Way* ☎ *702/293–2034* ⊕ *www.bouldercitychamber.com* ⊙ *Weekdays 9–5.*

Hoover Dam

❷ *8 mi northeast from Boulder City via U.S. 93.*

In 1928, Congress authorized $175 million for construction of a dam on the Colorado River to control destructive floods, supply a steady water supply to seven Colorado River Basin states, and generate electricity. Considered one of the seven wonders of the industrial world, the art deco **Hoover Dam** is 726 feet high and 660 feet thick at the base. Construction required 4.4 million cubic yards of concrete—enough to build a two-lane highway from San Francisco to New York. Originally referred to as Boulder Dam, the structure was later officially named Hoover Dam in recognition of President Herbert Hoover's role in the project. Look for artist Oskar Hansen's plaza sculptures, which include the 30-foot-tall "Winged Figures of the Republic." Many people walk right over Hansen's most intriguing work: the plaza's terrazzo floor inlaid with a celestial map.

Fodor'sChoice
★

The Discovery Tour allows you to see the power plant generators and other features. Guide staff give talks every 15 minutes at each stopping point from 9 to 4:30 (early tours are less crowded). Cameras, pagers, tote bags, and cell phones are subject to X-ray screening. The top of the dam is open to pedestrians during daylight hours only; approved vehicles can cross the dam 24/7. Note: all specified hours are Pacific Time Zone. ⊠ *U.S. 93 east of Boulder City* ☎ *702/293–8000 Bureau of Reclamation* ⊕ *www.usbr.gov/lc/hooverdam* ☞ *Discovery Tour $10, parking $5* ⊙ *Daily 9–5* ☞ *Security, road, and Hoover Dam crossing information: 888/248–1259.*

Lake Mead

❸ *About 4 mi from Hoover Dam; travel west on U.S. 93 to the intersection with Lakeshore Dr. to reach the Alan Bible Visitors Center.*

★ **Lake Mead,** which is actually the Colorado River backed up behind the Hoover Dam, is the nation's largest man-made reservoir: it covers 229 square mi, is 110 mi long, and its irregular shoreline extends for 550

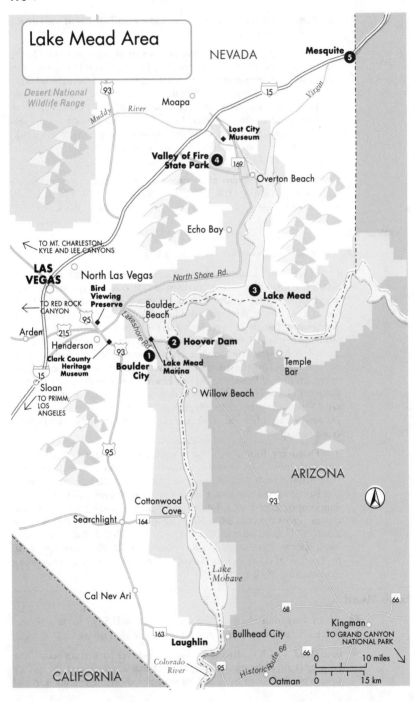

Lake Mead Area

NEVADA

Mesquite ⑤

Desert National
Wildlife Range

93

Muddy   River

Moapa ○

Lost City
Museum ◆

Valley of Fire
State Park ④   169

Overton Beach ○

Echo Bay ○

← TO MT. CHARLESTON,
KYLE AND LEE CANYONS

LAS
VEGAS

North Las Vegas   North Shore Rd.

Bird
Viewing
Preserve ◆

← TO RED ROCK
CANYON   95

Arden ○   215

Henderson ○   93

Clark County
Heritage
Museum ◆   Boulder
City ①   Lake Mead
Marina

15

Sloan ○

TO PRIMM,
LOS
ANGELES

95

Boulder
Beach

Lakeshore Rd.

② Hoover Dam

③ Lake Mead

Temple
Bar

Willow Beach ○

ARIZONA

95

Cottonwood
Cove ○

Searchlight ○   164

Lake
Mohave

93

Cal Nev Ari ○

66

68

Kingman ○
TO GRAND CANYON
NATIONAL PARK

163

Laughlin   Bullhead City

Colorado
River   Historic Route 66   66   0   10 miles

95   0   15 km

CALIFORNIA   Oatman ○

mi. You can get information about the lake's history, ecology, recreational opportunities, and accommodations available along its shore, at the **Alan Bible Visitors Center** (☎ 702/293–8990 ☾ Daily 8:30–4:30). People come to Lake Mead to swim: **Boulder Beach** is the closest to Las Vegas, only a mile or so from the visitor center; **Echo Bay,** roughly 40 mi beyond Boulder Beach, is the best place to swim in the lake because it has better sand and is less crowded than the other beaches. Angling and houseboating are favorite pastimes; marinas strung along the Nevada shore rent houseboats, speedboats, and ski boats. Divers can explore the murk beneath, including the submerged town of St. Thomas, a farming community that was inundated in 1937. ⊕ *www.nps.gov/lame* ⊠ *$5 per vehicle, good for 5 days; lake use fees $10 per vessel.*

At **Lake Mead Cruises** you can board the 300-passenger *Desert Princess,* a stern-wheeler that plies a portion of the lake; breakfast, cocktail, and dinner and dancing cruises are available. Daily 90-minute sightseeing cruises and dinner cruises are scheduled on weekends. ⊠ *Lake Mead Marina* ☎ *702/293–6180* 🖷 *702/293–0343* ⊕ *www.lakemeadcruises. com* ⊠ *$19–$55; reservations strongly recommended* ☾ *Tours Nov.–Mar., daily at noon and 2; Apr.–Oct., daily at noon, 2, and 4.*

Lake Mead Resort Marina has boat rentals, a beach, camping facilities, a gift shop, and a floating restaurant. ⊠ *322 Lakeshore Rd.* ☎ *702/293–3484 or 800/752–9669* ⊕ *www.sevencrown.com.*

A drive of about an hour will take you along the north side of the lake, where there are three more marinas. When you reach the upper arm of the lake, about a mile past Overton Beach, look for the sign announcing the Valley of Fire. Turn left here, and go about 3 mi to reach the Valley of Fire Visitors Center. At this juncture, it may also be possible to see some of the remnants of St. Thomas, as drought conditions have lowered lake levels dramatically.

Valley of Fire

50 mi northeast of Las Vegas; take I–15 north about 35 mi to Exit 75–Rte. 169 and continue 15 mi.

❹ The 56,000-acre **Valley of Fire State Park** was dedicated in 1935 as Nevada's first state park. Valley of Fire takes its name from its distinctive coloration, which ranges from lavender to tangerine to bright red, giving the vistas along the park road an otherworldly appearance. The jumbled rock formations are remnants of hardened sand dunes more than 150 million years old. You find petrified logs and the park's most photographed feature—Elephant Rock—just steps off the main road. Mysterious petroglyphs (carvings etched into the rocks) and pictographs (pictures drawn or painted on the rock's surface) are believed to be the work of the Basketmaker and ancestral Puebloan people who lived along the nearby Muddy River between 300 BC and AD 1150.

The **Valley of Fire Visitors Center** (☾ Daily 8:30–4:30) has displays on the park's history, ecology, archaeology, and recreation, as well as slide shows and films, an art gallery, and information about the 51 campsites within the park. The park is open year-round; the best times to visit, especially during the heat of summer, are sunrise and sunset, when the light is especially spectacular. ✉ *Rte. 169 (Box 515), Overton 89040* ☎ *702/397–2088* ⊕ *www.parks.nv.gov* ✉ *$6* ☉ *Daily.*

<table><tr><td>off the beaten path</td><td>**LOST CITY MUSEUM** – The Moapa Valley has one of the finest collections of ancestral Puebloan artifacts in the American Southwest. Lost City was a major outpost of the ancient culture, which disappeared around 1150. The museum's artifacts include baskets, weapons, a restored Basketmaker pit house, and black-and-white photographs of the 1924 excavation of Lost City. To get to the Lost City Museum from Valley of Fire, turn around on the park road and head back to the "T" intersection at the entrance to the Valley of Fire. Turn left and drive roughly 8 mi into Overton. Turn left at the sign for the museum. ✉ *721 S. Moapa Valley Blvd., Overton* ☎ *702/397–2193* ⊕ *www.comnett.net/~kolson* ✉ *$3* ☉ *Daily 8:30–4:30.*</td></tr></table>

Mesquite

⑤ *80 mi northeast of Las Vegas on I–15.*

The Virgin River valley, at the foot of snow-capped desert mountains, drew ancient people, Paiutes, Old Spanish Trail travelers, and Mormon farmers. Now other attractions are drawing everyone else to the fastest-growing small city in the West. As soon as you enter Mesquite, you can see its evolution from farmland to playground (especially for golfers—there are six courses). A field with an old dairy barn merges into parking lots and massive Las Vegas–style resorts surrounded by palm trees and fake-Mediterranean glitz. Strip malls mix with old houses, golf courses run off into the desert, and everywhere there's that sense of a small town trying on its big-city-sister's clothes.

Stop in at the **Nevada Welcome Center** for information on resorts, golf courses, trails, and adventures. You also can pick up a historical walking tour map. ✉ *460 N. Sandhill Blvd.* ☎ *702/346–2702 or 877/637–7848* 🖷 *702/346–2709* ⊕ *www.visitmesquite.com.*

The **Virgin Valley Heritage Museum & Fine Arts Center** might be the most oddly beautiful facility in Southern Nevada. A 1941 native-rock building, once a library and hospital and one of only two Pueblo Revival–style structures in Nevada, houses the museum. A giant art-metal farm silo, a shed clad in rusting metal, and a small courtyard sheltered by slanted, corrugated metal constitute the $830,000 arts center, which was designed by architect Eric Strain. ✉ *35 W. Mesquite Blvd.* ☎ *702/346–5705* ☉ *Museum Tues.–Sat. 9–5; Arts center Tues.–Sat. 9–4.*

The challenging course at **Wolf Creek Golf Club** winds through Paradise Canyon in the dry mud hills northwest of Mesquite like a broad green snake, starkly at odds with mountains, sky, and desert. The view from the course's Baileyi Bar and Grill, perched above the canyon, is mesmerizing. If you want luxury, you can stay on-site at the Paradise Canyon Resort. ✉ *401 Paradise Pkwy.* ☎ *702/346–1670* 🖨 *702/346–9094* ⊕ *www. golfwolfcreek.com* ⚓ *7,018 yards, par 72, 18 holes, 75.4 rating, 154 slope.*

Where to Stay & Eat

★ **$$-$$$** 🍴 **Paradise Canyon Resort.** The luxury golf getaway has the best view in town of the glowing desert mesas and far-off mountains. The resort has condos and houses perched above its upscale, highly ranked Wolf Creek Golf Club and offers time shares and rentals. ✉ *401 Paradise Pkwy., 89027* ☎ *866/484–6866* 🖨 *702/345–3187* ⊕ *www.trivistaresorts.com* ⤴ *4 1-bedroom condos, 12 2-bedroom condos, 1 2-bedroom villa, 7 3-bedroom villas* ♿ *Restaurant, room service, BBQs, in-room hot tubs, kitchens, refrigerators, cable TV with videos, 18-hole golf course, pool, exercise equipment, spa, bar, laundry facilities, Internet; no smoking* ☰ *AE, D, DC, MC, V.*

$-$$ 🍴 **Casablanca Hotel, Casino, Golf & Spa.** The Casablanca's hard to miss as you enter town from the south, with its towering, pastel-pink exterior, grass, and palm trees. Inside you find a casino with a tropical theme, and a courtyard out back has more palms and grass, a swimming pool and hot tub, and an outdoor faux lagoon filled with hot mineral water where spa goers paddle languidly. Rooms have indoor entries and are connected to the casino. ✉ *950 W. Mesquite Blvd., 89027* ☎ *702/346–7529 or 800/459–7529* ⊕ *www.casablancaresort.com* ⤴ *700 rooms, 18 suites* ♿ *4 restaurants, coffee shop, ice-cream parlor, room service, in-room data ports, some in-room hot tubs, cable TV with movies and video games, driving range, 18-hole golf course, putting green, 3 tennis courts, pro shop, pool, gym, hair salon, outdoor hot tubs, spa, steam room, volleyball, bar, lounge, cabaret, casino, free parking, no-smoking rooms* ☰ *AE, D, DC, MC, V.*

¢-$ 🍴 **Oasis Resort, Casino, Golf & Spa.** The purple and green Oasis is the casual, Western, family-oriented sister of the Casablanca resort. Rooms are done in bright colors and many have views of the mountains or a pool. A go-cart track zips around behind the parking lot, and a free shuttle service takes guests to horseback-riding and gun-club facilities north of town. The resort's Arnold Palmer–designed Palms Course is popular. ✉ *897 Mesquite Blvd., 89027* ☎ *702/346–5232 or 800/216–2747* ⊕ *www.oasisresort.com* ⤴ *1,000 rooms, 36 suites* ♿ *3 restaurants, pizzeria, ice-cream parlor, some in-room hot tubs, some kitchenettes, some microwaves, some refrigerators, cable TV with movies and video games, driving range, 18-hole golf course, golf privileges, miniature golf, putting green, 2 tennis courts, pro shop, 4 pools, gym, hot tubs, spa, horseback riding, lounge, sports bar, cabaret, casino, free parking, no-smoking rooms* ☰ *AE, D, DC, MC, V.*

GRAND CANYON NATIONAL PARK

240 mi east of Las Vegas; south on U.S. 93 to Kingman, east on I–40 to Williams, north on Rte. 64.

★ If you only make one side trip from Las Vegas, make it to **Grand Canyon National Park.** The Colorado River has carved through colorful and often contorted layers of rock, in some places more than 1 mi down, to expose a geologic profile spanning a time between 1.7 billion and 2.5 billion years ago—one third of the planet's life. There's nothing like standing on the rim and looking down and across at layers of distance, color, and shifting light. Add the music of a canyon wren's merry, descending call echoing off the cliffs and springwater tinkling from the rocks along a trail, and you may sink into a reverie as deep and beautiful as the canyon.

There are two main access points to the canyon: the **South Rim** and the **North Rim,** both within the national park, but the hordes of visitors converge mostly on the South Rim during the summer, for good reason. Grand Canyon Village is here, with most of the lodging and camping, restaurants and stores, and museums in the park, along with the airport, railroad depot, rim roads, scenic overlooks, and trailheads into the canyon. The East or North rims, which are less accessible and have fewer, though comparable, tourist services, are less crowded. The geology and vistas of the East Rim closely resemble what you see from the South Rim, and the entrance is accessible from both the South Rim and Flagstaff. The North Rim, by contrast, stands 1,000 feet higher than the South Rim and has a more alpine climate, with twice as much annual precipitation. Here, in the deep forests of the Kaibab Plateau, the crowds are thinner, the facilities fewer, and the views even more spectacular. ☎ 928/638-7888 ⊕ *www.nps.gov/grca* ✉ *$20 per car, $10 per individual* ☉ *North Rim, daily mid-May–mid-Oct.*

Numbers in the margin correspond to numbers on the Grand Canyon National Park map.

South Rim

❻ **Mather Point,** approximately 4 mi north from the south entrance, gives you the first glimpse of the canyon from one of the most impressive and accessible vista points on the rim; from it, you can see nearly a fourth of the Grand Canyon. The **Canyon View Information Plaza,** in Grand Canyon Village at Mather Point, orients you to many facets of the site, and it's an excellent place for gathering information, whether you're interested in escapist treks or group tours. If you'd like a little exercise and great overlooks of the canyon, it's an easy hike from the back of the visitor center to the El Tovar Hotel. Walk through a pretty wooded area for about ½ mi; from there the path runs along the rim for another ½ mi or so.

The **East Rim Drive,** relatively uncluttered by cars and tour buses, also has beautiful views of the canyon and the river. The 23-mi, 45-minute
❼ (one-way) drive along the East Rim takes you past **Lipan Point,** the widest and perhaps most spectacular part of the canyon, and continues to where you see partially intact ancient rock dwellings. On East Rim Drive, you find **Tusayan Ruin and Museum** (☉ Daily 9–5), which has exhibits about Native American tribes who have inhabited the region in the past 2,000 years. East Rim Drive ends at the East Rim Entrance
❽ Station and the 70-foot-tall **Desert View Watchtower,** which clings precariously to the lip of the chasm.

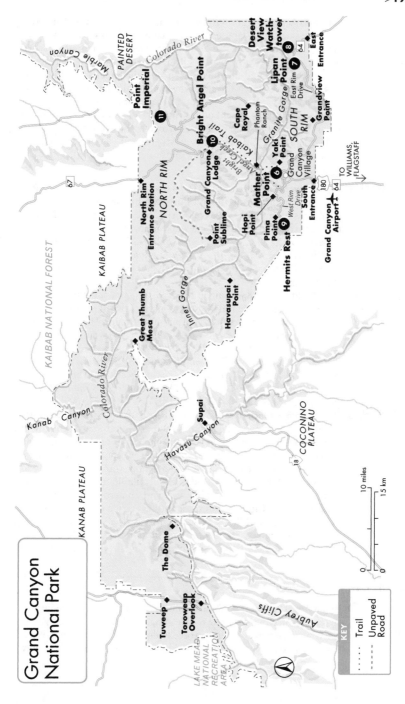

Grand Canyon
National Park

PAINTED DESERT

Marble Canyon

Colorado River

Point Imperial

11

Bright Angel Point

Cape Royal

Phantom Ranch

Desert View Watchtower

8

64

East Entrance

Lipan Point

7

Grandview Point

SOUTH RIM

East Rim Drive

Granite Gorge

Grand Canyon Lodge

10

Bright Angel Trail

Kaibab Trail

NORTH RIM

North Rim Entrance Station

67

Point Sublime

Hopi Point

Pima Point

9

Hermits Rest

West Rim Drive

Yaki Point

Mather Point

6

Grand Canyon Village

South Entrance

Grand Canyon Airport

180

64

TO WILLIAMS, FLAGSTAFF

KAIBAB PLATEAU

KAIBAB NATIONAL FOREST

Inner Gorge

Great Thumb Mesa

Havasupai Point

Colorado River

Kanab Canyon

Supai

Havasu Canyon

COCONINO PLATEAU

18

KANAB PLATEAU

The Dome

10 miles

15 km

0

0

Tuweep

Toroweap Overlook

LAKE MEAD NATIONAL RECREATION AREA

Aubrey Cliffs

KEY

· · · · Trail

– – – Unpaved Road

The **West Rim Drive** runs 8 mi west from Grand Canyon Village. Along this tree-lined, two-lane drive are scenic overlooks with panoramic views of the inner canyon—all popular sunset destinations. The West Rim Drive terminates at **Hermit's Rest.** Canyon views from here include Hermit's Rapids and the towering cliffs of the Supai and Redwall formations. From March through November, only the free shuttle bus is allowed on West Rim Drive. You can catch it at the West Rim Interchange near Bright Angel Lodge every 10 to 15 minutes 7:30 AM–sunset. The shuttle stops at all eight canyon overlooks on the 8-mi trip out to Hermit's Rest, but only stops at Mojave and Hopi Points on the inbound leg. A round-trip takes 80 minutes.

Where to Stay & Eat

$$-$$$$ ✕⊞ **El Tovar Hotel.** Built in 1905 of native stone and heavy pine logs, El Tovar is reminiscent of a grand European hunting lodge. For decades the hotel's restaurant ($–$$$) has served fine food in a classic 19th-century room of hand-hewn logs and wood-beam ceilings. ☒ *Grand Canyon Village, AZ* ☎ *303/297–2757 or 888/297–2757, 928/638–2631 hotel switchboard* 🖷 *303/297–3175* ⊕ *www.grandcanyonlodges.com* 🛏 *78 rooms, 11 suites* ♻ *Dining room, room service, cable TV, lounge; no smoking* ☰ *AE, D, MC, V.*

$-$$ ✕⊞ **Bright Angel Lodge.** Built in 1935, this log-and-stone structure a few yards from the canyon rim has rooms in the main lodge or in rustic cabins (some with fireplaces) scattered among the pines. The Arizona Room restaurant overlooks the abyss. ☒ *Grand Canyon Village, AZ* ☎ *303/297–2757 or 888/297–2757, 928/638–2631 hotel switchboard* 🖷 *303/297–3175* ⊕ *www.grandcanyonlodges.com/* 🛏 *11 rooms with bath, 13 rooms with ½ bath, 6 rooms with shared bath, 42 cabins with bath* ♻ *Restaurant, coffee shop, cable TV in some rooms, hair salon, bar; no a/c in some rooms, no TV in some rooms* ☰ *AE, D, MC, V.*

★ $ ✕⊞ **Phantom Ranch.** Popular with hikers and mule riders going to the bottom of the canyon, Phantom Ranch is the only lodging below the canyon's rim. These primitive quarters, built in 1922 along Bright Angel Creek, consist of cabins and dorm spaces. Cabins are included with the two-day mule trips (run only November through March), while segregated, dormitory-style lodging is available to backpackers. The Canteen has breakfast, sack lunches, and dinners served at two seatings. The early seating serves steak and vegetarian meals while the second seating serves hiker's stew. The rooms don't have TVs—there's plenty to see outside. ☒ *On the canyon floor, AZ* ☎ *888/297–2757* 🛏 *11 cabins, 2 bunks apiece; 20 dorm beds* ♻ *No a/c, no room TVs* ☰ *AE, D, MC, V.*

North Rim

➓ Bright Angel Point, on the North Rim, is one of the most awe-inspiring overlooks on either rim. The trail leading to it begins on the grounds of the Grand Canyon Lodge and proceeds along the crest of a point of rocks that juts into the canyon for several hundred yards. The walk is only 1 mi round-trip, but it's an exciting trek because there are sheer drops just a few feet away on each side of the trail.

For spectacular sunrise views of the eastern canyon and Painted Desert, ⑪ head to **Point Imperial.** The road to Point Imperial and Cape Royal intersects Route 67 about 3 mi north of Grand Canyon Lodge. The picture-perfect road winds 8 mi through stands of quaking aspen into a forest of conifers. When the road forks, continue 3 mi north to the overlook.

Where to Stay & Eat

$-$$ ✕⊞ **Grand Canyon Lodge.** The 1937 stone structure has comfortable, though not luxurious, rooms and is the only in-park lodging facility on the North Rim. The lounge area, with hardwood floors and high, beam ceilings, has a spectacular view of the canyon through massive plate-glass windows. Surprisingly sophisticated fare is served in the huge dining room ($-$$). There are two ADA-compliant cabins. ⊠ *North Rim, AZ* ☎ *303/297–2757 or 888/297–2757, 928/638–2631 hotel switchboard* 🖷 *303/297–3175* ⊕ *www.grandcanyonlodges.com* ➳ *40 rooms, 161 cabins* ♿ *Cafeteria, dining room, cable TV, bar, shop, laundry facilities, no-smoking rooms; no a/c* ⊟ *AE, D, MC, V.*

$-$$ ⊞ **Kaibab Lodge.** Rustic cabins with simple furnishings are in a wooded area just 5 mi from the park's entrance. When you're not lolling in the fine, big meadow outside, you can sit around a stone fireplace (it can be chilly up here even in the summer). The 1920s-era, pine-beam-supported lodge is open mid-May to mid-October. ⊠ *Box 2997, Flagstaff AZ 86003* ☎ *928/638–2389 reservations for summer, 928/526–0924 reservations for winter, 800/525–0924* ⊕ *www.canyoneers.com* ➳ *29 cabin-style units; limited group quarters available* ♿ *Restaurant, shop; no a/c, no room TVs* ⊟ *D, MC, V.*

Grand Canyon A to Z

To research prices, get advice from other travelers, and book travel arrangements, visit www.fodors.com.

CAR TRAVEL

It's a little less than 300 mi to the South Rim from Las Vegas. Take U.S. 93 to Kingman, Arizona; I–40 east from Kingman to Williams; then Route 64 and U.S. 180 to the edge of the abyss. The North Rim is about 282 mi from Las Vegas. Take I–15 east to Hurricane, Utah; Routes 59 and 389 to Fredonia; and U.S. 89 and Route 67 to the North Rim. The North Rim is closed to automobiles after the first heavy snowfall of the season (usually in late October or early November) through mid-May. All North Rim facilities close between October 15 and May 15, though the park itself stays open for day use from October 15 through December 1, if heavy snows don't close the roads before then.

🖪 **North Rim road conditions** ☎ *928/638–7888.*

LODGING

Lodging reservations at all Grand Canyon National Park facilities are made through a master concessionaire, Xanterra Parks and Resorts. Occasionally, reservations can be made at individual properties on the day of arrival, but arranging for that once-in-a-lifetime room far in advance—up to 23 months—is more likely to result in fewer disappointments. Contact Xanterra for dining information as well.

🏠 **Xanterra Parks and Resorts** ✉ 14001 E. Illiff, Suite 600, Aurora, CO 80014 ☎ 303/297-2757, 888/297-2757 lodging, 928/638-2631 dining 🖷 303/297-3175 ⊕ www.grandcanyonlodges.com

TIME

Hours of operation listed for the Grand Canyon use Arizona time.

The state of Nevada is in the Pacific Time Zone, while Arizona is in the Mountain Time Zone. Arizona does not use Daylight Savings Time, however, and as a result, during the summer, Nevada and Arizona observe the same hours.

TOURS

Air Vegas, Scenic Airlines, and Grand Canyon Tour Company offer air tours of the Grand Canyon from Las Vegas; each provides ground transportation around the South Rim, stopping at spectacular scenic overlooks and Grand Canyon Village. You can also take a helicopter tour with any of the four Las Vegas–based companies that take you out over Hoover Dam and Lake Mead for a thrilling trip that can last from two to four hours.

🏠 Air Tours **Air Vegas** ☎ 702/736-3599 or 800/255-7474 ⊕ www.airvegas.com. **Grand Canyon Tour Company** ☎ 702/655-6060 or 800/222-6966 ⊕ www.grandcanyontourcompany.com. **HeliUSA** ☎ 702/736-8787 or 800/359-8727 ⊕ www.heliusa.net. **Maverick Helicopter Tours** ☎ 702/261-0007 or 888/261-4414 ⊕ www.maverickhelicopter.com. **Papillon** ☎ 702/736-7243 or 888/635-7272 ⊕ www.papillon.com. **Scenic Airlines** ☎ 702/638-3300 or 800/634-6801 ⊕ www.scenic.com. **Sundance Helicopter** ☎ 702/736-0606 or 800/653-1881 ⊕ www.helicoptour.com.

VISITOR INFORMATION

🏠 **Grand Canyon Chamber of Commerce** ✉ Box 3007, Grand Canyon, AZ 86023 ☎ 928/638-2901 ⊕ www.grandcanyonchamber.org. **Grand Canyon National Park Visitors Services** ✉ Box 129, Grand Canyon, AZ 86023 ☎ 928/638-7888 recorded information 🖷 928/638-7797 ⊕ www.nps.gov/grca. **Kane County Office of Tourism** ✉ 78 S. 100 E, Kanab, UT 84741 ☎ 435/644-5033 or 800/733-5263 ⊕ www.kaneutah.com.

LAUGHLIN, NEVADA

90 mi south of Las Vegas.

Laughlin is a unique state-line city, separated from Arizona by the Colorado River. Its founder, Don Laughlin, bought an eight-room motel here in 1966 and basically built the town from scratch. By the early 1980s Laughlin's Riverside Hotel-Casino was drawing gamblers and river rats from northwestern Arizona, southeastern California, and even southern Nevada, and his success attracted other casino operators. Today Laughlin is the state's third major resort area, attracting more than 5 million visitors annually. The city fills up, especially in winter, with retired travelers who spend at least part of the winter in Arizona and a younger resort-loving crowd. The big picture windows overlooking the Colorado

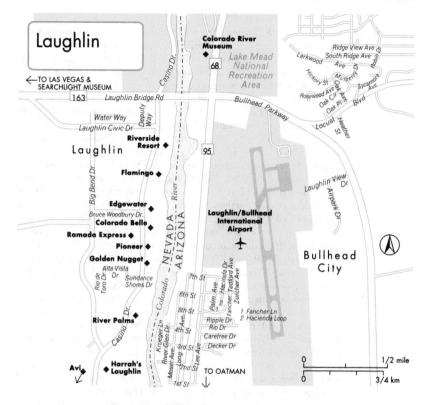

River lend a bright, airy, and open feeling particular to Laughlin casinos. Take a stroll along the river walk, then make the return trip by water taxi ($3 round trip; $2 one way). Boating, Jet Skis, fishing, and plain old wading are other options for enjoying the water.

★ Across the Laughlin Bridge, ¼ mi to the north, the **Colorado River Museum** displays the rich past of the tristate region where Nevada, Arizona, and California converge. There are artifacts from the Mojave Indian tribe, models and photographs of steamboats that once plied the river, rock and fossil specimens, and the first telephone switchboard used in neighboring Bullhead City. ✉ *2201 Rte. 68* ☎ *928/754–3399* ⊕ *www. bullheadcity.com/tourism/Hismuseum.asp* 🎟 *$1* ⊙ *Sept.–June, Tues.–Sun. 10 AM–4 PM.*

en route | **Searchlight Museum.** Searchlight was once the biggest boomtown in Southern Nevada, and this modern, one-room exhibit area inside the town hall details the area's rich mining and railroad history. It also exposes the lives of its most famous couple, legendary silent screen stars Rex Bell and Clara Bow. On the way to Laughlin from Las Vegas on U.S. 95, turn off at Cottonwood Cove Road, drive almost a mile to the end of town, and turn left on Michael Wendell Way. ✉ *200 Michael Wendell Way* ☎ *702/297–1642* 🎟 *Free* ⊙ *Weekdays 9–5, Sat. 9–1.*

Where to Stay & Eat

★ ¢–$ ✕▦ **Avi Resort & Casino.** The only tribally owned casino in Nevada is run by the Fort Mojave tribe. The 25,000-square-foot casino houses nearly 1,000 slot and video-poker machines; a 156-room tower with river views was opened in late 2003. The biggest draw, however, is the private white-sand beach where you can lounge or rent a watercraft. The resort has an eight-screen Brenden movie theater and plans to add a new marina, a convention facility, and a 5,000-seat showroom in 2005. Be sure to visit the **Moonshadow Grille,** preferably for the finest Sunday champagne brunch in the tristate area. ✉ *10000 Aha Macav Pkwy., 89029* ☎ *702/535–5555 or 800/284–2946* ⊕ *www.avicasino.com* ⇤ *456 rooms, 29 spa suites* ⏆ *5 restaurants, cable TV, 18-hole golf course, pool, gym, spa, beach, marina, bar, lounge, casino, cinema, children's programs (ages 6 wks–12 yrs), no-smoking rooms* ▭ *AE, D, DC, MC, V.*

¢–$ ✕▦ **Golden Nugget Laughlin.** A tropical atrium in this miniversion of the Las Vegas Golden Nugget has two cascading waterfalls and more than 300 types of plants from around the world. **The Deck** ($$–$$$) offers the only riverfront dining in town. ✉ *2300 S. Casino Dr., 89029* ☎ *702/ 298–7222 or 800/950–7700* 🖷 *702/298–7279* ⊕ *www.gnlaughlin.com* ⇤ *300 rooms* ⏆ *4 restaurants, cable TV, pool, hot tub, lounge, casino, nightclub, no-smoking rooms* ▭ *AE, D, DC, MC, V.*

¢–$ ✕▦ **Harrah's.** This is the classiest joint in Laughlin, and it even comes with a private sand beach. It also has two casinos (one is no-smoking) and big-name entertainers perform in the Fiesta Showroom and at the 3,000-seat Rio Vista Outdoor Amphitheater. **The Range Steakhouse** ($–$$$) serves Continental fare. ✉ *2900 S. Casino Dr., 89029* ☎ *702/ 298–4600 or 800/427–7247* 🖷 *702/298–6855* ⊕ *www.harrahs.com* ⇤ *1,571 rooms* ⏆ *5 restaurants, some in-room data ports, cable TV, 2 pools, gym, hair salon, hot tub, spa, beach, 3 bars, lounge, casino, showroom, shops, meeting rooms, no-smoking floors* ▭ *AE, D, DC, MC, V.*

¢–$ ✕▦ **Pioneer Hotel and Gambling Hall.** You can spot this small (by casino standards) hotel by looking for the neon mascot, River Rick—he's Vegas Vic's brother. While other casinos stress the new, the Pioneer retains its laid-back Western theme with checkered tablecloths and wagon-wheel light fixtures. **Granny's Gourmet Room** ($–$$$) serves Continental and American cuisine. ✉ *2200 S. Casino Dr., 89029* ☎ *702/298–2442 or 800/634–3469* 🖷 *702/298–5256* ⊕ *www.pioneerlaughlin.com* ⇤ *416 rooms* ⏆ *2 restaurants, cable TV, pool, hot tub, beach, lounge, casino, no-smoking rooms* ▭ *AE, D, DC, MC, V.*

¢–$ ▦ **Ramada Express.** Reserved for adults only, the Gamblers Tower in this Victorian-theme hotel and casino is a perfect refuge for those seeking a child-free escape. There are also adults-only hours at the pool. The 53,000-square-foot casino has state-of-the-art slots and a sports book. The American Heroes Museum focuses on the 1940s, and a miniature train takes you on a free ride around 27 landscaped acres. ✉ *2121 S. Casino Dr., 89029* ☎ *702/298–4200 or 800/243–6846* ⊕ *www. ramadaexpress.com* ⇤ *1,500 rooms* ⏆ *5 restaurants, cable TV, pool, hot tub, lounge, casino, no-smoking floors* ▭ *AE, D, DC, MC, V.*

¢–$ ▦ **River Palms Resort Casino.** A large balcony overlooks the table games in the 65,000-square-foot casino. The hotel's south wing, adjacent to the outdoor pool and hot tub, offers a quiet refuge away from the casino. ⊠ *2700 S. Casino Dr., 89029* ☎ *702/298–2242 or 800/835– 7904* 🖷 *702/298–2179* ⊕ *www.river-palms.com* 🛏 *1,003 rooms* 🖒 *4 restaurants, cable TV, pool, gym, hair salon, hot tub, spa, 5 bars, casino, showroom, meeting rooms, airport shuttle, no-smoking rooms* ⊟ *AE, D, DC, MC, V.*

¢ ✕🖭 **Colorado Belle.** The Mandalay Bay Resort Group owns this Nevada anomaly—a riverboat casino that's actually on a river. The 608-foot replica of a Mississippi paddle wheeler has nautical-theme rooms with views of the Colorado River. No-smoking gamblers will appreciate the smoke-free section in the slot machine area. The **Boiler Room Brew Pub** ($–$$), the only microbrewery in Laughlin, pumps out 155,000 gallons of beer each year. ⊠ *2100 S. Casino Dr., 89029* ☎ *702/298–4000 or 866/352–3553* 🖷 *702/298–3697* ⊕ *www.coloradobelle.com* 🛏 *1,177 rooms* 🖒 *6 restaurants, in-room data ports, cable TV, 2 pools, hot tub, casino, dry cleaning, laundry service, no-smoking rooms* ⊟ *AE, D, DC, MC, V.*

★ ¢ ✕🖭 **Riverside Resort.** Town founder Don Laughlin still runs this north-ernmost joint himself. Check out the Loser's Lounge, with its graphic homage to famous losers, such as the *Hindenburg,* the *Titanic,* and the like. And don't pass up Don's two free classic-car showrooms, with more than 80 rods, roadsters, and tin lizzies. The **Gourmet Room** restaurant serves Continental and American cuisine. ⊠ *1650 S. Casino Dr., 89029* ☎ *702/298–2535 or 800/227–3849* 🖷 *702/298–2614* ⊕ *www. riversideresort.com* 🛏 *1,440 rooms* 🖒 *6 restaurants, cable TV, 2 pools, hot tub, bowling, lounge, casino, nightclub, showroom, theater, children's programs (ages 3 months–12 yrs), no-smoking rooms* ⊟ *AE, D, DC, MC, V.*

¢ 🖭 **Edgewater Hotel Casino.** Like the Colorado Belle, this 26-story hotel is a property of the Mandalay Bay Resorts Group. The 60,000-square-foot casino includes nearly 1,400 machines. ⊠ *2020 S. Casino Dr., 89029* ☎ *702/298–2453 or 800/677–4837* 🖷 *702/298–5606* ⊕ *www.edgewater-casino.com* 🛏 *1,421 rooms* 🖒 *4 restaurants, cable TV, pool, hair salon, hot tub, lounge, casino, no-smoking rooms* ⊟ *AE, D, DC, MC, V.*

¢ 🖭 **Flamingo Laughlin.** The casino at the largest resort in Laughlin has 1,500 slot and video-poker machines and a sports book. The Flamingo's 3,000-seat outdoor amphitheater, on the bank of the Colorado River, hosts big-name entertainers. Standard rooms have two double beds or a queen-size bed. Suites are larger (650–1,000 square feet) and equipped with cof-feemakers, minibars, irons, and ironing boards. ⊠ *1900 S. Casino Dr., 89029* ☎ *702/298–5111 or 800/352–6464* 🖷 *702/298–5116* ⊕ *www. parkplace.com/flamingo/laughlin* 🛏 *1,824 rooms, 90 suites* 🖒 *4 restau-rants, cable TV, 3 tennis courts, pool, gym, 2 bars, lounge, casino, show-room, business services, no-smoking rooms* ⊟ *AE, D, DC, MC, V.*

off the
beaten
path

OATMAN – Wild burros, descendants of animals employed during the area's gold-mining era, freely roam the streets of modern-day Oatman. The main street is right out of the Old West, and the town served as a backdrop for several films, including *How the West Was Won.* While visiting the gift shops and munching on *churros* (sticks of deep-fried dough), visit the **Oatman Hotel** (⊠ U.S. 66) where Hollywood's

Clark Gable and Carole Lombard spent their honeymoon night. A climb up the steep, squeaking staircase leads to their famous room, still adorned with frilly lace. The hotel is on historic Route 66, the "Main Street of America." From the Laughlin Bridge, take Arizona Route 95 south about 15 mi to Boundary Cone Road. Turn left and go toward the mountains about 11 mi to reach Oatman.

GOLD ROAD MINE – Two miles east of Oatman is the Gold Road Mine, an active operation that dates back to 1900. A one-hour tour takes modern-day prospectors underground for a demonstration of drilling equipment and a visit to the "Glory Hole," where the vein structures in the rock are highlighted with a black light to show the gold. ⊠ *U.S. 66* ☎ *928/768–1600* ⊕ *www.goldroadmine.com* 🖾 *$12* ☉ *Daily 10 AM–5 PM.*

Laughlin A to Z

To research prices, get advice from other travelers, and book travel arrangements, visit www.fodors.com.

AIR TRAVEL
Sun Country flies from 50 cities in 18 states, including Seattle, Portland, Denver, Minneapolis–St. Paul, San Francisco, Phoenix, and Dallas–Ft. Worth. Several hotel-casinos also sponsor charter flights.

🗗 Airlines **Allegiant Charters** ☎ 800/594–6937. **Sun Country Airlines** ☎ 800/359–6786 ⊕ www.suncountry.com.

AIRPORTS
🗗 **Laughlin/Bullhead International Airport** ☎ 928/754–2134.

BUS TRAVEL
Greyhound buses stop at the Airport Chevron at 600 Route 95 in Bullhead City, Arizona. To get to Laughlin, walk to the boat dock across the highway and take a free ride to a Nevada hotel river landing. Individual hotel-casinos also sponsor bus trips from Las Vegas, Los Angeles, and other destinations.

🗗 **Greyhound** ☎ 800/231–2222 ⊕ www.greyhound.com.

CAR RENTALS
Avis, Enterprise, and Hertz vehicles are available at the Laughlin–Bullhead International Airport. Other agencies can be found in Bullhead City; some companies have separate locations in some of the Laughlin hotels. Fuel up in Arizona—all grades of gasoline can be as much as 30¢–50¢ per gallon less in Bullhead City than in Laughlin.

🗗 **Avis-Airport** ☎ 928/754–4686 ⊕ www.avis.com. **Enterprise-Airport** ☎ 928/754–2700 ⊕ www.enterprise.com. **Hertz-Airport** ☎ 928/754–4111 ⊕ www.hertz.com.

CAR TRAVEL
To get to Laughlin from Las Vegas, take U.S. 95–93 south (I–515 east) then exit where U.S. 95 veers off to the southwest. Drive for an hour, almost to the California border. A left turn onto Route 163 takes you east into Laughlin.

TIME

The state of Nevada is in the Pacific Time Zone, while Arizona is in the Mountain Time Zone. Arizona does not use Daylight Savings Time, however. As a result, during the summer, Nevada and Arizona observe the same hours.

TRAIN TRAVEL

Amtrak's *Southwest Chief* stops at Needles, California, which is 25 mi south of Laughlin. An Amtrak Thruway bus shuttles passengers to the Ramada Express in Laughlin.

🚆 **Amtrak** ☎ 800/872-7245 ⊕ www.amtrak.com.

VISITOR INFORMATION

🚆 **Laughlin Chamber of Commerce** ✉ 1585 S. Casino Dr., 89029 ☎ 702/298-2214 or 800/227-5245 🖷 702/298-5708 ⊕ www.laughlinchamber.com. **Laughlin Visitors Bureau** ✉ 1555 Casino Dr., 89029 ☎ 702/298-3321 or 800/452-8445 ⊕ www. visitlaughlin.com.

MT. CHARLESTON AREA

45 mi northwest of Las Vegas on U.S. 95.

★ In winter Las Vegans crowd the upper elevations of the Spring Mountains to throw snowballs, sled, cross-country ski, and even slide downhill at a little ski area. In summer they return to wander the high trails and escape the valley's 115°F heat (temperatures are at least 20°F cooler than in the city), and maybe even make the difficult hike to **Mt. Charleston,** the range's high point. Easier trails lead to seasonal waterfalls or rare, dripping springs where dainty columbine and stunted aspens spill down ravines and hummingbirds zoom. Or they might lead onto high, dry ridges where ancient bristlecone trees have become twisted and burnished with age. For camping information, contact the **U.S. Forest Service** (☎ 702/515-5400). For snow reports and winter road conditions, call the **Las Vegas Ski and Snowboard Resort** (☎ 702/593-9500).

At the intersection of U.S. 95 and Route 157, turn left to Kyle Canyon. The first stop on Kyle Canyon Road (about 17 mi up) is the **Mt. Charleston Hotel,** built in 1984. The large, lodgelike lobby has a big hearth, bar, and spacious restaurant with a mountain view. ✉ *2 Kyle Canyon Rd.* ☎ *702/872-5500 or 800/794-3456* ⊕ *www.mtcharlestonhotel.com.*

If you take Route 157 to its end you reach the **Mt. Charleston Lodge.** At 7,717 feet above sea level, the lodge overlooks Kyle Canyon; it has a fireside cocktail lounge and log cabin rentals and is close to hiking trails. ✉ *1200 Old Park Rd.* ☎ *702/872-5408 or 800/955-1314* 🖷 *702/872-5403* ⊕ *www.mtcharlestonlodge.com.*

The **Las Vegas Ski and Snowboard Resort** in Lee Canyon has two campgrounds (at around 8,500 feet), the Bristlecone Trail, and a ski area with 10 runs on 40 acres. Depending on snowfall, ski season can last from Thanksgiving to Easter. ☎ *702/645-2754* ⊕ *www.skilasvegas.com.*

RED ROCK CANYON AREA

16 mi west of Las Vegas on W. Charleston Blvd. (Rte. 159).

From any vantage point in Las Vegas, your gaze is inevitably drawn to the Spring Mountains, that big limestone and sandstone wall hemming in the west side of the Las Vegas Valley. The range's centerpiece is the ★ **Red Rock Canyon National Conservation Area**, whose red-and-cream, water-carved canyons, jutting gray massifs, and fey, polka-dot boulders bring solace to many a city-fried Las Vegan. A 13-mi loop road winds past world-famous climbing areas and rolls up through the Mojave Desert shrubscape to a high viewing perch before rambling back down through the hills. A 30-minute drive west on West Charleston Boulevard (Route 159) delivers you there.

The first stops on the one-way loop road are the easy Calico Vistas 1 and 2 trails, where you can walk along the pretty path or grab a handful of sandstone and hoist yourself high (well, not too high, unless you ⟳ have the gear and training). Red Rock's **BLM Visitors Center** exhibits the flora and fauna of the Mojave Desert and the history of past inhabitants. A turnoff for Willow Springs–Lost Creek is 6 ½ mi past the vista ⟳ pullouts. Take this road to reach **Lost Creek Discovery Trail**, an easy ¾-mi loop trail with Native American pictographs and a seasonal waterfall. There are 20 tables and a partly shaded picnic site next to the rocks. Arrive early to get a table. ⊠ *W. Charleston Blvd.* ☎ *702/515–5350* ⊕ *www.redrockcanyon.blm.gov* ⛁ *$5 per car* ☉ *Visitor Center Nov.–Mar., daily 8–4:30; Apr.–Oct., daily 8–5:30. Loop road Nov.–Feb., daily 6 AM–5 PM; Mar. and Oct., daily 6 AM–7 PM; Apr.–Sept., daily 6 AM–8 PM.*

Some of the buildings at **Spring Mountain Ranch State Park** date to 1860, but for centuries groups as varied as the Paiute Indians, Spanish Trail travelers, and cattle-raiding mountain men used the spring-fed meadows flourishing at the base of the colorful Wilson Range. The ranch has passed through many hands, including those of German actress Vera Krupp and millionaire Howard Hughes. The red ranch house, white picket fences, and long green lawns make this a perfect place for a picnic. **Super Summer Theater**, from June through August, transforms the sprawling grassy grounds into a playhouse under the stars. ⊠ *Rte. 159, 2½ mi past Red Rock Canyon scenic loop exit* ☎ *702/875–4141 ranch, 702/594–7529 theater* ⊕ *parks.nv.gov/smr.htm* ⛁ *Ranch, $6 per car; theater, prices vary, advanced purchase required* ☉ *Daily 8 AM–dusk. Ranch house 10–4, walking tours of old ranch weekdays at noon, 1, and 2, also at 3 on weekends and holidays.*

⟳ At **Bonnie Springs Ranch/Old Nevada,** Old West kitsch meets a petting zoo (with a noisy duck pond) and a cozily eccentric restaurant and bar (note the artful floor embedded with tree stumps and the dance-hall costumes on the bathroom-stall doors). There's also a 50-unit motel. You can rent horses from the stable and take a one-hour guided trail ride through cacti, yucca, and Joshua trees. The theme park includes an opera house, two museums, a cemetery, a stamp mill, several stores, and a wedding chapel. Three times a day actors stage gunfights and hangings in the street. On weekends you can ride a miniature train that chugs its way between the parking lot and the entrance. The free train runs from 10:30 to 5. ☒ *1 Bonnie Springs Ranch Rd.* ☎ *702/875–4191* 🖷 *702/875–4424* ⊕ *www.bonniesprings.com* ☒ *$7 per car weekdays, $10 per car weekends; horseback riding $25* ☉ *Labor Day–Memorial Day, daily 10:30–5; Memorial Day–Labor Day, daily 10:30–6.*

Tip: As with travel in all desert areas, be on the lookout for stormy weather any time of year. A winter storm can drop snow on the higher elevations, and a sudden summer rain can turn normally dry washes into deadly torrents.

en route   **Goodsprings, Nevada.** Before outlet malls and casinos, there were cattle and mines, and you can sidestep into a scrap of that past in this tiny semi-ghost town. The **Pioneer Saloon,** built in 1913 and still clinging to life, is clad inside and out in painted, molded tin ordered from Sears Roebuck. In a side room, you can read newspaper accounts of the 1942 plane crash into Mt. Potosi that killed actress Carole Lombard. Actor Clark Gable, her husband, waited in the Pioneer Saloon while the search for survivors ensued. Ask the bartender to show you the photo of Cheech and Chong when they came to town. ☒ *Rte. 161, 7 mi west of Jean.*

PRIMM & JEAN, NEVADA

Jean is 30 mi south of Las Vegas on I–15; Primm is another 12 mi south.

Las Vegas has optimum shopping and gawking, but those looking for a less-crowded alternative to the Strip's shops and sights can head out to Primm, Nevada, a 30-minute drive south on I–15 to the California border. Jean, Nevada, 12 mi before Primm, is a good place to watch wide-winged gliders soaring on desert thermals. Two casinos, the Gold Strike and Nevada Landing, flank the highway.

In Primm, stop at the **Nevada Welcome Center** (☎ 702/874–1360 ☉ Daily 9–6) for information and brochures about the state. Then shop for bargains at Fashion Outlets Las Vegas or take a heart-pounding ride on Desperado, one of the world's tallest and fastest roller coasters. If you're in the mood to gamble or hungry for an inexpensive meal, stop by one of three casinos: Primm Valley Resort, Buffalo Bill's, or Whiskey Pete's. Two challenging Tom Fazio–designed 18-hole championship golf courses are just across the state line in California.

Fashion Outlets Las Vegas is a circular building connected to the Primm Valley Resort & Casino. Designed like a cartoon city, complete with car kiosks and streetlights, the 360,000-square-foot mall is anchored by famous-name outlet stores. Take time to see Bonnie and Clyde's shot-up car (yep, the real one) and the last shirt (bloodstains and all) worn by Clyde. This minimuseum is up the escalators, just before you enter the casino. Catch a $13 round-trip shuttle at New York–New York or MGM Grand. Shuttles leave six times each day (three times each from MGM and New York–New York); the first shuttle leaves the New York–New

York at 9:15 AM and the last leaves the MGM at 3:15 PM. ⊠ *I–15, at Exit 1* ☎ *702/874–1400, 888/424–6898 shuttle reservations* 🖷 *702/874–1560* ⊕ *www.fashionoutletlasvegas.com* ☉ *Daily 10 AM–8 PM.*

Once you've shopped, you can drop, literally, by riding one of **Buffalo Bill's Rides.** The Desperado roller coaster promises G-forces of 4.0, near-zero gravity, and speeds of 90 mph in less than three minutes—two steep drops add even more thrills. Passengers board inside Buffalo Bill's Casino. Buffalo Bill's also has the Venture Canyon Log Flume Ride (go splash, then travel the indoor river), the Turbo Drop (a 170-foot drop at 45 mph), a virtual roller coaster, and motion-simulator rides. ⊠ *31900 Las Vegas Blvd. S* ☎ *702/386–7867 or 800/386–7867* ⊕ *www. primadonna.com* ✍ *Rides $3–$6; half-day wristband $22, all-day wristband $30* ☉ *Mon. through Thurs. 11–9 PM, Fri. 11 AM–midnight, Sat. 10 AM–midnight, Sun. 10 AM–10 PM* 🖃 *D, MC, V.*

off the beaten path

SANDY VALLEY – Maybe your cowboy hat looked out of place in the fine new joints of Vegas, but in Sandy Valley it's a given. Here you can don the hat, climb onto a trusty steed, and round up some cows in the wide open mesquite scrub of a classic mountain-ringed, big-sky Nevada valley. Then eat campfire grub out under the stars and curl up in a tepee. Or, stay in the quirky, Victorian-decorated covered wagon for a romantic evening. ⊠ *Sandy Valley Rd., 6 mi west of Jean on Rte. 161, 89019* ☎ *702/631–0463 or 877/726–3998* ⊕ *www.sandyvalleyranch.com.*

Where to Stay

¢–$$ 🏨 **Gold Strike Hotel and Gambling Hall.** The Gold Strike has spacious rooms—with either two queen-size beds or one king and a pull-out sofa—that look out over the Nevada desert. On the inside, the casino has a predictable Old West design, but the weird white, red, and bright-blue facade outside is at odds with the brownish desert hues. ⊠ *1 Main St., Jean 89019* ☎ *702/477–5000 or 800/634–1359* 🖷 *702/671–1655* ⊕ *www.stopatjean.com* ☝ *812 rooms* ♨ *3 restaurants, cable TV, pool, lounge, casino, no-smoking rooms* 🖃 *AE, D, DC, MC, V.*

¢–$ 🏨 **Buffalo Bill's Hotel and Casino.** The towering barn-red structure encircled by a roller coaster is one of the three hotel-casinos right at the California border. Owned by the parent company of MGM–Mirage, the trio are a little world all their own, connected by a free monorail. To get people out here from Las Vegas, Bill's has to make it worth their while, and does so with inexpensive rooms and food and coupon funbooks thrown in. Rooms feel like the inside of a cabin, with log wallpaper and rustic furniture, and have great views of the surrounding mountains. Check out the buffalo-shape swimming pool. ⊠ *I–15 at state line, Primm 89019* ☎ *702/386–7867 or 800/386–7867* 🖷 *702/679–5424* ⊕ *www.primadonna.com* ☝ *1,242 rooms* ♨ *4 restaurants, cable TV, pool, spa, casino, cinema, showroom, meeting room, no-smoking floors* 🖃 *AE, D, DC, MC, V.*

¢–$ 🏨 **Nevada Landing Hotel and Casino.** Right across I–15 from the Gold Strike (on the westbound side), Nevada Landing closely resembles its neighbor, except it's smaller and looks like a stranded riverboat. Both the Gold Strike and Nevada Landing are owned by Mandalay Resort Group. ⊠ *2 Goodsprings Rd., Jean 89019* ☎ *702/387–5000 or 800/ 628–6682* 🖷 *702/671–1407* ⊕ *www.primadonna.com* 🛏 *303 rooms* ♨ *3 restaurants, pool, lounge, casino, no-smoking rooms* ▭ *AE, D, DC, MC, V.*

¢–$ 🏨 **Primm Valley Resort & Casino.** Faux ivy, latticework, and the green-and-white interior approximate a country-club theme. Top-notch lounge entertainment complements Buffalo Bill's 6,000-seat Star of the Desert Arena and Whiskey Pete's 700-seat showroom. The outlet mall is accessible from the resort's casino. ⊠ *I–15 at state line, Primm 89019* ☎ *702/386– 7867 or 800/386–7867* 🖷 *702/679–5424* ⊕ *www.primadonna.com* 🛏 *624 rooms* ♨ *3 restaurants, cable TV, pool, piano bar, casino, convention center, no-smoking floors* ▭ *AE, D, DC, MC, V.*

¢ 🏨 **Whiskey Pete's Casino and Hotel.** It's a noisy, surprisingly busy, state-line hotel-casino, with lounge bands, cheap food, and large, inexpensive rooms with king-size beds. When you're headed for Las Vegas from the west, an overnight stop at Pete's will leave you with just a short drive to those lavish Vegas breakfast buffets. ⊠ *I–15 at state line, Primm 89019* ☎ *702/386–7867 or 800/386–7867* 🖷 *702/679–5424* ⊕ *www. primadonna.com* 🛏 *777 rooms* ♨ *3 restaurants, cable TV, pool, casino, showroom, no-smoking floors* ▭ *AE, D, DC, MC, V.*

DEATH VALLEY

At 3.4 million acres, **Death Valley National Park** is the largest national park outside Alaska. The topography of Death Valley is a mini geology lesson. Two hundred million years ago, seas covered the area, depositing layers of sediment and fossils. Between 35 million and 5 million years ago, faults in the Earth's crust and volcanic activity pushed and folded the ground, causing mountain ranges to rise and the valley floor to drop. The valley was then filled periodically by lakes, which eroded the surrounding rocks into fantastic formations and deposited the salts that now cover the floor of the basin. Today the area has 14 square mi of sand dunes, 200 square mi of crusty salt flats, hills, 11,000-foot-high mountains, and canyons of many colors. The lowest point in the Western Hemisphere is here. There are more than 1,000 species of plants and trees—21 of which are unique to the valley, such as the yellow Panamint daisy and the blue-flowered Death Valley sage. Distances are deceiving, and mirages trick your eyes so that seeming bodies of water appear, shift, expand, and then disappear as you drive by. As with any desert travel, you should always carry plenty of water, sunblock, a hat, a mirror, and other potentially lifesaving items. In summer avoid extended activity during the day. ⊕ *www.nps.gov/deva* 🎫 *$10 per vehicle, $5 per motorcycle; valid for 7 consecutive days from purchase date* ⊙ *Daily.*

Lodging facilities at Furnace Creek Ranch and Inn and Stovepipe Wells Village are managed by a master concessionaire, **Xanterra Parks and Resorts.** During the cooler period, October through May, accommodations sell out early, especially over holiday weekends. ⊠ *14001 E. Illiff, Suite*

600, Aurora, CO 80014 ☎ *303/297–2757 or 888/297–2757* 🖷 *303/ 297–3175* ⊕ *www.xanterra.com.*

en route

Rhyolite. Shorty Harris and Ed Cross struck gold here in 1904, and the fever grew a town of close to 10,000 people. But by 1919, in typical boom-bust fashion, it had all blown away. The best of what's left includes Tom Kelly's bottle house, built in 1906 almost entirely of glass bottles and mortar, and the train depot. You also find the remains of a school, jail, general store, and bank. The town, managed by the Bureau of Land Management, is 4 mi southwest of Beatty off Route 374.

Before you reach Rhyolite, you pass **Goldwell Open Air Museum** (☎ 702/498–7057 ⊕ www.goldwellmuseum.org), an eerie assortment of life-size ghostly sculptures. In 1984, Belgian artist Albert Szukalski created *The Last Supper,* a series of plaster-and-fiberglass human figures representing Christ and his disciples. A similar ghostly white figure on a separate platform hovers over a real, old-fashioned bicycle. When Szukalski died in 2000, friends created the nonprofit museum, and the site is slowly becoming a bizarre little hub of arts and culture amid the lonely expanse of the Amargosa Desert as more artists contribute to the collection.

Before descending into Death Valley, stop at **Beatty Museum** for exhibits on the old Bullfrog Mining District. Shelves are laden with old radios and Victrolas, war radios, and "troubleshooter" manuals, and one exhibit details the Department of Energy's plans to ship and store nuclear waste nearby. ✉ *417 Main St., Beatty* ☎ *775/553– 2303* ⊕ *www.beattymuseum.com* ☉ *Daily 10–2.*

Numbers in the margin correspond to numbers on the Death Valley map.

Stovepipe Wells Village

148 mi northwest of Las Vegas; take U.S. 95 north 113 mi to Beatty, then take Rte. 374 SW for 27 mi to Rte. 190 W 8 mi.

⓬ Stovepipe Wells Village was the first resort in Death Valley. The tiny outpost, which dates back to 1926, takes its name from the stovepipe that early prospectors left to indicate that they'd found water. The area contains a motel, a restaurant, a grocery store with unleaded fuel, a landing strip, and campgrounds. Minutes away are sand dunes (familiar perhaps from their role in the *Star Wars* films); Devil's Corn Field; Salt Creek, a brackish year-round flow from an underground spring that provides a breeding ground for the endangered pupfish; and colorful Mosaic Canyon.

Where to Stay & Eat

$ ✕🖫 **Stovepipe Wells Village.** An aircraft landing strip is an unusual touch for a motel, as is a heated mineral pool, but the rest is standard. Still, this is the best lodging bargain inside the park, offering pleasant rooms at a reasonable rate, as well as a campground and RV park. The

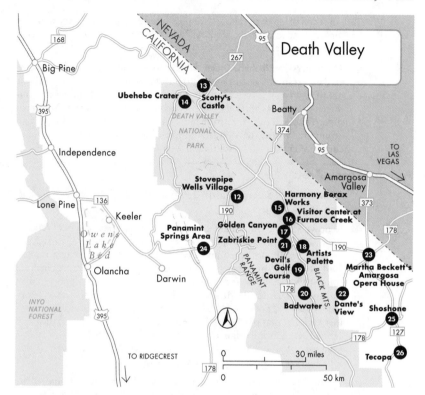

Old West–style Toll Road Restaurant ($) serves steaks, prime rib, and salmon. ⊠ *Rte. 190, Death Valley National Park, 92328* ☎ *303/297–2757 or 888/297–2757* 🖷 *303/297–3175* ⊕ *www.xanterra.com* 🖘 *83 rooms* ♿ *Restaurant, cable TV, tennis courts, pool, bar, shop, Internet* ▭ *AE, D, MC, V.*

Scotty's Castle Area

46 mi north of Stovepipe Wells Village; head east on Rte. 190, then north at signs for castle.

🔟 Scotty's Castle is an odd apparition rising out of a canyon. This $2.5-mil-
Fodor'sChoice lion Moorish mansion, begun in 1924 and never completed, is named after
★ Walter Scott, better known as Death Valley Scotty. An ex-cowboy, prospec-
tor, and performer in Buffalo Bill's Wild West Show, Scotty always told
people the castle was his, financed by gold from a secret mine. That secret mine was, in fact, a Chicago millionaire named Albert Johnson, who
was advised by doctors to spend time in a warm, dry climate. The house,
which functioned for a while as a hotel—guests included Bette Davis and
Norman Rockwell—contains works of art, imported carpets, handmade
European furniture, and a tremendous pipe organ. Costumed rangers portray life at the castle in 1939. Fifty-minute tours are conducted frequently,

but waits of up to two hours are possible. To avoid delays, try to arrive for the first tour of the day. ☎ 760/786–2392 ⊕ *www.nps.gov/deva/ pphtml/facilities.html* ⊒ *$9* ⊗ *Grounds daily 7–6, tours daily 9–5.*

⓮ The impressive **Ubehebe Crater,** 500 feet deep and ½ mi across, was created as a result of violent underground steam and gas explosions about 3,000 years ago; its volcanic ash spreads out over most of the area, and the cinders are as thick as 150 feet around the crater's rim. You have superb views of the valley from here, and you can take a fairly easy hike around the rim at the west side to Little Hebe Crater, one of a smaller cluster of craters to the south and west.

Furnace Creek Area

54 mi south of Scotty's Castle, 25 mi southeast of Stovepipe Wells Village on Rte. 190.

⓯ Renowned mule teams hauled borax from the **Harmony Borax Works** to the railroad town of Mojave, 165 mi away, and were truly a sight to behold: 20 mules hitched up to two massive wagons, each carrying a load of 10 tons of borax through burning desert. The teams plied the route between 1884 and 1907, when the railroad finally arrived in Zabriskie. The **Borax Museum** (⊠ Rte. 190, 2 mi south of the borax works ⊒ Free) houses original mining machinery and historical displays in a building that once served as a boardinghouse for miners; the adjacent structure is the original mule-team barn. The works are open anytime for self-guided tours. ⊠ *Harmony Borax Works Rd., west of Rte. 190* ⊒ *Free* ⊗ *Borax Museum daily 8–4.*

Exhibits on the desert, trail maps, and brochures can be found at the
⓰ **Visitor Center at Furnace Creek.** ⊠ *Rte. 190* ☎ *760/786–3200* ⊕ *www. nps.gov/deva* ⊗ *Daily 8–6.*

⓱ A mild hike into the spacious **Golden Canyon** landform leads to glowing yellow-and-orange rock walls. Farther up the canyon, you encounter a colorful formation called Red Cathedral. ⊠ *Badwater Rd., 3 mi south of Furnace Creek; turn left into parking lot.*

⓲ The **Artists Palette,** named for the brilliant array of pigments in the rocks, mirrors similar colors spread across a larger scale elsewhere in Death Valley. Artists Drive, the approach to the area, heads one-way north off Badwater Road, so if you're visiting Badwater it's more efficient to come here on the way back. The drive winds through foothills composed of colorful sedimentary and volcanic rocks: the reds, pinks, and yellows come from iron salts; the green is decomposing mica; and the purple is manganese. ⊠ *8 mi north of Badwater, Badwater Rd. to Artists Dr.; 10 mi south of Furnace Creek, Rte. 190 to Badwater Rd. to Artists Dr.*

Looking like a white-capped sea of brown mud frozen into heaved-up
⓳ broken waves, **Devil's Golf Course** is solid rock salt poking skyward. You don't want to venture off the road because the jagged spires have been known to shred tennis shoes and produce severe scrapes and broken bones should you take a tumble. ⊠ *Badwater Rd., 5 mi north of Badwater, 14 mi south of visitor center at Furnace Creek.*

② As you approach **Badwater,** you see a shallow pool lying against an expanse of desolate salt flats—a sharp contrast to the expansive canyons and elevation not too far away. Legend has it that one of the early surveyors saw that his mule wouldn't drink from the pool and noted "badwater" on his map. The water contains mostly sodium chloride and is saltier than the sea. But tiny pupfish live there, and a new boardwalk with interpretive signs takes you within peering distance of them. Badwater is the lowest spot in the Western Hemisphere—282 feet below sea level—and also one of the hottest. On the rock face behind the road, a marker indicates sea level. ⊠ *Badwater Rd., 19 mi south of visitor center at Furnace Creek.*

② **Zabriskie Point** is one of Death Valley National Park's most scenic spots. Not particularly high—only about 710 feet—it overlooks a striking badlands panorama with wrinkled, multicolor hills. Film buffs of a certain vintage may recognize it (or at least its name) from the film *Zabriskie Point.* ⊠ *Rte. 190, 5 mi south of Furnace Creek.*

② From atop **Dante's View,** more than 5,000 feet up in the Black Mountains, you can see most of the valley's 110-mi expanse. The oasis of Furnace Creek is a green spot to the north. The view up and down is equally astounding: the tiny blackish patch far below is Badwater; on the western horizon is Mt. Whitney, the highest spot in the continental United States at 14,494 feet. ⊠ *Dante's View Rd. off Rte. 190, 21 mi south of Zabriskie Point.*

② **Marta Beckett's Amargosa Opera House** is an unexpected pleasure in an unlikely place. Marta Beckett is an artist and dancer from New York who first saw the town of Amargosa while on tour in 1964. Three years later she impulsively bought a boarded-up theater amid a complex of run-down Spanish colonial buildings, and began performing there in 1968. To make up for the sparse attendance in the early days, Becket painted an audience, turning the walls and the ceiling of the theater into a trompe l'oeil masterpiece. Today the hamlet's population is still in single digits (cats outnumber people here), but it swells when cars, motor homes, and buses roll in to catch the show. Becket often performs her blend of classical ballet, mime, and 19th-century melodrama to sellout crowds, so advance reservations are strongly encouraged. After the show you can meet her in the adjacent art gallery. ⊠ *Rte. 127, Death Valley Junction, 92328* ☎ *760/852–4441* 🖷 *760/852–4138* ⊕ *www.amargosa-opera-house. com* 🎫 *$15* ⊙ *Performances Oct.–May, Sat. 7:45 PM* ▭ *MC, V.*

Where to Stay & Eat

★ **$$$$** ✕🏨 **Furnace Creek Inn.** The 1927 early mission-style inn, with adobe brick walls accented by stone, was built into the side of a hill amidst a desert oasis, where palm trees tower over a hot spring-fed pool and a cascading creek. The pool tiles make a large palm-frond pattern, and you can swim until 11 PM under bright stars framed by real palm fronds, while mesquite burns in two outdoor fireplaces and coyotes yip-yip in the desert. The hallways of the inn, leading to exquisite rooms, are hung with oil portraits of Death Valley 49ers painted by Leslie B. DeMille. Rooms have coffeemakers and bathrobes. **The Inn Dining Room** ($$–$$$) serves elegant, and sometimes unusual, fare (try the rattlesnake) and has creamy adobe walls, two fireplaces, grand wood-frame images of Death Valley on the walls, and many windows with views of the looming Panamint Mountains. ⊠ *Rte. 190 (Box 1), Death Valley National Park, 92328* ☎ *760/786–2345, 303/297–2757 reservations* 🖷 *760/786–2514* ⊕ *www.furnacecreekresort.com* ⮧ *66 rooms* ⚘ *Restaurant, cable TV, 4 tennis courts, pool, lounge, meeting room, no-smoking rooms* ⊟ *AE, DC, MC, V* ⊘ *Closed mid-May to mid-Oct.* ☞ *Energy surcharge.*

$–$$$ ⊡ **Furnace Creek Ranch.** Originally the crew headquarters for a borax company, the ranch has four two-story buildings with motel-style rooms. The adjacent Furnace Creek golf course, 214 feet below sea level, guarantees the "lowest" round of golf. The general store sells supplies and gifts, and the visitor center is a short walk away. ⊠ *Rte. 190 (Box 1), Death Valley National Park, 92328* ☎ *760/786–2345, 303/297–2757 reservations* ⮧ *224 rooms* ⚘ *Restaurant, coffee shop, cable TV, 18-hole golf course, 2 tennis courts, pool, basketball, horseback riding, bar, shop, playground, meeting room* ⊟ *AE, DC, MC, V* ☞ *Energy surcharge.*

Panamint Springs Area

㉔ *31 mi west of Stovepipe Wells Village on Rte. 190, 48 mi east of Lone Pine, CA on U.S. 395.*

Added to the park in 1994, this remote spot is an ideal destination for backcountry enthusiasts, especially those with high-clearance or four-wheel-drive vehicles. To the east and south on Emigrant Canyon Road is Skidoo, the remains of a once-thriving mining town, and Wildrose Charcoal Kilns, which look like giant rock beehives and produced fuel from 1877 to 1878 for silver ore processing. To the west lies Father Crowley Point, a lava landscape that looks out on the colorful Rainbow Canyon. Just outside town is Darwin Falls, a rare water hole in the desert.

Where to Stay & Eat

$–$$ ✕⊡ **Panamint Springs Resort.** Though inside the park, this privately owned property is not associated with the National Park Service. It overlooks the nearby awesome geological formations as well as the Panamint Valley Sand Dunes. A campground and RV park are available. Summertime barbecues are served outdoors on the porch, which has a spectacular view of Panamint Valley. ⊠ *Rte. 190 (Box 395), Ridgecrest, CA 93556* ☎ *775/482–7680* 🖷 *775/482–7682* ⊕ *www.deathvalley.com/reserve/reserve.shtml* ⮧ *14 rooms, 1 cottage* ⚘ *Restaurant, cable TV, bar, shop, some pets allowed* ⊟ *MC, V.*

Shoshone–Tecopa Area

㉕–㉖ *Shoshone is 28 mi south of Death Valley Junction on Rte. 127 and 80 mi west of Las Vegas via Pahrump (Rte. 160 east to Rte. 372 to Rte. 178). Tecopa is 13 mi south of Shoshone via Rte. 127.*

Both fresh and mineral water have drawn people here for thousands of years. Paiute and Shoshone Indians lived here (the name "Tecopa" comes from Chief Tecopet, who died in 1905). Early Europeans came along the Old Spanish Trail that linked water holes from Santa Fe, New Mexico, to California. Horse thieves stirred up the dust awhile. The gold rush and, later, borax discoveries brought miners, and the Tonopah & Tidewater Railroad followed. Today the railroad's but a memory and mining's mostly gone bust, but the hot springs are still drawing people. There are a few year-round residents and many seasonal "snowbirds" who motor across the nation in their RVs year after year to spend the winter here. Shoshone has a general store, two cafés, and a motel. Tecopa has several hot-spring resorts. The area is also the southern gateway to Death Valley.

The displays at the **Shoshone Museum and Death Valley Chamber of Commerce** include artifacts of the region's mining and railroad history, the bones of fossilized mammoths discovered nearby, and stories of Death Valley women—including Susan Sorrells, who inherited the town. ⊠ *Rte. 127, Shoshone, CA 92384* ☎ *760/852–4414* ✉ *Donation* ⊙ *Wed.–Sun. 8–4.*

The water at the **Inyo County Tecopa Hot Springs & Campground** is 104°F, and regulars declare its quality is second only to the waters of Baden-Baden along the France-Germany border. Nudity is required for cleanliness, and you're likely to be admonished by a regular soaker if you don't shower first. Baths are separate for men and women. The county has 250 RV spaces nearby, with some electrical hookups. You can camp up to six months. ⊠ *Rte. 127, Tecopa, CA 92389* ✉ *Free* ☎ *760/852–4264.*

off the beaten path

CHINA RANCH DATE FARM – The story goes that in the 1890s a Chinese man, possibly named Ah Foo, raised hogs, chickens, and veggies down in this creek-fed, stark-hilled canyon to feed local miners. In the 1920s, current owner Brian Brown's great aunt and uncle started to convert the 218-acre ranch to date palms. By 1989 Brown and his wife Bonnie were planting dozens more varieties of the trees. Today there's a huge orchard (with colorful dresses strung on the trees to scare off birds) and a shop selling dates, fresh date-nut bread, decadent date shakes, and handmade gifts. The private farm is surrounded by public land and wilderness. Hiking trails take you along the old railroad bed, or up onto the spare mud hills, or deep into another cliff-banked canyon where the Amargosa River intermittently flows and creates a lush strip of life. ⊠ *Box 61, off Old Spanish Trail Hwy., Tecopa, CA, Take Furnace Creek Rd. off old Spanish Trail Hwy.* ☎ *760/852–4415* ⊕ *www.chinaranch.com* ⊙ *Daily 9–5.*

Interior designer Cynthia Kienitz has turned this 1920s cottage at China Ranch into a colorful B&B, which sits amid a grove of big cottonwoods adjacent to the date farm. Here, you're on Tecopa time—the opposite of Las Vegas. There's one clock, one phone, no TV, no e-mail, and little tolerance for cell-phone addicts. You might sit all day on the lawn and watch the light change the colors of the bare, dry, mud-and-crag hills, now and then consuming something delicious cooked up inside the ranch house. Here, conversation becomes an art, and you might philosophize late into the night with fellow guests or locals. You're likely to run into authors, artists, scientists, or movie makers (*The Sum of All Fears* was partly filmed here). ✉ *Box 14, Tecopa, CA 92389* ☎ *760/852–4358* ⊕ *www. ranchhouseinn.com* ➟ *2 rooms without bath, 1 suite* ☒ *$98* ⚑ *No room phones, no room TVs, gift shop* ⊟ *D, MC, V* ⦿*CP* ⊙ *Closed June–mid-Sept.*

Where to Stay & Eat

$ ✕ **Cafe C'est Si Bon.** Step into David Washum's fanciful cafe in the middle of the desert for espresso, crepes, vegetarian gourmet food, cheeses, and fresh croissants and other breads. The tiny, airy outpost, done in white, minty green, and rose tones, is also the only solar Internet cafe for miles. Odd or dainty sculptures lurk and dangle everywhere, and pretty plants and rocks fill the garden and porch. ✉ *Rte. 127 (Box 37), Shoshone, CA* ☎ *760/852–4307* ⊙ *Closed Tues. No dinner.*

$ ✕ **Crowbar Cafe & Saloon.** The restaurant dates to the 1930s, is distinctly Western, and serves hearty meals, including breakfast. The train-rail footrest is adorned with the names of local mines, which were welded on by local iron artist Jill "Lady Buffalo" Thacker. ✉ *Rte. 127, Shoshone, CA* ☎ *760/852–4180.*

$$ ☷ **Delight's Hot Springs Resort.** At first the rows of tiny cabins and resident trailers are rather plain looking, but Delight's lives up to its name as soon as you step into one of the baths, which sparkle with clean, 104°F water. With blue sky or stars overhead, you may think you're in your own private paradise. You can buy a day pass for just the tubs ($12), or rent a cabin with the soak included. ✉ *368 Tecopa Hot Springs Rd., Tecopa, CA 92389* ☎*760/852–4343 or 800/928–8808* ⎙*760/852–4301* ⊕*www.delightshotspringsresort.com* ➟*6 cabins, 3 motel units* ⚑ *Kitchenettes, refrigerators, outdoor hot tubs, massage, hiking, recreation room, laundry facilities, free parking, some pets allowed (fee); no kids, no room phones, no room TVs, no smoking* ⊟ *AE, D, MC, V* ⊙ *Tubs daily 10–8.*

$ ☷ **Shoshone Inn.** Simple, modest, and comfortable, this motel was built in 1956 and has a warm, spring-fed pool. ✉ *Box 67, Rte. 127, Shoshone, CA 92384* ☎ *760/852–4335* ➟ *16 rooms* ⚑ *Some kitchenettes, cable TV, pool, laundry facilities, no-smoking rooms* ⊟ *AE, D, MC, V.*

LINCOLN COUNTY

Lincoln County, with U.S. 93–Great Basin Highway as its transportation spine, has been long overlooked as a Vegas getaway. No glaring neon or rush-hour freeway traffic here; rather, an occasional dim streetlight in one of the county's four tiny communities breaks up the vast star-studded sky or a sputtering hay-baler negotiates the lonely asphalt ribbon.

Lincoln County encompasses ghost towns and near-ghost towns, national wildlife refuges, large ranches, and abundant water. The five state parks in the area are ideal destinations for just plain relaxing or for more strenuous activities like boating, fishing, hiking, and mountain biking.

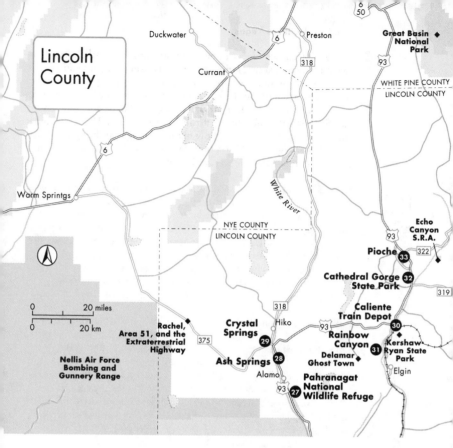

Plan your trip and make reservations well in advance; the entire county is "tourist-challenged," meaning that it has less than 100 hotel–motel rooms and less than a half-dozen restaurants. Contact the Bureau of Land Management for a map of off-highway travel. And be sure to bring a coat or sweater; it can get chilly, since the elevation varies from 3,200 to 6,200 feet.

Pahranagat Valley

92 mi from Las Vegas via I–15 to U.S. 93.

Desert vistas of creosote bushes and towering mountain ranges line the first 65 mi of this drive out of Las Vegas. But after cruising through a narrow volcanic rock pass, the world changes. Underground aquifers turn the landscape from stark to lush.

★ ㉗ The 5,380-acre **Pahranagat National Wildlife Refuge** is a chain of three lakes, marshes, and meadows that provides a convenient stop on the Pacific Flyway for ducks, herons, egrets, eagles, and other species. The Upper Lake is the most accessible, with campsites, picnic tables, and observation points. ⊠ *Box 510, Alamo 89001* ☎ *775/725–3417* ✉ *Free.*

28 Two geological wonders can be seen north of Alamo **Ash Springs,** formerly a famous spa site, is now fenced and abandoned, but you can still get a glimpse of an active hot spring across from the gas station–convenience store. Early in the morning, when the air is cool, steam rises **29** from the bubbling cauldron. **Crystal Springs** is a large cool-water spring that fills several ponds before it runs off to the east. This oasis under tall cottonwood trees shows how natural springs can bring the desert to life. It's easily accessible on foot from the junction of Routes 375 and 318, less than a half-mile west of U.S. 93.

off the
beaten
path

AREA 51 – Known as Dreamland, this is a tiny nub in the northeast corner of the vast 3.5-million-acre Nellis Air Force Base. According to sketchy and unconfirmed media reports, Area 51 is a super-secret military installation where the Air Force has tested top-secret aircraft (such as the U-2 spy plane and the Stealth bomber). Some people also believe the government stores and does research on UFOs and even collects and studies extraterrestrial beings here. It's illegal to approach the installation; military police have complete authority (including deadly force, if necessary) to prevent intrusions.

Route 375, a 98-mi road that runs through southeast Nevada from U.S. 93 to U.S. 6, was named the "Extraterrestrial Highway" in 1995. Signs along the road promote the eye-catching label—though they are frequently stolen. A desolate 36 mi from the junction of U.S. 93 is the tiny town of Rachel, about as close as you can get to Area 51. Today, thanks to its proximity to the secret area (and to the mysterious "Black Box" where the installation's mail was supposedly delivered), Rachel is a pilgrimage site for UFO enthusiasts from around the world. ⊠ *143 mi northeast of Las Vegas, west on Rte. 375.*

Little A'Le'Inn. The main gathering spot in Rachel has photos of UFOs on the walls and an Alien Burger on the restaurant menu. Its rooms have TVs, but there's no TV reception; you can rent videos, including UFO and Area 51 documentaries, from the inn's library. ⊠ *Rte. 375, HCR 61, Box 45, Rachel 89001* ☎ *775/729–2515* 🖨 *775/729–2551* ⊕ *rachel.dreamlandresort.com.*

Where to Stay

¢–$ 🛏 **Alamo Meadow Lane Motel.** You get basic prices for basic rooms here. Alamo Meadow is the only place to stay on the drive from Vegas to Caliente, and the only dining in town is at Del Pueblo Restaurant across the highway. ⊠ *300 N. Rte. 93, Alamo 89001* ☎ *775/725–3371 or 888/ 740–8009* 🖨 *775/725–3372* 🛏 *15 rooms* ♿ *Cable TV, some pets allowed, no-smoking room* 🖃 *AE, D, MC, V.*

Caliente

149 mi from Las Vegas via I–15 to U.S. 93.

Caliente used to be an important layover stop for water-thirsty steam locomotives making the trek through the steep, narrow canyons surrounding the town. Today, Lincoln County's largest community has 1,100 residents and serves as a hub for visitors striking off in all directions to see the five nearby state parks, the county seat of Pioche, or the ghost town of Delamar. And, as the name implies, it's hot here—not because of oppressive temperatures, but from the hot springs where townsfolk can relax.

㉚ The **Caliente Train Depot,** built in 1923, is a classic Mission-style station. Having outlived its usefulness as a depot, it now houses the Caliente Chamber of Commerce, the library, and an art gallery. ✉ *101 Depot St.* ☎ *775/726-3129* ⊕ *www.lincolncountynevada.com.*

Head north on Spring Street to **Company Row.** The railroad company built these 18 homes in 1905 for workers manning this major refueling site for steam locomotives. The historic buildings are still in use today as privately owned homes.

㉛ On the south side of town, Route 317 leads to the magnificent **Rainbow Canyon.** You pass between towering cliffs of red and orange, gold, and even deep green, where spring water drips from cracks in some places. Ancient petroglyphs have been pecked into some of the rocks. The bank-robbing duo of Butch Cassidy and the Sundance Kid hid out from the law deep inside some of the side canyons. You can also catch a close-up glimpse of a long diesel train winding its way through the chasm on the railroad's mainline. **Kershaw-Ryan State Park,** which is part of Rainbow Canyon, is a destination for picnickers and hikers. ✉ *HC 64 Box 3, Caliente 89008* ☎ *775/726-3564* ⊕ *www.parks.nv.gov* 🎫 *$4 per vehicle.*

㉜ Erosion has shaped the bentonite clay of **Cathedral Gorge State Park** into odd formations, with twisting, tall, damp corridors of solidified mud leading to caves, more passageways, and sudden high perches. Step inside one of the curtains of wavy mud to escape the hot sun. **Miller Point Overlook** is about 2 mi north of the park's entrance. The overlook reveals part of the ancient lake bed. Eagle View Trail, which starts at the overlook, is one of several park trails leading hikers closer to the formations. The visitor center for Cathedral Gorge is the regional center for all state parks in Lincoln County. ✉ *Box 176, Panaca 89042* ☎ *775/728-4460* ⊕ *www.parks.nv.gov* 🎫 *$4 per vehicle.*

off the beaten path

DELAMAR GHOST TOWN – Some dilapidated buildings and rusted-out equipment are all that remain of this former silver-mining town that had a population of 3,000 around 1900. The so-called "Delamar Dust" inhaled by miners was actually silica dust, and the town earned a reputation as the "Maker of Widows" from the resulting deaths. Four-wheel-drive vehicles are recommended for the 16-mi jaunt over the bumpy gravel and rock road that's chopped with several dry washes along the way. ✉ *South off U.S. 93, 16 mi west of Caliente* ⊕ *www.ghosttowns.com/states/nv/delamar.html* ☞ *No services.*

Where to Stay & Eat

¢–$ ✕ **Brandin' Iron Restaurant.** Two rooms are separated by an island bar in this rustic downtown café on the south side of the railroad tracks. It's open all day, but go at dinner, when you can have twice-baked potatoes. ✉ *190 Clover St., Caliente 89008* ☎ *775/726–3164* 🖃 *AE, D, MC, V.*

¢–$ ✕ **Knotty Pine Restaurant.** The walls are done in tongue-and-groove knotty pine at this eatery on the north side of the tracks. It's a good place to eat breakfast (try the excellent pancakes) and watch the train chug by, cutting the town in half. ✉ *690 Front St., Caliente 89008* ☎ *775/ 726–3767* 🖃 *AE, D, MC, V.*

¢–$ 🏨 **Caliente Hot Springs Motel.** The rooms may be usual, but what's unusual is the bathhouse with natural hot springs to soothe tightened, car-cramped muscles. The bathhouse is open daily from 8 AM to 10 PM. For those willing to spend a little extra, five rooms have mineral baths inside. Access to the motel is off a side street (look for the directional sign); the motel is set back a distance from the highway and nestled against the mountain to the rear. ✉ *451 N. Spring St., Caliente 89008* ☎ *775/726–3777* 🛏 *17 rooms* ⚷ *Cable TV, some pets allowed* 🖃 *AE, D, MC, V.*

¢ 🏨 **Shady Motel.** The newest, largest, and tallest motel in Lincoln County has twin two-story buildings on a modern-looking complex. They face each other and not the highway, giving visitors peace and quiet throughout the night. ✉ *450 Front St., Caliente 89008* ☎ *775/726–3107* 🛏 *28 rooms* ⚷ *Cable TV, some pets allowed, no-smoking rooms* 🖃 *AE, D, MC, V.*

Pioche

➌ *174 mi from Las Vegas via I–15 to U.S. 93.*

Fodor'sChoice
★

A mining town dating back to the 1870s, Pioche once had the reputation of being more recklessly lawless than the notorious Western towns of Tombstone, Bodie, and Dodge City. According to legend, more than 70 gunfight victims were buried in Boot Hill cemetery before anyone who had died of natural causes found a place there. Relics of the boom-and-bust mining periods—from silver mining in the late 1800s to zinc and lead in the 1940s—are more prevalent on the streets today than gunplay, however. At 6,064 feet, walking around hilly Pioche can take your breath away—literally. Walk slowly and enjoy the sights.

The **Lincoln County Museum** on Main Street houses thousands of rock specimens, photos, and artifacts. The antique X-ray machine, with its long, pointy "arm," looks like something out of a Ray Bradbury novel. ✉ *69 Main St., Pioche 89043* ☎ *775/962–5207* 🎟 *Free* ☉ *Daily 10–4.*

The **Million Dollar Courthouse** is so named because that's how much it cost to pay off the building's debt of $16,400 over the course of 66 years. The 1st floor has restored offices, and the 2nd floor is the original courtroom with fancy old light fixtures, ornate woodwork, and a molded-tin ceiling. The only ones holding court these days are life-size dummies dressed in old-timey garb representing the judge, jury, attorneys for the prosecution and defense and, of course, the suspect. Outside the courtroom is the jail, with tiny holding cells made of stone and iron. ✉ *Lacour St.* ☎ *702/962–5182* 🎟 *Donations* ☉ *Mid–Apr.–mid Oct., daily 11–4.*

There are several old buildings along Main Street that you can view from the outside. The **Mountain View Hotel** is a three-story wooden structure built in 1895. Former president Herbert Hoover, himself a mining engineer, stayed here on a visit to the town.Other buildings include the **Old Commercial Building and Fire Hall, Thompson Opera House,** and the **Gem Theater.** On the outskirts of town are the **Glory Holes and Pioche Aerial Tramway,** which hauled ore by gravity from the Treasure Hill mine to the mill in the valley below, and **Boot Hill,** where graves and carved wooden headstones recall the past.

The 65-acre reservoir at **Echo Canyon State Park** is a favorite for fishing and boating. The park has a campground and picnic area. Jackrabbits, bobcats, coyotes, hawks, eagles, and even, on occasion, tundra swans call this lake-centered haven of Great Basin scrub, piñon, and juniper home. ⊠ *12 mi east of Pioche via Rtes. 322 and 323* ☎ *775/962–5103* ⊕ *www.parks.nv.gov* 🖾 *$4 per vehicle.*

off the beaten path

GREAT BASIN NATIONAL PARK – The state's last remaining glacier is in a scooped-out rock bowl just below the tip of the second highest peak in Nevada, the 13,063-foot-high Wheeler Peak in White Pine County. Underground, water dripping through limestone over the ages has created the fantastic and lovely configurations which make up Lehman Caves. It's one of the most remote and diverse national parks in the nation, taking you from sagebrush steppes up into cool forests with creeks, and on up through the high groves of 5,000-year-old bristlecone pine trees until you ascend beyond the tree line. A jacket and treaded walking shoes are recommended for all adventures here—it can snow in July—and, inside the caves, the "weather" is a constant 50°F and 90% humidity. Take U.S. 93 81 mi north to the U.S. 6–50 junction, turn right (east) and go 28 mi to the Route 487 turnoff. Turn right (south) and go 5 mi to Baker, where you turn right (west) on Route 488 into the park. ⊠ *Rte. 488, Baker 89311* ☎ *775/234–7331* ⊕ *www.nps.gov/grba* 🖾 *Free* ⊙ *Visitor center June–Aug., daily 7:30–6; Sept.–May, daily 8:30–5; Lehman Cave tours daily, call 775/234–7331 Ext. 242 for departure times.*

Where to Stay & Eat

¢–$ ✕ **Silver Cafe.** The building dates back to 1907, and the restaurant has been in operation for nearly as long. Owners Sal and Barbi Cammarano serve hearty and plentiful meals at skinny prices. It's pure Lincoln County here: there's a cozy pot-bellied stove, historic photos on the wall, a tin bucket on the counter with issues of the local newspaper (just drop a quarter in), and cowboys murmuring at nearby tables. ⊠ *97 Main St. 89043* ☎ *775/962–5124* ▤ *No credit cards.*

¢–$ 🏨 **Overland Hotel & Saloon.** This relic from Pioche's past was rebuilt in the 1940s after the original building was destroyed in one of the town's numerous fires. The rooms are quaint, not fancy. You have to climb a long set of creaky stairs to get to them. ⊠ *85 Main St., 89043* ☎ *775/962–5895* 🖷 *775/962–5177* ↪ *13 rooms* ⌂ *Cable TV, some pets allowed, no-smoking room* ▤ *AE, D, MC, V.*

Lincoln County A to Z

CAR TRAVEL

Take I–15 north 22 mi from downtown Las Vegas to the U.S. 93 turnoff. Most of the Lincoln County sights, including Caliente and Pioche, are along 93.

Given the remoteness of the area and the lack of services, make sure that you have plenty of fuel, water, food, and supplies before leaving any town. A good rule is to keep your gas tank at least half-full at all times. Also, the weather can be tricky in eastern Nevada. Monitor weather reports frequently and check road conditions, even in July, especially before leaving U.S. 93.

The Bureau of Land Management publishes a detailed map for off-highway travel in Lincoln County.

🚩 **BLM Caliente Field Station** ⊠ *1400 Front St., Caliente 89008* ☎ *775/726-8100* 🖷 *775/726-8111* ⊕ *www.nv.blm.gov/ely* ⊙ *Weekdays 7:30–4:30* 🖃 *AE, D, DC, MC, V.*

LODGING

Most Lincoln County motels observe a strict, no-nonsense no-smoking policy that can result in heavy fines ($50–$100 is common) and immediate eviction, no questions asked, if the smell of smoke is detectable or lingers in no-smoking rooms.

VISITOR INFORMATION

🚩 **Caliente Chamber of Commerce** ⊠ *Caliente Train Depot, 89008* ☎ *775/726-3129* 🖷 *775/726-3447* ⊙ *Weekdays 10–2.* **Greater Lincoln County Chamber of Commerce** ⊕ *www.lincolncountynevada.com.* **Pahranagat Valley Chamber of Commerce** ⊠ *Box 421, Alamo 89001* ☎ *775/725-3483.* **Pioche Chamber of Commerce** ⊠ *55 Main St., 89043* ☎ *775/962-5544* ⊙ *May–early Sept., Mon.–Thurs. 11–3.*

PLAYING
THE GAMES

By Deke
Castleman
Revised by Bill
Burton

OVER THE PAST 60 YEARS the name Las Vegas has become synonymous with gambling. Nine out of 10 visitors gamble while they're in town. It's almost perverse to visit Las Vegas and *not* gamble. But while unreasonable expectations can lead to disappointment or, worse still, the loss of a lot of money, the key to having a good time is to approach the casinos with the idea that, contrary to popular opinion, you *can* win or, at the very least, get much more than your money's worth of playing time. Your success depends less on being lucky than on being familiar with the rules of the games, being aware of the concepts *behind* the games, and being conversant with the strategies that enable you to play not only with confidence but also with a fair shot at walking away a winner.

CASINO STRATEGY

The House Advantage

The first important concept to understand about gambling in Las Vegas is that the odds for all the games provide an advantage for the casino ("house"), generally known, appropriately enough, as the "house advantage" (or "edge" or "vigorish"). The casino is a business, and wagering is its product. Because the house establishes the rules, procedures, and payoffs on every game, it builds an automatic commission into every bet to ensure a profit margin.

Here's how it works. Let's pretend that I'm the house and you're the customer and we're betting on a series of coin flips. The deal that I make with you is that every time the coin lands heads up, I win and you pay me a dollar. Every time the coin lands tails up, you win—but I only pay you 90¢. The law of averages maintains that out of every 100 coin tosses, heads will win 50 times and tails will win the other 50. If I take a dime out of every one of your winning payoffs, the longer you play, the more dimes will wind up in my pocket. If you started with a $50 bankroll, after 1,000 tosses, *even if you win half of them,* you'd be busted out. (Because it requires two trials—win one, lose one—for the house to make its 10¢ "commission," your "negative expectation," or house edge, in this example is 5%.)

The second important gambling concept is known as "fluctuation" (or "variance"). In plain English, we're talking about "luck." Looking at our coin-toss game through the lens of averages, if you and I flip a coin 1,000 times, it's reasonable to expect that the coin will land heads up and tails up close to 500 times each. However, if we flip the coin only 10 times, it's conceivable that the coin could land heads up only once or twice or as many as 8 or even 10 times. Now let's say that we made the same betting deal as above but we limited the number of tosses to 10. This would largely eliminate your 5% disadvantage and leave it up to "the luck of the toss"—in other words, the fluctuation. Thus, a short-term fluctuation in the law of averages eliminates the long-term threat of the negative expectation.

How do these concepts—the house advantage and negative expectation, and the short-term fluctuation—apply to the choices that you make as a casino customer? Your decisions, based on these concepts, will determine not only what you play, but also how you play; how long you play; and, ultimately, how well you play.

Luck Versus the Edge

The average "bankroll" (cash carried for the sole purpose of gambling) of a Las Vegas visitor who plans to spend some time in the casino is roughly $500. This is a crucial statistic. The amount of your bankroll and your preferred style of "action" (how you risk your bankroll) define your relationship to luck and the house edge.

Basically, the parameters of gambling action are fast and slow. Some people, though they're in the minority, like their action fast and loose and high-risk; these are true "gamblers," in the old-fashioned sense of the word. The extreme version of this type of action is to take the whole $500 bankroll and lay it down on a single play—say, red or black on the roulette table. The odds are not quite even. The green 0 and 00 on the roulette table give the house an advantage of 5.26% (⇨ Roulette). Still, even though the odds are less than fair, the immediate result will be the same: double or nothing.

Making one play eliminates both the law of averages and the long-term threat of the house advantage; here you rely solely on the luck of the draw. If you want to go on a roller-coaster ride of luck, with a minute or so of adrenaline-pumping, heart-pounding excitement, lay it all down at once. In a matter of moments, you either have twice the money you arrived with or none of it.

A less extreme version of this wild ride is to break your bankroll into two units, and make two bets. Here you can either double your money, lose it all, or break even. Similarly, if you separate your $500 bankroll into five units and make five bets, or 10 units and make 10 bets, your ride lasts a little longer and your outcome is a little less black and white: You can double, bust out, break even, or come out somewhat ahead or behind. Still, the cumulative danger of the house advantage barely comes into play.

Luck can supersede the house advantage, but only in the short run. And though luck accounts for winners big and small—such as the local cocktail waitress who, in January 2000, lined up three Megabucks symbols on the $3 payline to win $35 million, or the $2 dice shooter who parlays a hot hand into a couple of hundred bucks—the lack of luck can obliterate a bankroll faster than a crooked S&L.

Besides, most people who come to Las Vegas like to gamble for as long as they can without running out of money. These people take their $500 bankrolls and split them into 100 units to make $5 bets, 250 units for $2 bets, 500 units for $1 bets, or even 2,000 units for 25¢ bets. This guarantees plenty of time for the law of averages to even out the fluctuations. On the other hand, it puts the house advantage and the negative expectation right back into the game.

So how do you play as long as you like without the certainty of the house advantage grinding your bankroll into dust?

The Good Bets

The first part of any viable casino strategy is to risk the most money on wagers that present the lowest edge for the house. Blackjack, craps, video poker, and baccarat are the most advantageous to the bettor. The two types of bets at baccarat have a house advantage of a little more than 1%. The basic line bets at craps, if backed up with full odds, can have a house advantage of as low as 0.5%. Blackjack and video poker, at times, can not only put you even with the house (a true 50-50 proposition) but actually give you a slight long-term advantage.

How can a casino possibly provide you with a 50-50 or even a positive expectation at some of its games? First, because a vast number of suckers make the bad bets (those with a house advantage of 5% to 35%, such as roulette, keno, and slots) day in and day out. Second, because the casino knows that very few people are aware of the opportunities to beat the odds. Third, because it takes skill—requiring study and practice—to be in a position to exploit these opportunities. However, a mere hour or two spent learning strategies for the beatable games will put you light-years ahead of the vast majority of visitors who give the gambling industry an average 12% to 15% profit margin.

THE GAMES

Each of the casino games has its own rules, etiquette, odds, and strategies. When you've decided on the kind of action you wish to pursue, you can choose a game that best suits your style. Then, if you take the time to learn the basics and fine points thoroughly, you'll be adequately prepared to play with as much of an edge as the game, combined with comps and coupons if possible, provides. In the meantime, good short-term fluctuation can add to your winnings. Some of the casinos offer free lessons to teach you how to play the most popular casino games, including blackjack, craps, roulette, and mini-baccarat. These lessons are a good way to become familiar with the rules of the games and table etiquette.

Baccarat

The most "glamorous" game in the casino, American baccarat (pronounced *bah*-kuh-rah), is a version of *chemin de fer,* popular in European gambling halls. The Italian word *baccara* means "zero"; this refers to the point value of 10s and picture cards. Most Las Vegas casinos like to surround baccarat with an aura of mystique: the game is played in a separate pit, supervised by personnel in tuxedos; the game's ritual is somewhat esoteric; and the minimum bet is usually $20–$100. Some casinos have forgone the larger baccarat pits in favor of the smaller mini-baccarat tables. Many players prefer mini-baccarat because it's less intimidating and can be played for lower limits. Mini-baccarat is essentially the same game, only it's played in the main blackjack pit, sans tuxedos and ritual, and with $5 minimums.

Up to 15 players can be seated around a baccarat table (six or seven at mini-baccarat). The game is run by four pit personnel. Two dealers sit side by side in the middle of the table; they handle the winning and los-

Baccarat Table

ing bets and keep track of each player's "commission" (explained below). The "caller" stands in the middle of the other side of the table and dictates the action. A pit boss supervises the game and acts as final judge if any disputes arise.

Baccarat is played with eight decks of cards dealt from a large "shoe" (or card holder). Each player is offered a turn at handling the shoe and dealing the cards. Two two-card hands are dealt: the "player" and the "bank" hands. The player who deals the cards is called the banker, though the house, of course, banks both hands. The players bet on which hand, player or banker, will come closest to adding up to 9 (a "natural"). The cards are totaled as follows: Ace through 9 retain face value, while 10s and picture cards are worth zero. If you have a hand adding up to more than 10, the number 10 is subtracted from the total. For example, if one hand contains a 10 and a 4, the hand adds up to 4. If the other holds an ace and 6, it adds up to 7. If a hand has a 7 and 9, it adds up to 6.

Depending on the two hands, the caller either declares a winner and loser (if either hand actually adds up to 8 or 9), or calls for another card for the player hand (if it totals 1, 2, 3, 4, 5, or 10). The bank hand then either stands pat or draws a card, determined by a complex series of rules depending on what the player's total is and dictated by the caller. When one or the other hand is declared a winner, the dealers go into action to pay off the winning wagers, collect the losing wagers, and add up the commission (usually 5%) that the house collects on the bank hand. Both bets have a house advantage of slightly more than 1%.

The player-dealer (or banker) continues to hold the shoe as long as the bank hand wins. As soon as the player hand wins, the shoe moves counterclockwise around the table. Players are not required to deal; they can refuse the shoe and pass it to the next player. Most players bet on the bank hand when they deal, because they "represent" the bank, and to do otherwise would seem as if they were betting "against" themselves. This isn't really the case, but it seems that way.

Making a bet at baccarat is very simple. All you have to do is place your money in either the bank, player, or tie box on the layout (⇨ Baccarat Table illustration), which appears directly in front of where you sit at the table. If you're betting that the bank hand will win, you put your chips in the bank box; bets for the player hand go in the player box. (Only real suckers bet on the tie, which has a house advantage of 14.4%.)

Because the caller dictates the action, the player responsibilities are minimal. It's not necessary to know any of the card-drawing rules, even if you're the banker. Playing baccarat is a simple matter of guessing whether the player or banker hand will come closest to 9, and deciding how much to bet on the outcome.

Bingo

Bingo is one of the world's best-known and best-loved games. It's also responsible for raising more money for charities, service organizations, religious institutions, and Native American tribes than any other fund-raiser.

One of the least profitable games for casinos, bingo was originally included in the roster of games for the same reason that extravaganzas were introduced to the showrooms, cheap steaks and breakfasts appeared in the restaurants, and coupons for free souvenirs began to be distributed via funbooks: to attract people to the casino. Simply by offering bingo, casinos can fill large halls with players, who have to pass by the pit and slots on the way in and out and often drop a few bucks on a roulette wheel or in a slot machine.

Bingo is derived from the Italian game lotto but is similar to the original Chinese game keno. Both use numbered cards, numbered Ping-Pong balls blown from a cage, a caller, and a master board. There, however, the similarities pretty much dissolve. Bingo is played on paper cards marked with a "dauber" or on two-ply cardboard "boards" marked with little round plastic tabs. Bingo cards contain 25 squares. Five horizontal columns are topped with the letters B-I-N-G-O. Under the B are five boxes, with a number in each box between 1 and 15; under the I, five boxes with numbers between 16 and 30; under the N, four boxes numbered between 31 and 45; and a "free" box in the center of the card; under the G, five numbers between 46 and 60; and under the O, five numbers between 61 and 75.

The caller announces the letter and number of each ejected Ping-Pong ball and illuminates them on the master board. For example, if the caller announces "G-58" or "Number 58, under G," the players check their cards under the column topped by the G for the number 58. If it appears, they mark the number with the ink dauber or the plastic tabs. A winning card will have five numbers lined up in a row, either horizontally, vertically, or diagonally. The "free" square is always considered marked, so frequently you only need to match four numbers to win a game.

When a player lines up a card with the proper configuration of markings, he or she yells out "Bingo!" A floor person picks up the card and verifies the player's numbers by those on the big board, then declares the player the winner. The caller gives the other players a few moments to determine whether they, too, have won; if there's another winner, the two split the total prize money. Most of the time, however, there's only one winner per game, because great pains are taken to ensure that each card is unique. Prize money can range from $10 on a regular bingo game up to $50,000 for a progressive jackpot.

The variety of patterns for bingo games is vast, from the "no-number" card, where not a single number on the card has been called, to the "coverall" or "black-out," where every number on the card is marked. Configurations such as "inside corner," "outside corner," and shapes such as "diamond," "square," "picture frame," or the letters "L," "X," "T," "H," and "U" are announced by the caller at the start of each game, and the patterns illuminated on secondary boards around the room.

There are almost as many different buy-ins as there are patterns. Cards start at 25¢ and can go up to $500 and higher for special promotions and tournaments. Different-color cards have different buy-in denominations (for example, blue costs $3, green $6, orange $9, etc.); the prize money is determined by the card's worth. "Game packs" or "booklets" consist of a given number of paper cards stapled together and used up in a "session." A quick call to the bingo room can tell you which sessions are played when.

Each game moves fairly quickly. The numbers are called one right after the other, leaving the players just enough time to look for them on their cards. Old bingo hands can play dozens of cards simultaneously, but beginners should limit themselves to a half dozen at most. When you buy in, if it's a paper session (i.e., one played on paper cards), make sure you have a dauber on hand when the game starts; they're for sale at the bingo cashier for $1 or so. By watching, asking your neighbors or a floor person a quick question about something you don't quite understand, and playing, you'll be in the swing of things after the first few games of a session.

Though the pace of bingo can often be blistering, the games start out fairly relaxed—with empty cards and players gearing up for the pattern. Tension mounts as more numbers are called, cards fill up, and players await the magic number or two that will make them winners. Finally, someone yells, "Binnnnnngooooo!" and for a brief moment the tension remains while the other players catch up on the last number or two. Then, as people realize they're not co-winners, the room deflates like a popped balloon. Quickly, the winner is verified and a new game starts the tension building all over again.

Blackjack

Blackjack is the most popular table game in the casino. It's easy to learn, fun to play, and it involves skill, and therefore presents varying levels of challenge. Blackjack also has one of the lowest house advantages. Furthermore, it's the game of choice when it comes to qualifying for comps: you can play for as long as you like and stand a real chance of breaking even or winning.

Because blackjack is the only table game in the casino in which players can gain a long-term advantage over the house, it is the only table game in the casino (other than poker) that can be played professionally. And because blackjack can be played professionally, it is the most written-about and discussed casino game. Dozens of how-to books, trade journals, magazines, newsletters, computer programs, videos, theses, and novels are available on every aspect of blackjack, including how to add to 21, when to stand or hit, how to play against a variety of shuffles, and the Level-Two Zen Count. Blackjack pros can spend hours debating whether the two-deck game at the Las Vegas Hilton has a starting house edge of 0.03 or 0.0275 because of the doubling-down-after-splitting option, or whether the Hi-Opt II count system's 88% betting efficiency correlation makes it stronger than the unbalanced count's perfect insurance indicator. Training someone to play blackjack professionally is beyond the scope of this guide. Contact the **Gambler's Book Club**

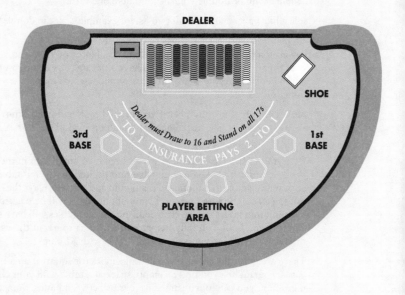

Blackjack Table

DEALER

3rd
BASE

Dealer must Draw to 16 and Stand on all 17s

2 TO 1 INSURANCE PAYS 2 TO 1

1st
BASE

SHOE

PLAYER BETTING
AREA

(☎ 702/382–7555) for a catalog of gambling books, software, and videotapes, including the largest selection on blackjack around.

The Rules

Basically, here's how it works: you play blackjack against a dealer, and whichever one of you comes closest to a card total of 21 without going over is the winner. Number cards are worth their face value, picture cards count as 10, and aces are worth either 1 or 11. (Hands with aces in them are known as "soft" hands. Always count the ace first as an 11; if you also have a 10, your total will be 21, not 11.) If the dealer has a 17 and you have a 16, you lose. If you have an 18 against a dealer's 17, you win (even money). If both you and the dealer have a 17, it's a tie (or "push") and no money changes hands. If you go over a total of 21 (or "bust"), you lose immediately, even if the dealer also busts later in the hand. If your first two cards add up to 21 (a "natural"), you're paid 3 to 2. However, if the dealer also has a natural, it's a push. A natural beats a total of 21 achieved with more than two cards.

You're dealt two cards, either face down or face up, depending on the custom of the particular casino. Two cards go to the dealer—one face down and one face up. Depending on your first two cards and the dealer's up card, you can:

stand, or refuse to take another card.

hit, or take as many cards as you need until you stand or bust.

double down, or double your bet and take one card.

split a like pair; if you're dealt two 8s, for example, you can double your bet and play the 8s as if they're two hands.

buy insurance if the dealer is showing an ace. Here you're wagering half your initial bet that the dealer does have a natural; if so, you lose your initial bet but are paid 2 to 1 on the insurance (which means the whole thing is a push).

surrender half your initial bet if you're holding a bad hand (known as a "stiff") such as a 15 or 16 against a high up card like a 9 or 10.

Buying In & Playing 21

First you must select a table at which to play. A small sign in the left-hand corner of the "layout" (the diagram printed on the felt tabletop) indicates the table minimum and maximum and often displays the house rules. You can be sure that the $2-minimum tables will be packed, the $5-minimum tables will be crowded, and the $25 tables will have some empty seats. Look carefully before you sit, so as to avoid the embarrassment of parking yourself at a $25 table with $1 chips.

There are generally six or seven betting circles (or squares) on a blackjack layout. When you find an empty space at a table with your chosen minimum, you can join a game in progress between hands. Sometimes you have to squeeze in and the other players might not be too eager to make room for you for one reason or another. The dealer should help make room for you. If everybody is particularly unfriendly, feel free to leave at any time, but it's to your advantage to spend as much time as possible playing at a crowded table. The more crowded the table, the fewer hands will be played every hour, which reduces your risk. If everybody makes plenty of room for you to be comfortable and the dealer is friendly, you've got it made for hours.

Once you're settled, it's time to "buy in" (convert your cash to casino chips). Place your money on the layout between the betting circles or in the insurance space. If you lay cash *inside* the betting area, the dealer will say something like, "Money plays," and you might wind up betting your whole buy-in amount on the next hand! The dealer should exchange your cash for chips and deposit the bills in the drop slot, using a small plastic "pusher."

Now you can place your wager in the betting circle. You're dealt your two cards. If they're face down, you can pick them up, with one hand, and hold them. If they're face up, don't touch them. If you have a natural, turn them over and the dealer will pay you immediately and take your cards. Otherwise, everyone plays out his or her hand one at a time, from the right side of the table ("first base") to the left ("third base").

BLACKJACK BASIC STRATEGY CHART									
YOUR HAND	**DEALER'S UP CARD**								
	2	**3**	**4**	**5**	**6**	**7**	**8**	**9**	**10**	**A**
5	H	H	H	H	H	H	H	H	H	H
6	H	H	H	H	H	H	H	H	H	H
7	H	H	H	H	H	H	H	H	H	H
8	H	H	H	H	H	H	H	H	H	H
9	D	D	D	D	D	H	H	H	H	H
10	D	D	D	D	D	D	D	D	H	H
11	D	D	D	D	D	D	D	D	D	D
12	H	H	S	S	S	H	H	H	H	H
13	S	S	S	S	S	H	H	H	H	H
14	S	S	S	S	S	H	H	H	H	H
15	S	S	S	S	S	H	H	H	H	H
16	S	S	S	S	S	H	H	H	H	H
17	S	S	S	S	S	S	S	S	S	S
18	S	S	S	S	S	S	S	S	S	S
19	S	S	S	S	S	S	S	S	S	S
20	S	S	S	S	S	S	S	S	S	S
21	S	S	S	S	S	S	S	S	S	S
A,2	H	H	D	D	D	H	H	H	H	H
A,3	H	H	D	D	D	H	H	H	H	H
A,4	H	H	D	D	D	H	H	H	H	H
A,5	H	H	D	D	D	H	H	H	H	H
A,6	D	D	D	D	D	H	H	H	H	H
A,7	S	D	D	D	D	S	S	H	H	H
A,8	S	S	S	S	S	S	S	S	S	S
A,9	S	S	S	S	S	S	S	S	S	S
A,A	SP	SP	SP	SP	SP	SP	SP	SP	SP	SP
2,2	H	SP	SP	SP	SP	SP	H	H	H	H
3,3	H	H	SP	SP	SP	SP	H	H	H	H
4,4	H	H	H	D	D	H	H	H	H	H
5,5	D	D	D	D	D	D	D	D	D	H
6,6	SP	SP	SP	SP	SP	H	H	H	H	H
7,7	SP	SP	SP	SP	SP	SP	H	H	H	H
8,8	SP	SP	SP	SP	SP	SP	SP	SP	SP	SP
9,9	SP	SP	SP	SP	SP	S	SP	SP	S	S
10,10	S	S	S	S	S	S	S	S	S	S

If you opt to stand, slide your two cards under your chips, then sit back and relax. If you want to hit, scratch the cards on the layout (seeing this done once will show you how). When you're ready to stand, slide the cards under the chips; if you bust, turn the cards over and the dealer will collect them and your bet. When everyone else has played, the dealer turns over her down (or "hole") card and plays out her hand, then settles up with all the players according to whether they won, lost, or pushed. Then the whole process starts all over again.

Playing blackjack is not only knowing the rules and etiquette, it's also knowing *how* to play. Many people devote a great deal of time to learning strategies, two of which are discussed in the sections that follow. However, if you don't have the time, energy, or inclination to get seriously involved, the following basic rules, which cover more than half the situations you can face, should allow you to play the game with a modicum of skill and a paucity of humiliation:

1) When your hand is a stiff (a total of 12, 13, 14, 15, or 16) and the dealer shows a 2, 3, 4, 5, or 6, always stand.

2) When your hand is a stiff and the dealer shows a 7, 8, 9, 10, or ace, always hit.

3) When you hold a 17, 18, 19, or 20, always stand.

4) When you hold a 10 or 11 and the dealer shows a 2, 3, 4, 5, 6, 7, 8, or 9, always double down.

5) When you hold a pair of aces or a pair of 8s, always split.

6) Never buy insurance.

Basic Strategy

Available to anyone with an interest in the game, a system called "basic strategy" consists of a large set of exact decisions for optimum play at blackjack based on a player's hand versus the dealer's up card. These decisions have been developed via computer simulations of hundreds of millions of blackjack hands; they're not open to debate. You must spend several hours memorizing the basic strategy chart and then spend another several hours practicing basic strategy with playing cards. And then you must make the correct play on every hand, regardless of your "hunches" or what the person sitting next to you might recommend.

The accompanying Basic Strategy Chart lists all the possible combinations of blackjack hands against the dealer's up card. Here's how to read it. Say you're dealt a 7 and a 5 and the dealer is showing a 9. First look at the left-hand column, under YOUR HAND for the total, 12. Then follow the line across to the column under the number 9. The "H" stands for hit. So you would hit this hand. Now, suppose you're then dealt a 4. Look back at the left-hand column for the new total, 16. Then follow it across to the number-9 column again. Again you have to hit. (Pray for a 5 or less, your only way out of this worst-case blackjack scenario. Most of the time you'll bust.)

Say you're dealt, on the next hand, an ace and a 4 against the dealer's 3; counting the ace as 11, you have a total of 15. Find the A,4 listing in the YOUR HAND column and follow it across to the dealer's 3. According to basic strategy, you should hit. If you get a 6, you've got 21, not 12. If you get a 5, you've got 20; of course you should stand. (If you're in doubt, look up the A,9 listing.) If you get a 9, however, you'll have to count the ace as a 1, for a total of 14; otherwise you'd bust with 23. Now you look up the proper play for 14 against a dealer's 3; you'd stand.

Finally, suppose you're dealt a pair of 7s against a dealer's 7. The chart tells you to split the pair. Here you place both cards face up near your initial bet (don't worry about the exact position; no matter how close you place them, the dealer will *always* rearrange them slightly) and then place a second bet equivalent to the first. Then you play each 7 as its own hand. What if you're dealt a 4 on your first 7 for a total of 11? Some casinos will let you double down after splitting. Ask the dealer if she doesn't volunteer this information. What if you're dealt another 7? Again, some casinos will let you split the new pair and play out three hands.

Rules vary from house to house and city to city. In Las Vegas, some places allow you to surrender; some don't. At some places, dealers stand on soft 17; some places they don't. Basic strategy can get fairly advanced, and there are times when certain variations apply. But for most sets of rules at most Las Vegas joints, basic strategy will put you way ahead of the pikers who swell the casino coffers.

Card Counting

Card counting is an exacting technique for tracking the cards that have been played during a blackjack round and thereby determining whether the cards remaining to be played are favorable or unfavorable to the player. Card counters designate different plus or minus values for cards that are removed from the deck in play; based on the count, players can make better-informed decisions about playing and betting strategies. *Knock-Out Blackjack—The Easiest Card-Counting System Ever Devised* delivers what it promises in the subtitle: a card-counting system that takes only a few hours to learn and a few more to perfect, without sacrificing any of the power of the most complex and difficult counts. It's available from **Huntington Press** (✉ 3687 S. Procyon Ave., Las Vegas, NV 89103 ☎ 702/252–0655 or 800/244–2224).

Card counting is something the dealers, pit bosses, and video surveillance teams are constantly on the lookout for. In some casinos, if a player is suspected of card counting he will be asked to leave the table ("backed off") or, in some cases, to leave the premises ("barred"). However, some casinos don't sweat card counters too much. Others counter the card counters' edge by using "six-deck shoes"; that is, they combine six decks, which reduces the value of tracking the deck till deep into it. A common misconception is that counters keep track of more than 300 cards in a six-deck shoe; in fact, you're only counting the point totals (2s through 6s are worth +1, 7s and 8s are worth 0, 10s and aces are worth -1). Also, the casinos rarely deal all the way to the bottom of a single deck, two decks, or six decks, because it's easier to figure out what cards are left once you get towards the bottom of the pile. Using multideck shoes is just one of myriad countermeasures that casinos employ to foil card counters. Early and unbalanced shuffling, low table limits, and controlled betting spreads are among the many others. It's a tough business, and only a select few card counters are good enough to consistently win enough money to make a living at it.

Craps

Craps is a dice game played at a large rectangular table with rounded corners. Up to 12 players can crowd around the table, all standing. The layout (⇨ Crap Table illustration) is mounted at the bottom of a surrounding "rail," which prevents the dice from being thrown off the table and provides an opposite wall against which to bounce the dice. It's important, when you're the "shooter," to roll the dice hard enough so that they bounce off the end wall of the table; this ensures a random bounce and shows that you're not trying to control the dice with a "soft roll." The layout grid is duplicated on the right and left sides of the table, so players on either end will see exactly the same design. The top of the railing is grooved to hold the bettors' chips; as always, keep a close eye on your stash to prevent victimization by rail thieves.

It can require up to four pit personnel to run an action-packed, fast-paced game of craps. Two dealers handle the bets made on either side of the layout. A "stickman" wields the long wooden "stick," curved at one end, which is used to move the dice around the table; the stickman also calls the number that's rolled and books the proposition bets made in the middle of the layout. The "boxman" sits between the two dealers and oversees the game; he settles any disputes about rules, payoffs, mistakes, etc. A slow craps game is often handled by a single employee, who performs stick, box, and dealer functions. A portable end wall can be placed near the middle of the table so that only one side is functional.

To play, just join in, standing at the table wherever you can find an open space. You can start betting casino chips immediately, but you have to wait your turn to be the shooter. The dice move around the table in a clockwise fashion: the person to your right shoots before you, the one to the left after (the stickman will give you the dice at the appropriate time). If you don't want to roll the bones, motion your refusal to the stickman and he'll skip you.

Playing craps is fairly straightforward; it's betting on it that's complicated. The basic concepts are as follows: if the first roll turns up a 7 or 11, that's called a "natural"—an automatic win. If a 2, 3, or 12 comes up on the first throw (called the "come-out roll"), that's termed "crapping out"—an automatic lose. Each of the numbers 4, 5, 6, 8, 9, or 10 on a first roll is known as a "point": the shooter has to keep rolling the dice until that number comes up again. If a 7 turns up before the number does, that's another loser. When either the point (the original number thrown) or a 7 is rolled, this is known as a "decision"; one is made on average every 3.3 rolls.

But "winning" and "losing" rolls of the dice are entirely relative in this game, because there are two ways you can bet at craps: "for" the shooter or "against" the shooter. Betting "for" means that the shooter

Crap Table

DEALER

DEALER

BOXMAN

STICKMAN

PASS LINE

Don't Pass Bar

Don't Come Bar

4 5 SIX 8 NINE 10

COME

2 • 3 • 4 • 9 • 10 • 11 12

FIELD

Pass   Double   Double

Don't Pass Bar

PASS LINE

PASS LINE

Don't Come Bar

10 NINE 8 SIX 5 4

COME

12 2 • 3 • 4 • 9 • 10 • 11

FIELD

Double   Pass   Double

Don't Pass Bar

PASS LINE

5 for 1 Seven 5 for 1

10 for 1   8 for 1
10 for 1   8 for 1

15 for 1   30 for 1
15 for 1   30 for 1

15 for 1   15 for 1

8 for 1 Any Craps 8 for 1

will "make his point" (win). Betting "against" means that the shooter will "seven out" (lose). (Either way, you're actually betting against the house, which books all wagers.) If you're betting "for" on the come-out, you place your chips on the layout's "pass line." If a 7 or 11 is rolled, you win even money. If a 2, 3, or 12 (craps) is rolled, you lose your bet. If you're betting "against" on the come-out, you place your chips in the "don't pass bar." A 7 or 11 loses; a 2 or 3 wins (a 12 is a push). A shooter can bet for or against himself or herself, as well as for or against the other players.

At the same time, you can make roughly two dozen wagers on any single roll of the dice. In addition to the "for" and "against" (pass and don't pass) bets, you can also make the following wagers at craps:

Come/Don't Come: After a pass-line point is established, the "come" bet renders every subsequent roll of the dice a come-out roll. When you place your chips in the come box, it's the same as a pass line bet. If a 7 or 11 is rolled, you win even money. If a 2, 3, or 12 is rolled, you've crapped out. If a 4, 5, 6, 8, 9, or 10 is rolled, it becomes another point, and the dealer moves your chips into the corresponding box on the layout. Now if that number comes up before the 7, you win the come bet. The opposite is true for the "don't come" box: 7 and 11 lose; 2, 3, and 12 win; and if the 7 is rolled before the point, you win.

Odds: The house allows you to take odds on whether or not the shooter will make his or her point, once it's established. The house pays off these bets at "true odds," rather than withholding a unit or two to its advantage, so these are the best bets in a crap game. Odds on the 6 and 8 pay off at 6 to 5, on the 5 and 9 at 3 to 2, and on the 4 and 10 at 2 to 1. "Back up" your pass line bets with single, double, triple, or up to 100 times odds (depending on the house rules) by placing your chips behind your line bet. For example, if the point is a 10 and your bet is $5, backing up your bet with single odds ($5) returns $25 ($5 + $5 on the line and $5 + $10 single odds); taking triple odds returns $55 ($5 + $5 on the line and $15 + $30). To take the odds on a come bet, toss your chips onto the layout and tell the dealer, "Odds on the come."

Place: Instead of waiting for a point to be rolled on the come, you can simply lay your bet on the number of your choice. Drop your chips on the layout in front of you and tell the dealer to "place" your number. The dealer puts your chips on the number; when it's rolled you win. The 6 and 8 pay 7 to 6, the 5 and 9 pay 7 to 5, and the 4 and 10 pay 9 to 5. In other words, if you place $6 on the 8 and it hits, you win $7. Place bets don't pay off at true odds, which is how the house maintains its edge (1.51% on the 6 and 8, 4% on the 5 and 9, and 6.66% on the 4 and 10). You can "call your place bet down" (take it back) at any time; otherwise the place bet will "stay up" until a 7 is rolled.

Buy: Buy bets are the same as place bets, except that the house pays off at true odds and takes a 5% commission if it wins. Buy bets have an edge of 4.7%, so you should only buy the 4 and 10 (rather than place them at a 6.6% disadvantage).

Big 6 and 8: Place your own chips in these boxes; you win if the 6 or 8 comes up, and lose on the 7. Because they pay off at even money, rather than true odds, the house edge is large—9.09%.

Field: This is a "one-roll" bet (a bet that's decided with each roll). Numbers 3, 4, 9, 10, and 11 pay even money, while 2 and 12 pay 2 to 1 (the 12 or "boxcars" pays 3 to 1 in Reno). The house edge on the field is 5.5%.

Proposition Bets: All the proposition bets are booked in the grid in the middle of the layout by the stickman. "Hardways" means a pair of numbers on the dice (two 3s for a hardways 6, two 4s for a hardways 8, etc.). A hardways 4 or 10 pays 7 to 1 (11.1% edge), and 6 or 8 pays 9 to 1 (9.09%). If a 7 or a 4, 6, 8, or 10 is rolled the "easy way," hardways bets lose. "Any seven" is a one-roll wager on the 7, paying 4 to 1 with a whopping 16.6% edge. "Yo'leven" is also a one-roll wonder paying 14 to 1 with a 16.6% edge. "Any craps" is a one-roll bet on the 2, 3, or 12, paying 7 to 1 (11.1%). Other bad proposition bets include the "horn" (one-roll bet on 2, 3, 11, or 12 separately; 16.6%), and "c and e" (craps or 11; 11.1%).

Note: the players place their own pass line, field, Big 6 and 8, and come bets. Players must drop their chips on the table in front of the dealers and instruct them to make their place and buy bets, and to take or lay the odds on their come bets. Chips are tossed to the stickman, who makes the hardways, any craps, any seven, and c and e bets in the middle of the layout.

Keno

Craps, blackjack, baccarat, and roulette arrived in Nevada casinos from Europe, but an early version of keno was brought over in the mid-1800s from China, where this bingo-type game was popular. It was rapidly Americanized in Reno casinos in the 1930s shortly after gambling was legalized.

Keno games are played once every seven or eight minutes. You participate by using a black crayon (provided) to mark a "ticket," imprinted with 80 boxes numbered 1 through 80, with 1 to 15 "spots" or numbers of your choice. You decide how many spots you want to mark based on how much money you're willing to bet. Eighty numbered Ping-Pong balls lying in a round plastic or wire bowl (the "goose") are mixed by an electric fan; the forced air blows the balls into two elongated tubes that hold 10 balls each. The numbers on the balls are announced over a public address system to the players in the keno "lounge" and are displayed on keno video monitors that hang all around the casino—in the coffee shop, restaurants, and bars. If enough of your numbers match the board's numbers, you win an amount enumerated in the keno payoff booklet (⇨ Keno Payoffs chart).

You can bring your ticket to the central keno "counter," where a "writer" gives you a duplicate ticket and books your wager, or you can fill out a ticket at one of the casino's bars and restaurants, which are served by keno "runners," who collect tickets and bets and run them to the central counter where they are processed. The runners then deliver the duplicate tickets to you. After the game has been played and

KENO PAYOFFS (FOR A BET OF $1)

NUMBERS MARKED	WINNING NUMBERS	PAYS $	NUMBERS MARKED	WINNING NUMBERS	PAYS $
1	1 number	3	11	5 numbers	1
				6 numbers	8
				7 numbers	72
2	2 numbers	12		8 numbers	360
				9 numbers	1,800
				10 numbers	12,000
3	2 numbers	1		11 numbers	28,000
	3 numbers	42			
			12	6 numbers	5
4	2 numbers	1		7 numbers	32
	3 numbers	4		8 numbers	240
	4 numbers	112		9 numbers	600
				10 numbers	1,480
5	3 numbers	2		11 numbers	8,000
	4 numbers	20		12 numbers	36,000
	5 numbers	480			
			13	6 numbers	1
6	3 numbers	1		7 numbers	16
	4 numbers	4		8 numbers	80
	5 numbers	88		9 numbers	720
	6 numbers	1,480		10 numbers	4,000
				11 numbers	8,000
7	4 numbers	2		12 numbers	20,000
	5 numbers	24		13 numbers	40,000
	6 numbers	360			
	7 numbers	5,000	14	6 numbers	1
				7 numbers	10
8	5 numbers	9		8 numbers	40
	6 numbers	92		9 numbers	300
	7 numbers	1,480		10 numbers	1,000
	8 numbers	18,000		11 numbers	3,200
				12 numbers	16,000
9	5 numbers	4		13 numbers	24,000
	6 numbers	44		14 numbers	50,000
	7 numbers	300			
	8 numbers	4,000	15	7 numbers	8
	9 numbers	20,000		8 numbers	28
				9 numbers	132
10	5 numbers	2		10 numbers	300
	6 numbers	20		11 numbers	2,600
	7 numbers	132		12 numbers	8,000
	8 numbers	960		13 numbers	20,000
	9 numbers	3,800		14 numbers	32,000
	10 numbers	25,000		15 numbers	50,000

the winning numbers are displayed, the runner returns to check if there are any winners. If there are, the runner redeems the winning tickets for her customers—at which point it's customary to tip her.

There are six different types of keno tickets, the most common of which are the "straight," "replay," and "split" tickets. On a straight ticket, you mark off your chosen numbers—say, eight of them (remember, you're allowed to mark as many as 15). Looking at the payout chart, you can see that if four or fewer of your numbers match the called numbers, you lose. If five out of the eight match, you win $9 (on the $1 bet). If all eight match, you're an $18,000 winner. If you mark 15 spots and all 15 match (fat chance!), you win the big jackpot, usually $50,000.

A replay ticket uses the same numbers that you bet on with a previous ticket. Simply hand your bet (which doesn't have to be for the same amount) and the duplicate ticket from a prior game to the writer. A split ticket means that you're making two straight bets on a single ticket. Mark your numbers for the first straight bet and draw a line to separate them from the numbers for the second straight bet. Be sure to tell the writer that this is a split ticket.

Like the split ticket, "way" and "combination" wagers use one ticket to make what are often large and complex numbers of bets—a method of reducing paperwork. But these bets are really just a fancier and faster way to lose money at keno. If you want to try them out, most keno lounges have a booklet explaining the way and combination bets.

Keno has the highest house advantage in the casino, but this doesn't seem to have much of an effect on its popularity. Even though you can expect to lose 25¢ to 40¢ on every dollar you wager, many people like keno. Why? It's easy to play and slow-paced; you can sit in the lounge, drink, and visit with your fellow suckers. You can also maintain a level of action while eating or drinking in a restaurant or bar. But mostly it's a long-shot game, at which you can win $25,000; $50,000; and, at some places, even $100,000 by risking only a few dollars.

Video keno is played similarly to "live" keno. You drop your nickel or quarter into the machine, then use the attached "pen" to touch your numbers of choice. When you press the button that says "play" or "start," the machine illuminates the winning numbers, usually accompanied by a beep. If enough of your numbers match the machine's, you're paid off either in coins or credits.

Poker Games

Over the last several years video poker has grown to be one of the most popular games in the casinos. It's no wonder that many of the newer table games that have made their way onto the casino floor are also based on poker. Let it Ride and Caribbean Stud are two of the fastest-growing table games, and Pai Gow Poker has been attracting new players to the tables. These games are fairly easy to learn; however, a player will need a general knowledge of the ranking of poker hands. From this, you'll understand what makes a winning hand and how to interpret the pay tables used for some of the bonus bets. Following is a hierarchy of poker hands, from strongest to weakest:

Royal Flush: This is the best hand, which is composed of a Ten (T), Jack (J), Queen (Q), King (K), and Ace (A) of the same suit.

Straight Flush: Five cards of the same suit that are in sequence.

Four-Of-A-Kind: Four cards of equal rank, one in each suit.

Full House: Three of a kind and a pair.

Flush: Any five cards of the same suit.

Straight: Five cards of any suit that are in sequence.

Three-Of-A-Kind: Any three cards of equal rank.

Two Pair: Two different pairs of the same rank.

One Pair: Two cards of the same rank.

Let It Ride

Let It Ride was first introduced to the casinos in 1993. The game is popular because it offers a potential for high payouts, but also because the players are not playing against each other or trying to beat the dealer, camaraderie develops among the players, creating a fun atmosphere. The game and the correct playing strategy can be learned quickly. In essence, each player is trying to put together a winning hand.

The game is played on a blackjack-size table. There are three circles on the table in front of each player. The circles are marked with the numbers 1 and 2, and a dollar sign ($). To start the game a player places three equal bets in each circle. The Shuffle Master machine deals out cards three at a time.

The dealer distributes a three-card hand to each player and retains the last hand. The dealer looks at the dealer's hand, discarding one of the three cards; the two remaining dealer's cards—still face down at this point—become the "community cards" for all the players. More about those in a moment.

The machine counts out the remaining cards into the discard tray. When this is finished, the players are all allowed to look at their three-card hands. At this point each player has the option to take back the bet in circle No. 1 or "let it ride." To take back your bet, you scrape your cards on the table toward you or make a brushing motion with your hand. If you let your bet ride, then it becomes part of your cumulative bet for the hand.

After all the players have made their decisions, the dealer will turn up the first of the two community cards. This card is used as the fourth card for all the players' hands. The players now have the option of taking down their second bet or letting it ride. You may take down the second bet even if you let the first bet ride, but you cannot take down the first bet if you passed on the last round or put it back up if your hand now has more promise than you originally expected.

After all the players make their decisions, the dealer will turn up the second community card. This card completes the five-card hand for all players. At this point, the dealer will pay all the winning bets according to the following Payout schedule:

LET IT RIDE PAYOUT SCHEDULE	
HAND	**PAYOUT**
Pair of Tens or Better	1 to 1
Two Pairs	2 to 1
Three of a Kind	3 to 1
Straight	5 to 1
Flush	8 to 1
Full House	11 to 1
Four of a Kind	50 to 1
Straight Flush	200 to 1
Royal Flush	1,000 to 1

The "house edge" for the basic game is approximately 3.5% when you play the correct strategy. You must know which hands you should take down and when to "let it ride." Here is the proper strategy for the game:

Let bet #1 ride if you have:

1) A winning hand—one pair of tens or better.

2) A three-card royal flush.

3) A three-card straight flush.

Let bet #2 ride if you have:

1) A winning hand—one pair of 10s or better.

2) A four-card royal flush or straight flush.

3) A four-card flush.

4) Four high cards (10 or better).

5) A four-card open-ended straight (any four cards in sequence, where you could have a straight by adding a card at either end).

There's a dollar side bet that can be made for a bonus payoff when certain hands are made. The pay tables for the bonus vary from casino to casino. The house edge ranges from 15% to 30% on these bets. As with most side bets offered by the casino, these should be avoided.

Let It Ride can be a fun game for the recreational player. The game is slower than blackjack. You will be dealt about 40 hands per hour, and some casinos offer lower-limit games. If you take the time to learn the simple strategy, you can enjoy the excitement of this table game.

Caribbean Stud

Caribbean Stud is played on a blackjack-size table. It's another poker-based game, so you need to know the ranking of hands. You are playing against the dealer, and your hand must beat the dealer's hand. You do not have to worry about beating the other players' hands.

The game starts with each player making an ante bet equal to the table minimum. This is placed in the circle marked "ante" in front of the player. At this time the player also has the option of making an additional dollar side bet for the bonus jackpot. An automatic shuffler is used, and the dealer distributes a five-card hand to each player face down. The dealer retains a hand and turns one card face up.

Players look at their cards and decide to fold and forfeit their ante bet or call by making an additional bet, which is twice the size of the ante. For example, at a $5 table your ante bet would be $5 and your call bet would be $10.

After the players have made their decision to fold or call, the dealer's hand is turned over. The dealer must qualify by having a hand with ace plus king or better. If the dealer does not qualify, the players are paid even money for their original ante bet and the second call bet is a "push," which means it does not win or lose.

If the dealer qualifies and the player wins the hand, he or she is paid even money for the ante bet, and the call bet is paid based on the winning hand according to the table below:

CARIBBEAN STUD PAYOUT SCHEDULE	
HAND	PAYOUT
One Pair or Less	1 to 1
Two Pairs	2 to 1
Three of a Kind	3 to 1
Straight	4 to 1
Flush	5 to 1
Full House	7 to 1
Four of a Kind	20 to 1
Straight Flush	50 to 1
Royal Flush	100 to 1

The player must act before the dealer. This means there will be times when you fold a hand only to have the dealer not qualify. This does not mean you should play every hand. A simple strategy is to play your hand if it contains Ace-King or better, and fold anything else.

The house edge for the main game is about 5%, but the pace of the game is fairly slow. Because of this the house edge won't hurt your bankroll too much if you play for smaller stakes.

The same is not true of the side bet for the progressive jackpot. As with all so-called bonus bets, the bonus jackpot has a high house edge. You need a flush or higher to qualify for one of the bonus payouts, and the money you win when you receive one of these hands is not close to the odds of doing so. If you look at the chart below, you will see that you

CARIBBEAN STUD PROGRESSIVE JACKPOT PAYOUT SCHEDULE		
HAND	DOLLAR JACKPOT	ODDS AGAINST
Flush	$50	508 to 1
Full House	$75	693 to 1
Four of a Kind	$100	4,164 to 1
Straight Flush	10% of progressive jackpot	64,973 to 1
Royal Flush	100% of progressive jackpot	649,740 to 1

will make a flush once every 508 hands, and for this the casino will pay you $50. You can see why this is a bad bet.

If you decide to make the side bet, you should know that you are eligible for the jackpot even if the dealer's hand does not qualify. You must inform the dealer immediately before she picks up the cards. Normally the dealer will pick up all the cards without turning them over. Make sure you speak up.

Caribbean Draw

The rules for Caribbean Draw are similar to those for Caribbean Stud. The payouts and betting strategies are the same. The difference is that after looking at their cards, players have the option of discarding and drawing replacements for up to two cards.

The dealer must have a pair of eights or better to qualify. If not, only the ante bet will be paid. A simple strategy is to call with a pair of eights or better and fold all other hands.

Pai Gow

Pai Gow is played with a standard 52-card deck and one joker, which can be used as an ace or a wild card to complete only a straight, flush, or straight flush. The game is played on a blackjack-size table with up to six players and a banker. The players are playing against the banker. In most cases the casino acts as the banker, although players can choose to bank the game if they wish to. This would require having enough money to cover all of the other player's bets. The casino collects a 5% commission on all winning bets.

To start the game, the players make their bets according to the table minimum. The dealer shuffles the cards and deals out seven stacks containing seven cards. This is done no matter how many players there are. The banker shakes a cup containing three dice to determine who gets the first hand.

You look at your seven cards and set them into a two-card hand and a five-card hand. There is a place marked on the table to place your hands. The two-card hand is placed in front and the five-card hand is placed behind it. If both hands beat the banker's two hands you win. If one of your hands beats the banker's and one loses, it's a "push," and there are no winners. If either of your hands has the exact same value as the banker's hand it is a tie, which is called a "copy," and the banker wins.

When you are setting your hands, your five-card hand must be a higher value than your two-card hand (based on the values of hands). If you make a mistake and the two-card hand is higher it is a "foul," and you lose automatically. When the casino acts as the banker, the dealer must set the house hands according to certain rules, which is called the "House Way." If you are unsure of how to set your hand, you can ask the dealer to set it the "House Way." This will keep you from making a mistake.

Pai Gow is a slower-pace game than most table games. Since you must utilize only the seven cards dealt to you, there are many pushes. The bank has a slight edge because it wins the copies.

Here is a Pai Gow strategy:

The **Back** is the five-card hand; the **Front** is the two-card hand. A **Complete Hand** is a poker hand that requires all five cards to win (i.e., a straight, flush, or straight flush). A **Set** is just a casino term for three of a kind.

No Pair: Use the highest card in the Back and second- and third-highest in Front.

One Pair: Place the pair in Back, the highest other two cards in Front.

Two Pair: If the "big" (i.e., higher-value) pair is **jack through ace,** place the "small" pair in Front. If the big pair is **7s through 10s,** place both pairs in Back if you can put Ace in Front. If the big pair is **2s through 6s,** place both pairs in Back if you can put King in Front. Otherwise, **split** the pairs, always putting the bigger pair in Back.

Three Pair: Place the big pair in Front.

Three-of-a-Kind: If you have **aces,** place an ace and the next-highest card in Front. If you have **kings and below,** place the three of a kind in Back, the two highest remaining cards in Front.

Two Sets: Place the pair from the higher set in Front; the remaining set goes in the Back.

Straight, Flush, or Straight Flush: If you have **no pair,** place the two highest cards in Front that leave a complete hand in Back. If you have **one pair,** place the two highest cards possible (pair or no pair) in Front that leave a complete hand in Back. If you have **two pair,** use "two-pair" strategy above. If you have **three of a kind,** place a complete hand in Back, a pair in Front.

Full House: Put the pair in Front, the set in Back.

Four-of-a-Kind: If you have **jacks through aces,** always split the pairs, putting one in Front and one in Back. If you have **7s through 10s,** place the four of a kind in Back if you can put ace or king in front; otherwise split into two pair. If you have **6s or below,** never split. If you **also have a pair,** play four of a kind in Back, the pair in Front. If you **also have three of a kind,** put the highest pair in Front, a full house in Back.

Five aces: Place a pair of aces in front.

Roulette

Roulette is a casino game that utilizes a perfectly balanced wheel with 38 numbers (0, 00, and 1 through 36), a small white ball, a large layout with 11 different betting options (⇨ Roulette Table illustration), and special "wheel chips." The layout organizes the 11 different bets into six "inside bets" (the single numbers, or those closest to the dealer) and five "outside bets" (the grouped bets, or those closest to the players).

The dealer stands between the layout and the roulette wheel, and chairs for five or six players are set around the roulette table. At crowded times, players also stand among and behind those seated, reaching over and around to place their bets. *Always* keep a close eye on your chips at these times to guard against "rack thieves," clever sleight-of-hand artists who can steal from your pile of chips right in front of your nose.

To buy in, place your cash on the layout near the wheel. Inform the dealer of the denomination of the individual unit you intend to play (usually 25¢ or $1, but it can go as high as $500). Know the table limits (displayed on a sign in the dealer area); don't ask for a 25¢ denomination if the minimum is $1. The dealer gives you a stack of wheel chips of a different color from those of all the other players and places a chip marker atop one of your wheel chips on the rim of the wheel to identify its denomination. Note that you must cash in your wheel chips at the roulette table before you leave the game. Only the dealer can verify how much they're worth.

The dealer spins the wheel clockwise and the ball counterclockwise. When the ball slows, the dealer announces, "No more bets." The ball drops from the "back track" to the "bottom track," caroming off built-in brass barriers and bouncing in and out of the different cups in the wheel before settling into the cup of the winning number. Then the dealer, who knows the winning bettors by the color of their wheel chips, places a marker on the number and scoops all the losing chips into his or her corner. Depending on how crowded the game is, the casino can count on roughly 50 spins of the wheel per hour.

How to Place Inside Bets

You can lay any number of chips (depending on the table limits) on a single number, 1 through 36 or 0 or 00. If the number hits, your payoff is 35 to 1, for a return of $36. You could, conceivably, place a $1 chip on all 38 numbers, but the return of $36 would leave you $2 short, which divides out to 5.26%, the house advantage.

If you place a chip on the line between two numbers and one of those numbers hits, you're paid 17 to 1 for a return of $18 (again, $2 short of the true odds).

Betting on three numbers returns 11 to 1, four numbers returns 8 to 1, five numbers pays 6 to 1 (this is the worst bet at roulette, with a 7.89% disadvantage), and six numbers pays 5 to 1.

How to Place Outside Bets

Lay a chip on one of three "columns" at the lower end of the layout next to numbers 34, 35, and 36; this pays 2 to 1. A bet placed in the

Roulette Table

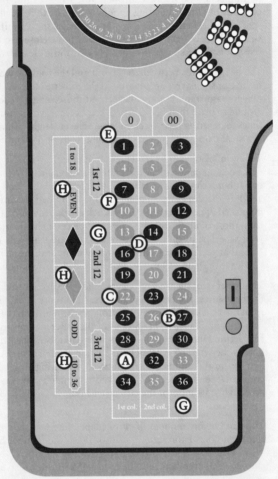

	Bet	Payoff
A	Single number	35 to 1
B	Two numbers	17 to 1
C	Three numbers	11 to 1
D	Four numbers	8 to 1
E	Five numbers	6 to 1
F	Six numbers	5 to 1
G	12 numbers (column)	2 to 1
G	1st 12, 2nd 12, 3rd 12	2 to 1
H	1-18 or 19-36	1 to 1
H	Odd or Even	1 to 1
H	Red or black	1 to 1

first 12, second 12, or third 12 boxes also pays 2 to 1. A bet on red or black, odd or even, and 1 through 18 or 19 through 36 pays off at even money, 1 to 1. If you think you can bet on red *and* black, or odd *and* even, in order to play roulette and drink for free all night, think again: the green 0 or 00, which fall outside these two basic categories, will come up on average once every 19 spins of the wheel.

The house advantage of 5.26% on every roulette bet (except, as noted, the five-number bet) is five times the advantage at craps and five times less than the average advantage at keno. European-style wheels, including those at Monte Carlo, have a single green 0, which slashes the house edge in half to 2.7%.

Slot Machines

Of all the games in the casino, slot machines are the most American: around the turn of the 20th century, Charlie Fey built the first mechanical slot in his San Francisco basement. Today, slot machines (along with video poker, keno, and blackjack machines) occupy more casino floor space and since 1992 have accounted for more gross casino winnings than all the table games combined. Once machine profits surpassed those of table games on the tony Las Vegas Strip, there was no looking back. You soon realize that slot machines aren't confined to casinos, though. They're everywhere—in airports, supermarkets, bars, coin laundries, and minimarts.

Slot-machine technology has exploded in the past 20 years, and now there are hundreds of different models, which accept everything from pennies to specially minted $500 tokens. The old "mechanical" or "electromechanical" slots—all more than 30 years old—can still be found in some casinos, as antique or nostalgia pieces. They feature small skinny reels with fruit symbols; usually accept only one coin; don't have any lighting or sound effects; have a single pay line; and pay back minor amounts. "Multipliers" are machines that accept more than one coin (usually three to five, maximum) and are mostly electronically operated—with flashing lights, bells and whistles, and spin, credit, and cash-out buttons. Multipliers frequently have a variety of pay lines: three horizontal for example, or five horizontal and diagonal.

One advance in the game, however, has been the progressive jackpot. Banks of slots within a particular casino are connected by computer, and the jackpot total is displayed on a digital meter above the machines. Generally, the total increases by 5% of the wager. If you're playing a dollar machine, each time you pull the handle (or press the spin button), a nickel is added to the jackpot. Progressive slots in many casinos are also connected by modem to other casinos throughout the state, and these jackpots often reach into the millions of dollars. The largest slot jackpot ever paid—$35 million, won by a 34-year-old cocktail waitress from the Monte Carlo Hotel-Casino at the Desert Inn in January 2000—was on a Megabucks progressive, which is competitive with surrounding state lotteries. (One form of gambling that is specifically illegal in Nevada is the lottery.) Nevada Nickels and Quartermania are lower-denomination versions of the statewide progressive. Lately, super high-tech slot machines have been emerging from manufacturers at a rapid clip, with large video screens and high-resolution graphics, games-within-a-game bonusing, and video clips (such as on the hot Elvis machines). Some of the new machines have such gimmicky themes as 1960s television programs (*I Dream of Jeannie, The Addams Family*); a Chinese-theme machine features firecrackers, fortune cookies, and MSG symbols. In addition, some slots are beginning to resemble video-poker machines, in which you choose symbols to hold or discard.

An innovation has been the introduction of the multi-denomination machines. Players can choose to play for pennies, nickels, quarters, or dollars without having to switch machines. Instead of dropping coins in a tray, these machines pay out in vouchers that can be redeemed at the casino cage.

Insert your coins or dollar tokens—or slip your paper dollars into the bill receptor. Pull the handle or press the spin button, then wait for the reels to spin and stop one by one, and for the machine to determine whether you're a winner (occasionally) or a loser (most of the time). It's pretty simple—but because there are so many different types of machines, be sure you know exactly how the one you're playing operates. If it's a progressive machine, you must play the maximum number of coins to qualify for the jackpot. For example, the maximum bet at Megabucks is $3. You can play $1; this limits the action to the first-coin pay line (usually the middle line across the reels). The same goes for $2 and the second-coin pay line (the top line). But to win the progressive total, the three Megabucks symbols must be lined up on the third-coin pay line (not surprisingly, the bottom line). Can you imagine lining up three Megabucks symbols on the third pay line with only a dollar or two played? Instead of winning at least $5 million, you wind up with bupkis!

Slot Candles: Many people have placed a quarter in a slot machine only to see it drop through into the tray below. At that point they realize it was a dollar machine that they were putting the quarter in. The denomination of the slot machine is posted on the machine, although many times it's hard to see. There's an easy way to determine the denomination of a slot machine. Look at the circular light on the top of the machine. This light is called a **candle.** The top half of the candle is white and lights up when you press the change button. The bottom half of the candle is colored. The color denotes the denomination of the machine. The candles are blue for the dollar machines, yellow for quarters, and red for nickel machines. By knowing the color of the candles, you can spot the denomination of the machine you want to play from across the casino floor. This little bit of knowledge will save you time when searching for a slot machine.

The house advantage on slots varies widely from machine to machine, from 2% to 25%. Casinos that advertise a 97% payback are telling you that at least one of their slot machines has a house advantage of 3%. Which one? There's really no way of knowing. Generally, $1 machines pay back at a higher percentage than quarter or nickel machines. On the other hand, machines with smaller jackpots pay back more money more frequently, meaning that you'll be playing with more of your winnings. One good thing to keep in mind is this: in a nationwide study of slot-machine paybacks, a major gambling publication determined that downtown Las Vegas has the "loosest" slots. This means that from all the available data—specifically the ratio between the "handle" (total action wagered) and the "hold" (what the casino keeps) on slot machines (which is published by the Gaming Control Boards in most casino jurisdictions)—year after year downtown Las Vegas's is the lowest. In other words, they hold the smallest percentage of the total wagered.

One of the all-time great myths about slot machines is that they're "due" for a jackpot. Slots, like roulette, craps, keno, and the big six, are subject to the Law of Independent Trials, which means the odds are permanently and unalterably fixed. If the odds of lining up three sevens on a 25¢ slot machine have been set by the casino at 1 in 10,000, then those odds remain 1 in 10,000 whether the three 7s have been hit three times in a row or not hit for 90,000 plays. Don't waste a lot of time playing a machine that you suspect is "ready," and don't think that if someone hits a jackpot on a particular machine only minutes after you've finished playing on it that it was "yours."

If you have the hots for slots, remember to join as many slot clubs as you can. You're paying a pretty hefty commission for your romance with cherries, lemons, and 7s, so you might as well be rewarded with comps and perks.

Sports Betting

In Las Vegas, the word "book" rarely denotes a work of literature. More often than not, book isn't even used as a noun, but when it is, book almost always refers to the large room attached to the casino, where sports wagers are made and paid, the odds on sporting events are displayed, and sports bettors (often called "wise guys") watch the main events on large TV screens and video monitors. Bookmakers (or bookies) are people in the business of taking wagers. Book as a verb is the action of accepting and recording a wager, primarily on sporting and racing events, but also on casino games; the house books your blackjack, crap, and slot machine action.

The first race and sports book in a casino opened in 1975. Today nearly every major casino books race and sports bets. A book can be as small as a table with a clerk who quotes the odds and writes your receipt for a bet by hand, or as large as the Las Vegas Hilton's "super book," which has 46 video screens and 500 seats.

In Nevada you can bet on professional football, baseball, basketball, and hockey; college football and basketball; boxing matches; horse racing; and special events. But of all the sports, pro football draws the most action.

Football Betting

A wager made on a football game is one of the best gambling (and entertainment) bargains in the business. It costs you all of $1 in commission to the house to place a $10 bet on a team; the return is several hours

PARLAY BETTING ODDS		
NUMBER OF TEAMS	**PAYOUT ODDS**	**TRUE ODDS**
2	13–5	3–1
3	6–1	7–1
4	10–1	15–1
5	20–1	31–1
6	35–1	63–1
7	50–1	127–1
8	100–1	225–1
9	200–1	511–1
10	400–1	1023–1

of heightened excitement while the game is played. As anyone who's made a casual bet with a friend or group of coworkers knows, having a little money riding on a game introduces a whole new level of energy and interest to it.

There are four ways to bet on a football game: point spread, money line, parlay, and teaser. A wager based on the point spread (or a "straight bet") means that you're not only betting that one team will beat the other, but that it will win by a predetermined number of points. The point spreads are calculated for all pro football games by an outside "handicapper" (or oddsmaker) based on the relative strengths or weaknesses of the teams playing. For example, when a strong team, say, the Jacksonville Jaguars, plays a weak team, say, the Detroit Lions, the spread will favor the Jags by, say, 17 points. This means that the Jags have to beat the Lions by 18 points in order for a wager placed on Jacksonville to win. If the Jags beat the Lions by 10 points, they didn't "cover" the spread, so a bet on the Lions would win. If the Jags win by 17 points exactly, it's a "push" or a tie, and the original bet (including the commission) is returned.

The "money line" bet on a pro football game uses odds instead of points and is determined simply by who wins and who loses. The money line for the Jacksonville–Detroit game might be a "minus 240 plus 180." This means you have to bet $24 to win $10 (for a total of $34)

TEASER BETTING ODDS			
NUMBER OF TEAMS	**6 points**	**6$\frac{1}{2}$ points**	**7 points**
2	even	10–11	1–12
3	9–5	8–5	3–2
4	3–1	5–2	2–1
5	9–2	4–1	7–2
6	7–1	6–1	5–1

on the heavily favored Jags; conversely, a bet of $10 on the underdog Lions will win you $18 (for a total of $28).

A "parlay" is a bet on two, three, or four teams (sometimes more), all of which have to cover the point spread for you to win (⇨ Parlay Betting Odds chart). If two out of the three teams cover and the third team wins but doesn't cover, you lose the whole bet. The payout on a two-team parlay is generally 13 to 5, on a three-team parlay 6 to 1, and on a four-team parlay 10 to 1.

A "teaser" is similar to a parlay, except that the point spreads are more variable than for a straight or parlay bet (⇨ Teaser Betting Odds chart). If you win a three-team teaser after taking an additional 6 points on the spread, you're paid at 9 to 5; with 6½ additional points it's 8 to 5; and with 7 points, 3 to 2.

Football bets are usually made in denominations of $11, which includes the house's 10% commission for booking the bet. Winning bets pay off in denominations of $10. So, for example, you might bet $33 on the 49ers to cover the point spread. If the Jags cover, you win $30 (for a total payback of $63).

To make a football bet (or a bet on any sporting event), go to the sports book and step up to the counter. Study the board that lists all the games, and pick out the one(s) you want to put your money on. The teams are numbered. Give the team number, amount of the bet, and type of bet (points or money line) to the "writer," who inputs your bet into a computer and prints out your "ticket" or receipt. (Parlay and teaser cards are filled out and presented to the writer.) Check your ticket carefully to make sure the writer has given you the exact bet that you intended to make.

Then sit back and root for your money. If you lose, wallpaper your bathroom with the rest of your losing tickets. If you win, return to the casino where you made the bet, present the ticket to the sports book cashier, and receive your due.

Video Poker

Like blackjack, video poker is a game of strategy and skill, and at select times on select machines, the player actually holds the advantage, however slight, over the house. Unlike with slot machines, you can determine the exact edge of video-poker machines (or in gambler's lingo, "handicap" the machine). Like slots, however, video-poker machines are often tied into a progressive meter; when the jackpot total reaches high enough, you can beat the casino at its own game.

The variety of video-poker machines is already large, and it's steadily growing larger. All the machines are played in a similar fashion, but the strategies are different. This section deals only with straight-draw video poker.

You must first ascertain what denomination of coin a straight-draw video-poker machine accepts. Thousands of penny, nickel, quarter, and dollar machines occupy casinos in Las Vegas. Five-dollar machines are

9/6 VIDEO POKER PAYOUT SCHEDULE					
Royal Flush	250	500	750	1000	4000
Straight Flush	50	100	150	200	250
Four of a Kind	25	50	75	100	125
Full House	9	18	27	36	45
Flush	6	12	18	24	30
Straight	4	8	12	16	20
Three of a Kind	3	6	9	12	15
Two Pair	2	4	6	8	10
Jacks or Better	1	2	3	4	5

becoming more popular around the state, and $25 and $100 machines can be played at places such as the Mirage, Golden Nugget, and Caesars Palace. Then there are the new multigame machines, where you can play 3, 5, 10, even 50 hands of video poker at the same time.

The schedule for the payback on winning hands is posted on the machine, usually above the screen. It lists the returns for a high pair (generally jacks or better), two pair, three of a kind, a straight, flush, full house, straight flush, four of a kind, and royal flush, depending on the number of coins played—usually 1, 2, 3, 4, or 5. (The machine assumes you're familiar with poker and its terminology.) Look for machines that pay with a single coin played: 1 coin for "jacks or better" (meaning a pair of jacks, queens, kings, or aces; any other pair is a stiff), 2 coins for two pair, 3 for three of a kind, 4 for a straight, 6 for a flush, 9 for a full house, 25 for four of a kind, 50 for a straight flush, and 250 for a royal flush. This is known as a 9/6 machine: one that gives a nine-coin payback for the full house and a six-coin payback for the flush with one coin played (⇨ 9/6 Video Poker Payout Schedule chart). Some machines pay a unit for a pair of 10s but get you back by returning only one unit for two pair. Other machines are known as 8/5 (8 for the full house, 5 for the flush), 7/5, and 6/5.

The return from a standard 9/6 straight-draw machine (with a 4,000-coin "flattop" or royal-flush jackpot) is 99.5%; you give up a half percent to the house. An 8/5 machine with a 4,000 flattop returns 97.3%. On 6/5 machines (such as those you find in supermarkets, 7-Elevens, and coin laundries around the city), the figure drops to 95.1%, slightly better than roulette. The return from a 25¢, 8/5 progressive machine doesn't reach 100% until the meter hits $2,200—a rare sight. (You can figure nickel, $1, and $5 progressives by the $2,200 figure. A 100% payback on nickels is $440; on $1 it's $8,800, and on $5 it's $44,000.) Machines with varying paybacks are scattered throughout the casinos. In some you see an 8/5 machine right next to a 9/6, and someone will be blithely playing the 8/5 machine!

As with slot machines, it's always optimal to play the maximum number of coins in order to qualify for the jackpot. You insert five coins into the slot and press the "deal" button. Five cards appear on the screen—

say, 5, J, Q, 5, 9. To hold the pair of 5s, you press the "hold" buttons under the first and fourth cards. The word "hold" appears underneath the two 5s. You then press the "draw" button (always the same button as "deal") and three new cards appear on the screen—say, 10, J, 5. You have three 5s; with five coins bet, the machine will give you 15 credits. If you want to continue playing, press the "max bet" button: five units will be removed from your number of credits, and five new cards will appear on the screen. You repeat the hold and draw process; if you hit a winning hand, the proper payback will be added to your credits. Those who want coins rather than credit can hit the "cash out" button at any time. Some older machines don't have credit counters and automatically dispense coins for a winning hand.

Like blackjack, video poker has basic strategies that have been formulated by the computer simulation of hundreds of millions of hands. The most effective way to learn it is with a video poker computer program that deals the cards on your screen, then tutors you in how to play each hand properly. The best program is *WinPoker,* available from **Huntington Press** (⌧ 3687 S. Procyon Ave., Las Vegas, NV 89103 ☏ 702/252–0655 or 800/244–2444).

If you don't want to devote that much time to the study of video poker, memorizing these six rules will help you make the right decision for more than half the hands you'll be dealt:

1) If you're dealt a completely "stiff" hand (no like cards and no picture cards), draw five new cards.

2) If you're dealt a hand with no like cards but with one jack, queen, king, or ace, always hold on to the picture card; if you're dealt two different picture cards, hold both. But if you're dealt three different picture cards, only hold two (the two of the same suit, if that's an option).

3) If you're dealt a pair, always hold it, no matter what the face value.

4) Never hold a picture card or an ace ("kicker") with a pair of 2s through 10s.

5) Never draw two cards to try for a straight or flush.

6) Never draw one card to try for an inside straight.

Wheel of Fortune (Big Six)

Prize wheels are among the oldest games of chance and among the easiest to play and lose. Nevada-style big six is modeled after the old carnival wheels that attracted suckers on the midway. The standard wheel, usually 6 feet across, is divided into nine sections and 54 individual slots or stops. Fifty-two of the stops are marked by dollar denominations: 23 $1, 15 $2, 8 $5, 4 $10, and 2 $20 stops. The other two stops are marked by a joker or the casino logo. A leather "flapper" mounted at the top of the wheel clicks as it hits the wood or metal pegs that separate each slot. When the wheel stops, the flapper falls between two pegs and indicates the winning number.

You lay your bet on a glass-covered table in front of the wheel. The layout display consists of the actual currency, which matches the numbers on the wheel (a Washington, Lincoln, Hamilton, Jackson, etc.). To play, you simply place a chip or cash atop the bill you think will be the winner. The payoff is a multiple of the denomination: a $1 bet on the $1 bill pays a buck; a $1 bet on the $2 bill pays $2; a $5 bet on the $20 pays $100. The joker, casino logo, or other non-numerical symbol on the wheel, however, pays 40 to 1: a successful $1 bet on one of these will get you back $40.

The house advantage starts at 11.1% on the $5 bet and rockets to 22.2% on the $20 bet and 24% on the joker. This isn't a game you want to play all night, or for more than a few spins. But the big six often draws a crowd. Even hardened gamblers like to stop and watch and listen to the wheel spin, with its hypnotic clicking of flapper against pegs, to see where it stops. They'd probably even lay down a buck or two, but they'd be too embarrassed in front of the dealer!

UNDERSTANDING LAS VEGAS

LAS VEGAS AT A GLANCE

GLITTER, GAMBLING, GROWTH

BOOKS & MOVIES

LAS VEGAS AT A GLANCE

Fast Facts

Nickname: Sin City
Type of government: The Las Vegas Valley metropolitan area has four cities: Las Vegas, Henderson, North Las Vegas, and Boulder City. Each has a council-manager form of government, with an elected mayor. The rest of Clark County is governed by the county commission, with an appointed county manager.
Population: City 528,617, Clark County 1.6 million
Population density: 93.7 people per square mi in Clark County
Median age: Female 34, male 35

Crime rate: 679 violent crimes and 4,132 property crimes per 100,000 people
Infant mortality rate: 6.4 per 1,000 live births
Ethnic groups: Caucasian 60%; Hispanic 23%; African American 9%; Asian–Pacific Islander 7%
Religion: Unaffiliated 65%; Catholic 16%; Other Christian 8%; Mormon 6%; Jewish 5%

"Las Vegas has become, just as Bugsy Siegel dreamed, the American Monte Carlo . . ."
—Tom Wolfe, Kandy-Kolored Tangerine-Flake Streamline Baby

Geography & Environment

Latitude: 36°N (close to those of Algiers, Algeria; Athens, Greece; and Gibraltar)
Longitude: 115°W (close to those of Calgary, Alberta; San Diego, CA; and Tucson, AZ)
Elevation: 2,030 feet
Land area: City 81 square mi; Las Vegas Valley urban area 516 square mi; Clark County 8,060 square mi
Terrain: Desert, mountain
Natural hazards: Earthquakes
Environmental issues: The level of Lake Mead, which supplies about 90% of

Southern Nevada's water, has dropped more than 70 feet since 1999. The decline is expected to continue due to low snowpack on the western slope of the Rocky Mountains. When the snowpack melts, the runoff feeds the Colorado River, which in turn supplies Lake Mead.

"Breasts are more than a body part here. They're entertainment."
Comedian Rita Rudner

Economy

Per capita income: $28,922
Unemployment: 4.6%
Work force: 934,800; service industries 81%; government 10%; construction 9%
Major industries: Gaming, tourism, construction, military

"We are never one thing. We are whatever we need to be next to get people here."
Hal Rothman, chairman of the history department at the University of Nevada, Las Vegas

Did You Know?

• Nine of the ten largest hotels in the United States are in Las Vegas. They are the MGM Grand, Luxor, Excalibur, Circus Circus, Flamingo, Mandalay Bay, Las Vegas Hilton, Venetian, and Bellagio.

• The cities of Las Vegas, Henderson, and North Las Vegas were among the 10 fastest-growing incorporated places (with populations of 100,000 or more), according to the 2000 U.S. Census.

• Caesars Palace serves around 7,700 eggs, 427 pounds of coffee, and more than 3,000 ounces of orange juice every day.

• Famous natives and residents of Las Vegas include Andre Agassi, Benjamin "Bugsy" Siegel, and Orson Welles.

• While the odds of rolling 27 straight passes, or wins, at craps are 12,467,890 to 1, an anonymous sailor did just that at the Las Vegas Desert Inn in 1950. Today the dice sit regally atop a velvet pillow under glass.

• If you were to string together all the lighted neon tubing from the signs on the Strip and downtown Las Vegas, it would measure more than 15,000 mi.

• The pyramid-shape Luxor Hotel is covered by 13 acres of glass. A specially designed window-washing device takes 64 hours to clean the four slanted walls.

THE LAS VEGAS OF THE STRIP and downtown is Wayne Newton, the Blue Man Group, and Cirque du Soleil. It's cards, dice, roulette wheels, and slots. It's harried keno runners and leggy cocktail waitresses, grizzled pit bosses and nervous break-in dealers. It's cab and limo drivers, valet attendants, and bellmen. Las Vegas is showgirls with smiles as white as spotlights and head wear as big and bright as fireworks. It's a place where thousands of people earn their livings counting billions in chips, change, bills, checks, and markers.

Gimmicks, glitz, and gigawatts of electrical power are what keep Las Vegas humming day and night—as do the more than 36 million casino-bound visitors who arrive every year and bed down in some of the world's largest, showiest hotels (the city has 18 of the 21 biggest in the world). Vegas Vic, the 50-foot-tall ambassador of Glitter Gulch, is forever duded up in high Western style to give gamblers a flashy welcome.

While the Strip and downtown are the best known and principal tourist areas of the city, more than 1 million people live—and lead "normal" lives—within 5 mi of them. Endless subdivisions enclose rows and rows of pink-stucco and red-tile, three-bedroom-two-bath houses, most of them fewer than 10 years old and occupied by transplants hoping to cash in on the boom. "Lost Wages" is a city of dreamers: gamblers hoping to beat the odds and get rich; dancers, singers, magicians, acrobats, and comedians praying to make it in the Entertainment Capital of the World; and increasingly real estate agents, supermarket cashiers, computer techs, credit card accounting clerks, shoe salespeople, and librarians seeking a better way of life.

For all the local talk about Las Vegas citizens being average people who just happen to live and work in an unusual city, living here is undeniably different.

The town is full of people whose jobs involve catering to strangers 24 hours a day, 365 days a year. Las Vegas probably has the largest graveyard shift in the world. And the notion that locals never gamble and rarely see a show or eat at a buffet is also largely a myth—residents are a large and active part of the total market that relishes 99¢ breakfasts and $5 prime ribs, slot clubs, casino paycheck-cashing promotions, and free lounge entertainment. Indeed, the casinos that cater primarily to locals (Palace Station, Boulder Station, Texas Station, the Rio, Gold Coast, Orleans, Santa Fe, Green Valley Ranch, Cannery, Arizona Charlie's, and Fiesta) are among the most successful in town. Surprisingly, Las Vegas is also a religious town—about a third of the 450 congregations here are Mormon—which adds a somewhat incongruous conservative dimension to local politics and morals.

* * *

GAMBLING AND TOURISM are not the only games in town. Nellis Air Force Base employs thousands of people. The construction industry is huge. Large corporations and small manufacturing firms frequently relocate to southern Nevada, which offers tax incentives as well as a lower cost of living. But local life is merely a curiosity to the 35 million tourists whose primary concern is choosing among more than 60 major hotel-casinos, dozens of shows, a mind-boggling list of gambling options, limitless dining, and spectacular day trips.

Las Vegas is the largest city in Nevada and one of the most remote large cities in the country: the nearest major population center to the west is Barstow, California, 2½ hours away; St. George, Utah, is two hours to the east. Through the years Las Vegas has wrested the political and economic power of Nevada away from Reno,

448 mi to the northwest, the city where legalized gambling first became popular and where the early casinos were built.

Las Vegas is surrounded by the Mojave Desert, and Las Vegas Valley is flanked by mountain ranges. Among them are the Spring Mountains, including Mount Charleston (11,918 feet), which has skiing and snowboarding, and Red Rock Canyon, characterized by stunning Southwest sandstone. The Las Vegas Wash drains the valley to the southeast into Lake Mead and the Colorado River system.

Average high temperatures in Las Vegas rise to 105°F in July and August; lows drop to 30°F in January and February. The heat is saunalike throughout the summer, except during electrical storms that can dump an inch of rain an hour and cause dangerous flash floods. Heavy rains any time of year exacerbate two of Las Vegas's major problems: a lack of water drainage and a surplus of traffic. The summer blaze often makes it very uncomfortable to be outside for any length of time. Winters can be surprisingly chilly during the day and especially cold after the sun goes down. But in September and October and April and May it doesn't get any better.

Las Vegas is the largest U.S. city founded in the 20th century—1905 to be exact. Some might argue that the significant year was 1946, when Bugsy Siegel's Fabulous Flamingo opened for business. But the beginnings of modern Las Vegas can be traced back to 1829, when Antonio Armijo led a party of 60 on the Old Spanish Trail between Santa Fe and Los Angeles. While his caravan camped about 100 mi northeast of the present site of Las Vegas, an advance party set out to look for water. Rafael Rivera, a young Mexican scout, left the main party, headed due west over the unexplored desert, and discovered an oasis. The abundance of artesian spring water here shortened the Spanish Trail to Los Angeles by allowing travelers to go directly through, rather than around, the desert and eased the rigors of travel for the Spanish traders who used the route. They named the oasis Las Vegas, Spanish for "the meadows."

The next major visitor to the Las Vegas Springs was John C. Fremont, who in 1844 led one of his many explorations of the Far West. Today he is remembered in the name of the principal downtown thoroughfare—Fremont Street.

Ten years later a group of Mormon settlers were sent by Brigham Young from Salt Lake City to colonize the valley. They built a large stockade; a small remnant of it—a 150-square-foot, adobe-brick fort— still stands. The fort is the oldest building in Las Vegas. The Mormons spent two years growing crops, mining lead, and converting the indigenous Paiutes, but the climate and isolation defeated their ambitions and by 1857 the fort was abandoned.

* * *

THINGS DIDN'T START HOPPING here until 1904, when the San Pedro, Los Angeles, and Salt Lake Railroad laid its tracks through Las Vegas Valley, purchased the prime land and water rights from the handful of homesteaders, and surveyed a town site for its railroad servicing and repair facilities. In May 1905 the railroad held an auction and sold 700 lots. Las Vegas became a dusty railroad watering stop with a few downtown hotels and stores, a saloon and red-light district known as Block 16, and a few thousand residents. It remained just that until 1928, when the Boulder Canyon Project Act was signed into law, in which $165 million was appropriated for the building of the world's largest antigravity dam, 40 mi from Las Vegas.

Construction of Hoover Dam began in 1931, a historic year for Nevada. In that year Governor Fred Balzar approved the "wide-open" gambling bill that had been introduced by a Winnemucca rancher, Assemblyman Phil Tobin. Gambling had been outlawed several times since Nevada became a state in 1864, but it had never been completely eliminated. Tobin maintained that controlled gaming would be good for tourism and the state's economy; people were going to gamble anyway, so why shouldn't the state tax the profits? Thus, he was able to convince lawmakers to make gambling permanently legal. Also in 1931, the legislature reduced the residency requirement for divorce to a scandalous six weeks, immediately turning Nevada into a "divorce colony."

The early 1930s marked the height of the Great Depression and Prohibition. The construction of the dam on the Colorado River (bridging the gap between Arizona and Nevada) brought thousands of job seekers to southern Nevada. Because the federal government didn't want dam workers to be distracted by the temptations of Las Vegas, it created a separate government town, Boulder City—still the only community in the state where gambling is illegal.

At this time Nevada's political and economic power resided in the northern part of the state: the capital in Carson City and the major casinos (notably Harold's Club and Harrah's) in Reno. But the completion of the dam in 1935 turned southern Nevada into a magnet for federal appropriations, thousands of tourists and new residents, and a seemingly inexhaustible supply of electricity and water. In addition, as the country mobilized for World War II, tens of thousands of pilots and gunners trained at the Las Vegas Aerial Gunnery School, opened by the federal government on 3 million acres north of town. Today this property is Nellis Air Force Base and the Nevada Test Site.

By the early 1940s downtown Las Vegas boasted several luxury hotels and a dozen small but successful gambling clubs. In 1941 Thomas Hull, who owned a chain of California motor inns, decided to build a place in the desert just outside the city limits on Highway 91, the road from Los Angeles. El Rancho Vegas opened with 100 motel rooms, a Western-motif casino, and, right off the highway, a large parking lot with an inviting swimming pool in the middle. El Rancho's quick success led to the opening a year later of the Last Frontier Hotel, a mile down the road. Thus, the Las Vegas Strip was established.

Benjamin "Bugsy" Siegel, who ran the New York mob's activities on the West Coast, began to see the incredible potential of a remote oasis where land was cheap and gambling was legal. He struggled for two years to build the Flamingo, managing to alienate his local partners and silent investors with his lavish overspending. He opened the joint prematurely, on a rainy night, the day after Christmas 1946 with fanfare and a who's who guest list. But the Flamingo flopped— the casino paid out more money than it took in, and six months later Bugsy was dead. Ironically, Bugsy's murder made the Flamingo infamous, and suddenly the big pink hotel was hopping.

The success of the Flamingo paved the way for gamblers and gangsters from all over the country to invest in Las Vegas hotel-casinos, one after another. The Desert Inn, Horseshoe, Sands, Sahara, Riviera, Dunes, Fremont, Tropicana, and Stardust were all built in the 1950s, financed with mob money. Every new hotel came on like a theme park opening for the summer with a new ride. Each was bigger, better, more unusual than the last. The Sahara had the tallest freestanding neon sign. The Riviera was the first highrise building in town. The Stardust had 1,000 rooms and the world's largest swimming pool.

That the underworld owned and ran the big joints only added to the allure of Las Vegas. And the town's great boom in the 1950s couldn't have happened without the mob's access to millions of dollars in cash. Under the circumstances, no bank, corporation, or legitimate investor would have touched the gambling business.

In time, however, the state began to take steps to weed out the most visible undesirables. The federal government assisted in the crackdown, using its considerable resources to hound the gangsters out of business. And, finally, an eccentric man arrived on a train and soon revolutionized the nation's image of Las Vegas.

Howard Hughes had just sold Trans World Airlines for $546 million, and he either had to spend half the money or turn it in as taxes. During a three-year stay in Las Vegas he bought the Desert Inn, Frontier, Sands, Landmark, and Silver Slipper hotels, a television station, an airfield, and millions of dollars' worth of real estate. His presence in Las Vegas gave gambling its first positive image: As a former pilot and aviation pioneer, Hollywood mogul, and American folk hero, Hughes could in no way be connected with gangsters.

Hughes's presence also opened the door to corporate ownership of hotel-casinos. In 1971 Hilton Corporation purchased the International (now the Las Vegas Hilton) and the Flamingo, becoming the first major publicly traded hotel chain to step onto the Las Vegas playing field. Ramada, Holiday Inn, Hyatt, Sheraton, and others have since followed suit.

* * *

AS VEGAS FELT THE EFFECTS of both the legalization of gambling in Atlantic City in the late 1970s and of the national recession of the early 1980s—but not for very long. Through the years the city has carved a secure niche for itself as a destination for national and international tourists; a winter sojourn for snowbirds from the north; a weekend getaway for gamblers and families from California, Arizona, and Utah; and convention central. Las Vegas has expanded at a ferocious pace since the 1990s: more than 65,000 hotel rooms have been added and more than a half million people have moved to the area, many of them fleeing California.

And why not? Though inching up, room rates are lower than in any other major U.S. city. There are lavish gourmet spots, but the inexpensive restaurants and buffet dining here can be cheaper than preparing a meal at home. Entertainment is abundant and reasonably priced. Las Vegas is possibly the easiest place in the world to receive freebies—the ubiquitous "comps." And best of all, gambling promotions such as coupons, slot clubs, paycheck bonuses, and drawings provide a fighting chance to win in the casino. In the back of everyone's mind is the idea that a trip to Las Vegas can be free or even a money-making vacation. That kind of thinking keeps the corporations smiling as they add a few more finishing touches to their $2-billion hotels.

BOOKS & MOVIES

Books

History & Biography. *Learning from Las Vegas–The Forgotten Symbolism of Architectural Forms,* by Robert Venturi et al., and *Viva Las Vegas—After Hours Architecture,* by Alan Hess, are readable analyses of the shapes, sizes, and placement of Las Vegas's signs, casinos, parking lots, and false fronts. *Literary Las Vegas,* edited by Mike Tronnes, is a superb collection of work by well-known writers—Tom Wolfe, Joan Didion, Michael Herr, Hunter S. Thompson, among them—about the neon jungle. Of course, Hunter S. Thompson's *Fear and Loathing in Las Vegas* is the famous psychedelic account of the gonzo journalist's late-1960s trip to Las Vegas. For the most savage indictment of Las Vegas and its mobsters, payoffs, cheating, corruption, and prostitution, read *Green Felt Jungle,* by Ovid Demaris and Ed Reid. The book that Reid and Demaris used as their model to expose the seamy underside of Las Vegas was *The Great Las Vegas Fraud* by Sid Meyers, published in 1958, the first—and most vicious—in a long series of books that came to be called the Las Vegas Diatribe.

For the antidote to *Green Felt Jungle* and *The Great Las Vegas Fraud,* try to find *Playtown, U.S.A.,* by Katherine Best and Katherine Hillyer, a snapshot of Las Vegas written in 1955—one of the most insightful and colorful portraits of Sin City ever written. *Las Vegas—As It Began, As It Grew,* by Stanley Paher, covers in detail the popular early history of Las Vegas, from the Old Spanish Trail up through the building of Hoover Dam. *Resort City in the Sunbelt,* by Eugene Moehring, is a comprehensive, academic, and heavily footnoted history of Las Vegas's development since the 1930s. A more recent history of Las Vegas is *The Money and the Power: The Making of Las Vegas and Its Hold on America* by Sally Denton and Roger Morris. *Fly on the Wall—Recollections of Las Vegas' Good Old, Bad Old Days,* by Dick Odessky, is the personal account of a newspaper-reporter-turned-casino-publicist who lived through the transition from mob-run to corporate-owned Las Vegas. *Las Vegas—A Desert Paradise,* by Ralph Roske, is a large-format pictorial that covers Las Vegas's historical highlights. *Cult Vegas,* by *Las Vegas Review-Journal* entertainment columnist Mike Weatherford (a contributor to this book), delves into the offbeat entertainment history of the Entertainment Capital of the World. *Howard Hughes in Las Vegas,* by Omar Garrison, concerns the four years the enigmatic billionaire spent sequestered on the 9th floor of the Desert Inn. *No Limit—The Rise and Fall of Bob Stupak and the Stratosphere Tower,* by John L. Smith, is the fascinating biography of Las Vegas's most flamboyant modern casino operator. *Easy Street* is the sad and gripping autobiography of Susan Berman, only child of David Berman, one of the earliest mobsters to relocate in Las Vegas.

Fiction. Most of Mario Puzo's novels contain an enormous amount of inside dirt on Las Vegas, but *Fools Die* is centered on the city and contains some excellent descriptions of casino color and scams. *The Death of Frank Sinatra,* by L.A. novelist Michael Ventura, is a dark and disturbing but brilliant fictional look at the meaning of Las Vegas. Larry McMurtry's *Desert Rose,* conversely, is an affectionate and poignant character study of an aging showgirl and her ties to Las Vegas. *Last Call,* by Tim Powers, is a strange, suspenseful, violent tale about chaos and randomness, the patron saints of Las Vegas. *Devil's Hole,* by Las Vegas novelist Bill Branon, concerns a hit man hired by a Las Vegas casino to take out a wildly successful sports bettor. *Neon Mirage,* by Max Allan Collins, is a novel about Bugsy Siegel, as is *Las Vegas Strip,* by Morris Renek. *The Big Night* is a story about a notorious gambler who assembles a team of five women to beat Las Vegas out of a million bucks, by Ian Andersen, one of the world's most success-ful high-stakes blackjack players. Ander-sen's book is one of a long list of pulp fiction titles based on "the great Las Vegas heist" theme: *The Vegas Trap,* by Hal Kantor; *Fortune Machine,* by Sam Ross; *Snake Eyes,* by Edwin Silberstang; and *Murder in Las Vegas,* by renaissance man Steve Allen, are other examples.

Gambling. *Comp City—A Guide To Free Las Vegas Vacations,* by Max Rubin, ex-poses the guarded world of the casino complimentary system. *Knock-Out Black-jack,* by Olaf Vancura and Ken Fuchs, is the easiest card-counting system ever de-vised. Ian Andersen, who's made his liv-ing at high-stakes blackjack for nearly three decades, tells all in two books, *Turn-ing the Tables on Las Vegas* and *Burning the Tables in Las Vegas. The Man with the $100,000 Breasts and Other Gambling Stories,* by Michael Konik, takes readers deep inside the world of high rollers, hus-tlers, card counters, and poker champions. The best low-roller guide to gambling ever written is *The Frugal Gambler,* by Jean Scott. *Casino Secrets,* by Barney Vinson, is a gambling primer and Las Vegas guide.

Movies

Frank Sinatra made his feature-film debut in the 1941 picture *Las Vegas Nights.* Bar-bara Stanwyck loses house and husband after becoming a gambling addict in the melodrama *The Lady Gambles* (1949). Sinatra gangs up with the rest of the Rat Pack for a heist in the cornball *Ocean's Eleven* (1960). Elvis Presley plays a race-car driver on the loose in Las Vegas, meet-ing up with Ann-Margret, in the famous *Viva Las Vegas* (1964).

The James Bond film *Diamonds Are For-ever* (1971) mixes footage of real-life casi-nos with shots from a fictional, studio-built casino. The main action in *The Electric Horseman* (1979) centers on Caesars Palace. *Melvin and Howard* (1980) tells

the tale of Melvin Dummar, who pre-sented for probate a will supposedly writ-ten by Howard Hughes. Much of the Albert Brooks comedy *Lost in America* (1985) takes place at the Desert Inn. Burt Reynolds stars as a Vegas private investi-gator in *Heat* (1987). On their way across the country in *Rain Man* (1988), Tom Cruise and Dustin Hoffman make a stop in Vegas to count cards.

Flying Elvises drop from the sky in the light comedy *Honeymoon in Las Vegas* (1992), part of which is set at Bally's casino. Robert Redford makes the titular *Indecent Proposal* (1993) to married couple Demi Moore and Woody Harrelson; some footage of the Las Vegas Hilton is in-cluded. Much of the campy, schlocky *Showgirls* (1995) takes place at the Star-dust. Nicholas Cage plays an unrepen-tant drunk in the bleak but moving *Leaving Las Vegas* (1995). Two of the better films about the role of organized crime in Las Vegas are *Bugsy* (1991), which traces the early days of mob involvement, and the Martin Scorcese movie *Casino* (1995), a look at how greed in the 1970s killed the goose that laid the Mafia's golden egg.

For scenes of present-day Las Vegas, check out *The Great White Hope* (1996), a satire about boxing that was shot at the MGM Grand; *Mars Attacks!* (1996), which in-corporates real-life footage of the implo-sion of the Landmark Hotel-Casino (and also includes shots of the Luxor); *Con Air* (1997), whose closing action is set at the Sands Hotel; and *Austin Powers: Interna-tional Man of Mystery* (1997), with Mike Meyers as a swingin' secret agent from the 1960s who was cryptogenetically frozen and defrosted in 1997, shagging his way through Las Vegas. The fountains of the Bellagio mesmerize George Clooney and his gang of thieves in Steven Soderbergh's 2001 remake of *Ocean's Eleven.*

INDEX